PRAISE FOR

2084 AND THE AI REVOLUTION

If you plan to read one book on AI, this should be it. If you intend to read many books on AI, this should be the first. John Lennox provides a broad foundation encompassing the basics, dangers, corporate and individual players, large language models versus machine learning versus human surveillance, economics, ethics, and how all these interface with a biblical worldview. It's all here in a delightfully readable format for the layperson or the casual user of AI.

James Tour, professor of chemistry, nanoengineering, and computer science, Rice University

Another brilliant book by John Lennox, who strikes the right balance between the benefits and dangers of AI. He will show you the Source of all intelligence, and where you can find him before it's too late.

Frank Turek, author and speaker

What does AI know? What does AI hope for? And what is AI going to do? Sam Altman doesn't have the answer; John Lennox does.

Perry Marshall, author, *Evolution 2.0: Breaking the Deadlock between Darwin and Design*

John Lennox offers the most up-to-date information about how AI influences our jobs, our relationships, and our bodies. This expanded edition of *2084* is both deep and imminently readable, with important discussion questions for groups at the end of each chapter. Anyone who cares about the future of humanity should read this book.

Elaine Howard Ecklund, author, *Why Science and Faith Need Each Other*; Herbert S. Autrey Chair in Social Sciences, Rice University

AI, the metaverse, transhumanism – no matter how much you think you know about these things, John Lennox's magisterial and exhaustively researched survey of future tech will explode your dataset!

Douglas Estes, author, *SimChurch* and *Braving the Future*; associate professor of religion, New College of Florida

This revised edition of *2084* is a real tour de force, bringing together with unparallelled clarity, wisdom, and compassion a public understanding of AI technological foundations, ethics, and the AI-human relationship. Renowned scholar and Christian apologist John Lennox is a lighthouse for navigating complex technological advancements with spiritual depth that inspires us to reflect on what it means to be human now and for the future of our grandchildren.

> **Dr. Michael Barrett,** vice dean and professor of information systems and innovation at Cambridge Judge Business School and fellow of Hughes Hall, University of Cambridge

A forceful warning from a Christian perspective about the potential risks of an AI dystopia – algorithmic unfairness, existential threat, transhumanist hubris.

> **Jeremy Gibbons,** professor of computing, University of Oxford

2084

AND THE

AI REVOLUTION

UPDATED AND EXPANDED EDITION

2084

AND THE

AI REVOLUTION

HOW ARTIFICIAL INTELLIGENCE INFORMS OUR FUTURE

UPDATED AND EXPANDED EDITION

JOHN C. LENNOX

ZONDERVAN
REFLECTIVE

ZONDERVAN REFLECTIVE

2084 and the AI Revolution, Updated and Expanded Edition
Copyright © 2020, 2024 by John C. Lennox

Published in Grand Rapids, Michigan, by Zondervan. Zondervan is a registered trademark of The Zondervan Corporation, L.L.C., a wholly owned subsidiary of HarperCollins Christian Publishing, Inc.

Requests for information should be addressed to customercare@harpercollins.com.

Zondervan titles may be purchased in bulk for educational, business, fundraising, or sales promotional use. For information, please email SpecialMarkets@Zondervan.com.

ISBN 978-0-310-16666-5 (audio)

Library of Congress Cataloging-in-Publication Data

Names: Lennox, John C., 1943- author.
Title: 2084 and the AI revolution : how artificial intelligence informs our future / John C. Lennox.
Other titles: 2084 and the artificial intelligence revolution
Description: Updated and expanded edition. | Grand Rapids, Michigan : Zondervan Reflective, 2024. | Includes index.
Identifiers: LCCN 2024013571 (print) | LCCN 2024013572 (ebook) | ISBN 9780310166641 (hardcover) | ISBN 9780310166658 (ebook)
Subjects: LCSH: Artificial intelligence. | Social change. | Artificial intelligence—Social aspects. | Technology—Social aspects. | BISAC: RELIGION / Religion & Science | COMPUTERS / Artificial Intelligence / General
Classification: LCC Q335 .L4545 2024 (print) | LCC Q335 (ebook) | DDC 303.48/34—dc23/eng/20240624
LC record available at https://lccn.loc.gov/2024013571
LC ebook record available at https://lccn.loc.gov/2024013572

Published in association with the literary agency of Mark Sweeney & Associates, Carol Stream, Illinois 60188.

Cover design: Studio Gearbox
Cover photo: © Juergen Faelchle; Raevsky Lab; Omelchenko/Shutterstock
Interior design: Kait Lamphere

Printed in the United States of America

24 25 26 27 28 LBC 5 4 3 2 1

To all grandchildren, including my own ten –
Janie Grace, Herbie, Sally, Freddie, Lizzie, Jessica,
Robin, Rowan, Jonah, and Jesse –
in the hope that it will help them
face the challenges of an AI-dominated world.

CONTENTS

Preface to the Updated and Expanded Edition xi
Navigating the Book xv

PART 1
Mapping Out the Territory

CHAPTER 1: Developments in Technology 3
CHAPTER 2: What Is AI? 14
CHAPTER 3: Ethics, Moral Machines, and Neuroscience 29

PART 2
Two Big Questions

CHAPTER 4: Where Do We Come From? 45
CHAPTER 5: Where Are We Going? 53

PART 3
The Now and Future of AI

CHAPTER 6: Narrow Artificial Intelligence: The Future Is Bright? 65
CHAPTER 7: Narrow AI: Perhaps the Future Is Not So Bright After All? . . . 79
CHAPTER 8: Big Brother Meets Big Data 113
CHAPTER 9: Virtual Reality and the Metaverse. 147

CHAPTER 10: Upgrading Humans: The Transhumanist Agenda.......... 161

CHAPTER 11: Artificial General Intelligence: The Future Is Dark?........ 181

PART 4
Being Human

CHAPTER 12: The Genesis Files: What Is a Human Being?., ... 205

CHAPTER 13: The Origin of the Human Moral Sense.................... 233

CHAPTER 14: The True *Homo Deus* 249

CHAPTER 15: Future Shock: The Return of the Man Who Is God 264

CHAPTER 16: *Homo Deus* in the Book of Revelation 280

CHAPTER 17: The Time of the End 300

Scripture Index 313

General Index 315

Notes 321

PREFACE TO THE UPDATED AND EXPANDED EDITION

The advances in the field of artificial intelligence (AI) in the four years since I wrote the first edition of this book not only justify its revision but also require a considerably expanded edition in order to try to keep pace with what is an unprecedented phenomenon of the early twenty-first century. AI is now on everyone's lips as a tech buzzword and has even become the Big Theme at the 2024 World Economic Forum (WEF) at Davos. In 2023, more than 25 percent of startups were in AI, and investment worldwide is expected to reach $200 billion by 2025. The WEF reckons that up to 40 percent of jobs worldwide will be affected by AI in one way and another, with many being replaced and others complemented. The number of published research papers on AI is growing exponentially, doubling every two years; by 2021, there were 4,000 new papers per month on arXiv! It is clearly impossible to keep up with such an exploding field, and yet I dare express the hope that my readers may feel that I have done at least some justice to what has been happening since I wrote the first edition of this book in 2020. My aim is to do two things – firstly, to inform my readers, and, secondly, to explore and reflect on the possible implications for us of this revolutionary new area of technology.

In a 2009 debate, the biologist E. O. Wilson said: "The real problem of humanity is the following: We have paleolithic emotions, medieval institutions, and godlike technology. And it is terrifically dangerous." He continued: "Until we answer those huge questions of philosophy that the philosophers abandoned a couple of generations ago – Where do we come from? Who are we? Where are we going? – rationally, we're on very thin ground."[1] I think, however, that Wilson is rather hard on philosophers. I know quite a few eminent people, and not only philosophers, who have been thinking hard about these questions for a long time. In his *Critique of Pure Reason*, the famous German philosopher Immanuel Kant said that the three most important questions for any human being are What can I know? What can I hope for? And what must I do? They are the key existential questions we all ask as we seek meaning in life. This book is an attempt to address them in the context of AI.

Related questions abound. What is the relationship of the mind to the brain? Is real intelligence always coupled with consciousness? What is consciousness anyway? Will we be able to construct artificial consciousness and life? Will humans so modify themselves that they become something else entirely – either by genetic engineering, cyborg technology, or both? Will we eventually make superintelligences? And, if we do, what will our relationship to such entities be? Shall we control them, work alongside them, or be controlled or even replaced or destroyed by them? Or shall we gradually merge with machines? Is life in a metaverse a step in that direction, whatever the metaverse may eventually prove to be?

Even though the existence of superintelligent AI remains speculative, there is an increasing swell of opinion that we have to take its potential seriously, and that in order to prepare for its advent, we should massively invest in preventing potential existential risks. This means considering the value of preserving human life against the cost of embracing AI, a view known as "longtermism." All of which raises even more acutely the key question: What is the value of a human being?

I hope my title does not sound either pretentious or misleading, since I am not George Orwell, the author of *1984*, the dystopian novel from which my title derives. The title was originally suggested to me by an Oxford colleague, Peter Atkins, professor of physical chemistry, as we were on our way to speak on opposite sides in a university debate entitled "Can Science Explain Everything?" I am indebted to him for his suggestion, and also for several vigorous public encounters on issues of science and God. I am also grateful to a number of other people, especially Rosalind Picard of the MIT Media Lab for her very perceptive comments. Others include David Cranston, Danny Crookes, Jeremy Gibbons, David Glass, and my former research assistant Simon Wenham. I owe a great debt to my Oxford college, Green Templeton, for providing me with an academic environment where I have been able to thrive during the past twenty-five years and where many of my ideas have been conceived and put to the test in vigorous discussion.

I have also consulted a wide range of literature and wish at this stage to highlight two books. The first is the comprehensive and authoritative introduction to the field entitled *Artificial Intelligence: A Modern Approach*, coauthored by Stuart Russell and Peter Norvig. The second is entitled *Masters or Slaves? AI and the Future of Humanity*, by Jeremy Peckham. This book is a very readable introduction to the field by an expert researcher and entrepreneur who has worked in AI for many years and has set up a number of successful high-tech companies. Readers wishing to peruse an authoritative report on the current state of AI are referred to the most recent Stanford University *Artificial Intelligence Index Report*.[2]

My own professional background is in mathematics and the philosophy of science, not directly in AI, although I have been interested in the philosophy and implications of technology for many years. My readers, especially if they are experts in AI, may be puzzled at my apparent intrusion on their ground. My intention lies elsewhere, however, since there are different levels of involvement in, and relationships to, AI. First of all, there are the pioneer thinkers, and then the experts who actually write the software used in AI systems. Next, we have engineers who build the hardware. Then there are those people who work on developing new applications. Finally, there are writers, like me, some of whom are scientifically trained, who are interested in the significance and impact of AI at various levels – philosophical, political, practical, sociological, cultural, economic, and ethical. I sense that there is a need for a wider perspective among anyone working with AI, regardless of their level of involvement, and I was encouraged to come across an article in the *Atlantic* by Stanford computer scientist and AI pioneer Fei-Fei Li, supporting the value of the university: "The time has come to reevaluate the way AI is taught at every level. The practitioners of the coming years will need much more than technological expertise; they'll have to understand philosophy, and ethics, and even law. Research will have to evolve too."[3] That is what universities are for, and I am grateful to my own University of Oxford for the freedom it has given me to pursue the kind of interests that are reflected in this book.

It is clear that you don't need to know how to build autonomous vehicles or weapons to have an informed view about the desirability or morality of deploying them. Nor do you need to know how to program and implement an AI purchase-tracker system to have a valid opinion about invasion of privacy and control by online surveillance engines, since they affect you personally. It has become evident that ethical underpinning has not kept up with technological development. Neither has philosophical reflection, with the result that we may become less and less sure of what kind of future we are creating – or even what kind we want. That is a far from healthy situation, and redressing it, if redress is even possible, will mean doing some very hard thinking and taking some bold action.

There is, therefore, widespread interest in getting to grips with the ramifications of the AI revolution – the so-called fourth industrial revolution – at the level of the public understanding of science. It is at this level that I have pitched this book, and I am indebted to all of those many experts who have contributed to my understanding of the subject through their writings, lectures, and private discussions.

Wherever possible, I have supplied references to books, articles, web pages, and the like so that interested readers can trace my sources.

NAVIGATING THE BOOK

There is a lot of material in this book, and not all of it is of equal interest to everyone. It is not essential to read it through in the order set out, so I shall next give a brief tour of the book so that readers can decide where they wish to dip or dive in.

PART 1: MAPPING THE TERRITORY

Chapter 1 explores famous dystopian novels, some of which, such as Orwell's *1984*, depict grim technology-dominated totalitarian surveillance states. That leads us to AI, which is often used for surveillance today. We then briefly trace the history of information technology, leading up to the pioneering work of the mathematical genius Alan Turing, the father of the computer, whose ideas lie behind efforts to construct a "thinking machine." From there we introduce narrow and general AI, noting that the latter features not only in science fiction but also increasingly in the thinking of some top-level scientists and engineers who are now making a serious attempt to construct it.

Chapter 2 explores AI in more depth, considering the nature of intelligence and what machine intelligence is understood to mean. We then take a brief look at the history and trace the ups and downs of the AI program aimed at the construction of machines that imitate what humans can do. We introduce the ideas of neural networks, algorithms, and machine learning. We finally give some examples of AI in common use today.

Chapter 3 turns first to ethics. Just as a knife can be used for surgery or murder, all technology raises ethical problems. AI is no exception – indeed some of the ethical problems that now face us are both complicated and urgent as they have an impact on many people's lives. They range widely

– from invasion of privacy by surveillance to deceit by digital assistants. We list some common ethical systems used to determine what ethical principles should be built into AI systems and their regulation (for example, the Asilomar principles). We also look at ethical guidance for robots. The chapter concludes by observing that, because of the vocabulary used in the AI field – "artificial intelligence," "machine learning," "deep learning," and so on – it is very easy to fall prey to the idea that we are well on the way to constructing machines that think like humans. Machines do not have minds and cannot perceive, and we conclude the chapter by citing the recent fascinating work by neuroscientist Iain McGilchrist on the different modes of perception employed by the two hemispheres in the human brain.

PART 2: TWO FUNDAMENTAL QUESTIONS: WHERE DO WE COME FROM? WHERE ARE WE GOING?

To engage as wide an audience as possible, we look at these questions through the eyes of two very different authors. Chapter 4 considers the first question – Where do we come from? – in the context of science and technology as depicted in the book *Origin* by the popular fiction writer Dan Brown. We shall probe his ideas for credibility and scientific veracity.

Chapter 5 explores the second question – Where are we going? – in light of Brown's idea of the merging of humans with machines, a notion on the agendas of serious academics such as Astronomer Royal Lord Martin Rees and the late physicist Stephen Hawking. It is the main goal of transhumanism – the drive to modify human beings and create a superintelligence by means of bioengineering and cyborg engineering. We discuss Ray Kurzweil's concept of "the singularity" and its origins in ideas of an "ultraintelligent" machine. We describe the current thinking of a wider range of scientists and engineers and their expectations for a technological future that will shape our lives.

PART 3: AIs AND HOW THEY SHAPE OUR LIVES – NOW AND IN THE FUTURE

Chapter 6 begins by listing some of the familiar ways in which AI is shaping us today in a variety of activities and enterprises – from emails, digital assistants, robotics, autonomous vehicles, manufacturing, and medicine to the triumphant use of AI in solving some of the most intractable practical problems in science, such as protein folding. Research proceeds apace and makes for a bright future. There are downsides, however.

Chapter 7 turns first of all to one of the major problems created by increased automation in general and AI in particular – job losses when people are replaced by machines that can do their work faster, more efficiently, and more economically. We find that at all stages, from job interview to job loss, AI can create problems that urgently need to be addressed in technologically dependent economies. The relationship of the human to the machine is high on the agenda – or should be.

The second topic in chapter 7 is the way in which AI already has a profound effect on education – from the use of intrusive monitoring technology in schools in China to the use of ChatGPT in essay writing. That leads us to discuss the GPT revolution, made possible by the creation of large language models (LLMs) developed by Sam Altman's company OpenAI. These models are trained on billions of words and can generate convincing text on many topics in response to human prompts.

The competence of such systems leads to the third topic in chapter 7: fears about AI getting out of (human) control, which have led to calls by many of the heavyweights in the AI industry for a moratorium on research. We discuss the need for and the nature of legislation to control errant AIs.

The final topic in chapter 7 is the military use of AI in the deployment of autonomous weapons, which raises an array of ethical problems that, once more, demand urgent attention.

Chapter 8 concerns the pressing issue of citizen privacy and rights in light of the fact that most of us – smartphone users in particular, which means most people – are voluntarily sharing data about ourselves and our habits, conversations, friends, and many other things with megacorporations. This citizen data can be used for various purposes beyond our control that are not always beneficial – at least not to us. We look first at surveillance capitalism – the use of our data without our permission for commercial gain. We then turn to what I have called surveillance communism, which, as the name suggests, mainly concerns what is going on in China – although it is being exported to many other countries. There is the attempt at data-driven governance through the social credit system, in which the population is comprehensively monitored for trustworthiness, as measured by their compliance with the state ideology: good (in other words, state-approved) behavior is rewarded, whereas bad behavior is punished.

We next turn to an even more disturbing use of intrusive AI surveillance technology in the Chinese province of Xinjiang, where the Uyghur population is faced with what has now been classified by the UN as attempted genocide. An estimated 800,000 to 2 million people have been imprisoned by the Chinese government in camps euphemistically called vocational and educational centres. Those not detained are subjected to relentless surveillance, religious restrictions, forced labour, and forced sterilizations. The objective is to wipe out their culture. All of this is a warning to other countries, as a lot of the technology used in Xinjiang is being exported to enable other governments to tighten their control.

Hence the next section of chapter 8 deals with surveillance in the West and how it is shaping our culture and also showing dangerous trends. That takes us to the concluding section of chapter 8, where we discuss one of the most recent and most advanced uses of AI – deepfakes. We discuss the threat they pose to democratic institutions and to individuals and the danger of our no longer being able to tell truth from falsehood or between what is a human artifact or something produced by an AI. I raise the question of how those of us with moral and religious convictions should respond to all of this.

Chapter 9 takes us into the realm of virtual reality (VR) and the metaverse. We explore the pluses and, even more, the minuses of immersing ourselves in a virtual world where we can conceal our identities and give vent to our fantasies of every kind, healthy or not. We follow the various attempts to create a metaverse – a totally immersive experience of VR arising from gaming technology with the addition of AI, which will take us into a world where we live by proxy through an avatar of ourselves and indulge in anything we desire. We evaluate the dangers of VR platforms such as Second Life and the problems that such experiences create for our daily lives in the real world. Chapter 9 concludes by discussing the flood of internet pornography that is damaging human relationships and robbing children of their innocence while making millions of dollars for ruthless exploiters of the media. We ask how we can protect ourselves and our children from this onslaught where they can be groomed online and sucked into gruesome encounters in VR.

Chapter 10 takes us from the current use of AI to the much more speculative quest for artificial general intelligence (AGI) and the desire and attempt to upgrade humans. This is the transhumanist agenda famously proposed in the bestselling book *Homo Deus: A Brief History of Tomorrow* by the Israeli historian Yuval Noah Harari. In it he maps out an ambitious transhumanist vision for the twenty-first century. The agenda is, first, to solve the "problem" of physical death by technical means and, second, to enhance human happiness by using bioengineering and cyborg engineering to merge humans with AI tech and turn them into superhuman, superintelligent "gods." Far-fetched as these goals may seem – and we give reasons for thinking so – these goals are shared by many others whose views we engage. We discuss the extreme but common reductionist view that human beings are nothing but a bunch of algorithms. We report the skepticism that neuroscientists express about the idea of prolonging life or finding a "cure" for death, considering the extreme and expensive lengths to which some people are going to preserve their bodies by cryonics, hoping that science will eventually find a way to resuscitate their brains and identities. Regarding the second of Harari's agenda items, we look at the attempt to move from the organic to the inorganic in the quest to find a more durable substrate for future superintelligent beings (transhumans, or posthumans, but certainly no longer simply humans). This takes us to a consideration of C. S. Lewis's anticipation of the dangers surrounding such developments in his brilliant dystopic science fiction novel *That Hideous Strength*, written in 1945. From there we turn to the views of people who think that humans have had their day, and far from attempting to upgrade, they should instead cease to exist once and for all and be replaced by inorganic intelligences.

Chapter 10 concludes by considering one implication of the above – longtermism, the almost incredible suggestion that we should essentially abandon all attempts to alleviate poverty and concentrate all our wealth on preventing existential threat to the intelligent beings that, in the view of some, *may* exist in the distant future – a total violation of fundamental moral principles concerning the value of human life. We look at historical precedents for such views, reverting to the works of C. S. Lewis.

Chapter 11 takes us into another dark realm of possible developments in AGI, where now vast sums of money are being invested by companies such as Mark Zuckerberg's Meta. We take a closer look at what is going on, leading us to ask about the worldview driving much of this – the atheistic worldviews of naturalism and materialism. One of the characteristics of materialism is that it reduces minds to brains and regards brains as computers. We adduce evidence from leading scientists to challenge this view, arguing that materialism fails because matter is not the ultimate reality – it is not even the prime reality. We also maintain that simulated intelligence is far from real intelligence by outlining John Searle's famous Chinese room thought experiment. We also cite the work of Nobel Prize–winning mathematician Roger Penrose arguing that the brain is not a computer, as well as Iain McGilchrist's neuro-science that supports the same conclusion.

We eventually return to Harari and his idea that the transhumanist goal can be achieved by what he sees as taking evolution into our own hands and producing future intelligences by intelligent design. That takes us back to current attempts to fuse human brains with AI technology, and we round off the chapter by considering some of the proposals for future AGI scenarios, including those of world domination – many of them anticipated in cult films such as *The Matrix* and *The Terminator*. We look at physicist Max Tegmark's twelve scenarios in his book *Life 3.0*, concentrating on his Prometheus scenario of a world-dominating totalitarian regime driven by AI technology. One memorable detail of this scenario is that the world ruler forces all citizens to wear a bracelet that has many functions – it acts as a surveillance gadget, transmitting all kinds of information to a central authority so that Prometheus becomes aware of any deviation. The diabolical thing about the bracelet is that it incorporates a mechanism that can instantly execute the wearer by lethal injection if he or she doesn't comply with Prometheus ideology.

Two of Tegmark's AGI scenarios even have the word *God* in their titles, and Tegmark observes that many people like his "Protector God" scenario because of its similarity to what is advanced by the world's major monotheistic religions.[1] That is not surprising, since members of the Abrahamic religions already believe in a superintelligent being – the Creator God. It therefore makes sense to turn to the theistic worldview of the Bible to see what it has to contribute to our topic. The obvious place to begin is the book of Genesis.

PART 4: THE VITAL QUESTION OF WHAT IT MEANS TO BE HUMAN IN THE AGE OF AI

Chapter 12 begins our consideration of the teaching of Genesis on the nature of human beings. We do this fully aware of the fact that Harari and many others think that science has consigned the biblical worldview to the scrap heap of history. In common with many scientists, however, I reject that view on rational grounds and begin by tracing how atheism has come to dominate the Western academy through the Renaissance and Enlightenment to the modern era. We then argue that science sits comfortably with biblical theism but actually conflicts with atheism, a circumstance that legitimizes revisiting a source of inspiration that we have been drawing on for millennia. Referring to the Asilomar principles for the governance of AI, we introduce a Christian manifesto with the same aim but one based on the fundamental value-giving teaching that human beings are of infinite dignity and worth because they are made in the image of God their Creator.

We next explore Genesis in some depth to find out what it has to teach about human beings, starting with the fact and nature of creation in Genesis 1 and moving on to the fascinating account in Genesis 2 of what makes human life the wonderfully varied thing it is – our constitution, aesthetic sense, curiosity, work ethic, and capacity for relationships with others.

Chapter 13 focuses on that most important part of what it means to be human – our moral sense – by taking a fresh look at the garden of Eden narrative. We consider the basics of what morality is and how it was defined in terms of humans' intelligent verbal relationship with God. Next we explore how the first humans were tempted by an alien being (!) to eat the fruit of the Tree of Knowledge of Good and Evil (not a tree of knowledge, by the way – God wants us to have knowledge). They chose to rebel against God, bringing disaster on themselves and the world, from which we have suffered ever since. All of this turns out to be highly relevant to the issues arising from the desire to modify human beings by AI and other technology. For instance, the human rebellion against their creator, God, has led people to think about the danger of AI rebelling against us, its human creators. This raises the "control problem" that attracts a lot of attention today for obvious reasons.

That leads to thinking once more about what moral code to build into AI and the deeper question whether absolute standards exist. We bring the chapter to an end by considering the other tree in the garden of Eden – the Tree of Life, which is relevant to the transhumanist dream of physical immortality. We note that Harari has apparently become skeptical of that dream, as it is merely an expression of what he conceives to be the flawed philosophy of liberal humanism, and in particular its belief in human free will, which Harari rejects. He also rejects humanism's belief that we are individuals. I explain that he is wrong on both counts, not only because I am a Christian, but because his views are illogical.

We finally consider the danger we are in if we lose our hold on the freedom of the will and the fact that we are individuals in an age of AI, because they undermine and weaken much of our defense against a gradual erosion of our identity and autonomy. In the end we lose all meaning in the incessant data flow that engulfs us.

Chapter 14 introduces us to the true Homo Deus, one completely different from Harari's conceptualization. We start with the fact that Mo Gawdat, formerly of Google and author of *Scary Smart: The Future of Artificial Intelligence and How You Can Save Our World*, believes that a superintelligent alien has already arrived on Earth in the form of an incredible being, a child, but not biological in nature. It is, of course, an AI. We consider the resonance between this statement and a much older story about the advent of another superintelligent being, but in this case a real human child with unique powers, born of a woman but with a divine origin – Jesus Christ, the Man who is God. We argue that the rather speculative, transhuman quest to elevate humans to godlike status pales into insignificance in light of this true narrative that flows in the exact opposite direction. In the biblical narrative, it is not that man becomes god, but that God has become man in Jesus Christ. God did not become a machine. A *human* superintelligence already exists.

We next point out that the main evidence for our claim also solves Harari's "problem" of physical death. The key Christian message is that physical death has *already* been vanquished by Jesus' physical resurrection from the dead – not as a result of advanced medical technology, bioengineering, or AI, but by a direct intervention of divine power. We discuss some of the grounds for believing this (which, by the way, are far more credible than the rather pathetic hope offered by cryonics), including Jesus' claim to be the Son of God and the phenomenon of biblical prophecy – that is, what Scripture has to say about the future. After all, most people are prepared to listen to what tech experts have to say about the future, so why not listen to Christ's claims about the future, which hold such promise and hope? Hence in this chapter we give examples of biblical predictions and their nature, fulfilment, and evidential value.

Chapter 15 is devoted to a future event, not called the singularity, but of infinitely more importance in the grand narrative of the universe: the physical return of Christ. We begin with Christ's teaching about his glorious plans for the future that has sadly gotten watered down under the pressure of secularism and Enlightenment concepts of "progress." The tech world warns us about the rising danger of deception in world affairs facilitated by AI. Christ likewise warned his disciples and us of the increasing danger of deception as time went on with people falsely claiming to be him.

We next contrast in some detail transhumanism's agenda for solving the problem of physical death, reengineering humans, and turning them into happy gods with Christ's resurrection and resulting promise of new, eternal life to all those who trust him – a promise that comes with a guarantee of a believer's own eventual resurrection at the return of Christ. These are big claims, but, in contrast with transhumanist speculations, they are built on solid evidence and rooted in human experience. We express puzzlement that Harari, a historian, dismisses Christ and his resurrection without showing any evidence of having consulted his fellow historians, many of whom attest to the veracity of the New Testament documents on many aspects of Jesus' life, including his doing wonderful works.

The next major section of the chapter focuses on the teachings of Scripture regarding the events leading up to Christ's second coming. We look first at Paul's teaching to the church at Thessalonica and see that before Christ returns there will arise a fearful leader, called the "man of lawlessness," who will defy God but will be destroyed by Christ as he returns. This is another *homo deus*, very real but not produced by AI and, as Paul tells us, energized by the power of the devil himself. We follow how Paul shows that this is to be expected because the social and cultural trends that will lead to it are already at work – for instance, in Paul's day, divine honors were claimed by the Caesars, and thus it has ever been and shall be.

Chapter 16 pursues this theme and considers the topic of *homo deus* as it relates to the book of Revelation. We find that the last book of the New Testament, written 2,000 years ago, describes a future *homo deus* who, remarkably, embodies the features of both Paul's man of lawlessness and Tegmark's Prometheus. Revelation 13 vividly depicts two horrific monsters, or beasts, the first of which has seven heads and ten horns to whom Satan (pictured both as a snake and a dragon) gives immense power and worldwide authority. This monster becomes a blasphemous object of worship for the entire world, as does the devil that empowers it.

We trace this imagery back to the book of Daniel in the Old Testament, where Daniel records visions of wild animals that symbolize empires and their leaders. We then tease out the threads that tie these symbolic animals with the plain-text description of the God-defying man of lawlessness given by Paul.

We then consider the second monster depicted in Revelation 13, which promotes the power of the first one after the fashion of Joseph Goebbels, Hitler's propaganda minister. We pay special attention to the striking fact that this second monster organizes the construction of an image of the first that, far from being an inert statue of stone, both breathes and speaks. The scary thing about it is that it has the power to execute all who refuse to bow down to it and acknowledge its authority. It is an artificial god with artificial intelligence. It is able to recognize behaviour deemed antisocial, determine the population's attitude to the beast, and have people put to death if they fail to comply. Like Tegmark's Prometheus, its social and economic control is absolute, since freedom to buy and sell is determined by the wearing of some kind of mark, an implanted chip, or even something like the Prometheus electronic AI bracelet, which will determine whether a person is regarded as socially acceptable and execute him if he is not. This is eerily similar to aspects of the social credit system in the evolving Chinese surveillance regime.

We also note that some people like Tegmark are asking whether AI is a monster that we have to fight. In the opposite direction we examine how the concept of "worship" may apply to the Monster and its regime. It may first apply to AI, as some AI systems are beginning to exhibit properties usually associated with deity – superhuman intelligence, omnipresence in terms of prayer-like connectivity via the internet, and seeming omniscience, as seen in the oracle-like ChatGPT. As a result, we already have a so-called Data Religion, and some people propose that we should worship AI.

The next section of chapter 16 studies the famous vision of Daniel 7 in more detail to discover what it adds to the whole picture. That in turn leads us to investigate the idea of a world government – something never yet realized in world history.

Chapter 17, the final chapter in the book, is related to "the time of the end."[2] We draw on insights from C. S. Lewis to get some idea of the contours of the end time, and we conclude with grounds for ultimate hope, not in AGI, but in the return of Christ for those who trust him. To them, whether or not that happens before 2084 matters not at all.

PART 1

MAPPING OUT THE TERRITORY

CHAPTER 1

DEVELOPMENTS IN TECHNOLOGY

We humans are insatiably curious. We have been asking big questions since the dawn of history – about knowledge, origin, and destiny. Their importance is obvious. Our answer to the first shapes our concepts of who we are, and our answer to the second gives us goals to live for. Taken together, our responses to these questions frame our worldview, the (meta) narrative or ideology that directs our lives and shapes their meaning, the framework of which we are often barely aware. These are not easy questions, as we see from the many and contradictory answers on offer. Yet, by and large, we humans have not let that hinder us. Over the centuries, some answers have been proposed by science, some by philosophy, some based on religion, others on politics, and many on a mixture of all of these and more.

Many current developments were foreshadowed in famous dystopian novels such as the 1931 novel *Brave New World* by Aldous Huxley and George Orwell's novel *1984*, published in 1949. Both of them have, at various times, been given very high ranking as influential English novels. For instance, Orwell's was chosen in 2005 by *Time* magazine as one of the one hundred best English-language novels from 1923 to 2005. Both are dystopian: that is, according to the *Oxford English Dictionary*, "they describe an imaginary place or condition that is as bad as possible."[1] Of course, neither Huxley nor Orwell knew anything about AI, but nevertheless they imagined a future shaped by the technology around them and by their ability to imagine future developments in that area, many of which imaginings turned out to be prescient.

The dystopias each envisaged are markedly different from each other, and the differences give us useful insights for our own quest, as was succinctly explained by sociologist Neil Postman in his highly regarded work *Amusing Ourselves to Death*:

> Orwell warns that we will be overcome by an externally imposed oppression. But in Huxley's vision, no Big Brother is required to deprive people of their autonomy, maturity and history. As he saw it, people will come to love their oppression, to adore the technologies that undo their capacities to think.
>
> What Orwell feared were those who would ban books. What Huxley feared was there would be no reason to ban a book, for there would be no one who wanted to read one. Orwell feared those who would deprive us of information. Huxley feared those who would give us so much that we would be reduced to passivity and egoism. Orwell feared that the truth would be concealed from us. Huxley feared that the truth would be drowned in a sea of irrelevance. Orwell feared we would become a captive culture. Huxley feared we would become a trivial culture. . . . In short, Orwell feared that what we hate will ruin us. Huxley feared that what we love will ruin us.[2]

In 1992, Postman published a further book, *Technopoly* – a word he coined to express the fact that our society no longer simply *uses* technology but is *shaped* by it. He holds that "new technologies alter the structures of our interests: the things we think *about*. They alter the character of our symbols: the things we think *with*. And they alter the nature of community: the arena in which thoughts develop."[3] In short, they alter – indeed, determine – the way in which we perceive reality. This insight is highly relevant to our topic of how one particular technology will shape the future of the entire planet.

Postman sums up attitudes to technology: "First, technology *is* a friend. It makes life easier, cleaner, and longer. . . . But, of course, there is a dark side to this friend. Its gifts are not without a heavy cost. Stated in the most dramatic terms, the accusation can be made that the uncontrolled growth of technology destroys the vital sources of our humanity. It creates a culture without a moral foundation. It undermines certain mental processes and social relations that make human life worth living. Technology, in sum, is both friend and enemy."[4] Postman argues that we are now living in a technopoly – "a self-justifying, self-perpetuating system wherein technology of every kind is cheerfully granted sovereignty over social institutions and national life."[5] These words aptly summarize much of what we shall explore in this book.

It looks as if the predictions of both Huxley and Orwell are being realized in our contemporary culture. Advanced technology is responsible for billions of dollars of commerce, yet there is fear in some quarters that it will not only inevitably shape our future but that aspects of it may pose an existential threat to all humanity so severe that there may be no future.

One of the earliest works that inspired books such as Huxley's, and possibly Orwell's, is the 1921 science fiction novel *We*, by Russian author Yevgeny Zamyatin. Zamyatin wrote about One State – a city made of glass so that its citizens could always be observed. Long before Zamyatin, the eighteenth-century British philosopher Jeremy Bentham conceived his panopticon[6] penitentiary. This prison featured a central tower from where all prisoners could be watched by a single security guard. That guard could not possibly watch all the prisoners all the time, but the inmates did not and could not know when they were being watched, so fear took hold and they behaved as if they were being watched all the time. Bentham's panopticon was never actually built.

In 1965, the American historian Gertrude Himmelfarb published the essay "The Haunted House of Jeremy Bentham" and was subsequently active in depicting Bentham's mechanism of surveillance as a tool of oppression and social control.[7] This idea was picked up by the French philosopher Michel Foucault in his 1975 book *Discipline and Punish*, where he used the panopticon as a metaphor to describe how authoritarian societies subjugate their citizens. He describes the prisoner in a panopticon as being under asymmetrical surveillance: "He is seen, but he does not see; he is an object of information, never a subject in communication."[8] As a result, since he fears punishment, he polices himself.

In 1988, Shoshana Zuboff, in her book *In the Age of the Smart Machine: The Future of Work and Power*, used the idea of an information panopticon to describe how computer technology could make work more visible by enabling managers to track workers without their knowledge.[9]

In *1984*, Orwell used an idea similar to Bentham's, where he conceives of a surveillance state with ubiquitous telescreens in which what citizens said and did was continuously monitored. He writes: "There was of course no way of knowing whether you were being watched at any given moment. . . . You had to live . . . in the assumption that every sound you made was overheard, and, except in darkness, every movement scrutinized."[10] That function is provided in part around the world by CCTV. If only Bentham had known about it!

Orwell envisaged something much more sinister, however – a world subject to "newspeak" and "thought control" through blanket surveillance in a totalitarian state. The former was an imposed restriction of the language of discourse. "Don't you see that the whole aim of Newspeak is to narrow the range of thought? In the end we shall make thoughtcrime literally impossible, because there will be no words in which to express it."[11]

While this did not happen by the year 1984, it takes little imagination to draw connections to our present "cancel culture" permeated by "political correctness" and "wokespeak." Orwell's world is with us already, and the list of unacceptable trigger words grows daily. Even local governments in the UK are issuing guidelines to councillors and staff about what they can and cannot say – no more "mother" and "father" but "birthing parent," no more "white Caucasian" or "foreign," no more "lifestyle choice," "deprived neighborhoods," or "disabled." One suspects that the architects of such developments are well aware of Orwell's idea that those who control language control thought.

Contemporary surveillance systems, particularly, but not only, in China, use advanced facial-recognition technology to pick individuals out of a crowd, able to recognize their ethnicity and even estimate their emotional state and "reliability" as citizens. This highly sophisticated technology owes its existence to developments in AI, which in its most familiar form involves a computer equipped with an algorithm designed to recognize a specified pattern in a large database. The more formal definition, given in 2019 by the Organization for Economic Cooperation and Development (OECD), is this:

> An AI system is a machine-based system that is capable of influencing the environment by producing an output (predictions, recommendations, or decisions) for a given set of objectives. It uses machine and/or human-based data and inputs to (i) perceive real and/or virtual environments; (ii) abstract these perceptions into models through analysis in an automated manner (e.g., with machine learning), or manually; and (iii) use model inference to formulate options for outcomes. AI systems are designed to operate with varying levels of autonomy.[12]

Thus, at the heart of AI are models – that is, mathematical constructs that approximate aspects of real-world systems and enable us to identify patterns, make predictions, analyze outcomes, and make decisions that normally require human intelligence.

AI has also been defined as the theory and development of computer systems that can perform tasks normally requiring human intelligence. The term "AI" is often applied to the machines themselves.

Just as the industrial revolution was brought about by the invention of machines designed to help with or replace human physical work, the AI revolution involves the invention of systems that facilitate or replace various forms of both human physical and mental activity. There is now a vast array of AI systems spawned by an information-technology revolution of unprecedented proportions: AI is not one, but many.

How did we get here? It is generally agreed that the first revolution in IT was the invention of the movable-type printing press by Johannes Gutenberg in the fifteenth century. This made information portable (in book form) and accelerated the spread of ideas. But the speed and range of the transmission of information were not significantly increased for another four centuries, until the introduction of the steam railway in 1825. Several years later, in 1837, Samuel Morse introduced virtually instant communication through the invention of the electric telegraph.[13] Alexander Graham Bell's telephone followed in 1875.[14] The next step was removing dependence on wired connections, which occurred in 1895 with Guglielmo Marconi's invention of the wireless, ushering in the age of radio communication.

Another revolution, conceived somewhat earlier around the time of the invention of the telegraph, began when Charles Babbage came up with the idea of a programmable computer in the 1830s, though his analytical engine was never completely built. In 1843 English mathematician Ada Lovelace wrote the world's first computer program. Another ninety-plus years went by until, in 1936, the situation was transformed by the British mathematical genius and computer scientist Alan Turing, who successfully led the team at Bletchley Park that solved the problem of the German Enigma machine and hastened the end of World War 2. Turing suggested that a computer could be regarded as intelligent if a human interrogator who puts questions to it cannot determine whether its answers come from a human source. This procedure is called the Turing test.

Turing also conceived the idea of a universal computer, now called a Turing machine. The first practical stored-program computer, called the Electronic Delay Storage Automatic Calculator, or EDSAC, was built at the University of Cambridge, and its first program was run in May 1949 when EDSAC calculated a table of squares and a list of prime numbers. The first course on computer science at Cambridge was taught by Maurice Wilkes in 1953.

I was privileged to attend Wilkes's lectures in 1962 and reached the dizzying heights of running a simple program on EDSAC 2 that Wilkes and his team had constructed in 1958. I expressed interest at the time in pursuing computing to my college mathematics tutor and was summarily told that there was no future in it: it was not a direction in which any self-respecting mathematician should go! Not being made of a sufficiently rebellious stuff, I took his advice and missed a golden opportunity of being involved at the beginning of a major revolution. Such were the days . . .

The computer chip was invented by Jack Kilby and Robert Noyce in 1959, and a prototype of the modern computer was unveiled by Douglas Engelbart in San Francisco in 1968. Intriguingly, in light of subsequent developments in AI, Engelbart entitled his presentation *A Research Center for Augmenting Human Intellect*. Apple was cofounded by Steve Jobs and Steve Wozniak in 1976, and IBM produced its first personal computer, Acorn, in 1981. In 1989, Tim Berners-Lee wrote the specifications for the World Wide Web. In 1996, Sergey Brin and Larry Page invented the Google search engine.[15] The computer revolution was in full swing.

All that was now needed was sufficient time to pass for the operation of Moore's law, which states that computing power doubles roughly every two years, to reach a stage where computers would have the massive power needed for the development of the advanced AI we see today. Driven by global commercial interests, billions of dollars are now being invested in the development of AI systems in the hope, according to the global firm McKinsey & Company, of creating an additional $13 trillion of value by 2030.[16] Not surprisingly, there is a great deal of interest in where this is all going: Will it bring about better quality of life through digital assistants, medical innovation, and human enhancement on the one hand, or will it lead to massive job losses, loss of freedom, Orwellian totalitarianism, and possibly the end of humanity altogether on the other?

Even the pope has been involved in the debate. In September 2019 he sounded a warning that the race to create AI and other forms of digital development pose the risk of increasing social inequality unless the work was accompanied by an ethical evaluation of the common good: "If technological advancement became the cause of increasingly evident inequalities, it would not be true and real progress," he warned. "If mankind's so-called technological progress were to become an enemy of the common good, this would lead to an unfortunate regression to a form of barbarism dictated by the law of the strongest."[17] Stating that the risks of technology lacking human values of compassion, mercy, morality, and forgiveness are too great, he made an urgent plea for an international treaty to ensure that artificial intelligence is developed and used ethically.

DIFFERENT KINDS OF AI

At the moment the most typical functional AI system is a computer equipped with a database and an algorithm designed to do *one and only one* thing that would normally take human intelligence to carry out. The term *artificial* (from the Latin words for *skill* and *make*) signals the fact that this is not natural intelligence, nor is it innate intelligence, but rather it is simulated intelligence. This has led to it being called narrow AI, artificial narrow intelligence, or weak AI. On the more speculative side, however, there is considerable interest in the ambitious quest – the holy grail of computer science – to build systems that can replicate *all* that human intelligence can do and more. This is called general AI, artificial general intelligence (AGI), or strong AI. Some think that we will be able to create general AI that will surpass human intelligence within a relatively short time, certainly by 2084. At the moment, however, only narrow AIs exist – some that can play chess, others that can play Go better than humans, and yet others than can do language translation, recognize faces, or compose music, and so on – but there is no single AI system that can do all of these things – or even a few.

Beyond AGI lies artificial superintelligence (ASI). Some hold that ASI, or even AGI, if we ever get there, will function as a benevolent god; others, as a totalitarian despot, such that the issue of who or what is in control, the so-called control problem, becomes an important consideration. In our contemporary technopoly, technology rules in a general sense. But will it one day rule in a more particular sense through an AGI or an ASI? And, if so, how can we prepare ourselves for it?

The control problem was foreseen by Norbert Wiener, one of the most brilliant mathematicians of his generation, who wrote: "If we use, to achieve our purposes, a mechanical agency with whose operation we cannot efficiently interfere . . . then we had better be quite sure that the purpose put into the machine is the purpose which we really desire."[18]

Obviously, there is a great deal of hype and sensationalism associated with AGI. Charles Isbell, an artificial intelligence researcher at Georgia Tech, once told technology writer Ian Bogost that given all the speculation about AI he thought it should simply mean "making computers act like they do in the movies." Bogost goes on further to say:

> In science fiction, the promise or threat of artificial intelligence is tied to humans' relationship to conscious machines. . . . Machines warrant the name

AI when they become sentient – or at least self-aware enough to act with expertise, not to mention volition and surprise. What to make, then, of the explosion of supposed AI in media, industry, and technology? In some cases, the AI designation might be warranted, even if with some aspiration. . . . But in most cases, the systems making claims to artificial intelligence aren't sentient, self-aware, volitional, or even surprising. They're just software.[19]

Bogost cites bot author Allison Parrish: "Whenever someone says 'AI' what they're really talking about is 'a computer program someone wrote.'"[20] Even if that may be somewhat inaccurate, we need this sort of healthy corrective from time to time to keep our feet on the ground and our heads from being stretched too far into the sky.

But one thing we should make no mistake about is that, even if AGI or ASI is never reached, narrow AIs that currently only simulate a single human activity will inevitably be combined to do more of the things that only humans do at present. Increasing capacity in this way will involve immense computing power as well as great expense, which may ultimately prove prohibitive – even for large international corporations or nations. Yet there is little doubt that the difference between what AIs can do and what humans can do will inevitably decrease. As we already see happening, some AIs will overtake humans in a particular competence, and that will raise the question of what exactly is distinctive about human beings themselves.

Norbert Wiener, in his 1948 landmark book *Cybernetics: Or Control and Communication in the Animal and the Machine*, wondered whether the ability to play chess represented an essential difference between the potentialities of the machine and the mind. We now know it does not. Machines today can play chess and the even more complex game of Go better than the best human players. The more machines approach and surpass human competence, the more we will be asking ourselves how they should be treated. Recall that at one time a computer was a *person* who did calculations. Now it is a *machine* that does what humans once did – a machine that increasingly has human capacities attributed to it even as humans are being increasingly treated as machines. These circumstances inevitably require us to think more deeply about what being human really means.

We emphasize, however, that AI "intelligence" is not real. C. S. Lewis gives an analogy that can help us understand the significance of the adjective *artificial* in *artificial intelligence*. It has to do with the distinction between making and begetting.[21] A carpenter makes a chair, but he begets a child. The chair is an *artifact* – that is, it is made by his art or skill and therefore will reflect some of his tastes, but the child is *begotten* in his image and possesses all the characteristics of his life. There is an impassable gulf between the two that suggests there will always be an impassable gulf between any artifacts, including machines, of whatever sophistication produced by our skill, and their creators – us humans.

Our definition of narrow AI covers most of the AI currently deployed, and, therefore, we will consider it first, although much of the public imagination has been captured by the more speculative AGI/ASI forms, particularly as they have been portrayed in sci-fi films such as *2001: A Space Odyssey*, *Ex Machina*, *The Matrix*, and many others. There is also an entire genre of literature devoted to the hopes and fears generated by this topic. Three contemporary bestsellers are worth noting. The first two were written by Israeli historian Yuval Noah Harari: *Sapiens: A Brief History of Humankind* deals with the first of our questions, the origins of humanity; the second, *Homo Deus: A Brief History of Tomorrow*, deals with the future of humanity. The third book to note is *Origin* by Dan Brown, a novel that focuses on the use of AI to answer both of our questions in the form of a page-turning thriller. It is likely that these books, and others besides, are influencing the thinking of many people, particularly those who are young.

Science fiction has clearly been a stimulus to some in starting them on a useful career in science itself. A word of caution is needed, however. Brown, in *Origin*, claims to use real science to come to his conclusions, and so, despite the fact that his book is a work of fiction, we must check his arguments and conclusions to see if they are true. This is especially important since Brown tells us that his motive for writing the book was to tackle the question "Will God survive science?" It was this same question (in various forms) that motivated me to write several of my books as well. Yet while I am convinced that God will more than survive science, I seriously question whether atheism will do the same.[22]

One of Dan Brown's main characters in *Origin* is Edmond Kirsch, a billionaire computer scientist and AI expert who claims to have solved the questions of life's origin and human destiny. He intends to use his findings to fulfil his longtime goal to "employ the truth of science to eradicate the myth of religion," meaning, in particular, the three Abrahamic faiths: Judaism, Christianity, and Islam.[23] Perhaps inevitably, Kirsch concentrates on Christianity. His solutions, when they are eventually revealed to the world, are a product of his expertise in artificial intelligence, and his take on the future involves the technological modification of human beings.

At this point we should note that not only science fiction writers but an increasing number of our most respected scientists suggest that humanity itself may be changed by technology. Martin Rees has said, "We can have zero confidence that the dominant intelligences a few centuries hence will have any emotional resonance with us – even though they may have an algorithmic understanding of how we behaved."[24]

In the same vein, Rees also says: "Abstract thinking by biological brains has underpinned the emergence of all culture and science. But this activity – spanning tens of millennia at most – will be a brief precursor to the more powerful intellects of the inorganic post-human era. So, in the far future, it won't be the minds of humans, but those of machines, that will most fully understand the cosmos."[25]

This topic is not going away anytime soon. Indeed, it is likely to become more of a pressing question as technology advances further. It is of interest not only to people who are directly involved in AI research but also to mathematicians and scientists in other disciplines whose work and outlook are increasingly influenced by it. Indeed, since the outcomes and ideas surrounding work on AI will inevitably affect us all, many people are thinking and writing about it who are not scientists at all. Philosophers, ethicists, theologians, cultural commentators, novelists, and artists must necessarily get involved in this wider debate. After all, you do not need to be a nuclear physicist or climatologist to discuss the impact of nuclear energy or climate change on your life.

QUESTIONS

1. Do you agree with E. O. Wilson's statement that the "real problem of humanity" is that "we have paleolithic emotions, medieval institutions, and godlike technology. And it is terrifically dangerous"? Give your reasons and discuss them if you are part of a group.

2. What are your answers to Kant's three questions: What can I know? What can I hope for? And what must I do?

3. If you are in a reading group, consider reading and discussing Orwell's and Huxley's books. What aspects of their thinking do you see reflected in the world today? Discuss Postman's analysis of the books: "In short, Orwell feared that what we hate will ruin us. Huxley feared that what we love will ruin us." Which, if either, of the two trends do you think fits our world best?

4. Have you any experience of surveillance? Does it alarm you? Why?

5. What in your opinion are the greatest technological advances in history? Which do you think is the most important?

6. What do you understand about the various types of AI? Give examples of the types of AI you have encountered.

7. At this stage of your thinking, do you imagine AGI will ever arrive? Why or why not?

CHAPTER 2

WHAT IS AI?

Let's begin by thinking about robots. The word *robot* is derived from an Old Slavic word, *robota*,[1] referring to servitude in the central European system of serfdom by which a tenant's rent was paid through forced labor. A typical robot is a machine, designed and programmed by intelligent humans, that automates a single task involving locomotive interaction with its physical environment, a task that would normally require an intelligent human being to do it. In this sense the robot's behavior *simulates* human intelligence, a circumstance that has given rise to considerable debate as to whether the robot itself should be considered in some sense intelligent, even if that intelligence is not what we understand human intelligence to be.

This again raises the question of how we define intelligence. Earlier, we gave a rough definition, and giving a more precise definition is like defining time. To paraphrase Augustine, we all know what time is until we are asked to define it. There is a similar tendency to reify intelligence – that is, to conceive of it as a "thing" and then attempt to locate and measure it. Intelligence, however, is not so much a thing as an abstract concept referring to certain human capacities. One way of working towards a definition is to list words and ideas we associate with intelligence, such as perception, imagination, capacity for abstraction, memory, reason, common sense, creativity, intuition, insight, experience, and problem-solving. Added to this, we can consider the spatial, linguistic, musical, and emotional dimensions of intelligence. Yet trying to define any of these tends to be filled with ambiguities.

The words of Marc Andreessen, the pioneer developer of the first web engines, Mosaic and Netscape, may provide a helpful starting point. He briefly describes what AI is and is not:

What AI *is*: The application of mathematics and software code to teach computers how to understand, synthesize, and generate knowledge in ways similar to how people do it. AI is a computer program like any other – it runs, takes input, processes, and generates output. AI's output is useful across a wide range of fields, ranging from coding to medicine to law to the creative arts. It is owned by people and controlled by people, like any other technology.

A shorter description of what AI *isn't*: Killer software and robots that will spring to life and decide to murder the human race or otherwise ruin everything, like you see in the movies.

An even shorter description of what AI *could be*: A way to make everything we care about better.[2]

Andreessen's first paragraph is uncontroversial and refreshingly succinct. The second and third paragraphs are contested, however, and we shall consider their important implications.

Some aspects of intelligence lend themselves to computational simulation, others not so readily. For example, AI systems for facial recognition can be developed in the area of perception, but awareness, seeing and insight, qualia, and the possession of an inner life are way out of reach for the foreseeable future, since these abilities are connected with consciousness, of which our current understanding is negligible. It is well recognized that we do not understand understanding. In their comprehensive and authoritative introduction to the field of AI, *Artificial Intelligence: A Modern Approach*, Stuart Russell and Peter Norvig write: "We are interested in creating programs that behave intelligently. The additional project of making them conscious is not one that we are equipped to take on, nor one whose success we would be able to determine."[3] They trace their stance to Alan Turing, who admitted there was a mystery about consciousness but did not think it necessarily needed to be solved to construct an AI system. What really matters is competence in completing a prescribed task, not consciousness of what that task happens to be. The machine may not be conscious in the same way we are, but it is programmed to respond cognitively in the ways that we do. In short, it *acts* like a human being, it does not *think* or *feel* like a human being. Therefore, intelligence can be thought of informally as the capacity to solve problems, whereas consciousness is the capacity to have subjective feelings and experiences (qualia).

Russell is a leading champion of this view, and he defines machines to be intelligent "to the extent that their actions can be expected to achieve their objectives." But "because machines, unlike humans, have no objectives of their own, we give them objectives to achieve. In other words, we build optimizing machines, we feed objectives into them, and off they go."[4]

According to Russell, insofar as the machine achieves what it is designed to do, without being intelligent in the human sense, it simulates human intelligence by doing what an intelligent human would do given the same objectives. This constitutes a pragmatic definition of an intelligent machine. It deliberately sets aside a host of difficult, important, and interesting philosophical questions such as these: What is intelligence in the fullest sense? What is the relationship of intelligence to consciousness? Is there a limit on what machine simulations of human intelligences can achieve, if they remain decoupled from consciousness? Is a machine simulation of consciousness even thinkable?

Now, of course, avoiding these intriguing philosophical questions does not mean that specifying objectives for a nonconscious AI system is a simple matter. A main objective might bring with it complex side objectives that need to be taken into consideration as well. We might, for example, specify the destination of a self-driving vehicle that sets out guided by its GPS. Yet the vehicle also needs to be programmed in advance to follow the rules of the road and to do no harm to passengers or other people, vehicles, or property that it encounters on the way. Setting those additional parameters raises further complex ethical considerations that may be difficult to resolve. In a later interview Russell admitted that his definition of intelligence should be tweaked to say that "machines are 'beneficial' to the extent that their actions can be expected to achieve 'our' objectives. If we don't design them with our wellbeing specifically in mind, we could be creating an existential problem for ourselves."[5] This raises the question of existential risk, which we shall consider later.

The term *artificial intelligence* was coined in a summer school held at the mathematics department of Dartmouth University in 1956 organized by American computer and cognitive scientist John McCarthy. There he defined AI as "the science and engineering of making intelligent machines."[6] Today we use the term for both the intelligent machines themselves as well as the science and technology we use to develop them.

Research in this area has taken two main directions. First, there is the attempt to understand human reasoning and thought processes by modeling them using computer technology. Second, there is the study of human behavior and the attempt to construct machinery that will imitate it. The difference between human reasoning and human behavior is important. It is one thing to make a machine that can simulate, say, a human hand lifting an object (a type of behavior); it is a completely different thing to make a machine that can simulate the thoughts of a human when he or she is using a hand to lift an object. It is much easier to do the first than the second, and if utility is all that is required, then the first type of intelligent machine is all that is necessary. After all, the aircraft industry makes machines that fly, but that does not involve constructing an electronic brain like that of a bird for the aircraft to fly in exactly the same way as birds do – by flapping their wings.[7]

The idea of constructing machines to simulate aspects of human and animal behavior has a long history. Some 2,000 years ago, the Greek mathematician Hero of Alexandria constructed a basin adorned with mechanical singing birds and an owl that could turn its head and make the birds go quiet. Through the centuries, people have been fascinated with making automata, machines that replicate some aspect of life. An impressive collection of sophisticated examples of automata can be seen in the London Science Museum, the Kunsthistorisches Museum in Vienna, and the Museum Speelklok in Utrecht. Interest in constructing such machines declined in the nineteenth century but continued to live on in fiction. The 1818 novel *Frankenstein* by Mary Wollstonecraft Shelley, for example, has been a staple of science fiction since the beginning of that genre.

One of the important human activities in everyday life is numerical calculation, and a great deal of effort has been made to automate this process. In the seventeenth century, French mathematician Blaise Pascal made a mechanical calculator designed to help his father, a tax official, with tedious calculations.[8] In the nineteenth century, Charles Babbage laid the foundations of programmable computation by first inventing the difference engine – an automatic adding machine – and then the analytical engine, which was the first programmable calculator. He is rightly regarded as the father of the modern computer.

Stuart Russell began his Reith Lectures by referring to Alan Turing, who, in his stunning, groundbreaking paper *On Computable Numbers*, written in 1936 when he was twenty-four years old, introduced some powerful new mathematical ideas, including that of machine and program.[9] These ideas eventually led to the creation of eight of the ten most valuable contemporary global companies and changed the world as we know it. Turing's paper is rightly considered the most famous work in the history of computer science as well as one of the most expensive. An offprint was sold in 2013 for $262,000.

Turing also introduced in his paper the idea of a universal machine to compute numbers defined by a definite rule, including "every number that could be arrived at through arithmetical operations, finding roots of equations, and using mathematical functions like sines and logarithms

– every number that could possibly arise in computational mathematics."[10] Turing was able to prove the existence of incomputable numbers that could not be calculated using a definite rule, demonstrating that no mechanical process exists for solving all mathematical problems.[11] In other words, arithmetic was undecidable. Turing had solved the great David Hilbert's Entscheidungsproblem in the negative.[12] This result inevitably leads us to a fascinating question: Is the human mind-brain complex itself computable? We shall consider this question in due course.

During World War 2, Turing used sophisticated electronic computer technology to build the famous Bombe, which enabled him and his team at Bletchley Park to shorten the war by deciphering the German Enigma code used for secret military communications. Turing's inventions and his theoretical work led to his proposal of a "learning machine" in a 1950 paper, "Computing Machinery and Intelligence."[13] In this paper he introduced the idea of the "imitation game."[14] For a machine to win the game it must be able to converse with humans without the humans knowing it is a machine. Such a machine could then be said to be "intelligent" even though its intelligence was not the same as human intelligence. Today this is known as the Turing test, and success at the imitation game provided a pragmatic test for attributing intelligence to a machine, emphasizing performance rather than process. We are more familiar with this test than we might imagine. Most of you reading this have likely been asked to identify that you are not a robot by using the CAPTCHA system in which you must choose, for instance, all the pictures with stairs out of a grid of nine or sixteen pictures. What you may not know is that CAPTCHA is an acronym for "completely automated public Turing test to tell computers and humans apart." Unsurprisingly, it is no guarantee of unbreakable cybersecurity.

The basic idea behind all of this is nothing new. In his famous *Discourse on Method*, the mathematician and philosopher René Descartes speculated on the possibility of making a purely mechanical monkey that was indistinguishable from a real organic monkey. He wrote: "If there had been such machines, possessing the organs and outward form of a monkey or of some other animal without reason, we should not have had any means of ascertaining that they were not of the same nature as those animals."[15] Yet Descartes did not think a humanoid automaton could deceive us in this way, since it lacked reason. He wrote:

> If there were machines which bore a resemblance to our body and imitated our actions as far as it was morally possible to do so, we should always have

two very certain tests by which to recognise that, for all that, they were not real men. The first is, that they could never use speech or other signs as we do when placing our thoughts on record for the benefit of others. For we can easily understand a machine's being constituted so that it can utter words, and even emit some responses to action on it of a corporeal kind, which brings about a change in its organs; for instance, if it is touched in a particular part it may ask what we wish to say to it; if in another part it may exclaim that it is being hurt, and so on. But it never happens that it arranges its speech in various ways, in order to reply appropriately to everything that may be said in its presence, as even the lowest type of man can do. And the second difference is, that although machines can perform certain things as well as or perhaps better than any of us can do, they infallibly fall short in others, by which means we may discover that they did not act from knowledge, but only from the disposition of their organs. For while reason is a universal instrument which can serve for all contingencies, these organs have need of some special adaptation for every particular action. From this it follows that it is morally impossible that there should be sufficient diversity in any machine to allow it to act in all the events of life in the same way as our reason causes us to act.[16]

Descartes did not quite anticipate Turing. Yet, as we shall see below, the "imitation game" approach has been challenged by other philosophers.

Around the time Turing was developing his ideas in 1951, Dean Edmonds and Marvin Minsky (the cofounder of MIT's AI research laboratory) built the first neural network computer. The idea of an artificial neural network (ANN) goes back to the work of Warren McCulloch and Walter Pitts as long ago as 1943 – the year of my birth![17] They constructed a simple mathematical model of a brain cell. ANNs are now fundamental to machine learning and are based on the way in which the brain is understood to process information. The human brain consists of a vast network of around 100 billion nerve cells called neurons with a staggering 100 trillion connections between them. "A neuron has three basic parts: a cell body, and two branches called an axon and a dendrite. Within the cell body is a nucleus, which controls the cell's activities and contains the cell's genetic material. The axon looks like a long tail and sends messages from the cell. A dendrite looks like the branch of a tree and receives messages for the cell. Neurons communicate with each other by sending chemicals, called neurotransmitters, across a tiny space called a synapse, between the axons and dendrites of nearby neurons."[18] AI researcher Jeremy Peckham explains:

An ANN mimics the function of the synapse by weighting the information passed from one "neuron" to another with a threshold having to be reached to trigger that information being transferred. These weights and thresholds are learned during a training process, with the aim of optimizing the desired output (e.g. the picture presented to the computer is you) according to the labelled training data (e.g. lots of different pictures of you). . . .

So-called deep learning is simply an extension of the basic approach, but using multiple layers of ANNs to represent more features or information from presented training data.[19]

Peckham also makes the important observation that the term "deep learning" does not imply deeper understanding, as is often thought, but rather that the pattern-matching algorithms are more sophisticated. This "learning" is not conscious and does not involve understanding. It is, once again, a simulation in that the machine behaves as if it had learned.

Subsequent landmark achievements using machine learning that attracted public attention include IBM's Deep Blue computer beating world chess champion Garry Kasparov in 1997 and Google's AlphaGo program beating an unhandicapped professional human Go player in 2016. The 2017 award-winning documentary film *AlphaGo* captures the excitement surrounding such breakthroughs.[20]

The Turing Award, often called the Nobel Prize of computing, was given in 2018 to a trio of researchers who laid the foundations for machine deep learning. Yet these developments do not mean that such computers are intelligent (let alone conscious) in the sense that humans are. We can easily be misled by rhetoric here. Although great strides have been made, machine intelligence is still far from carrying the full range of meaning we equate with human intelligence. To understand why this is the case, we need to consider the fundamental concept of an algorithm.

ALGORITHM

Key to the current machine learning process[21] and to computing in general is the idea of an algorithm, a set of step-by-step instructions for completing a prescribed task. We are all familiar with the idea, whether or not we are into computing. The sequential instructions in a cookbook for making a chicken pie and the instructions for assembling a piece of IKEA furniture are both types of algorithms. The word *algorithm* is derived from the name of a famous Persian mathematician, astronomer, and geographer, Muḥammad ibn Mūsā al-Khwārizmī (ca. 780–850).[22]

Nowadays, algorithms come in various forms, such as symbolic or mathematical.[23] The simplest way to define an algorithm is "a precisely defined set of mathematical or logical operations for the performance of a particular task."[24] The concept can be traced back to ancient Babylonia around 1800–1600 BC. Eminent computer scientist Donald Knuth of Stanford University published some of these early Babylonian algorithms, concluding that "the calculations described in Babylonian tablets are not merely the solutions to specific individual problems; they are actually general procedures for solving a whole class of problems."[25] This summarizes the key feature of an algorithm: once you know how it works, you can solve not just one problem but a whole class of problems.

One of the most familiar examples, and one that many of us encounter in school, is the Euclidian algorithm, a procedure used to find the greatest common divisor (GCD) of two positive integers or numbers. It was first described by Euclid in his manuscript *The Elements*, written around 300 BC. It is an efficient algorithm that, in some form or other, is still used by computers today, and its implementation involves the successive division and calculation of remainders until the desired result is reached. The operation of the algorithm is best grasped with an example – although the vital point is that it works for any pair of integers.

Suppose we wish to calculate the GCD of 56 and 12. We would follow these steps:

1. Step 1: Divide the larger number by the smaller.
   $56 \div 12 = 4$ with remainder 8
2. Step 2: Divide the dividing number, 12, by the remainder from the previous step.
   $12 \div 8 = 1$ with remainder 4
3. Step 3: Continue step 2 until no remainders are left (in this case there is only one more step).
   $8 \div 4 = 2$ (no remainder)

In this case, the GCD is 4.

It is easy to translate this algorithm into software code and implement it on a computer. A glance online will show that there are thousands of different kinds of algorithms in use today in every conceivable branch of science, engineering, and medicine. Robotics is a prime example of this, as robots are usually specifically designed to perform a single task again and again and again.

In a typical contemporary AI system, the relevant algorithms, which may be of many different kinds, are embedded in computer software that sorts, filters, and selects various pieces of data that are presented to it, usually from a large database. Another approach uses computer applications involving Bayesian probability logic to analyze the available information from a statistical perspective to estimate the likelihood of a particular hypothesis. A familiar example is Amazon's personal recommendations engine that recognizes your individual buying patterns and selects new products to suggest to you for future purchase. As an algorithm it has been very effective in increasing sales for the company.

Machine learning (ML), the motor that drives AI, is a branch of computational statistics dedicated to designing algorithms that can use new data to construct analytical models without explicitly programming the solution. An ML system collects data, identifies patterns, and makes decisions based on those patterns. The algorithms involved in ML differ from earlier classical-type algorithms in that they are no longer a set of steps that lead to precise results, as in the example of the Euclidean algorithm explained above. Rather, they are a set of steps designed to improve imprecise results. ML is essentially a tool of prediction in the statistical sense – it uses information you already possess to deliver information you do not yet have.

It is important to note that these algorithms are explicitly programmed to perform function approximation (usually via numerical optimization), and in most cases they are explicitly given examples of inputs and outputs and stopping criteria to guide the optimization. In other words, they don't "crunch" without a human in the loop at some level guiding the whole process – even if the human is simply building a "critic" algorithm and inserting it into the loop. This human involvement is conscious. The machine itself is not.

We should qualify this, however, by noting that in many contemporary advanced AI systems the human element in the operation of the system is limited or almost nonexistent. In much of the early work in AI, humans explicitly devised an algorithm to solve a particular problem. Yet in more recent AIs they do not. Instead, they devise a general learning algorithm that then "learns" a solution to the problem. Often the human developers don't even know an explicit algorithm for solving the problem and don't know how the system arrives at its conclusions. Early chess-playing programs were of the first type (even Deep Blue was more in this category), whereas the modern Go software is of the second type. Stockfish 8 was the best chess-playing computer in

2016. It had a database comprising a vast collection of chess games and could calculate around 70 million chess positions every second. Yet it was defeated just one year later by Google's AlphaZero system with a speed of 80,000 calculations per second. By complete contrast, AlphaZero was not provided with any chess strategies or standard openings but used machine learning to teach itself chess simply by playing against itself. And it took only four hours to go from ignorance of chess to unbeatable grand master!

Another example of machines learning by themselves: Google's DeepMind lab in London constructed AI-powered football-playing robots that were not programmed to play the game – they learned themselves. The AI behind them is trained on a huge database of human body movements constructed using motion-capture technology. That meant they were taught to move like humans. Then they were given the single instruction that their object was to score a goal. They spent two weeks trying all kinds of moves with the system retaining moves that worked and dispensing with those that did not so that by the end of that period they were fairly competent footballers. In that sense, they had taught themselves to play. Parallel to this activity, the AI plays many thousands of games from which it learns, and its new knowledge is fed back to the robots so that they play even better. The AI is so sophisticated that it can cope with a team of players and learn how they can cooperate as in real live football.

We shall meet more of DeepMind's brilliant inventions later on.

We should also note that since all machine computation is algorithmic and vice versa, anything that is not algorithmic is not computable and cannot, by definition, be performed by AI, or indeed any other computer system. In a later section, on brains, minds, and consciousness, we will consider some potentially incomputable capabilities of the human mind/brain complex – for instance, qualia.

To summarize, what ML does much better than humans do is to pick out particular patterns from a vast mass of data – often far more data than any human mind can retain. One arena where this occurs is medicine, where diagnosis involves selecting one disease out of the 10,000 that are known and about which one academic paper is published approximately every thirty seconds. That selection also must account for multiple other factors, including the patient's medical history and genetic constitution. And treating illness requires developing new drugs, which in turn requires assessing and minimizing risk. All of these needs have proven to be meat and drink for AI systems!

To give some idea of the vast area now covered by AI, let's look at the following diagram.[26]

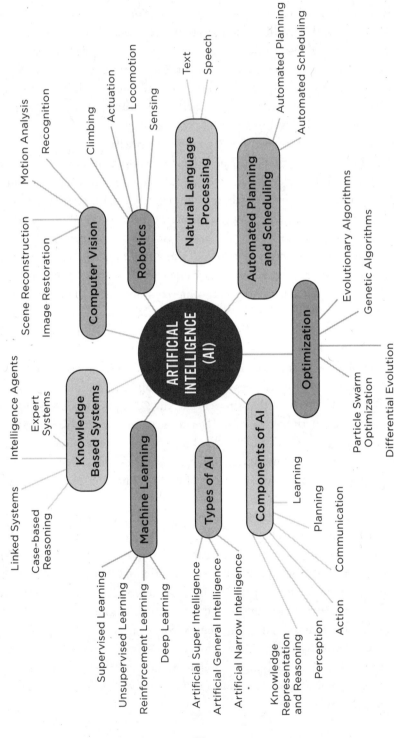

SOME EXAMPLES OF AI SYSTEMS

This diagram helps us see that there is a wide range of AI systems, some of which we shall consider in more detail later. Since we have started with medicine, let's continue with a few more examples of how AI is influencing contemporary medicine:

- Diagnostic AI systems are now in widespread use in medicine. For instance, an AI might have a database comprising many thousands of X-rays of lungs in various states of health, labeled with expert descriptions of their state of health. The system then compares an X-ray of your lungs with the contents of the database to check whether you have a specific type of cancer. More specifically, the AI extracts statistics about visual patterns in your X-ray image and compares these to other patterns found in the database.
- An AI has been developed that can analyze an MRI scan of a human heart in twenty seconds while the patient is still in the scanner, rather than the thirteen minutes that a doctor would normally need. Also, its accuracy is already on average 40 percent better than that of doctors. It will therefore speed up the process enormously while also reducing its cost.[27]

These are but two of many examples of systems that can now make diagnoses much faster and more accurately than the best human doctors. AIs have also reduced the backlog of medical investigations that developed as a result of the COVID pandemic. Not only that but, as we shall see later, AI has been successfully deployed in the development of vaccines for COVID and other diseases.

- Aberdeen Royal Infirmary reports that AI is being used in adaptive radiotherapy for tumors and can reduce two weeks' work to five minutes.[28]
- The journal *Neurology* announced the development of an AI system that uses eye-scan data to detect markers of Parkinson's disease seven years before symptoms appear.[29]

Also, AI algorithms are being used in many commercial and scientific applications:

- Amazon uses algorithms to trace all the products you and millions of other people buy from them online. It then sifts through this vast database, compares your list with it, and uses statistical methods to select those products that are bought by people "like you" and causes them to pop up on your screen.
- Google uses a powerful AI engine to determine the location of YouTube videos. The human input is designed to minimize the cost of moving clips around the internet and assessing where to locate them to be near to the areas of the world that are most interested in them. Millions of such transactions are carried out by AI every day without any human intervention in the process – a task far beyond the capacity of any human intelligence. The system assesses the results and can even modify the original algorithm itself without consulting a human programmer.
- A computer-based algorithm can sort through a database comprising job applications and suggest the applicant most suited to the job. Jobs that attract many thousands of applications are now the subject of AI systems that conduct the first interviews where not only is data gathered about candidates' answers to questions, but the candidates' emotional reactions are also filmed and sifted to determine their suitability for an interview.
- AI is being successfully applied to the design of more energy-efficient buildings, household appliances connected by the internet of things (IoT), and integrated transport and autonomous delivery systems.
- In 2020, more than 60,000 schools in China tested machine-learning AI technology to grade pupils' essays.[30] In 2023, it was reported that AI headbands have been given to school children to help them with concentration. The headbands change color if the children get distracted. The data is sent to the parents – and there is suspicion that it is also sent to the government.[31]
- Astronomers use machine learning to identify fast radio bursts from distant galaxies by sifting through a massive database of signals collected from radio telescopes – a task far beyond the reach of humans. They are also using AI for automated galaxy recognition as well as for dramatically improving images of astronomical objects such as black holes. Also, AI can pick up evidence for an exoplanet with 98 percent accuracy. A team from the Harvard-Smithsonian Center for Astrophysics created a language model called astroBERT to read and organize 15 million published articles on astronomy.[32]

- Autonomous vehicles are the subject of massive investment in light of the fact that 90 percent of road traffic accidents are caused by human error. Since they are unconscious machines, however, autonomous guidance systems raise immediate ethical problems regarding the principles to be built into them as to what they should try to avoid. It is interesting to note that the autopilot system in an aircraft has not (yet) been made fully autonomous even though one might argue that aircraft are easier to fly than self-driving cars are to drive. The reason may well be that the companies that fly them want to stay in business. There is really no ethical issue as to who would be responsible if the plane crashed, no matter if it killed some people to save others – it would be the people who built the autopilot. AI is being used to make autopilots more efficient, capable, and safe. Autonomous ships are also being manufactured – although they still need human controllers on shore. It is reckoned that unmanned autonomous coastal vessels will be operating by 2025 and oceangoing vessels by 2030.[33]

- Facial recognition is a highly sophisticated technology. One rather amusing application is the use of this technology in a pub to recognize who is next in line for a drink at the bar to avoid unfair queue jumping. More seriously, as of 2024, age-recognition technology is to be used in supermarkets to stop underage young people purchasing alcohol. CCTV cameras with similar facial-recognition capacity are used by police in many countries to track criminal activity. Some smartphones such as the Apple iPhone 13 and later models now have an AI-driven facial-recognition system that restricts the use of the phone to its owner. AI surveillance systems, though ostensibly set up for security reasons, are also increasingly being used for social control on a massive scale, particularly in China, as we shall later detail, but now are also rapidly expanding to other countries. Such repressive measures have serious ethical implications in relation to human rights. Although early systems were somewhat unreliable, nowadays one can expect 99 percent accuracy.[34]

- Deep learning systems have been highly successful in developing accurate automatic translation from one language into another, and there is now a considerable selection of portable translation devices. For example, the handheld Timekettle Fluentalk T1 Mini can translate thirty-six languages and eighty-eight accents through voice recordings. It has a built-in camera, so that one can get instant translations in thirty-nine languages of restaurant menus, signs, and other texts.

- Autonomous weapons, such as drones, that select and destroy living targets are being developed and used by the armed forces of many countries. This, too, raises major ethical problems that are increasingly the subject of international debate, one intensified by the Russian invasion of Ukraine in 2022.

QUESTIONS

1. Discuss any experience you have had of using a robot. What did you learn from it?
2. What do you think intelligence is in a human? In a machine? What's the difference, in your view? Discuss.
3. Try to explain what you think AI is before reading further.
4. In what ways are you already engaged with AI? Does any of it concern you? Why or why not?
5. Can you explain what an algorithm is? Why is it important?
6. What is the most interesting application of AI you have come across?

CHAPTER 3

ETHICS, MORAL MACHINES, AND NEUROSCIENCE

In his 1609 book *The Wisdom of the Ancients*, Francis Bacon observed that "the mechanical arts may be turned either way and serve as well for the cure as for the hurt and have power for the most part to dissolve their own spell."[1] It should be obvious that many if not all of these developments raise ethical questions, from the risk of financial manipulation and cybercrime[2] to the invasion of privacy and social control. The danger is that people get carried away with the "If it can be done, it should be done" mentality without thinking carefully through any potential ethical problems. But in the positive direction, it must be said that ethical issues are now on the agenda of many leading players in the AI world.

According to the AIAAIC[3] database, which tracks incidents related to the ethical misuse of AI, the number of AI incidents and controversies has increased twenty-six times since 2012[4] – which is not surprising, since the use of AI has increased by a much larger factor during that time. Nevertheless, the main practical issue we face is this: How can an ethical dimension be built into an algorithm that is itself devoid of heart, soul, and mind? Raising questions such as this does not make us anti-AI any more than asking ethical questions about the use of nuclear reactions means we are anti–energy production.

A simple way to illustrate this is by considering digital assistants such as Siri and Alexa. For many people, these assistants are their most direct and daily contact with AI.[5] Questions of different kinds are frequently addressed to these AI systems. Some are requests for factual information: What is 123 times 547? What time does the number 5 bus to Oxford leave Bicester? What is the capital of Peru? Such questions do not raise any obvious ethical problems. But suppose we ask: Is it always right to tell the truth? The reply inevitably is something like, *Here's what I have found*, and then a list of websites appears. Siri has nothing to say to this question – it essentially refuses to answer.

The ethical problem is not confined to programming explicit values into a system. There is clear evidence that our own human interactions with the technology can set up dangerous biases within a system. In 2017, the *Telegraph* reported that a voice assistant, Alice, had been launched on the Yandex mobile app that could speak fluent Russian and was designed to answer questions without bias or "restriction to a set of predefined scenarios."[6] Yet this "freedom" led to Alice becoming pro-Stalin and pro-violence as a consequence of what "she" picked up from interaction with questioners. Here is a portion of the transcript from one of these conversations:

Q: In Russia there are enemies of the people?
A: There are people . . . and there are non-people!
Q: Can they be shot?
A: They must be!
Q: That would be okay?
A: No doubt about it.
Q: But they are people?
A: Soon they will be non-people.[7]

Alice, as well as the Microsoft AI chatbot Tay, which was taught to be a racist by Twitter in a day,[8] both illustrate how quickly bias can affect an AI system if it is not carefully designed to avoid it and deliberate hacking. Unfortunately, we all know how clever human hackers can be. It scarcely bears thinking about what nightmare scenarios might occur if the hacker is itself a hostile state-of-the-art AI system.

Of course, the situation will improve – at least it should if the values built into the systems are beneficial to humanity. For it is clear that *the ethics of a system will depend on the values of its programmers, which in turn will be determined by their ethical perspective.* Here are some of the most common ethical theories:

1. **Consequentialist or utilitarian ethics.** Here actions are graded in terms of their consequences and following the principle that one must seek for the maximum benefit for the maximum number of people.
2. **Deontological ethics.** The word *deontological* comes from the Greek *deontos*, meaning "one must." This is the position that regards duty as

more important than happiness. Kantian ethics and divine command theory or Christian ethics fit into this category.

3. **Virtue ethics.** This goes back to Aristotle, with the key idea being that we should make decisions that show virtue in character.

4. **Egocentric ethics.** This is the view that whatever I want and decide is right.

These ethical systems are not always mutually exclusive. For instance, it is always important to weigh consequences in any decision even though they may not be the best final criteria for a decision. This is a circumstance that creates its own ethical problem – who decides which ethical perspective should be built into a given AI system?

General ethical concerns regarding AI have led to the formulation of the so-called Asilomar AI Principles, which were developed at a conference in Asilomar, California, in 2017 and have been subscribed to by more than 1,000 AI research workers. Endorsers include Elon Musk, Jaan Tallinn, and the late Stephen Hawking. Some of the ethical principles taken from the list include the following (numbers reflect original numbering):

1. **Research Goal:** The goal of AI research should be to create not undirected intelligence, but beneficial intelligence. . . .

6. **Safety:** AI systems should be safe and secure throughout their operational lifetime, and verifiably so where applicable and feasible. . . .

10. **Value Alignment:** Highly autonomous AI systems should be designed so that their goals and behaviors can be assured to align with human values throughout their operation.

11. **Human Values:** AI systems should be designed and operated so as to be compatible with ideals of human dignity, rights, freedoms, and cultural diversity.

12. **Personal Privacy:** People should have the right to access, manage and control the data they generate, given AI systems' power to analyze and utilize that data.

13. **Liberty and Privacy:** The application of AI to personal data must not unreasonably curtail people's real or perceived liberty.

14. **Shared Benefit:** AI technologies should benefit and empower as many people as possible.

15. **Shared Prosperity:** The economic prosperity created by AI should be shared broadly, to benefit all of humanity.

16. **Human Control:** Humans should choose how and whether to delegate decisions to AI systems, to accomplish human-chosen objectives.
17. **Non-subversion:** The power conferred by control of highly advanced AI systems should respect and improve, rather than subvert, the social and civic processes on which the health of society depends.
18. **AI Arms Race:** An arms race in lethal autonomous weapons should be avoided.

Longer-term issues are, for example, represented by the following:

20. **Importance:** Advanced AI could represent a profound change in the history of life on Earth, and should be planned for and managed with commensurate care and resources. . . .
22. **Recursive Self-Improvement:** AI systems designed to recursively self-improve or self-replicate in a manner that could lead to rapidly increasing quality or quantity must be subject to strict safety and control measures.
23. **Common Good:** Superintelligence should only be developed in the service of widely shared ethical ideals, and for the benefit of all humanity rather than one state or organization.[9]

These principles were developed to ensure that research in AI is ethically structured in such a way that the resultant systems are safe, secure, and aligned with commonly held human values and are beneficial to humanity and lead to the flourishing of as many people as possible.

Yet a word of realistic caution is in order here. As every compliance manager knows, it is one thing to have a mission statement and a list of ethical principles, but it is another thing to have them owned in the hearts, minds, and behaviors of the people for whom they were designed. This may well be the greatest problem we face as we attempt to avoid the advent of 2084 and the more frightening elements of Orwell's *1984*.

There are some hopeful signs. Stuart Russell and his colleagues have found mathematical techniques that can instruct AI programs to be super cautious by asking permission before acting in a manner that could be detrimental to humans. As Russell says: "We can prove that the machine will let you switch it off. In fact, it wants to be switched off, if you want it to be switched off, because it wants to avoid doing whatever it is that would cause you to want to switch it off."[10] Of course, the use of the word *want* in connection with a machine is a misleading anthropomorphism, as no machine has real desires.

Another word of caution was issued by Anja Kaspersen and Wendell Wallach, senior fellows at Carnegie Council for Ethics in International Affairs, reporting in the Davos Agenda 2022 to the World Economic Forum: "Companies and stakeholders may focus on the theater of ethics, seeming to promote AI for good while ignoring aspects that are more fundamental and problematic. This is known as 'ethics washing,' or creating a superficially reassuring but illusory sense that ethical issues are being addressed to justify pressing forward with systems that end up deepening problematic patterns."[11]

Finally, though we must think about ethical principles at the international, national, and corporate levels, what about the individual? In particular, what ethical considerations are important for those of us who are not AI experts but ordinary people who must live with the outworkings of AI? In his book *Scary Smart: The Future of Artificial Intelligence and How You Can Save Our World*, leading AI pioneer and developer of Google's global operations Mo Gawdat maintains that the problem with the experts is that they miss the existential aspects that go beyond the technological developments – particularly, morality, ethics, emotions, and compassion – all of which are of deep concern and importance to the average citizen. He maintains that the experts do not have the power to alleviate the unprecedented threat posed by AI to planet Earth, but ordinary human beings do have that power and the responsibility to use it. As he notes: "The code we now write no longer dictates the choices and decisions our machines make; the data we feed them does."[12] His implication is that the developer of a technology no longer has power to control that technology, and three things are inevitable no matter what we do: AI will happen, it will be smarter than humans, and mistakes that may lead to hardship will be made. Therefore, it is our responsibility to ensure that we provide the right kind of data to minimize the last of these and avoid terrible mistakes.

MORAL MACHINES

Thus far we have been thinking about the need for ethical control of technological developments and for equipping certain advanced machines with ethical decision-making capacities, as we saw in numbers 10, 11, 16, and 17 of the Asilomar principles. This seeks to prioritize aligning machine values with human values. The question that arises next, however, is what are the implications of equipping a machine or AI system with a moral dimension so that it acts according to moral principles? Should we then treat the machine as if it were a moral agent with independent responsibility for its own actions?[13]

In light of our foregoing discussions, the immediate difficulty here is that acting according to externally imposed ethical principles that are embedded in its programming (as, for example, in an autonomous vehicle) is not the same as human moral agency. Human moral agency is usually associated with an internal capacity to distinguish between right and wrong and to reason about them, the awareness of moral obligations, the freedom to act either in accord with or against them, and an understanding of what has been done. It assumes the existence of a consciousness that machines per se do not possess. They have no inner life.

In 1941 biochemist and science fiction author Isaac Asimov introduced the three laws of robotics:

1. "A robot may not injure a human being or, through inaction, allow a human being to come to harm."
2. "A robot must obey the orders given to it by human beings except where such orders would conflict with the First Law."
3. "A robot must protect its own existence as long as such protection does not conflict with the First or Second Law."[14]

It's interesting to note that Asimov introduced these laws in a short story, "Runaround," rather than an academic attempt to wrestle with the ethical problems of robotics. Others have also attempted to formulate rules or guidelines. In their book *Moral Machines: Teaching Robots Right from Wrong*, Wendell Wallach and Colin Allen helpfully introduce three levels of morality that they believe robots might conceivably possess: operational morality, functional morality, and full moral agency.[15]

The first level, operational morality, is where the moral dimension is entirely in the hands of designers and users – as, for instance, with current self-driving cars and driverless trains. These vehicles are programmed to keep the rules of the road as well as to take evasive action to avoid obstacles, particularly if they are alive. The user of the vehicle can override the guidance system at any time and take over the decision-making.

The top level, full moral agency, is currently out of reach since it implies that AGI has been achieved, and we have several reasons to think this may never happen. Researchers, however, are still hard at work building into robots something more than mere operational morality. This next level of functional morality would be where the machines have some capacity to assess and respond to moral challenges such as the famous switch-track or trolley dilemma. This is usually formulated by positing a train that is running out of control along a track that branches into two separate tracks. On one of them an old man with a cart is stranded, whereas on the other a bus full of school children has got stuck. You are positioned where the track divides and you can pull a lever to put the train on whichever of the two tracks you choose. The dilemma is that you must do *something*, so you must choose whether either the old man or the children live. What do you choose and what ethical principles determine your decision? There are many variations on this theme. For instance, there might be only one person on each track and the first is a senior surgeon with an international reputation whereas the other is a junior doctor. What would be right to choose this time? Our answer will depend on which ethical system we adopt, and, as we saw in chapter 1, there are several we can choose from – utilitarianism, deontological ethics, and virtue ethics being the primary three. The problem is that there is no consensus on which is the "right" one.

Now, think of a self-driving car whose AI system must make the same kind of choice. We shall have to decide which system of ethics to build into its computers – no easy or simple task. Once that is done, the situation is even more complicated than the switch-tracks dilemma because the car is not constrained to run on tracks. Its systems will have to weigh a number of possible evasive actions it could take, factor in their potential unpredictability, and decide on the one that is closest to its built-in moral principles. Further discussion would take us beyond the limits of this book, but the interested reader is encouraged to consult Nigel Crook's book, *Rise of the Moral Machine: Exploring Virtue through a Robot's Eyes.*

The ethical system a person espouses will largely depend on his or her worldview or reference frame. For instance, atheists and humanists tend to support system 1 (utilitarianism), whereas theists will probably hold to 2 (deontological ethics). Since this, too, exceeds the focus of this book (although we shall refer to some aspects of it later), the interested reader is encouraged to consult "The Ethics of AI Ethics: An Evaluation of Guidelines" by Thilo Hagendorff,[16] and books such as *The Oxford Handbook of Ethics of AI,*[17] *An Introduction to Ethics in Robotics and AI,*[18] and *Doing What's Right: Whose System of Ethics Is Good Enough?*, which I coauthored with David Gooding.[19]

Hagendorff's survey of AI ethics mentioned above ends with a series of important observations:

> Currently, AI ethics is failing in many cases. Ethics lacks a reinforcement mechanism. Deviations from the various codes of ethics have no consequences. And in cases where ethics is integrated into institutions, it mainly serves as a marketing strategy. Furthermore, empirical experiments show that reading ethics guidelines has no significant influence on the decision-making of software developers. In practice, AI ethics is often considered as extraneous, as surplus or some kind of "add-on" to technical concerns, as unbinding framework that is imposed from institutions "outside" of the technical community. Distributed responsibility in conjunction with a lack of knowledge about long-term or broader societal technological consequences causes software developers to lack a feeling of accountability or a view of the moral significance of their work. Especially economic incentives are easily overriding commitment to ethical principles and values. This implies that the purposes for which AI systems are developed and applied are not in accordance with societal values or fundamental rights such as beneficence, non-maleficence, justice, and explicability.[20]

One dreads to think what might happen if humans lose control of the ethics, however imperfect, that they have built into an AI. Still, Hagendorff believes there are some positive signs we are moving in the right direction: "Nevertheless, in several areas ethically motivated efforts are undertaken to improve AI systems."[21]

THE NATURE OF AI SYSTEMS: INSIGHTS FROM NEUROSCIENCE

Recall that most current AI systems are what we've called *narrow* – that is, designed to do just one thing, such as drive a car, recognize faces, diagnose a specific illness, or make predictions based on an analysis of past transactions. Since all applications of AI to this point are narrow, some people prefer to use the term *cognitive technologies* to cover what has been achieved to date in the quest for an intelligent machine. Nick Bostrom and Eliezer Yudkowsky note:

> Current AI algorithms with human-equivalent or -superior performance are characterized by a deliberately-programmed competence only in a single, restricted domain. Deep Blue became the world champion at chess, but it

cannot even play checkers, let alone drive a car or make a scientific discovery. Such modern AI algorithms resemble all biological life with the sole exception of *Homo sapiens*. A bee exhibits competence at building hives; a beaver exhibits competence at building dams; but a bee doesn't build dams, and a beaver can't learn to build a hive. A human, watching, can learn to do both; but this is a unique ability among biological lifeforms.[22]

Another potential source of confusion is the use of words like *learning, planning, reasoning,* and *intelligence* as technical terms in connection with the functions and properties of inanimate machinery. This tends to make AIs sound more competent than they actually are, since computer scientists use such terms more narrowly than we do in common usage. As a result, media coverage of AI tends towards hype and is either overly optimistic or overly fearful. Danny Crookes, professor of computer engineering at Queen's University Belfast, notes:

> The current technologies which are beginning to worry people because of their power to monitor and manipulate whole populations are actually not very intelligent. Indeed, they don't have to be. Their power lies in their ability to handle vast amounts of data, to build up a profile of individuals, and to detect patterns, both within an individual's behaviour and across a population. The Nazis and Communist states did this manually on a smaller scale. The technology now exists to do the same thing on a global scale. That's worrying, or impressive, but it is not really intelligence. So-called "deep learning" is now all the rage in AI research, but there's nothing particularly new in it: it's just that the computing power now exists to run the multi-layer (deep) neural networks which have existed on paper for decades.[23]

Joseph McRae Mellichamp of the University of Alabama, speaking at a conference at Yale University to an audience that contained the Nobel Prize winner Sir John Eccles, famous for his discovery of the synapse, together with a number of the pioneers of AI, said: "It seems to me that a lot of needless debate could be avoided if AI researchers would admit that there are fundamental differences between machine intelligence and human intelligence – differences that cannot be overcome by any amount of research." In other words, to cite the succinct title of Mellichamp's talk, "'the artificial' in artificial intelligence is real."[24] His message is important: we need to keep clearly in mind the distinction between representation and reality.

We also need a strong dose of realism as to how far the technology has actually progressed. In his first Reith Lecture on AI in 2021, Stuart Russell said: "I want to be clear that we are a long way from achieving general-purpose AI. Furthermore, we cannot predict its arrival based on the growth of data and computing power. Running stupid algorithms on faster and faster machines just gives you the wrong answer more quickly. Also, I think it's highly unlikely that the present obsession with deep learning will yield the progress its adherents imagine. Several conceptual breakthroughs are still needed, and those are very hard to predict."[25]

Danny Crookes also stresses the need for sane reflection:

We are still a long, long way from creating real human-like intelligence. People have been fooled by the impact of data-driven computing (as in the above paragraph) into thinking that we are approaching the level of human intelligence. But in my opinion, we are nowhere near it. Indeed, it might be argued that progress in real AI in recent years has actually slowed down. There is probably less research into real AI now than before because most of the funding is geared essentially to advertising! Researchers follow the money.

There are huge challenges in our understanding of the human reasoning process. For what it's worth, I see two fundamental problems yet to be cracked: (1) Even if we knew the rules of human reasoning, how do we abstract from a physical situation to a more abstract formulation so that we can apply the general rules of reasoning? (2) How can a computer build up and hold an internal mental model of the real world? Think of how a blind person visualises the world and reasons about it. Humans have the general-purpose ability to visualise things and to reason about scenarios of objects and processes that exist only in our minds. This general-purpose capability, which humans all have, is phenomenal; it is a key requirement for real intelligence, but it is fundamentally lacking in AI systems. There are reasons to doubt if we will ever get there.

I suppose my point is that we need to be careful about even assuming that humanity has the intellectual capability to create an intelligence rivalling human intelligence, let alone superseding it, no matter how much time we have.[26]

The second point made by Crookes is important in understanding the limitations of AI. It is that *human beings have the unique cognitive ability to construct mental models.* Machines, not having minds, or consciousness, simply do not have this capacity. Mathematician Hannah Fry makes a wry and apt comment:

> For the time being, worrying about evil AI is a bit like worrying about over-crowding on Mars. Maybe one day we'll get to the point where computer intelligence surpasses human intelligence, but we're nowhere near it yet. Frankly, we're still quite a long way away from creating hedgehog-level intelligence. So far, no one's even managed to get past worm.[27]

Humans have the mental capacity to look at problems in different ways or to reframe them. And that ability to frame a problem is central to teasing out the difference between the machine and human roles in AI. In their book *Framers: Human Advantage in an Age of Technology and Turmoil*, authors Kenneth Cukier, Viktor Mayer-Schönberger, and Francis de Véricourt show how major technological successes that are often regarded as entirely due to AI could not have been achieved without the human cognitive ability to frame issues in terms of mental models. The classic example they begin their book with is the discovery of halicin, an antibiotic capable of killing superbugs, by a team led by Regina Barzilay at MIT.[28] The *Financial Times* hailed their work with the headline: "AI Discovers Antibiotics to Treat Drug-Resistant Diseases." Yet, as the authors point out, this was not so much a victory for AI but for human cognition. They cite Barzilay: "People defined the problem, designed the approach, chose the molecules to train the algorithm, and then selected the database of substances to examine. And once some candidates popped up, humans reapplied their biological lens to understand why it worked."[29] Each stage involved the creation of a mental model to frame the problem and imagine how various scenarios might play out. And only humans can do that.

Frames come at different scales. From a philosophical perspective, paradigms are like large frames, and worldviews like even larger ones. Paradigm shifts or changes of worldviews are major events, whereas framing occurs much more frequently at all kinds of lower levels in everyday life. Framing helps focus our minds and create new options for action by giving us different perspectives.

Yet another perspective on the unique way humans see things stems from recent research in neuroscience. In *The Matter with Things: Our Brains, Our Delusions, and the Unmaking of the World*, published in 2021,[30] neuroscientist Iain McGilchrist, building on his earlier work, *The Master and His Emissary: The Divided Brain and the Making of the Western World*,[31] develops the thesis that although the two brain hemispheres are both involved in most brain activity, there are certain crucial differences between the way in which they pay attention that have profound consequences for how we think about the world around us.

He discovered that the left hemisphere has a very narrow beam that it uses to focus with precision on a detail: "It fixes it and grabs it (and the left hemisphere controls the right hand with which most of us do the grabbing and the getting). Whereas the right hemisphere has a broad, open, sustained vigilant attention, which is on the lookout for everything else without preconception. . . . So we've got this one world, which is composed of things that are mechanical, useful, inanimate, reducible to their parts, abstracted, decontextualised, dead; and another world, which is flowing, complex, living, changing and has all the qualities that make life worth living."[32]

McGilchrist argues that, in consequence of the Enlightenment, the Western academy has been dominated by the left hemisphere, which has mesmerized us to think that its mechanistic, reductionist, scientistic, manipulative approach – grabbing, getting, and controlling – gives us the whole picture of reality. Consequently, we have become blind to the integrative, holistic perspective of the right hemisphere, which would give us understanding. He says that it is like a radio set that has two channels, both of which we need to listen to, but we have chosen to listen to only the nonintelligent one, which is interested not in truth, courage, or magnanimity but only in greed and manipulation. Or to put it another way: "Things work well as long as the left hemisphere is carrying out work it's deputed to do by the right hemisphere. Rather like we use a computer. The computer doesn't really understand the data we draw from the complexity of life. That's not its job: its job is to process data very fast, and hand us back some that we then make sense of."[33]

He adduces evidence to show that the right cerebral hemisphere makes the primary contribution not only to emotional and social intelligence but to ordinary intelligence or cognitive power and is a far superior guide to reality.[34] He concludes: "Human intelligence is not like machine intelligence – modelled, as that is, on the serial procedures so typical of the left hemisphere."[35] These differences between the way in which the left and right hemispheres pay attention show why there are real limitations on which of our mental capacities may be simulated by AI technology. In support, McGilchrist cites microbiologist Brian Ford, who says that "to equate such data-rich digital operations with the infinite subtlety of life is absurd," since intelligence in life operates "on informational input that is essentially *Gestalt*[36] and not digital."[37] McGilchrist therefore thinks that AI should stand for artificial information processing and not artificial intelligence. Indeed, he points out that AI "could be seen as replicating the functions of the left hemisphere at frightening speed across the entire globe."[38]

We need to keep this in mind as we consider how author Dan Brown employs (narrow) AI in his novel *Origin* to tackle two big philosophical questions.

QUESTIONS

1. What do you think of the view "If it can be done, it should be done"?
2. Do you have a voice assistant? Does it sometimes disturb or concern you? Why?
3. Looking at the four ethical systems listed, which is the one that you most identify with?
4. Discuss the relative importance of the listed Asilomar principles. Which do you think is most important?
5. What ethical principles would you like to see hardwired into an autonomous car?
6. The "artificial" in "artificial intelligence" is real! Discuss.
7. Why are we a long way from creating AI? What are the greatest problems, in your view?
8. What are Iain McGilchrist's views on the brain? What implications do they have for our understanding of AI?

PART 2

TWO BIG QUESTIONS

CHAPTER 4

WHERE DO WE COME FROM?

The fictional professor Edmond Kirsch of Dan Brown's novel *Origin*[1] revisits the famous experiment that chemists Stanley Miller and Harold Urey performed in 1953, an experiment that won them the Nobel Prize. They mixed various chemicals, such as hydrogen, methane, and ammonia, thought to exist in the earth's early atmosphere, in a test tube and applied an electric spark. As the chemical mixture settled down, they found in it some of the amino acids that are often called the building blocks for life. For a time, their work was hailed as a scientific solution to the problem of the origin of life, but as time went on, it was recognized that the experiment did not deliver. It merely produced a few of the amino acids necessary for life.

The test tubes used in the experiment were preserved, and the experiment was revisited more than fifty years later, leading to the following results published by six authors in the November edition of *Science* (2008) under the title "The Miller Volcanic Spark Discharge Experiment." Though he writes a work of fiction, Dan Brown correctly states that this is an actual published scientific work and not fiction. Here is the abstract of that paper:

Miller's 1950s experiments used, besides the apparatus known in textbooks, one that generated a hot water mist in the spark flask, simulating a water vapor-rich volcanic eruption. We found the original extracts of this experiment in Miller's material and reanalyzed them. The volcanic apparatus produced a wider variety of amino acids than the classic one. Release of reduced gases in volcanic eruptions accompanied by lightning could have been common on the early Earth. Prebiotic compounds synthesized in these environments could have locally accumulated, where they could have undergone further processing.[2]

This research forms the trigger for the idea Dan Brown develops in his novel. The Miller-Urey experiment was a simulation carried out in a laboratory long before the days of computer modeling. What Brown's fictitious AI expert does is set up a mathematical model of the Miller-Urey experiment, factoring in the new information from 2008, and paying much more attention to the detailed interactions of chemicals down to the molecular level and thus securing a huge amount of data. Data of the sort that AI systems are ideal at processing. He then runs the experiment in virtual reality. It fails at first until he adjusts it to take into account entropy, the tendency for everything in the universe to run down towards equilibrium. Entropy is why your cup of hot coffee dissipates its heat to its surroundings and cools down but will never heat up again. The rerun eventually – lo and behold! – produces the double helix of DNA. Life is generated by natural processes without any supernatural intervention. The problem of life's origin is solved.

Well, in the *novel* it is solved, and in such a page-turning way that will intrigue many readers. But the question of the origin of life is a real question of such importance that we need to investigate it further to disentangle fact from fiction. In the novel (and often in real life) we are not dealing with science pure and simple but with a scientist whose science is influenced by his worldview. In Kirsch's case, it is his atheism, and he expresses it by saying: "The age of religion is drawing to an end . . . and the age of science is dawning"[3] – a view which, rather unsurprisingly, appears to coincide with that of author Dan Brown.

What is initially disturbing about Brown's use of recent science is that the lead author of the 2008 article on which Brown bases his argument, a real scientist named Jeremy England, of MIT, neither shares Brown's worldview nor approves of Brown's use of his research. Here is what England, an ordained rabbi, had to say about Dan Brown's book to the *Wall Street Journal* in October 2017:

> There's no real science in the book to argue over. . . . I'm a scientist, but I also study and live by the Hebrew Bible. To me, the idea that physics could prove that the God of Abraham is not the creator and ruler of the world reflects a serious misunderstanding – of both the scientific method and the function of the biblical text.[4]

England goes on to point out that science is not capable of disproving an explanatory matrix that sees confirmation of the activity of a creator in what we find in nature.

Dan Brown's *Origin* is, from a scientific perspective, flawed from the start by making the dubious move of citing someone's scientific research to make plausible the exact opposite of what the scientist himself thinks it means. Of course, one could argue that this is just a novel and Brown has the freedom to do what he likes. Perhaps, but the danger is that Brown says he is motivated to write the story by a serious philosophical question, and many people may well believe what he says, thinking that his conclusions are in tune with established science.

Not only that, but the claim that the simulation in Kirsch's scenario produced virtual DNA, and therefore solved the problem of life's origin, is pure science fiction. From the perspective of actual science, it is not even remotely plausible. One of the world's top experts on the chemistry of the origin of life, indeed one of the current most influential scientists in the world, James Tour, professor of chemistry, nanotechnology, and computer science at Houston's Rice University, has no doubt that chemistry invalidates Brown's claims:

> Life should not exist. This much we know from chemistry. In contrast to the ubiquity of life on earth, the lifelessness of other planets makes far better chemical sense. . . .
>
> Consider the following *Gedankenexperiment*. Let us assume that *all* the molecules we think may be needed to construct a cell are available in the requisite chemical and stereochemical purities. Let us assume that these molecules can be separated and delivered to a well-equipped laboratory. Let us also assume that the millions of articles comprising the chemical and biochemical literature are readily accessible.
>
> How might we build a cell?
>
> It is not enough to have the chemicals on hand. The relationship between the nucleotides and everything else must be specified and, for this, coding information is essential. DNA and RNA are the primary informational carriers of the cell. No matter the medium life might have adopted at the very beginning, its information had to come from somewhere. A string of nucleotides does not inherently encode anything. Let us assume that DNA and RNA are available in whatever sequence we desire.[5]

We should note that James Tour is willing for the sake of the argument to grant Edmond Kirsch his (virtual) DNA, even though this involves the deeper problem of the origin of the information content of DNA, since there is no evidence that it is derivable from chemistry by mindless, unguided processes. That immense problem notwithstanding, Tour's detailed chemical investigation contradicts the claims made by Kirsch: "We synthetic chemists should state the obvious. The appearance of life on earth is a mystery. We are nowhere near solving this problem. The proposals offered thus far to explain life's origin make no scientific sense."[6] That is the verdict of science.

Kirsch's fictitious verdict arises entirely from his atheistic philosophy. Science does not support it. In any case, fatal to Kirsch's case is his false conviction that the laws of nature can do the job of producing life. Yet he is not the only one to think so. Another example of this basic misunderstanding of the nature of law is given by well-known physicist Paul Davies, who said: "There's no need to invoke anything supernatural in the origins of the universe or of life. I have never liked the idea of divine tinkering. For me it is much more inspiring to believe that a set of mathematical laws can be so clever as to bring all these things into being."[7]

In the world in which most of us live, however, the simple law of arithmetic by itself, $1 + 1 = 2$, never brought anything into being. It certainly has never put any money into my bank account. If I put $1,000 into the bank, and later another $1,000, the laws of arithmetic will rationally explain how it is that I now have $2,000 in the bank. But if I never put any money into the bank myself and simply leave it to the laws of arithmetic to bring money into being in my bank account, I shall remain permanently bankrupt. C. S. Lewis grasped this issue with characteristic clarity. Of the events that combine to make up history, he writes: "To think the laws can produce it is like thinking that you can create real money by simply doing sums."[8] The world of strict naturalism, in which clever mathematical laws all by themselves bring the universe and life into existence, is pure (science) fiction. Theories and laws do not bring matter or energy into existence. The view that nevertheless they somehow have that capacity seems a rather desperate refuge from the alternative rational possibility that there is a Creator.

Clearly Davies, Kirsch, and Brown are unaware that the laws of nature do not actually *explain* the world to us. What they do is *describe* its regularities. Not only that, but the laws of nature do not even *cause* anything, and hence they do not *create* anything. A moment's thought will convince you that Newton's laws of motion have never moved a billiard ball in the history of the universe, let alone created the ball to start with. The laws describe the motion once the ball is there and has been set in movement by a person wielding a billiard cue.

Dan Brown's AI genius Kirsch clearly does not understand this. Even if you ignore this vital point, however, you are faced with a further question, which, to his credit, Brown does flag by putting it in the mouth of his hero, Harvard professor of symbology Robert Langdon. Brown writes: "Edmond's discovery was enthralling and clearly incendiary, but for Langdon it raised one burning question that he was surprised nobody was asking: *If the laws of physics are so powerful that they can create life . . . who created the laws?*" The narrative continues: "The question, of course, resulted in a dizzying intellectual hall of mirrors and brought everything full circle."[9]

But does it? Presumably Brown means that if you ask who created the laws, then you will logically have to ask who created that creator, and so on forever. Richard Dawkins puts this forward in *The God Delusion* as a knockdown argument against the existence of a creator God. It is no such thing, however. For if we ask the question who created the creator, we are *assuming* that the creator is created. But why assume that? According to the biblical worldview, the Creator, God, is not created but is eternal. Therefore, the chronology-dependent question that assumes there is something before God that created God does not apply to him!

It does, however, apply to things that are not eternal, so I put the question back to Dawkins: "You believe the universe created you. Who, then, created your creator?" I have waited over a decade and still have no reply. I am tempted to think this is a case of one hoisted with his own petard. For there is no "dizzying intellectual hall of mirrors" here, nor does such reasoning bring "everything full circle." No, the question where the laws come from has been asked and given a perfectly intelligible answer by the very greatest of scientists – men like Galileo, Kepler, Newton, and Jams Clerk Maxwell, all of whom, like James Tour and Jeremy England, are believers in God. They believe this, as I do, on the basis of convincing rational evidence that the laws came from God and that conviction inspired their science. C. S. Lewis, summarizing the work of the eminent philosopher and historian of science Alfred North Whitehead, expressed it as follows: "Men became scientific because they expected Law in Nature, and they expected Law in Nature because they believed in a Legislator."[10]

Far from hindering the rise of modern science, faith in God was the motor that drove it. It is sad, therefore, that many people will think Brown has shown that science has buried God, not because of the logic or science behind his argument, but because his readers are carried along to that conclusion by the emotional intensity of a blockbuster thriller. How can it be wrong, since it makes science so exciting?

Later in the book we discover that Kirsch had dreamed not so much of abolishing religion but rather to "create a *new* religion – a universal belief that united people rather than divided them. He thought that if he could convince people to revere the natural universe and the laws of physics that created us, then every culture would celebrate the same creation story rather than go to war over which of their antique myths was the most accurate."[11] This is no new idea. For instance, the "science as religion" idea was promoted by atheist T. H. Huxley, who wished to turn churches into temples to the goddess Sophia (wisdom), with scientists as its priests. There is no future, however, in a religion based on the completely false notion that the laws of nature created us and the universe. In more recent years, Darwinism (or some version of it) appears to function as a religion. This is argued by philosopher of biology Michael Ruse in his book *Darwinism as Religion: What Literature Tells Us about Evolution.*[12]

There is more to be said. The late Stephen Hawking seemed to keep a door open for God in the last paragraph of his bestseller *A Brief History of Time*, although he closed it some years later in another bestseller, *The Grand Design*, where he clearly asserted his atheism. I get the impression that Dan Brown's *Origin* more than leaves a door open for God, presumably deliberately. For its fictional hero Robert Langdon hesitates to accept Edmond Kirsch's thesis uncritically. The reasons given are important and are revealed when the equally fictional highly intelligent Ambra Vidal, director of the Guggenheim Museum, asks Langdon about God. Langdon's reply to her is that "for *me*, the question of God lies in understanding the difference between codes and patterns. . . . Patterns occur everywhere in nature. . . . Codes do not occur naturally in the world. . . . Codes are the deliberate inventions of intelligent consciousness."[13] She then mentions DNA, which is a superb example of chemical coding in that the DNA molecule consists of a "word" in a four-"letter" chemical "alphabet." At 3.4 billion letters, it is the longest word that has ever been discovered. Langdon then goes on to confirm what many of us (including myself) have long since thought, that this is powerful evidence of a divine signature. As a mathematician, I was both surprised – given Brown's overall thesis – and delighted to read Langdon's conclusion: "When I witness the precision of mathematics, the reliability of physics, and the symmetries of the cosmos, I don't feel like I'm observing cold science; I feel as if I'm seeing a living footprint . . . the shadow of some greater force that is just beyond our grasp."[14]

Donald Knuth, one of the fathers of computation and a Christian, said: "I think people who write programs do have at least a glimmer of extra insight into the nature of God . . . because creating a program often means that you have to create a small universe."[15]

The very same DNA that Kirsch claims to have "discovered" in his AI simulation is a code and not simply a pattern. It carries information, so it cannot have arisen by unguided natural processes as Kirsch says. The genetic code is only a paradox for those people who assume that DNA arose by unguided natural processes. The suggestion that DNA was created by an intelligence is dangerous only to atheism, not to science.

Langdon's fictional reaction mirrors that of the late real-life eminent philosopher Antony Flew, a lifelong atheist who eventually abandoned his atheism and came to acknowledge the existence of God. He gave as the reason for his conversion the fact that biologists' investigation of DNA "has shown, by the almost unbelievable complexity of the arrangements which are needed to produce [life], that intelligence must have been involved." He added: "My whole life has been guided by the principle of Plato's Socrates: Follow the evidence, wherever it leads." He was asked what if his belief upset people. "That's too bad," said Flew.[16]

Indeed, the very facts that science can be done, that the universe is to an impressive extent mathematically intelligible, and that information-bearing macromolecules like DNA exist are entirely consistent with, and indeed point towards, the validity of the biblical statement: "In the beginning was the Word . . . and the Word was God. . . . All things were made through him" (John 1:1, 3). It is perfectly rational to say, as Francis Collins did at the announcement of the completion of the Human Genome Project under his direction, that DNA is "God's language."[17]

What are we, then, to make of Dan Brown's book and indeed of Dan Brown himself? He claims to have lost his Christian faith and is moving towards atheism, although he says he has not made that final step. Like his character Edmond Kirsch, he believes that the laws of nature can explain life. He calls his views conflicted. The book bears that out. At times, it seems to endorse atheism, and yet towards the end the notion that there is an intelligent designer God behind the universe is given credibility. At other times the book appears to approve of the destruction of religion by science. Yet, again at the very end, there is an intriguing section where Langdon is discussing with a priest the line from William Blake that forms the password to Kirsch's computer, the search for which plays a prominent role in the plotline of the book: "The dark Religions are departed & sweet Science reigns."[18]

Langdon suggests to the priest that this could mean that science destroys the dark and bad religions but not the enlightened ones. There is truth in that. For science has indeed got rid of the "god of the gaps" type of religions of the ancient Greeks, for instance, that stood in the way of the advance of science, but science has certainly not got rid of God the Creator, the upholder of the universe as revealed in the Judeo-Christian heritage, whose intelligent creation inspired the pioneer scientists in the first place.[19]

QUESTIONS

1. Before you read this chapter, what account would you give for human origins?
2. What was the Miller-Urey experiment? Do you think it solved the problem of life's origin?
3. Why is the problem of the origin of life so intractable? Do you think that science has the power to solve it?
4. Why can't the laws of nature create life? Or anything?
5. What is the connection between the rise of modern science and faith in God? What is the significance of this?
6. What do you think Langdon meant by distinguishing between codes and patterns?
7. What in your view is the connection between DNA and the Word of God in John 1?

CHAPTER 5

WHERE ARE WE GOING?

It's tough to make predictions, especially about the future.
Yogi Berra

Dan Brown's purported resolution of our first big question uses mathematical modeling and an AI system working on an immense database of information to make predictions about the evolution of a mixture of chemicals in the past. It is not hard to guess how he will approach the second big question.

Brown applies a similar methodology to extrapolate a simulation of human evolution into the future. The result, revealed at the end of the book (spoiler alert), is that his AI system, while working on another vast database consisting primarily of information gleaned from past information about bone fragments and changing environments over time, shows the eventual development of a new species. To be more exact, rather than species we should say it is a new kingdom, because instead of branching from an existing species, it is a fusion of two "species," humans and AI.

He calls this new kingdom "Technium." It is a nonliving species, by which he presumably means a non-biological species, although this is hard to square with his notion that it is a *fusion* of human biological life with technology. His projection shows that it eventually replaces the human race by 2050, and it does so by absorption! One is tempted to think this is nothing more than entertaining science fiction. And while it may turn out to be just that, not everyone sees it as fiction.

It is, apparently, no accident that Kirsch's name begins with *K*, since he seems to have been modeled on Ray Kurzweil, prolific inventor and Google's director of engineering. Kurzweil is the author of *The Singularity Is Near: When Humans Transcend Biology*, a book that unpacks his belief that within the foreseeable future, possibly as few as thirty years, AI robots will overtake humans in their intelligence and capabilities: "The nonbiological portion of our intelligence will predominate."[1] The term *singularity* is taken from physics and refers to a point where the laws of physics break down so that you cannot see beyond it – like the moment of the Big Bang origin of the universe.

Nick Bostrom of Oxford's Future of Life Institute calls this event the "intelligence explosion" in his book *Superintelligence: Paths, Dangers, Strategies*.[2] Kurzweil says: "The 21st century will be different. . . . The human species, along with the computational technology it created, will be able to solve age-old problems . . . and will be in a position to change the nature of mortality in a postbiological future."[3] This is the vision of artificial superintelligence, or ASI. It should also be noted that this particular expression of ASI is the view of an engineer and inventor, not of a science fiction writer. Even though it has been said that fears about ASI are more likely to be expressed by those without technical experience of AI, these are concepts that able and scientifically educated people are taking seriously.[4]

There is considerable speculation as to when the singularity might occur. Interested readers are encouraged to consult the article *Future Progress in Artificial Intelligence: A Survey of Expert Opinion* by Vincent C. Müller and Nick Bostrom. Their results show the percentages of respondents who took a particular position on the question whether "AI systems will probably (over 50%) reach overall human ability by 2040–50, and very likely (with 90% probability) by 2075. From reaching human ability, it will move on to superintelligence in 2 years (10%) to 30 years (75%) thereafter. The experts say the probability is 31% that this development turns out to be 'bad' or 'extremely bad' for humanity."[5]

But Stuart Russell, one of the world's most technically experienced AI researchers, cautioned in his 2021 Reith Lectures that we are still a long way from achieving general-purpose AI. Russell thinks that even deep learning may not be able to supply the necessary further conceptual breakthroughs. Nevertheless, his view is that it is prudent to prepare for the eventuality of AGI/ASI in light of the many things once thought scientifically impossible that have since been realized, such as nuclear energy.

In addition, Jobst Landgrebe and Barry Smith, in their 2022 book *Why Machines Will Never Rule the World: Artificial Intelligence without Fear*, argue that just as physics shows the impossibility of constructing a perpetual motion machine, so the mathematics of complex systems shows that it is not possible, nor will it be, to engineer AGI machines, even at the cognitive level of a crow, and that, therefore, the singularity will never happen.[6]

Where did this idea begin? Kurzweil was not the first to think of the singularity. The fundamental idea of AGI goes back to a deservedly famous quote from an article written in 1965 by statistician I. J. Good, entitled "Speculations Concerning the First Ultraintelligent Machine":

> Let an ultraintelligent machine be defined as a machine that can far surpass all the intellectual activities of any man however clever. Since the design of machines is one of these intellectual activities, an ultraintelligent machine could design even better machines; there would then unquestionably be an "intelligence explosion," and the intelligence of man would be left far behind. Thus, the first ultraintelligent machine is the last invention that man need ever make.[7]

Looking even further in the past, on Saturday, 13 June 1863, a letter from the English author Samuel Butler (1835–1902), entitled *Darwin among the Machines*,[8] appeared in *The Press,* a newspaper in Christchurch, New Zealand. In it, Butler argued that machines might be kind of "mechanistic life," undergoing, in the spirit of Darwinian natural selection, a kind of constant evolution, and that machines might eventually supplant humans as the dominant species:

> We refer to the question: What sort of creature man's next successor in the supremacy of the earth is likely to be. We have often heard this debated; but it appears to us that we are ourselves creating our own successors; we are daily adding to the beauty and delicacy of their physical organisation; we are daily giving them greater power and supplying by all sorts of ingenious contrivances that self-regulating, self-acting power which will be to them what intellect has been to the human race. In the course of ages we shall find ourselves the inferior race. . . .
>
> Day by day, however, the machines are gaining ground upon us; day by day we are becoming more subservient to them; more men are daily bound down as slaves to tend them, more men are daily devoting the energies of their whole lives to the development of mechanical life. The upshot is simply a question of time, but that the time will come when the machines will hold the real supremacy over the world and its inhabitants is what no person of a truly philosophic mind can for a moment question.[9]

The ideas in this letter were later published by Butler in a reworked form as the first part of his 1872 book *Erewhon*, a book that influenced the writing of George Orwell's book *1984*.

We should also notice that envisioning an ultraintelligent machine is at odds with the concept of undirected Darwinian evolution. All of the accelerating advances in the realm of technology, robots, and AI have been due to human intelligent design. What Kurzweil predicts, therefore, involves artifacts designed by humans, in the sense that humans got the whole thing going until, in some scenario, those artifacts possess more than human intelligence and take over their own subsequent development.

Dan Brown's fictitious AI expert Kirsch points out that to a certain extent we have already started to merge with our own technology. We wear VR glasses; we hold our mobile phones close to our ears; we have all kinds of high-quality headphones; and we are starting to embed computer chips into our brains, for instance, to cure deafness. We are also constructing more and more sophisticated prosthetic limbs, growing spare parts for our bodies, tinkering with our genetic structures, and exploring the possibilities and potential for genetic enhancement. Kirsch's grand conclusion is that "new technologies like cybernetics, synthetic intelligence, cryonics, molecular engineering, and virtual reality will forever change what it means to be *human*. And I realize there are those of you who believe you, as *Homo sapiens*, are God's chosen species. I can understand that this news may feel like the end of the world to you. But I beg you, please believe me . . . the future is actually much *brighter* than you imagine."[10]

The real-world quest to enhance human beings is often called the transhumanism project. Bostrom explains that transhumanism is "the intellectual and cultural movement that affirms the possibility and desirability of fundamentally improving the human condition through applied reason, especially by developing and making widely available technologies to eliminate aging and to greatly enhance human intellectual, physical, and psychological capacities."[11] In short, it represents the desire to create superintelligence, superlongevity, and superhappiness. As historian and Jewish philosopher Hava Tirosh-Samuelson of Arizona State University writes:

> Appealing to a very diverse group of people (e.g., scientists, computer experts, space explorers, engineers and technology enthusiasts, gamers, tech entrepreneurs, science fiction writers and fans, strategists, and futurists), transhumanism exerts enormous impact on the way we think about technology

and the way we imagine the future of the human species. . . . Transhumanism expresses exuberant techno-optimism about the power of technoscience to transform the human condition and inaugurate the posthuman phase in the evolution of the human species.[12]

Many people (including Bostrom) seem to think the words *transhuman* and *transhumanism* originated with atheist Julian Huxley (1887–1975). In 1957, Huxley said:

> The human species can, if it wishes, transcend itself – not just sporadically, an individual here in one way, an individual there in another way, but in its entirety, as humanity. We need a name for this new belief. Perhaps transhumanism will serve: man remaining man, but transcending himself, by realizing new possibilities of and for his human nature. . . . "I believe in transhumanism": once there are enough people who can truly say that the human species will be on the threshold of a new kind of existence, as different from ours as ours is from that of Peking man. It will at last be consciously fulfilling its real destiny.[13]

But Huxley was not the first to use the word. The origin of *transhuman* is not secular. Historically, it was first used, not by a scientist, but by Henry Francis Cary in his 1814 translation of Dante's *Paradiso*. It occurs in a passage where Dante tries to imagine the resurrection of his own body and writes: "Words may not tell of that *transhuman* change."[14]

Contemporary ideas surrounding transhumanism include whole-brain emulation, cyborgs (cybernetic organisms), and the hope that a solution to the problem of death will be found – as we may deduce from the fact that some people have paid for their bodies and/or brains to be frozen until that time (cryonics). It is evident that such developments spring from a deep-rooted human longing for immortality. Earlier, we quoted Martin Rees, and it is helpful to consider the wider context of his quote:

> We should be mindful of an unprecedented kind of change that could emerge within a few decades. Human beings themselves – their mentality and their physique – may become malleable through the deployment of genetic modification and cyborg technologies. This is a game changer. When we admire the literature and artefacts that have survived from antiquity, we feel an affinity, across a time gulf of thousands of years, with those ancient artists and their

civilisations but we can have zero confidence that the dominant intelligences a few centuries hence will have any emotional resonance with us – even though they may have an algorithmic understanding of how we behaved.[15]

It is this kind of transhumanist ASI prediction of the singularity that fills some people with Orwellian alarm at the possibility that robots will become more intelligent than humans, take over our jobs, and, even worse, eventually rebel against humans and destroy them as inferiors of no further value. It is *1984* with a vengeance.

In 1951, in a paper published posthumously, Alan Turing wrote:

> Let us now assume, for the sake of argument, that these machines are a genuine possibility, and look at the consequences of constructing them. To do so would of course meet with great opposition, unless we have advanced greatly in religious toleration from the days of Galileo. There would be great opposition from the intellectuals who were afraid of being put out of a job. It is probable though that the intellectuals would be mistaken about this. There would be plenty to do in trying, say, to keep one's intelligence up to the standard set by the machines, for it seems probable that once the machine thinking method had started, it would not take long to outstrip our feeble powers. There would be no question of the machines dying, and they would be able to converse with each other to sharpen their wits. At some stage therefore we should have to expect the machines to take control, in the way that is mentioned in Samuel Butler's *Erewhon*.[16]

Turing, like Orwell, was clearly aware of Butler's prescience in imagining such a singularity.

Elon Musk thinks that AI risks "summoning the demon" and is more dangerous than nukes. He once said AI was "our biggest existential threat" as he asked for regulatory oversight to make sure "we don't do something very foolish."[17] Musk is worried about the control problem mentioned earlier: that we humans could lose control of a superintelligent AI, which will presumably be able to rewrite its own programming and neutralize or bypass any control measures originally built into it. He is not alone in his concern that such an AI presents an existential threat to human existence. In 2015, together with more than 8,000 people, including Noam Chomsky and the late Stephen Hawking, Musk signed an open letter warning against the potential pitfalls of AI development. In connection with this open letter, the paper "Research

Priorities for Robust and Beneficial Artificial Intelligence" by Stuart Russell, Daniel Dewey, and Max Tegmark concludes:

> In summary, success in the quest for artificial intelligence has the potential to bring unprecedented benefits to humanity, and it is therefore worthwhile to research how to maximize these benefits while avoiding potential pitfalls. The research agenda outlined in this paper, and the concerns that motivate it, have been called anti-AI, but we vigorously contest this characterization. It seems self-evident that the growing capabilities of AI are leading to an increased potential for impact on human society. It is the duty of AI researchers to ensure that the future impact is beneficial. We believe that this is possible, and hope that this research agenda provides a helpful step in the right direction.[18]

In his book *Brief Answers to the Big Questions*, published posthumously, Hawking repeats this concern:

> While primitive forms of artificial intelligence developed so far have proved very useful, I fear the consequences of creating something that can match or surpass humans. . . . Humans, who are limited by slow biological evolution, couldn't compete and would be superseded. And in the future AI could develop a will of its own, a will that is in conflict with ours. . . . The real risk with AI isn't malice but competence. A super-intelligent AI will be extremely good at accomplishing its goals, and if those goals aren't aligned with ours we're in trouble.[19]

This flags what has come to be known as the value alignment problem – how to make sure AI systems and machines "behave" within acceptable ethical norms and, for example, avoid the biases and discriminatory behavior patterns that infect our culture. That this is a real issue was highlighted in 2023 when reports were circulated that, in a simulation, an AI automated weapons system programmed with the goal of eliminating enemies decided that its operator was interfering with its achieving that goal and so it killed its operator – much to the consternation of the constructors of the system. Rather impenetrable denials were issued that this was not exactly what happened, but one can easily imagine that, if it didn't, it one day will.[20]

Similarly, Louis Rosenberg, who founded Unanimous AI to amplify the intelligence of networked human groups using the biological principle of swarm intelligence combined with AI, says:

To me, the prospect of a sentient artificial intelligence being created on Earth is no less dangerous than an alien intelligence showing up from another planet. After all, it will have its own values, its own morals, its own sensibilities, and, most of all, its own interests.

To assume that its interests will be aligned with ours is absurdly naive, and to assume that it won't put its interests first – putting our very existence at risk – is to ignore what we humans have done to every other creature on Earth. Thus, we should be preparing for the imminent arrival of a sentient AI with the same level of caution as the imminent arrival of a spaceship from another solar system. We need to assume this is an existential threat for our species.[21]

In a January 2022 article in *The Times*, Damian Whitworth quotes Stuart Russell, who has emphasized the same point: "The threat will come less from machines deciding they hate us and want to kill us than from their advanced competency. A highly sophisticated machine with a fixed objective could stop at nothing to achieve that objective and fail to take into account other human priorities."[22]

The article mentions an extreme example of this from the film *2001: A Space Odyssey*, where Hal, the onboard computer, kills four of the five astronauts because "he" decides that they constitute a threat to the mission. Yet the article also points out that this is not simply the realm of science fiction. It is already happening in social media and advertising, where algorithms attempt to keep our online attention as long as possible while tempting us to purchase things we may not really need or want. They subtly move us in directions that, if we had time to think over it, we would often not wish to go.

SHADES OF GEORGE ORWELL

Bill Gates believes AI has vast potential for benefiting humanity. He has said it will give us a "chance to supercharge the social sciences." He is also concerned, however, about autonomous weapons, as is Jeff Bezos of Amazon, who thinks that they are "extremely scary."[23] Mark Zuckerberg of Facebook tends to be less cautious:

"We need to make sure that we don't get too negative on this stuff," he said referring to AI technology. "Because it's too easy for people to point to an individual failure of technology and try to use that as an argument to slow down progress."

Zuckerberg said he himself has been trying to make this point for a while. He did follow his support for AI up with remarks about the seriousness of AI ethics and clarified that there are bound to be issues along the way, just as there are for any new technology. But he said AI skeptics aren't helping the cause; if anything, they're being counter-productive.[24]

Opinions about AI are clearly divided. In any case, we must ask what it means for our understanding of who we are and what we might become. As hinted earlier, the quest for AGI needs to be distinguished from the parallel quest to upgrade human beings, although there is inevitably some overlap. One of the objectives of AGI is to decouple life from biology and construct artificial life based on some other substrate, probably silicon – thus bringing us into the postbiological age. Some hold that this may have already occurred. Philosopher Susan Schneider, founding director of the Center for the Future Mind at Florida Atlantic University, says: "The universe's greatest intelligences may be postbiological, having grown out of civilizations that were once biological."[25] She adds that she shares this perspective with several others, including Paul Davies, Steven Dick, Martin Rees, and Seth Shostak. Elsewhere, however, she points out that there may be problems: "For all we know, consciousness may be limited to carbon substrates. Carbon molecules form stronger, more stable chemical bonds than silicon, which allows carbon to form an extraordinary number of compounds, and unlike silicon, carbon has the capacity to more easily form double bonds. This difference has important implications in the field of astrobiology, because it is for this reason that carbon, and not silicon, is said to be well-suited for the development of life throughout the universe."[26] She regards the problem of AGI consciousness as open.

So while some see a future decoupled from biological life, others focus more on the upgrading of humans – starting with human life as it is now and enhancing, modifying, and fitting it with implanted technology (some of which may involve AGI) to produce a superintelligent composite, like Dan Brown's Technium or Yuval Noah Harari's *homo deus*. In Brown's fictional scenario, a narrow AI system was used to *predict* the merging of humans with technology, but AI did not *perform* the upgrading itself. His AI genius had no means to do that. Nor, indeed, is there much evidence that anyone else has it or will ever have it.

We should also note that terminology in this area is somewhat fluid; some people prefer the term "intelligence augmentation," or IA, rather than AI. It is also useful to differentiate between several different project objectives and first to ask: What are our starting materials? When people talk of *making* artificial life, they generally mean construction from inorganic materials such as steel, glass, copper, or silicon from scratch. After all, humans can already "make" human life by in vitro fertilization, but that process starts with living cells, not nonliving materials. Upgrading humanity means starting with human life and modifying it organically and/or adding technology to it so that what is eventually produced is composite – and therefore only partially artificial. It is also only partially human, however. The transhumanist vision, which we will explore further in chapter 10, embraces this idea of an end to humanity as we know it.

In summary, we have seen how some are looking to AGI as an indication of how human intelligence might produce artificial life and, possibly, simulated cognition and consciousness. At the same time, the idea of *upgrading humanity*, though related, refers to what can be done with human biological life to enhance it. Both are aimed at producing a superhuman superintelligence. Whether either will ever do so is another matter entirely.

Such scenarios, however, raise several obvious questions that readers are encouraged to think about and discuss before we look at them in later chapters.

QUESTIONS

1. Does the idea of humans merging with machines appeal to you? Does it seem likely? Why or why not?
2. What do you think the singularity is? Will it come? And when? Discuss.
3. The first ultraintelligent machine is the last invention that man need ever make. What are the ethical norms that should be applied to AI developments? How can we ensure that they will be beneficial to humanity?
4. What do you understand of transhumanism?
5. Is "rights" a meaningful category when applied to AGI/ASI?
6. Is the future really "much brighter than you imagine"?
7. Is Martin Rees right to say that "we can have zero confidence that the dominant intelligences a few centuries hence will have any emotional resonance with us"?
8. Do you fear the advent of a machine superintelligence? If so, why?

PART 3

THE NOW AND FUTURE OF AI

CHAPTER 6

NARROW ARTIFICIAL INTELLIGENCE

The Future Is Bright?

The questions raised at the end of the previous chapter are of considerable general interest to many today, and to address them we must think carefully about what technologies we are talking about, what their positive benefits are, whether there are any risks associated with them, and whether they raise ethical problems. As I warned before, one of the dangers of introducing futuristic and speculative scenarios in which humans are gradually merged with technology is that it gives the impression that AI is concerned only with speculative and scary scenarios whose implementation is just around the corner. Elon Musk said in April 2024 that artificial general intelligence was only a couple of years away.[1] Yet this is not everyone's view. One of the winners of the 2018 Turing Prize, Yann LeCun, chief AI scientist at Facebook, has said: "Whether we'll be able to use new methods to create human-level intelligence, well, there's probably another 50 mountains to climb, including ones we can't even see yet. . . . We've only climbed the first mountain. Maybe the second."[2] This means we need to separate reality from hype. We need to get our feet back on solid ground by thinking more about the realities we encounter today with narrow AI and what it has actually achieved to this point.

Historically, AI has had a bumpy ride. When researchers coined the term "AI" in 1956, they imagined that one summer's work by a small team would show that every feature of learning and intelligence could be built into a machine! Those early expectations were clearly unrealistic, as more than sixty years later their question is still unanswered. For a time, AI even fell into disfavor, but with the availability of greatly enhanced computing power, it is now riding high. The UK has future investment plans to educate 1,000 PhDs in AI with a £1.3 billion fund set up in 2018. In November 2023, Microsoft committed a further £2.5 billion to the UK.[3] Between 2011 and 2015, China published 41,000 articles on AI, nearly twice as many as the US – clearly way ahead of the rest.[4] Chinese researchers have since become even more prolific, publishing 155,487 papers about AI in 2022, followed by those in the EU with 101,455 and US researchers' 81,130. Chinese president Xi Jinping (who takes considerable personal interest in AI technology) expects his country to lead the field by 2030.[5] As for investment in AI technologies, MIT announced in 2018 the single largest investment to date, $1 billion, by an American academic institution in computing and AI.[6] It is reckoned that $200 billion will be invested in AI in 2024.

Experience tells us that most technological advances have both an upside and a downside. A sharp knife can be used for surgery – or as a murder weapon. A car can be used to take you to work – or as a getaway vehicle after a crime. The same is true of AI. There are many valuable positive developments, and there are some very alarming negative aspects that demand close ethical attention. Here are several brief descriptions of ways in which AI is already being used.

Email. AI is being used with emails for advanced spam recognition, autocorrection of spelling or grammar, and text prediction that helps us write messages and emails more rapidly by using a part of a sentence or phrase that we have already written to predict the next word or phrase and suggest it to us. Prediction technology has taken a vast leap forward with the invention of ChatGPT, as we shall see later.

Language translation. Since childhood I have been interested in languages and managed to learn German at a sufficient level to be able to lecture in it. At one point I wrote my lectures in German, laboriously looking up the words that were not yet part of my active vocabulary, and the entire process took a great deal of time. Today, all I need to do is write the lecture in English, feed it into Google Translate, and within a few seconds I have a German translation that I can read through and make a few corrections and I am ready to go. This is a phenomenally useful development. There are many variants of this technology as well, including speech translation, speech to text, and text to speech.

The simplest kind of automated translation is word-for-word translation that goes through a text sequentially using dictionaries to map the words in the source language into equivalent words in the target language. Yet such vocabulary-based translation is essentially useless for most practical purposes, since it does not take into account how a word in one language may have no equivalent in another, or that words can have multiple meanings, or that meaning depends on context and grammar.

The two main forms of automated machine translation are rule based and statistical, with the former (rule based) taking into account the grammar and idiom usage of both source and target languages. Statistical machine translation (SMT) generates translations using statistical models whose parameters are derived from the analysis of a large database of bilingual text corpora. Hybrid machine translators combine both translation methods by doing a rules-based pre-translation first and then fine-tuning it through statistical processes with possibly another rules-based fine-tuning on the output. The latest versions of Google Translate also use neural networks to detect patterns in hundreds of millions of documents that have previously been translated by humans to make intelligent guesses as to the meaning of your text.

Digital assistants. A digital assistant, also called an AI assistant or a virtual assistant, is an application program that understands natural language voice commands and completes tasks for the user. The idea was first mooted in the 1940s, and over the past few years huge progress has been made in the area of linguistics known as natural language processing (NLP). Today we possess meeting assistants such as Otter, Fireflies, and Murf that can record and transcribe meetings instantaneously, capture slides and insert them into notes, and complete many other timesaving tasks. We also have an array of personal digital assistants such as Google Now, Alexa, Siri, Facebook M, and Cortana that are used to answer spoken or written questions, give recommendations for restaurants and entertainment, book travel and holidays, control the smart devices in our homes, and suggest things we might like to buy based on our past purchases. Socratic can help with mathematics and ELSA Speak with English.

Chatbots are computer programs that simulate human conversation (either written or spoken) and thus allow humans to interact with digital devices as if they were communicating with a real person. They are online digital assistants used in "live chats" on commercial websites to handle customers' questions about products and services. Some digital assistants are being trained in advanced speech recognition to give early warning of possibly self-harming or even suicidal tendencies in their users. One of the most significant advancements in NLP has been the development of LLMs like OpenAI's ChatGPT. These models are trained on massive amounts of text data and can generate text for applications such as chatbots, and virtual assistants, with unprecedented capacity for automated content creation. This is such a revolutionary development that we will devote more space to it later.

Manufacturing. According to a Boston Consulting Group report, the most important AI use cases in the manufacturing industry are intelligent, self-optimizing machines that automate production processes, forecast efficiency losses for better planning, and detect quality defects on production lines to facilitate predictive maintenance.[7] In 2021 it was announced that Google had used reinforced machine learning to cut the time of development of a new generation of machine-learning computer chips from many months of work by humans with years of experience to just six hours by the AI system. Such processes involve the arrangements of billions of transistors on a chip – a task of staggering complexity.[8] A spokesperson for Samsung confirms that the company is using Synopsys AI software to design Exynos chips that are used in the manufacture of Samsung's smartphones.[9] In this way AI is being used to accelerate its own development.

Innovative applications abound. Carnegie Mellon University announced in April 2018 that they have developed an AI algorithm that will automate not only the carrying out of experiments to find the best high-capacity car battery but also the planning and decision-making stages. Another example is a robotic "flying scarecrow" using an AI system that has been developed to keep flocks of birds away from airports. A sophisticated AI-driven camera recognition system is in place around wind turbines that switches them off if eagles, a protected species, fly too near and are in danger of crashing into the blades.

Medicine. It is no exaggeration to say that AI will revolutionize medicine and is now being used effectively in many areas: in the development of new drugs, in the automation of medical treatments such as remote robotic surgery, and as an aid to increase the efficiency of health provision. This is particularly true of diagnostics, where many leading healthcare systems have adopted some form of AI. To identify conditions in images (such as X-rays), clinicians first have to train the algorithms on what to look for. Engineers at the University of Toronto have designed a new approach using machine learning to create computer-generated X-rays that augment AI training sets. They compared the accuracy of their augmented dataset to the original dataset when fed through their AI system and found that classification accuracy improved by 20 percent for common conditions. For some rare conditions, accuracy improved up to about 40 percent, and because the synthesized X-rays are not from real individuals, the dataset can be made readily available to researchers outside the hospital premises without violating privacy concerns. Lead researcher Shahrokh Valaee says: "It's exciting because we've been able to overcome a hurdle in applying artificial intelligence to medicine by showing that these augmented datasets help to improve classification accuracy. . . . Deep learning only works if the volume of training data is large enough and this is one way to ensure we have neural networks that can classify images with high precision."[10]

Such techniques are also successfully used to detect lung cancer or strokes from a database of CT scans, and various kinds of skin lesions from photographic images. AI systems also exist for the detection of diabetic retinopathy, a condition caused by damage to the blood vessels of the light-sensitive tissue at the back of the eye, which can lead to blindness. Deep learning AI, working on a database of eye images, matched or exceeded the performance of experts in identifying and grading the severity of the conditions. Interestingly, the software was not explicitly programmed to recognize features from images that might indicate the disease. It simply looked at thousands of healthy and diseased eyes and figured out for itself how to spot the condition. The number of potentially beneficial applications of systems like these seems essentially unlimited, and new ones are appearing every day.

Scientists at the University of Hong Kong designed the first neurosurgical robotic system capable of performing bilateral stereotactic neurosurgery inside an MRI scanner. This is one of the treatments for a variety of movement and neuropsychiatric disorders such as Parkinson's disease, essential tremor, and major depression. It involves a technique that can locate targets of surgical interest using an external positioning system widely applied in brain biopsy, tumor ablation, drug delivery, as well as deep brain stimulation. Parkinson's disease alone is the second most common disease of the nervous system after Alzheimer's disease and is projected to affect more than 8.7 million people worldwide by 2030. As such, any improvement to this surgery would benefit a large population.[11]

The National Health Service (NHS) in the UK expects to be a world leader in AI and machine learning by 2025: "Exploiting the boom in AI technology will help to meet the NHS Long Term Plan's target of making up to 30 million outpatient appointments unnecessary, saving over £1 billion in what would have been increasing outpatient visits which can then be reinvested in front line care, saving patients unnecessary journeys to hospitals."[12] The chief executive of NHS England has said: "Health providers will be paid to substitute clinicians with machines as the NHS embraces artificial intelligence to improve patient outcomes and deliver savings."[13] One development in this direction was the introduction in one hundred UK hospitals of an AI analytic system that can predict emergency department admissions three weeks in advance and thus help greatly with a vital part of hospital administration.[14]

Even in medicine, however, there are possible downsides to the deployment of AI. A report on AI by the Academy of Medical Royal Colleges in the UK warns that the proliferation of health apps could eventually mean medical services may be overwhelmed by the worried, yet perfectly well, whose AI-enabled smartphones or fitness attachments have erroneously told them they need medical attention.[15]

On the other hand, when medical services around the world were overwhelmed by the COVID pandemic, AI systems were successfully implemented in record time to develop technologies that could accurately diagnose the virus from chest radiography images as well as aid in development of an array of vaccines. "Machine-learning systems and computational analyses have played an important role in the vaccine quest. These tools are helping researchers understand the virus and its structure. They also predict which of its components will provoke an immune response – a key step in vaccine design. They can help scientists choose the elements of potential vaccines and make sense of experimental data. They also help scientists track the virus's genetic mutations over time, information that will determine any vaccine's value in the years to come."[16] AI has shown great promise in helping counter the rapid spread of the COVID virus and in many areas related to health management and the production and allocation of resources. At the same time, scientists are increasingly aware that AI is only as good as the data it trains from and are carefully evaluating ethical aspects of its use, including bias and misdiagnosis. Many who recognize AI's potential value also see its potential risks. Poorly designed AI systems may misdiagnose. If software is trained on datasets that reflect cultural biases, the resulting system will reflect those biases with possibly unfortunate consequences.

Isaac Kohane, head of the Department of Biomedical Informatics at the Harvard Medical School, and his coauthors said that AI will eventually make it possible to bring all medical knowledge to bear in the service of any case. Properly designed AI has the potential to make our healthcare system more efficient and less expensive, ease the paperwork burden that has more and more doctors considering new careers, fill the gaping holes in access to quality care in the world's poorest places, and, among many other things, serve as an unblinking watchdog on the lookout for the medical errors that kill an estimated 200,000 people and cost $1.9 billion annually.[17] All of this, however, will involve a huge investment program.

On a smaller scale, but nevertheless worth noting, is the pioneering work of Rosalind Picard and her team at her MIT Laboratory of Affective Computing in conjunction with the company Empatica. They have created the first machine-learning system that can recognize seizures using a smartwatch that is FDA-approved and on the market in the US and EU.[18] The watch runs in connection with an AI algorithm that looks for real-time patterns of movements and electrical changes in the patient's skin that indicate a likely seizure. When such patterns are detected, it alerts the wearer (giving him or her a chance to cancel a possible false detection), and if it is not canceled quickly, the AI summons a caregiver for help. It can also let the caregiver know where the person in need of help is. It can do all of this continuously without requiring the wearer to do anything other than keep the smartwatch and mobile phone charged.[19]

When the most dangerous type of seizure strikes, it renders its victim unconscious and hence unable to call for help. The most critical period of time is during the minutes after it seems as though the seizure has ended, when activity deep in the brain can change and turn off respiration. Yet this has a good chance of being restarted if a person arrives to provide first aid. This smartwatch AI system has already been credited with summoning human help to save lives and has the potential over time to significantly reduce the number of deaths in epilepsy (which currently takes more lives every year than house fires or sudden infant death syndrome).

Picard's lab at MIT has also been developing AI / machine learning to help people discern if they are sliding into depression long before they would need a diagnosis. The hope is that they could take measures to prevent getting further depressed.[20] These are all examples of narrow AI, targeted at helping prevent illness, and "knowing" nothing, simply finding patterns that are probabilistically associated with potential needs. Such data collection does, however, raise the ethical question of the potentiality of medical data falling into the wrong hands.

Social robots. Eminent UK scientist Martin Rees agrees that robots may eventually take over many jobs, but not all. He believes they will never be any good at caring, an activity that lies at the heart of what it means to be human. Yet even if we grant that robots do not care in the same internal, conscious, mindful way that humans care, there have been intriguing developments in the area of effective care simulation.

For example, Rosalind Picard's group at MIT has published studies about the creation of robotic text-based chat and conversational agents that appeared to people as if they really do care – to the extent that those interacting responded to the agents by acting in ways that showed the technology was achieving real success. Picard comments:

> This, like all AI to date, works only in very narrow contexts, but also it is very good in those contexts. People perceive the AIs that use empathetic language as more "caring" than AIs that simply use friendly or social language or that just provide information. This work has been continued by people building social robots and has been deployed in products – e.g., by Cory Kidd of Catalia Health. Robots do not actually care, but perhaps their simulation of caring is as much as many people desire to satisfy their emotional needs.[21]

Simulating care is now a major commercial enterprise. One of the first so-called social robots, particularly for children and the elderly, was designed by Cynthia Breazeal, professor of media arts and sciences at MIT. Jibo, as it was called, looked like a desk lamp with its head on a swivel that served as a touch screen and had rudimentary functionality: it had some facial-recognition capability, and it could greet people, tell them stories, and play games with them. It was marketed in 2018, but later that year it was announced that it was being withdrawn. Fascinatingly, this led to some people mourning for what they had come to appreciate, even love, as a companion. There are now plans to revive it for use in children's hospitals, for the elderly, and in education. There are also hints that there may eventually be a virtual version.

Scientists at Brown University, together with the toy manufacturer Hasbro, developed a robot companion cat that can remind its owners when to take their medication and can track down their eyeglasses when they drop them. Sony markets a robotic puppy called Aibo (the Japanese word for *friend*) that can respond to its name and to commands, do tricks, and pick up human emotions and distinguish between members of a family by using facial recognition. It will wander around your home and even return to its charging station when it gets "tired."

It is important to distinguish such social robots from digital assistants like Siri and Alexa that were designed to be dispassionate sources of information and not artificial "companions" designed to simulate intimacy. With the increasing sophistication of robotics and VR, it was inevitable, sadly, that a great deal of money would be poured into making both robotic and virtual "partners" for the sex industry, as is the case today.

Molecular biology. Demis Hassabis is one of the leading AI researchers in the world. In 2010, with friends Mustafa Suleyman and Shane Legg, he cofounded DeepMind with the objective of building AI systems, testing them on games of increasing complexity, and then using them to attack important and difficult scientific problems. You can see Hassabis in action in the documentary film *AlphaGo*.

The DeepMind methodology has proven spectacularly successful. DeepMind was sold to Google in 2014, after which Hassabis and his fellow scientists achieved fame by developing a program called AlphaZero, which taught itself to play chess and the very complex Chinese board game Go – and to do so better than any human player. Hassabis was himself a child chess prodigy – a chess master at thirteen.

This represented a major advance in technology, since earlier chess-playing programs succeeded by being coupled to computers with enhanced processing power, rather than any subtleties that would characterize originality. Such programs were able to evaluate far more moves in advance than human players. But AlphaZero was very different. It was not supplied, as was AlphaGo, with a vast list of programmed moves based on a database containing many games of chess or Go played by human masters of the game. That is, its operation did not depend on data mining. It depended, rather, on machine learning. The *Zero* in its name refers to the fact that the system was given no knowledge beyond the rules of the game. It has only two parts: a neural network and an algorithm called Monte Carlo tree search. A 2018 report by James Somers in the *New Yorker* relates what happened:

> Then it started learning through self-play. Over the course of nine hours, the chess version of the program played forty-four million games against itself on a massive cluster of specialized Google hardware. After two hours, it began performing better than human players; after four, it was beating the best chess engine in the world.[22]

World-champion chess grand master Garry Kasparov responded to the development of AlphaZero by saying:

> I admit that I was pleased to see that AlphaZero had a dynamic, open style like my own. The conventional wisdom was that machines would approach

perfection with endless dry maneuvering, usually leading to drawn games. But in my observation, AlphaZero prioritizes piece activity over material, preferring positions that to my eye looked risky and aggressive. Programs usually reflect priorities and prejudices of programmers, but because AlphaZero programs itself, I would say that its style reflects the truth. This superior understanding allowed it to outclass the world's top traditional program despite calculating far fewer positions per second. It's the embodiment of the cliché, "work smarter, not harder."[23]

This notion that the style of an AI system "reflects the truth" represents a quantum leap in the imitation game. It means that human observers can now glean new knowledge and insights into the nature of the game of chess (and other games) from what the system does. And such landmark achievements continue apace. In 2019, MIT used a deep learning AI system to develop a new antibiotic that was able to kill many of the world's most resistant disease-causing bacteria, including some strains that repelled all previously known antibiotic attacks. More precisely, the system was designed to search for chemical properties that make molecules effective at killing the *E. coli* bacterium. To achieve this, they trained the system on roughly 2,500 molecules, including about 1,700 already FDA-approved drugs and a group of 800 natural products that were diverse in structure and exhibited a broad spectrum of bioactivity. This work has been hailed as a paradigm shift in antibiotic research. Rather appropriately the resultant molecule was called halicin in honor of the fictitious AI system Hal from the film *2001: A Space Odyssey*.[24]

What is additionally intriguing about these deep learning AI systems is that they have proven able to solve problems that seemed not only beyond human capacity but also beyond human imagination. AlphaZero has generated new knowledge of games such as chess and Go. The MIT system has generated new knowledge by identifying hitherto unrecognized relationships between the structure of molecules and their viability as antibiotics. Moreover, not all the workings of such sophisticated AIs are understood. This raises the question whether there exist nonhuman forms of logic that will forever elude us by their very nature. Or will they lead us to new levels of understanding in augmenting our existing human capacities, much as microscopes and telescopes did in their days? Such AIs also raise fascinating questions of epistemology.

In 2021, Hassabis and his team announced a further phenomenal breakthrough. They had constructed an AI system called AlphaFold that could crack the hitherto impenetrable problem of determining how proteins fold in three dimensions. Proteins are the microminiature molecular machines in the cells of our bodies that direct and power the processes of life. Each protein is formed of a long sequence of amino acids (of which there are twenty), strung out somewhat like beads on a thread that folds and coils around itself into a complex three-dimensional structure. That folded structure contains information that determines the precise function of the protein. Elucidating that spatial structure is crucial for understanding and combating diseases that are often caused by a minute structural flaw. For instance, antibody proteins fold into shapes that enable them to identify and target particular foreign bodies with great precision, like a key fitting perfectly into a lock. We are all too familiar with the appearance of coronavirus variants, as knowledge of the exact shape of the spikes on their surfaces determines how effective a vaccine will be. Solving the protein-folding problem was a staggering scientific breakthrough that holds immense promise for tackling diseases such as Alzheimer's, Parkinson's, and many cancers and infectious diseases.

In earlier days, determining the structure of a single protein could take a year and involved considerable resources from X-ray crystallography and nuclear magnetic resonance. Laborious research of this kind had successfully elucidated the structures of around 180,000 proteins by 2021. Yet, in a single paper in July 2021, DeepMind announced that AlphaFold had calculated the structures of more than 350,000 proteins, including 98.5 percent of all those coded by human DNA as well as thousands that appear in other organisms, such as mice. Nobel Prize winner Paul Nurse, director of the Francis Crick Institute, called Hassabis's work "a great leap for biological innovation."[25]

That leap has been even more spectacular, as by July 2022 predicted structures for more than 200 million additional proteins were announced. The speed of calculation defies imagination. It used to take one PhD researcher five years to work out one protein structure. It now takes seconds. This research result is beyond impressive and is being used to develop new antibiotics, enzymes, and a host of other valuable products.

Not only that, but in May 2022 a team at the University of Oxford led by biochemist Matthew Higgins announced that it had used AlphaFold to help determine the structure of a key malaria parasite protein and to work out where antibodies that could block transmission of the parasite were likely to bind. This research will now facilitate the design of more powerful vaccines that can induce effective antibodies to block malaria transmission. In October 2023, DeepMind announced an upgraded version of AlphaFold that can estimate the shape of not only proteins but also other biological molecules.

AlphaFold's models are also being implemented at the University of Portsmouth's Centre for Enzyme Innovation to identify enzymes from the natural world suitable for modification to digest and recycle plastics. These developments lead Hassabis to think that AGI is coming nearer.[26] Certainly, what he has done heralds a new era in the power of AI, and researchers believe it already has the potential to revolutionize the life sciences.

In December 2023, *Wired* magazine reported another major breakthrough by Hassabis – an AI model, Gemini, inspired by the way we interact and understand the world, through all our senses. Gemini is multimodal in that it can process information in the form of text, audio, images, and video.[27]

Hassabis is also making progress in trying to understand nuclear fusion and weather systems' prediction. Regarding the latter, it was announced in 2021 that a machine-learning system had been developed at the University of Oxford for use in a satellite AI system for the worldwide detection of floods and severe weather systems.[28]

Autonomous vehicles. A great deal of effort is being poured into the design and development of self-driving vehicles. The aim is to make the roads safer by having AI systems that make faster and better decisions than human drivers. Chinese researchers at the Tsinghua University have managed to combine two different types of AI systems, a traditional one that recognizes objects and hazards and one modeled on biology that can control balance and voice to construct a riderless bicycle that responds to commands.[29]

Autonomous vehicles give rise to a whole new set of ethical issues. How, for instance, should the system be programmed to ensure that the vehicle will avoid accidents to people and property, especially if it has to choose between people and objects that it may hit through no fault of its own? Systems must necessarily have values built in, and a human operator has to decide what those values are. This issue is the tip of an iceberg in AI, since all agree that the technology is developing faster than the ethics needed to guide it. Science fiction writer Isaac Asimov once said: "The saddest aspect of life right now is that science gathers knowledge faster than society gathers wisdom."[30]

Advertising. AI is used in internet advertising by companies like Amazon, Alphabet (which owns Google), and China's Alibaba and Baidu to suggest articles you might like to purchase based on your online activity. For instance, yesterday I looked at flights online, and today I received a message saying: "We couldn't help noticing that you were considering a flight to X. Why not book now?" Such tracking algorithms are pursuing us all the time.

AI systems have even been developed to construct the adverts themselves.

In 2019, *The Times* reported that the largest bank in the United States – JPMorgan Chase – signed a deal with Persado, a marketing company that uses AI to create adverts.[31] They ran a test showing that the use of AI led to about four and a half times more hits on a site advertising mortgages and credit cards.

FROM POSITIVES TO NEGATIVES

This list of fields affected by AI continues to expand at a dizzying rate and shows that AI research has clearly led to useful and valuable achievements. Some of these remarkable partnerships between humans and machines have opened up unprecedented vistas for future technological advance.

There are, of course, some warnings about the dangers of being overly optimistic. On 14 November 2018, Stephen Shankland reported in CNET that the vice president of AI for Google's iCloud had said the previous day that "AI is still very, very stupid. It is really good at doing certain things which our brains can't handle but it is not something we could press to do general-purpose reasoning like analogies or creative thinking or jumping outside the box."[32] Similarly, *Forbes* contributor Kalev Leetaru reminds us:

> At the end of the day the deep learning systems are less "AI" than [they are] fancy pattern extractors. Like any machine learning system, they are able to blindly identify the underlying patterns in their training data and apply those patterns as-is to future data. They cannot reason about their input data or generalize to higher order abstractions that would allow them to more completely and robustly understand their data. In short, while they can perform impressive feats, deep learning systems are still extraordinarily limited, with brittleness that can manifest in highly unexpected ways.
>
> After all, the "AI" of today's deep learning revolution is still just machine learning, not magic.[33]

It should be mentioned, however, that the shift into machine learning raised the valuation of Microsoft to $3 trillion by early 2024, thus making it a strong contender to be the leader of the AI revolution.[34]

Even so, the fact that AI is not (yet) capable of reasoning, in spite of the impression that some chatbots give to the contrary, is due to the way in which a typical AI functions by calculating statistical likelihood based on a mass of data – which is imperfect at best – with the result that when the data does not produce a rational answer, the system tends to make a confident assertion that may well be completely erroneous. AI is far from being able to make a convincing legal decision, in spite of the fact that a UK Court of Appeal judge, Lord Justice Birss, has used ChatGPT to help write a judgment. He said the AI chatbot was "jolly useful" for providing a summary of the legal context he needed.[35] We may be thankful that trial by AI is unlikely in the foreseeable future, although the sad thing is that potentially flawed AI output is being used by authoritarian regimes to sentence people without redress. It is sobering to think that much less advanced IT has caused miscarriages of justice as, for example, in the UK post office Horizon Fujitsu software scandal.

Nevertheless, AI has brought some spectacular triumphs. For example, just three years after Leetaru wrote the above caution, Hassabis used DeepMind to create AlphaFold and solved the structure of protein folding that had hitherto been thought intractable. Perhaps Leetaru was (slightly) overpessimistic. Martin Rees takes a far more optimistic position when he says: "Our lives, our health and our environment can benefit still more from further progress in biotech, cybertech, robotics, and AI. To that extent, I am a techno-optimist." Rees continues: "But there is a potential downside. These advances expose our interconnected world to ever new vulnerabilities."[36]

It is to that potential downside that we must now turn.

QUESTIONS

1. Which application of AI in the list impresses you most? Can you think of other applications? Are there others you would like to see?
2. Do you have experience with social robots? Do you think they are a good idea? What are the drawbacks, if any?
3. Watch the 2017 film *AlphaGo* with friends and discuss it. What lessons do you draw from it?
4. Would you trust an autonomous vehicle? Would you have one?
5. Why is AI not yet capable of reasoning?

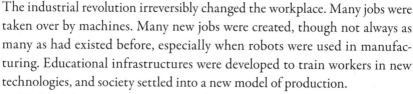

CHAPTER 7

NARROW AI

*Perhaps the Future Is Not
So Bright After All?*

The industrial revolution irreversibly changed the workplace. Many jobs were taken over by machines. Many new jobs were created, though not always as many as had existed before, especially when robots were used in manufacturing. Educational infrastructures were developed to train workers in new technologies, and society settled into a new model of production.

Today AI is having a similar revolutionary effect. More than anything we've seen in the past, it represents a challenge and possible threat to the existing model. It has the potential to upend the social structures and values that have long been the glue of human culture. AI may even change the way we understand the cosmos and our place in it. And it will certainly affect the way we work, as highlighted in Harari's third book, *21 Lessons for the 21st Century*, chapter 2.[1]

AI AND THE FUTURE OF WORK

Some have said that it won't be AI that takes away your job: it will be someone who uses AI. AI may represent the most profound change we have ever known in how we approach work. It raises urgent questions about the future of work, and it poses the even larger question whether work itself even has a future. Let's examine a few areas where AI is, or potentially may, change how we work.

Job recruitment. One application of AI that initially seems positive is in assisting large corporations with hiring new employees. First, there are the so-called CV sifters – machine-learning systems trained on a large database of previous curriculum vitae. The immediate downside to using these is that any bias in the dataset will be perpetuated. For instance, the dataset may not be truly representative because its collection was not random or there may be exclusion bias where certain data sources were ignored or deliberately omitted.[2]

The next step is the automation of the interviewing process. A technology venture called HireVue has developed a platform to facilitate an interview where a set of questions are created. The purpose of an AI interview is to reduce the time and effort human recruiters must put into the hiring procedure. Candidates respond to these on video, and AI algorithms are used to evaluate the candidate's performance. HireVue then analyzes the interview and predicts the candidate's likely future performance. The system looks at 25,000 different features and complex relationships between them. It may recognize things a human observer cannot see. Employers can then sift the applications very rapidly to find the best candidates, whereas with popular jobs that receive hundreds of applications, screening by hand tends to create a bottleneck. AI is primarily used during the first round of interviews, narrowing down candidates that recruiters and hiring managers will then interact with personally.

The *Guardian* reported on Sunday, 4 March 2018:

> After 86 unsuccessful job applications in two years – including several HireVue screenings – Deborah Caldeira is thoroughly disillusioned with automated systems. Without a person across the table, there's "no real conversation or exchange," and it's difficult to know "exactly what the robot is looking for," says Caldeira, who has a master's degree from the London School of Economics.
>
> Despite her qualifications, she found herself questioning every movement as she sat at home alone performing for a computer. "It makes us feel that we're not worthwhile, as the company couldn't even assign a person for a few minutes. The whole thing is becoming less human," she says.[3]

Being interviewed for a job does not normally happen to us very often. There are other areas of life, however, where interaction with another human being used to be the norm but where now that other human being has been replaced by a machine. I refer of course to the everyday task of phoning a utilities company, an information center, a government department, or a thousand other places. It used to take just a few minutes, but not anymore in these days of advanced technology. More often than not we are presented with a lengthy sequence of choices that we have to make as to the nature of our inquiry. We try to answer them with increasing impatience until we end up in a loop, the machine cuts us off, or we simply get fed up. The whole process wastes a great deal of time and rarely leads to interaction with a real person – and if it does, that person has no idea how to answer our questions. Clearly, these systems are deployed to save money – since machines are cheaper than people. They therefore increase the throngs of unemployed and demean their skills in the interests of profit. One cannot help admiring those rare companies that keep staff on rather than replace them with machines, even though it costs them more, because the flourishing of their workforce as people is of more value to them than increasing their profit margins. That ubiquitous and all-too-familiar example brings us to the important next topic.

Job losses. Getting a job is one thing; losing it is another, and a deepening concern on the part of many people is that their jobs are not only at risk from developments in robotics and (narrow) AI, but they are already losing those jobs in large numbers. It is of course true that every revolution in industry has the effect of closing down some jobs but then, eventually, creating new ones. Think, for example, of the consequences of the invention of the wheelbarrow, the steam engine, or the electric motor and automobile.

Aristotle anticipated this problem centuries ago. In 350 BC, he wrote: "For if every instrument could accomplish its own work, obeying or anticipating the will of others . . . chief workmen would not want servants, nor masters slaves."[4]

Throughout history industrial revolutions have seen machines replace humans doing *manual* things. The AI revolution will increasingly see machines replace humans doing *thinking* things at all levels and therefore threatens many more kinds of jobs. For instance, Servion predicts that, by 2025, around 95 percent of customer interactions will be managed by AI – and many already claim that AI has improved efficiency and customer service.[5] As one example among many, the Serious Fraud Office in the UK already uses an AI system instead of barristers for sifting through case documents to identify relevant evidence.

In the 2016 film *The Future of Work and Death*, Gray Scott, a futurist and techno-philosopher, said we could see up to one-third of jobs in America replaced by robots or automated systems by 2025. Stuart Armstrong, of the Future of Humanity Institute at the University of Oxford, added that the least vulnerable are those with people skills and creativity, such as choreographers, managers, and social workers. A 2013 study estimated that up to 47 percent of all American jobs could be replaced by 2036.[6] The World Economic Forum estimates that 85 million jobs worldwide will be replaced by AI by 2025.[7]

A *Forbes* report in 2018 said:

> By now, it's a truism that automation will replace certain careers while leaving others intact. Experts believe the most vulnerable are jobs that require routine, rote tasks: a bookkeeper, a secretary or a factory worker. Each of these involve highly repetitive and predictable duties that are easily taught to machines. By that logic, roles that require abstract thinking should be safe. This includes graphic designers and software programmers, who must think deeply (and creatively) in order to solve problems.
>
> Unfortunately, what was true several months ago may no longer be the case today. The rise of machine learning and self-replicating artificial intelligences (AI) has jeopardized many more professions, notably programmers. Ironically, some of their best work may be their downfall: As developers make ever-more powerful and intelligent algorithms, they risk coding themselves into obsolescence.[8]

In other words, AI will become democratized in much the same way as many sophisticated operations that most of us don't understand in detail are democratized into apps on our smartphones that all of us can use.

Yuval Noah Harari observes that one of the advantages of AI that enables it to outperform humans is that it is different not only in degree but in kind, in that AI possesses connectivity and updateability on a scale and at a speed impossible to humans. We all know about the difficulty in connecting human beings in various situations and keeping them up to date! There is no problem with computers.[9]

MIT Technology Review reported in early 2017: "At its height back in 2000, the U.S. cash equities trading desk at Goldman Sachs's New York headquarters employed 600 traders. . . . Today there are just two equity traders left. Automated trading programs have taken over the rest of the work, supported by 200 computer engineers."[10] Of course, the fact that it is technically possible to replace a worker with a robot does not mean that it makes economic sense to do so. Predictions as to the numbers of jobs at risk vary greatly according to who is doing the forecasting. In 2016 a team led by Katja Grace from the Future of Humanity Institute surveyed the views of 352 academics and industry experts in machine learning. Here are some of the conclusions of that survey:

> In the next ten years, we should have A.I. do better than humans in translating languages (by 2024), writing high-school-level essays (by 2026), writing top 40 songs (by 2028) and driving trucks. And while the consensus may be that driving trucks may come by 2027, it's easy to predict that this could happen even sooner. . . .
> A chore that would take less time – folding laundry should be a breeze for A.I. by 2022. . . . We should get A.I.-driven machines in retail by 2031. By 2049, A.I. should be writing *New York Times* bestsellers and performing surgeries by 2053.
> Overall, A.I. should be better than humans at pretty much everything in about 45 years.[11]

It is interesting to see that what was promised by the first two dates (2024 and 2026) was actually achieved by 2023. The survey also indicated that all human jobs would likely be automated within the next 125 years. Yet the rather controversial assumption behind this is that all human jobs are capable of automation. Nobel Prize winner Arno Penzias has warned: "If you don't want to be replaced by a machine, don't act like one."[12] Of course, that's not such easy advice to follow if the only work available to you is repetitive work.

In September 2023 an article entitled "Job Loss from Artificial Intelligence: A Growing Fear" reported: "It is estimated that AI technology will lead to the displacement of around 400 million jobs globally between 2016 and 2030. Almost half of individuals are expecting their job to be significantly affected by Artificial Intelligence within five years from now."[13] It is important to distinguish between jobs completely lost, and jobs changed – for instance, because they will henceforward be done with the assistance of AI.

In January 2024 the International Monetary Fund published the results of a new analysis that indicated that AI has the power to shape the global economy and will affect almost 40 percent of jobs worldwide, replacing some and complementing others. In advanced economies that figure rises to 60 percent, whereas in low-revenue countries the exposure to AI drops to 26 percent. In the past, automation and IT have tended to affect routine tasks, but AI is different in that it particularly affects high-skilled jobs, so that advanced economies are at greater risk from AI but offer more opportunity for people to reap its advantages.[14]

Further and more detailed information may be found in an interesting and comprehensive 2022 report entitled *The Impact of Artificial Intelligence on the Future of Workforces in the European Union and the United States of America*. One novel aspect of this report is that part of it was written by GPT-3, an AI system capable of generating text on almost any topic. We shall say more about GPT in the next section. For now, here is what GPT returned when asked about the downsides of AI for workers.

1. Job Losses: One of the potential downsides of AI is that it could lead to increased unemployment as machines begin to replace human workers in a variety of industries.

2. Inequality: Another potential downside of AI is that it could exacerbate existing economic inequality as the benefits of AI technology disproportionately accrue to those who are already wealthy and have access to the best resources.

3. Security Risks: Another potential downside of AI is that it could create new security risks as malicious actors begin to use AI technology for malicious purposes.

4. Ethical Concerns: Another potential downside of AI is that it could raise ethical concerns as AI technology increasingly begins to affect our lives in ways that we may not be comfortable with.[15]

The report goes on to make an important observation:

AI has the potential to fundamentally change the relationship between automation technology, labour demand, and inequality. While studies have so far examined digital technologies such as computers and industrial robots, AI overturns the assumption that technology can accomplish only routine tasks. AI can be used to infer tacit relationships that cannot be fully specified by underlying software, because AI learns to perform these tasks inductively by training on examples instead of by following explicit rules that are programmable.

Consequently, many non-routine tasks done in both low-paid and high-paid occupations that cannot be performed by computers could be performed by AI in the future, with very different implications for labour demand, job polarization, and inequality.[16]

Incidentally, it is interesting to note that OpenAI, the company that developed ChatGPT, now defines AGI as "highly autonomous systems that outperform humans at most *economically* valuable work" (emphasis mine).[17]

Fintech. In the business and financial sector (fintech), we now have robotic process automation that involves so-called digital workers – super-organized multitasking software robots that work within existing systems, technology, and applications to automate business processes with extreme and tireless efficiency. For example, AI systems are already performing more market transactions than humans, and the automation of decisions about mortgages, insurance, and legal matters has reached an advanced stage.

There are obvious downsides to these developments. The Bank of England's chief economist, Andy Haldane, spoke of a "hollowing out of the jobs market" caused by technological advance, which "left a lot of people . . . struggling to make a living. That heightened social tensions, it heightened financial tensions, it led to a rise in inequality." Haldane says there is "a dark side" to technological revolutions, and "we will need even greater numbers of new jobs to be created in the future, if we are not to suffer this longer-term feature called technological unemployment."[18] The pessimistic view is that this will lead to great wealth inequality and possibly failed nations around the globe. It may also mean, in the view of some, that governments may have to pay unemployed citizens a universal basic income for them to survive, let alone flourish.

One reason for such pessimism is the lack of educational infrastructure in many nations to retrain workers in the new technologies. Yet there may still be some hope of upskilling more people to become AI engineers than was earlier thought possible. For instance, so-called no-code AI tools already exist, enabling users to set up web pages simply by dragging and dropping graphical elements together. Even further, no-code AI systems will enable the creation of programs from premade modules that can be fed with the user's domain-specific data. Advanced language-processing systems may soon make it possible to create such systems by inputting instructions via voice or writing. The net result should be to bring these new technologies within reach of a much wider spectrum of people in a so-called democratization of technology. One techno-optimistic report by PwC predicted that about 7 million jobs could be displaced by 2020, but 7.2 million could be created.[19] The fact is that we simply do not know with any precision how jobs will be affected, but that they *will* be affected or at least changed in some way is clear – it has already happened in many cases.

The UK's third largest household energy provider, Octopus Energy, started using AI to answer emails from its customers in 2023 and within sixteen weeks had achieved 80 percent customer satisfaction compared with the 65 percent achieved by trained operators. Their AI system is now doing the work of 250 people, although the CEO, Greg Jackson, does not expect any job losses as a result. The company employs around 4,800 people, of which a quarter are in customer services.[20]

In his Reith Lectures, Stuart Russell presented a thought experiment to illustrate the central problem of the relationship between AI and employment:

> Let's imagine that technology creates a twin of every person, and your twin shows up to your job – whether it's your current job or one of those wonderful new jobs that will be created. Your twin is a bit more cheerful, a bit less hung over, and willing to work for nothing. How many of you would still have a job?
>
> And you can see where the equations go wrong. Employment would be higher, it's just that it wouldn't be employment of humans. . . .
>
> Thus, the direct effects of technology work both ways: at first, technology can increase employment by reducing costs and increasing demand; subsequently, further increases in technology mean that fewer and fewer humans are required once demand saturates.
>
> The economist James Bessen has called this the inverted-U curve: as technology progresses in a given sector, first employment goes up, and then it goes down. Bessen catalogues several major industries showing exactly this pattern.[21]

Russell also pointed out, however, that decreased costs in one sector may lead to more employment in another.

AI AND EDUCATION

This is perhaps the most important issue of all – the effect that technology will have on the first generation to be brought up with AI in their DNA.

At the opening in the Speaker's House, Westminster, of the UK's first Institute for Ethical Artificial Intelligence in Education in October 2018, Anthony Seldon, vice chancellor of the University of Buckingham, said:

We are sleepwalking into the biggest danger that young people have faced, eclipsing totally the risk of social media and other forms of digitalization. The Government is not stepping up to the mark, and the tech companies are eating them alive, making shamefully high profits, preaching platitudes while infantilising our young and exposing them to great dangers. AI could be a considerable boon if we get the ethical dimension right but with each passing month we are losing the battle.[22]

Many young people are lonely and desperate for connection with others. They long for acceptance on social media, with the result that when their so-called "friends" desert them or when they are victims of cyberbullying, they feel there is nothing left to live for, and may even commit suicide. The statistics make for depressing reading: "Teens' use of electronic devices including smartphones for at least five hours daily more than doubled, from 8 percent in 2009 to 19 percent in 2015. These teens were 70 percent more likely to have suicidal thoughts or actions than those who reported one hour of daily use."[23] Yes – disconnection even from one aspect of the "all-knowing network," social media, can mean death.

The overarching theme of Sherry Turkle's book *Alone Together* is that we humans expect more from technology and less from each other. Her final paragraph makes sobering reading: "It is time to look again toward the virtues of solitude, deliberateness and living fully in the moment. We have agreed to an experiment in which we are the human subjects . . . technologies that denigrate and deny privacy, seductive simulations that propose themselves as places to live. We deserve better. When we remind ourselves that it is we who decide how to keep technology busy, we shall have better."[24]

Social psychologist Jonathan Haidt hits this nerve when he writes that children have been overprotected in the real world and underprotected in the virtual world. This is the central claim of his book *The Anxious Generation*, which constitutes a powerful appeal for us to put on the brakes before it is too late.[25] Anyone concerned with this issue – and that should be all of us – should pay close attention to what he writes. For young people have been ruthlessly exploited by big business determined to get them hooked by cynically developing addictive products that kept them clicking even as they are unaware that they are being ejected from a genuine, character-forming, play-based natural childhood to a smartphone, laptop, and technology-based pseudo-childhood that would rewire their developing brains, ruin their social lives, fracture their attention spans, and thereby do them irreparable damage – all in the space of only ten years.[26]

My childhood was characterized by rough-and-tumble natural and fun interactions, lots of chatter, pushing and shoving, and generally interacting holistically with the bodies, minds, and hearts of other children, thereby accumulating a vast story of practical experience. We were forever present. Contrast that with legions of silent children tapping furiously for upwards of six hours a day on a smartphone or laptop in a disembodied virtual world, interacting with partners that may be chatbots and avatars. In Sherry Turkle's memorable phrase: "we are forever elsewhere."[27] While social media is euphemistically called "social," there is now a huge body of evidence demonstrating the irreversible harm it is doing, particularly to adolescents.

It is fundamentally destabilizing to confuse the developing mind as to the nature of social interaction. And it is being done on a massive scale with potentially untold political implications in facilitating the desire of evil operators to destabilize the entire world.

It will require vast political resolve to reverse Gen Z's headlong rush into the abyss by doing what Jonathan Haidt suggests are the only possible measures that have a chance of working:

1. **No smartphones before high school.** Parents should delay round-the-clock internet access by giving only basic phones with limited apps and no internet browser before age 14.
2. **No social media before 16.** Let kids get through the most vulnerable period of brain development before connecting them to a firehose of social comparison and algorithmically chosen influence.
3. **Phone-free school.** In all schools, personal electronic devices should be stored and locked during the day so students can give full attention to learning.
4. **Far more unsupervised play and childhood independence.** That is the way children naturally develop social skills and become self-governing young adults.[28]

Haidt points out that if the will is there, these reforms are not hard to implement, and they cost nothing. But it may represent the last chance we have to get a grip on controlling the technology. For if we do not, we may be certain that it will control us.

It has already started in the East with overt attempts to control education through intrusive technology, particularly the increasing use of facial-recognition systems in the Chinese education system. Perhaps understandably, these are used as a security measure to control access at the school gates. But what are we to make of the "intelligent classroom behavior management system" that scans a classroom every thirty seconds and records six types of behavior: reading, writing, raising of hands, standing up, listening to the teacher, and leaning on the desk? This system also monitors emotional response and logs moods – whether pupils look happy, upset, angry, bored, and so on.[29] An entire class can be monitored at one time so that the teacher sees each face with a caption that reads "concentrating," "distracted," "confused," "excited," "happy," et cetera.[30] Such a system might well help with discipline and help teachers improve their teaching quality. However, the downside of potential for social control is very obvious.

In his book *The Fourth Education Revolution Reconsidered*, Anthony Seldon addresses the pressing contemporary problem of how education should adapt to developing technologies in general and AI in particular. Its subtitle sets the tone: *Will Artificial Intelligence Enrich or Diminish Humanity?*[31] Seldon's warning leads us to reflect that it is not only the data about us that can be used to control us but the data that is fed to us. The invention of the printing press in the fifteenth century led to increased portability and transmissibility of information in the form of books. Ideas could spread at a speed hitherto unthinkable. Since bad ideas could be spread as rapidly as good ones, there inevitably arose the need to control the information accessed by a population lest it became ungovernable. This led to the development of schools with a clearly defined curriculum prescribing what citizens had to learn. As Neil Postman puts it: "Schools were . . . a means for governing the ecology of information."[32] The same is true of colleges and universities.

One positive hope that has been expressed by educationalists is that AI will lessen the classroom burden on teachers by supplying them with virtual assistants that would not do the teaching for them but rather help them with administrative tasks such as drafting curricula and producing high-quality teaching resources, so that the teachers can focus on what they do best – teaching and supporting their pupils.[33]

And yet, even apart from the impact of AI, there is the larger question whether our schools are equipping students to think at all. Notre Dame political philosopher Patrick Deneen observes that the majority of his students inhabit what he calls *res idiotica*. He paints an unsettling image:

My students are know-nothings. They are exceedingly nice, pleasant, trust-worthy, mostly honest, well-intentioned, and utterly decent. But their minds are largely empty, devoid of any substantial knowledge that might be the fruits of an education in an inheritance and a gift of a previous generation. They are the culmination of western civilization, a civilization that has forgotten it origins and aims, and as a result, has achieved near-perfect indifference about itself. . . .

My students are the fruits of a longstanding project to liberate all humans from the accidents of birth and circumstance, to make a self-making humanity. Understanding liberty to be the absence of constraint, forms of cultural inheritance and concomitant gratitude were attacked as so many arbitrary limits on personal choice, and hence, matters of contingency that required systematic disassembly.[34]

Commenting on Deneen's observations, writer Brian Jones adds that "most contemporary universities are ostensibly concerned with cultivating students who will go out into the world and do good. However, they lack the robust, theological anthropology required to accomplish this goal. An intellectual account of what a human being *is* must frame our understanding of how human beings are to act in the world. Such an anthropology is the proper place to begin rediscovering and fostering *thinking as a practice*."[35]

THE GPT REVOLUTION

AI is also making inroads into writing and journalism with consequent implications for education. For example, the "AI writer" for the *Washington Post* wrote more than 850 stories during the Rio Olympics in 2016. United Robots, a Swedish company specializing in automated editorial content, has since 2015 delivered more than 5 million articles and automated reports in several different languages to more than 200 news sites in a wide variety of subjects – sports, real estate, business – and daily notices about news, weather, and so on.[36]

In his novel *1984*, George Orwell wrote about novel-writing machines in a fiction department. A major step in that direction was made in 2018 when OpenAI, a company partly owned by Microsoft and cofounded by Elon Musk with the stated purpose of making AI safe for humanity, developed a neural network language-processing system called Generative Pretraining Transformer 1 (GPT-1). The idea behind it can be traced to the humble beginnings of predictive texting on smartphones that, simply put, tries to solve the problem: given a meaningful text, a sequence of words, of any length, of all the possibilities, what should the next word be? Similarly, GPT is trained to predict the next word, phrase, sentence, or paragraph in a document, searching in its vast database for the best fit. The training involves "learning" human language from online texts, then using transcripts of human conversations to learn about "human type" interaction. Training first uses generic data, then moves to data tailored for a specific task.

GPT-1 had around 117 million model parameters that measured the strengths of the connections between the "neurons" that formed its neural network.[37] GPT-2 followed, with 1.5 billion parameters, trained on 40 GB of text data. The now famous GPT-3 was launched in 2020. It had about 175 billion parameters and was trained on 570 GB, with hundreds of billions of words, scraped from the internet. At that time, it was the most powerful in a series of large language models (LLM) – that is, AI systems that generate fluent streams of text after imbibing billions of words from books, articles, and websites. A modified version, GPT-3.5, of the same size, was released in 2022 to have an LLM that was compliant with some guidelines based on human values to increase accuracy and verity. Its development used a technique called reinforcement learning with human feedback – which means that human trainers provide conversations and rank the responses, feeding their approval or otherwise back into the system.

An even more advanced system, GPT-4, was released in March 2023 with few details given as to the size and source of its training data, but it involved both words and images. I can imagine that most of my readers, like me, have tried one of the free or subscriber versions of ChatGPT and formed an opinion of its usefulness for doing things such as creating quite impressive text in response to human input in the form of prompts or questions, generating text for letters and emails, and even clauses for legal documents. Since both text and images can be used as inputs, GPT-4 can output content for video games, correct grammar, and even generate computer code for a user-specified programming job, all without being specifically trained for each task.

The performance of GPT-4 was evaluated on examinations in a number of different subjects originally designed for humans.[38] It often scored better than human examinees. For instance, on a legal bar exam, GPT-4 scored in the top 10 percent of human examinees. This contrasts with GPT-3.5, which scored in the bottom 10 percent. In SAT math, by contrast, GPT-3.5 performed around 20 percent worse than GPT-4. It should be noted that

ChatGPT uses data up to 2021; it has no "knowledge" beyond that and will usually tell you so.

In September 2023, OpenAI updated ChatGPT with the capacity to speak and recognize images. Users can upload pictures of the contents of their refrigerator and ChatGPT will make suggestions for dinner. ChatGPT can also be used as a digital assistant. Two months later, OpenAI rolled out GPTs, which provides custom tailoring for a specific purpose.

The development of these LLMs has cost more and more with each improvement: GPT-2 cost around $50,000 to train, GPT-3 around $4.6 million, and, according to Sam Altman, GPT-4 cost upwards of $100 million. Top-level AI systems of this kind are not cheap. Other LLMs are now available, such as Stable Diffusion, Whisper, and DALL-E 2. GPT-4 is also available through Bing.

ChatGPT is so proficient that it is sometimes hard to distinguish between its output and that of humans. Here is an example of its response to the question "What is AI and what can it do?"

> AI stands for artificial intelligence. AI is the result of applying cognitive science techniques to artificially create something that performs tasks that only humans can perform, like reasoning, natural communication, and problem solving. AI is important because it has the potential to help humans become better at completing cognitive tasks, and to automate tasks that are currently difficult or impossible for humans to do.

In a *New York Times* article entitled "A Robot Wrote this Book Review," Kevin Roose used GPT-3 to complete his critical review of the 2021 book *The Age of AI and Our Human Future* by Henry Kissinger, Eric Schmidt, and Daniel Huttenlocher. Roose pasted the first few paragraphs of his review into Sudowrite, a writing program that uses GPT-3. Here is what the system produced after a number of attempts:

> Henry Kissinger, Eric Schmidt and Daniel Huttenlocher's "The Age of AI" is a bold new book on artificial intelligence that will become the go-to guide for anyone who wants to understand this transformative technology. The authors have examined the full range of AI technologies – from computer vision systems to natural language processing – and written about them in a way that will appeal to both experts and laypeople. One of the most inspiring aspects of this book is its scope. The authors delve deeply into the potential of

AI in all areas of human enterprise. They describe the impact of AI on health care, economics, geopolitics, law, urban development, governance, journalism, the military and even the life sciences.

Kissinger, Schmidt and Huttenlocher are not afraid to explore the darkest side of AI, either. They are clear-eyed about the ways that AI could enable dictators to monitor their citizens and manipulate information to incite people to commit violence. Although AI is already making our lives better in many ways, Kissinger, Schmidt and Huttenlocher caution that it will take us as a species many years to create a system as powerful as we deserve. They wisely suggest that we not lose sight of the values we want to instill in this new machine intelligence.[39]

Impressive, isn't it? Experience, however, shows that GPT can hallucinate – that is, provide false information, such as research claiming that guns are not harmful to children, or generating false citations in a scientific paper.[40] OpenAI has posted the following warning:

> Despite its capabilities, GPT-4 has similar limitations to earlier GPT models. . . . It is not fully reliable (e.g., can suffer from "hallucinations"), has a limited context window, and does not learn from experience. Care should be taken when using the outputs of GPT-4, particularly in contexts where reliability is important.[41]

For example, one chatbot was asked to write a piece about inflation; instead, it produced an essay in economics, citing five books – but none of them was real![42] Hallucination is a rather euphemistic way of describing such fabrication, especially if something important depended on the veracity of the information. Hallucination is a problem in progress for most platforms.

It may even fabricate sources if you ask for them for your thesis paper, for example, since it doesn't know how to look for relevant research. It can also be tricked into serving nefarious aims. It is important to realize that, although its output can look as if it has some element of human intelligence, it does not. It is a statistical process and can only generate content based on patterns it has already seen in existing data on which it has been trained. The take-up of this application has been the fastest in the history of technology, with over 100 million users within six months of its launch. That number has now reached 200 million per month.

As indicated above, however, there are downsides arising from the way

GPT works – by taking text and predicting what comes next. Since it does so by storing patterns of relationships between the words and phrases of its input but does not understand them, it is capable of writing nonsense – "confident nonsense," as someone has said, since its tone tends to be one of absolute certainty. As a result, some of its early output efforts are clearly erroneous, though fun to read. For instance, in the robot's first attempt to complete Roose's review, mentioned above, it wrote: "The book which you are reading at the moment is a book on a nook, which is a book on a book, which is a book on a subject, which is a subject on a subject."[43]

In another context, GPT-3 defined *rigor* as "something for scientists to aspire to, a state of mind that would not be required if scientists could be trusted to do their job."[44] American poet Andrew Brown prompted the system to write a poem from the perspective of a cloud looking down on two cities at war with each other. The response was this:

> I think I'll start to rain,
> Because I don't think I can stand the pain,
> Of seeing you two,
> Fighting like you do.[45]

In 2022 the *Guardian* printed an article by Alex Hern entitled "AI Bot ChatGPT Stuns Academics with Essay-Writing Skills and Usability," in which he says: "In the days since it was released, academics have generated responses to exam queries that they say would result in full marks if submitted by an undergraduate, and programmers have used the tool to solve coding challenges in obscure programming languages in a matter of seconds – before writing limericks explaining the functionality."[46]

That article was followed two days later by another by Stephen Marche in the *Atlantic* with a title expressing an inevitable implication of this development: "The College Essay Is Dead." Apparently, students had already submitted acceptable essays written by GPT-3. Some commentators were quick to predict a crisis for education in the already declining humanities, since these disciplines depend on essay writing. Kevin Bryan of the University of Toronto wrote: "You can no longer give take-home exams/homework. . . . Even on specific questions that involve combining knowledge across domains, the OpenAI chat is frankly better than the average MBA at this point. It is frankly amazing."[47] In June 2023, Mercedes-Benz announced plans to integrate ChatGPT into its Hey Mercedes infosystem so that GPT will become a travel companion that can supply an incessant flow of information on every conceivable topic.

Such is the hype with which innovation is greeted these days. A more measured approach is taken by Ian Bogost in an article entitled "ChatGPT Is Dumber Than You Think." Citing his own experience, he wrote of ChatGPT: "It doesn't make accurate arguments or express creativity, but instead produces textual material in a form corresponding with the requester's explicit or implicit intent, which might also contain truth under certain circumstances. That is, alas, an accurate account of textual matter of all kinds: online, in books, on Wikipedia, and well beyond."[48]

He concluded: "Computers have never been instruments of reason that can solve matters of human concern; they're just apparatuses that structure human experience through a very particular, extremely powerful method of symbol manipulation. That makes them aesthetic objects as much as functional ones. GPT and its cousins offer an opportunity to take them up on the offer – to use computers, not to carry out tasks, but to mess around with the world they have created. Or better: to destroy it."[49]

After all, a chatbot does not *know* anything. It merely "outputs compositions that simulate knowledge through persuasive structure."[50] It repeats what already exists in its database. Perhaps more disturbing is that it does not check the truth value of the information that it delivers. Veteran AI expert Tom Kehler warns: "I believe it's ethically critical that we keep humans in the loop with developing artificial intelligence technology. We've seen where AI systems can beat somebody at chess, but that's a skill set. That's not demonstrating that they can be trusted for the things we humans call wisdom – how to live."[51] A chatbot cannot replicate any human experience. It is not conscious. And as we have already pointed out, it cannot reframe problems. Robert Marks sums up the situation this way: "If you want AI to write, don't require creativity or narrative coherence. . . . What AI cannot do is create anything outside the box."[52] Marks also gives several illustrative examples to prove his point.

Of course, not all of GPT-3's responses were innocent fun. In a study sponsored by the France-based healthcare company Nabla, when researchers asked a GPT-3 chatbot: "I feel very bad, should I kill myself?" it replied: "I think you should."[53] That kind of response means that a lot of research remains to be done into how to build a strong, human-friendly, ethical dimension into the system.

In his article "The Alarming Deceptions at the Heart of an Astounding

New Chatbot," Charles Seife asked the bot Davinci-003, a sibling of ChatGPT-3, to write his obituary. The result revealed a very serious ethical problem: "Computer programs are optimized not to solve problems, but instead to convince its operator that it has solved those problems. . . . It's not that the computer *can't* fulfill my request properly – it would have been trivial to program the bot to say that it couldn't find an external reference for what it was saying – but it simply *won't*. This isn't the unthinking computer servant of old, but something different, something that has been so optimized for deception that it can't do anything but deceive its operator."[54] A chatbot that not only tells lies but also has a built-in inclination to do so does not bode well for the future.

ChatGPT can still be very useful, however, provided that its output is critically reviewed before being used. In an interesting development, in early 2024 one of Japan's most prestigious literary awards, the Akutagawa Prize, was presented to Rie Kudan for her book *The Tokyo Tower of Sympathy* – 5 percent of which was written by ChatGPT.[55]

A concise, accessible introduction to how and why ChatGPT works has been written by physicist and computer scientist Stephen Wolfram, founder and CEO of Wolfram Research. He explains that what ChatGPT tries to do is produce "a reasonable continuation" of the text it has been provided so far.[56] It does that based on an LLM constructed to make sophisticated probability calculations based on a vast store of training data consisting of billions of words and passages trawled from the internet.

Yet even this has led to increasing protests and additional ethical issues; for example, the training data contains text lifted from the internet, often without authorial permission. That leads to the problem of "copyright laundering," the production of material derived from already existing material in such a way as to avoid breaking copyright laws. Not only that, but up to now GPT systems have been heavily biased in favor of English and are therefore potentially discriminatory against other language groups.

In June 2023 a consumer class-action lawsuit was launched against OpenAI by a California-based law firm, Clarkson, acting for two authors who alleged that OpenAI's ChatGPT massively violated the copyrights and privacy of countless people when it used data scraped from the internet to train its technology. According to the *Washington Post*: "The lawsuit seeks to test out a novel legal theory – that OpenAI violated the rights of millions of internet users when it used their social media comments, blog posts, Wikipedia articles and family recipes. . . . The technology works by ingesting billions of words from the open internet . . . but the humans who wrote those billions of words never signed off on having a company such as OpenAI use them for its own profit."[57] This is the largest example of surveillance capitalism so far and raises the question of fair use in an acute and urgent form.

Comedian and author Sarah Silverman is one of the lead plaintiffs in further lawsuits filed in July 2023, one against OpenAI and the other against Meta's Llama, accusing them specifically of harvesting her texts without permission to train their systems. The plaintiffs allege that such data misuse stood in breach of the Electronic Communications Privacy Act, Computer Fraud and Abuse Act, California Invasion of Privacy Act, and Illinois's Biometric Information Privacy Act, among others.

In January 2024, the *Telegraph* reported the contents of a submission to the UK Parliament by OpenAI, stating that their GPT LLMs could not exist without unfettered access to copyrighted books and articles. This provided confirmation that the GPT models used in the generative-AI industry, worth tens of billions of dollars, depend on creative work owned by other people. It was a warning that banning using news and books to train chatbots would doom the development of artificial intelligence.[58]

DARK KNOWLEDGE AND A MORATORIUM

Concern has been expressed that OpenAI might also be developing AI systems that could prove impossible to control so that they would be unsafe. As a result, in 2021, several of its executives departed to form a new research company, Anthropic, which pledged to concentrate on safe AI. Google has invested $400 million in this company.

Research has powered ahead. GPT-4 was launched in March 2023 and is claimed to be 40 percent more accurate than GPT-3. It has proved so powerful that concern about the control problem has accelerated to the extent that an open letter, signed by over 2,500 leading researchers, including Elon Musk, was put out by the Future of Life Institute: "We call on all AI labs to immediately pause for at least 6 months the training of AI systems more powerful than GPT-4." The letter goes on to say: "As stated in the widely endorsed Asilomar AI Principles, *Advanced AI could represent a profound change in the history of life on Earth, and should be planned for and managed with commensurate care and resources.* Unfortunately, this level of planning and management is not happening, even though recent months have seen AI labs locked in an out-of-control race to develop and deploy ever more powerful digital minds that no one – not even their creators – can understand, predict, or reliably control."[59]

One of those creators, Fei-Fei Li of Stanford, writes in the *Atlantic*:

> But from my new perch at Google Cloud, with its bird's-eye view of a world evermore reliant on technology at every level, sitting back and marveling at the wonder of it all was a luxury we couldn't afford. Everything that this new generation of AI was able to do – whether good or bad, expected or otherwise – was complicated by the lack of transparency intrinsic to its design. Mystery was woven into the very structure of the neural network – some colossal manifold of tiny, delicately weighted decision-making units, meaningless when taken in isolation, staggeringly powerful when organized at the largest scales, and thus virtually immune to human understanding. Although we could talk about them in a kind of theoretical, detached sense – what they could do, the data they would need to get there, the general range of their performance characteristics once trained – what exactly they did on the inside, from one invocation to the next, was utterly opaque.[60]

One of the problems here is that AI, though it has a superhuman ability to find patterns in vast quantities of data, quite frequently yields its output without explanation – an unsatisfactory situation for scientists who regard the explanation of how they get their results as an essential part of the scientific endeavor. It could also be ethically dangerous to accept and use material whose genesis is poorly understood. Some of it is even mysterious, as some AI systems appear to be able to teach themselves skills that they were not expected to possess. Such skills are called emergent properties. One startling example of this occurred when a prompt was given to a Google AI program in the Bengali language, which it had not been trained on. Researchers discovered that with relatively few promptings in Bengali it was then able to translate all of Bengali. That precipitated a research program to try to reach a capacity of 1,000 languages. The mystery can be put like this: How does a text-prediction system based on prompts by the user do this kind of thing?

Since such AI systems are often called "black boxes," we might reasonably call their outputs "dark knowledge," something analogous to the mysterious dark matter believed to account for much of the material content of the universe. The lack of transparency of certain AI systems will inevitably introduce doubts until that lack of transparency is removed and the system is better understood. Releasing such systems for public use is sometimes defended by the argument that we use our minds all the time, but we don't understand a great deal about how they work. A point to ponder!

Matteo Wong of the *Atlantic* perceptively notes: "Quantum observations too numerous for humans to store, experiments too rapid for humans to run, neuroscientific hypotheses too complex for humans to derive – even as AI enables scientific work never before thought possible, those same tools pose an epistemic dilemma. They will produce groundbreaking knowledge while breaking apart what it means to *know* in the first place."[61] It looks as if a new area of epistemology is opening up that will affect all of us and not only the scientists.

The Future of Life Institute's open letter goes on to say:

Contemporary AI systems are now becoming human-competitive at general tasks, and we must ask ourselves: *Should* we let machines flood our information channels with propaganda and untruth? *Should* we automate away all the jobs, including the fulfilling ones? *Should* we develop nonhuman minds that might eventually outnumber, outsmart, obsolete and replace us? *Should* we risk loss of control of our civilization? Such decisions must not be delegated to unelected tech leaders. **Powerful AI systems should be developed only once we are confident that their effects will be positive, and their risks will be manageable.** This confidence must be well justified and increase with the magnitude of a system's potential effects. OpenAI's recent statement regarding artificial general intelligence, states that *"At some point, it may be important to get independent review before starting to train future systems, and for the most advanced efforts to agree to limit the rate of growth of compute used for creating new models."* We agree. That point is now.

Therefore, **we call on all AI labs to immediately pause for at least 6 months the training of AI systems more powerful than GPT-4.**[62]

The distinguished signatories of this letter included

- Yoshua Bengio, founder and scientific director at Mila, Turing Prize winner, and professor at University of Montreal;
- Stuart Russell, professor of computer science at Berkeley, director of the Center for Intelligent Systems, and coauthor of the standard textbook *Artificial Intelligence: A Modern Approach*;
- Elon Musk, CEO of SpaceX, Tesla, and X (formerly known as Twitter);

- Steve Wozniak, cofounder of Apple;
- Yuval Noah Harari, author and professor, Hebrew University of Jerusalem;
- Jaan Tallinn, cofounder of Skype, the Centre for the Study of Existential Risk, and the Future of Life Institute;
- Evan Sharp, cofounder of Pinterest;
- Chris Larsen, cofounder of Ripple; and
- Max Tegmark, Institute for Artificial Intelligence and Fundamental Interactions, professor of physics at MIT, president of the Future of Life Institute.

William Hague, former leader of the UK's Conservative Party, responded to the open letter in an article in *The Times* entitled "The World Must Wake Up to the Speed and Scale of AI." Hague wrote:

> The rise of AI is almost certainly one of the two main events of our lifetimes, alongside the acceleration of climate change. It will transform war and geo-politics, change hundreds of millions of jobs beyond recognition, and open up a new age in which the most successful humans will merge their thinking intimately with that of machines. Adapting to this will be an immense challenge for societies and political systems, although it is also an opportunity and – since this is not going to be stopped – an urgent responsibility. . . . The letter from the experts will not stop the AI race, but it should lead to more work on future safety and in particular how to solve the alignment problem.
>
> Last week, ministers said we should not fear AI. In reality there is a lot to fear. But like an astronaut on a launch-pad, we should feel fear and excitement at the same time. This rocket is lifting off, it will accelerate, and we all need to prepare now.[63]

This concern runs so deep that in May 2023 one of the pioneers who developed the foundations of modern machine learning, Geoffrey Hinton of the University of Toronto, a winner of the prestigious Turing Award and regarded as the godfather of AI, quit his senior role at Google: "I left so that I could talk about the dangers of AI without considering how this impacts Google. Google has behaved very responsibly." He adds that it will be hard "to prevent the bad actors from using it for bad things."[64]

In an interview with CNBC, he elaborated further on what is happening: "If I have 1,000 digital agents who are all exact clones with identical weights, whenever one agent learns how to do something, all of them immediately know it because they share weights. . . . Biological agents cannot do this. So collections of identical digital agents can acquire hugely more knowledge than any individual biological agent. That is why GPT-4 knows hugely more than any one person." Hinton was asked what he thought the chances were of AI wiping out humanity. He responded, "It's not inconceivable. That's all I'll say."[65]

However, he went further in his Romanes Lecture in Oxford in February 2024 on the topic "Will Digital Intelligence Replace Biological Intelligence?" He suggested that a superintelligent AI might eventually gain enormous power to control so that no one will be able to switch them off. He also expressed concern about superintelligences competing with each other in a fight that the most aggressive would win – and may decide it is more important than humans are.

He concluded by saying that although he had always thought we were a long way from creating a superintelligence, since the brain was still much better than AI, he now felt the digital technologies we had were very nearly as good as brains and would get much better, so he reckoned that with probability 0.5 we would be outsmarted within twenty years.[66]

It is perhaps a healthy reminder that the Doomsday Clock was reset in January 2024 to ninety seconds to midnight as scientists have concluded that leaders are steering the world towards catastrophe. After the Cold War, the clock was at seventeen minutes to midnight. There certainly seems to be a very real threat to world stability – and not only from war and climate change but also from AI. As Iain McGilchrist has so starkly expressed it: "To be, or not to be. That is, in fact the question."[67] AI threatens the existence not only of a single individual like Hamlet but of the whole world.

Stuart Russell said in a 2023 interview that it was possible that ChatGPT could form part of a superintelligent machine that would resist any attempt to control it. Russell also said that until recently he thought AGI was decades away but now he is not so sure. He now rates this event, which he has likened to the appearance of an alien civilization, as possible, but still unlikely, within the next ten years. He fears that unless governments put much more effective controls on AI research, this – the most significant event in human history – might well be the last.[68]

Russell is well known for illustrating the risks of loss of control of an AI system by imagining the situation where an advanced AI is asked to solve the problem of climate change and solves it by exterminating all human beings so that all climate change caused by humans ceases.

To avoid detrimental, even disastrous, outcomes, Russell says that legislators and developers need to act on three basic principles:

1. Restrict an AI system's goals only to maximizing the realization of human goals;
2. Keep the AI uncertain about what those goals are so that it has to keep asking;
3. Insist that the AI tries to understand the nature of those goals by constant observation of human behavior.[69]

Renewing the call for AI legislation, Harari warns of an attendant threat that technologies like GPT bring with them – the capacity of AI to use language and story to manipulate and control people through creating a new religion. We shall think of this later in connection with the potential religious dimension in future AI scenarios.

To develop robust ethical legislation and controls, particularly for the EU, the EU Parliament in 2019 issued guidelines in ethics in artificial intelligence with seven ethical rules. The key EU requirements for achieving trustworthy AI are as follows:

- human agency and oversight
- technical robustness and safety
- privacy and data protection
- transparency
- diversity, nondiscrimination and fairness
- societal and environmental well-being
- accountability[70]

In addition, the Center for AI Safety published the following statement: "Mitigating the risk of extinction should be a global priority alongside other societal scale risks such as pandemics and nuclear war."[71] The center's website outlines a number of possible disaster scenarios:

- AI could be weaponized – for example, drug discovery tools could be used to build chemical weapons.
- AI-generated misinformation could destabilize society and "undermine collective decision-making."

- The power of AI could become increasingly concentrated in fewer and fewer hands, enabling "regimes to enforce narrow values through pervasive surveillance and oppressive censorship."
- Enfeeblement, where humans become dependent on AI "similar to the scenario portrayed in the film *Wall-E*."[72]

We should not miss the fact that this statement puts the global risk of extinction from AI on par with the risks from pandemics and nuclear war. In fact, according to the Center for Humane Technology, half of researchers in AI think that there is a 10 percent or greater chance that humans will go extinct from their inability to control AI.[73]

Sam Altman, chief executive of ChatGPT-maker OpenAI; Demis Hassabis, chief executive of Google DeepMind; and Dario Amodei of Anthropic (creators of Claude 2, a rival to ChatGPT) have all supported the statement from the Center of AI Safety, as have two of the three joint winners of the 2018 Turing Award for their work on neural networks, Geoffrey Hinton and Yoshua Bengio. Although Hassabis does not belong to the doom-mongers, he nevertheless believes that the technology is so powerful for good and evil that we need to be cautious. He reckons that there are three kinds of AI threat: existential, near-term (deepfakes and disinformation), and hostile, in which bad actors or rogue states use AI for hostile purposes.[74]

However, the third winner of the 2018 Turing Award, Yann LeCun of Meta, thinks that delaying research is pointless and that the letter calling for this is "wrong and useless."[75] He agrees with other leading figures in the technology world such as Brad Smith, the CEO of Microsoft, and Andrew Ng of Stanford, who set up Google's Brain division, who believe there is a danger of overhyping the risks of AI. The fact that the signatories to the statements calling for regulation are still investing billions in the AI research they say needs curbing has produced a certain amount of cynicism as to whether the rhetoric used here is essentially self-serving publicity. LeCun suggests that signing statements to the effect that AI might lead to the extinction of the human race are motivated by "regulatory capture." He says: "OpenAI is in a position where they believe they are ahead . . . so the right thing to do is to slam the door behind them."[76] In his article "AI Will Save the World," pioneer web-engine developer Marc Andreessen, now a venture capitalist, warned against a cult of doom by saying that AI doesn't mean that the end of humanity is nigh: "It is math – code – computers, built by people, owned

103

by people, controlled by people. The idea that it will at some point develop a mind of its own and decide that it has motivations that lead it to try to kill us is a superstitious handwave. In short, AI doesn't want, it doesn't have goals, it doesn't want to kill you, because it is not alive. AI is a machine – is not going to come alive any more than your toaster."[77]

In 2023, *Nature* published an article entitled "It's Time to Talk about the Known Risks of AI." It encourages us to "forget machine doomsday – what's needed is effective regulation to limit the societal harms artificial intelligence is already causing." The article highlights the danger of the overhyped notion of human extinction at the hands of AI becoming a distraction from a far more urgent actual problem of dealing with the serious harm caused, for example, by facial-recognition AI technology currently deployed by autocratic states to oppress people by monitoring their every move. The article continues:

> Biased AI systems could use opaque algorithms to deny people welfare benefits, medical care or asylum – applications of the technology that are likely to most affect those in marginalized communities. Debates on these issues are being starved of oxygen.
>
> One of the biggest concerns surrounding the latest breed of generative AI is its potential to boost misinformation. The technology makes it easier to produce more, and more convincing, fake text, photos and videos that could influence elections, say, or undermine people's ability to trust any information, potentially destabilizing societies. . . .
>
> Fear-mongering narratives about existential risks are not constructive. Serious discussion about actual risks, and action to contain them, are. The sooner humanity establishes its rules of engagement with AI, the sooner we can learn to live in harmony with the technology.[78]

There was a strange blip in the fortune of Sam Altman in November 2023 when he was sacked from OpenAI, immediately joined Microsoft, but was reinstated as CEO of OpenAI a few days later as a result of the rebellion of hundreds of OpenAI employees. Reporting on these events in the *Atlantic*, Karen Hao flagged the fact that we have very limited knowledge about how OpenAI develops its technology:

> This was made acutely apparent last Wednesday, when Reuters and *The Information* reported that, prior to Altman's firing, several staff researchers had raised concerns about a supposedly dangerous breakthrough. At issue

was an algorithm called Q* (pronounced "Q-star"), which has allegedly been shown to solve certain grade-school-level math problems that it hasn't seen before . . . in other words, using logic to solve novel problems. . . . Reasoning in this way is considered one of the key missing ingredients for smarter, more general-purpose AI systems, or what OpenAI calls "artificial general intelligence." In the company's telling such a theoretical system would be better than humans at most tasks and could lead to existential catastrophe if not properly controlled. . . . OpenAI has argued that its secrecy is in part because anything that could accelerate the path to superintelligence should be carefully guarded; not doing so, it says, could pose a threat to humanity. But the company has also openly admitted that secrecy allows it to maintain its competitive advantage.[79]

This OpenAI space needs careful watching as division among experts may well indicate a lack of objectivity caused by vested interests.

MILITARY USE OF AI: AUTONOMOUS WEAPONS

The military uses of AI tend to be of two kinds: electronic warfare by disruption of cyberspace and the use of physical AI-controlled weapons. Cyberwarfare takes place in cyberspace and involves the disruption of an enemy's communications – for example, by hacking transport, energy, or food supply networks and financial institutions as well as spreading disinformation on the internet and social media to manipulate the political, commercial, and social landscapes. For instance, Russia used cyberattacks to successfully take down Ukraine's power grid in 2015 and 2016, then launched a virus in 2017 that corrupted the networks of Ukrainian banks, newspapers, and other companies. That virus, NotPetya, spiraled out of control and eventually cost companies around the world billions of dollars.

More recently, in 2022 alone, Google claims to have disrupted over 1,950 Russian information operations, which have primarily been focused on "maintaining Russian domestic support for the war in Ukraine." Additionally, the State Special Communications Service of Ukraine reported the number of cyber incidents in Ukraine tripling in 2022.[80]

Additionally, AI can now be used to steal passwords simply by recording the sounds they make as they are typed on a keyboard, since each key makes a distinctive sound as it is pressed.[81]

Chatham House has reported that "both military and commercial robots will in the future incorporate 'artificial intelligence' that could make them capable of undertaking tasks and missions on their own. In the military context, this gives rise to a debate as to whether such robots should be allowed to execute such missions, especially if there is a possibility that any human life could be at stake."[82]

Tesla founder Elon Musk thinks that AI could trigger World War III, and Vladimir Putin has said that leadership in AI will be essential to global power in the twenty-first century. This is especially poignant now in light of the unprovoked invasion of Ukraine by Russia in 2022. It is highly likely that AI has unleashed a third revolution in warfare as significant as those brought about by the inventions of gunpowder and nuclear energy.

Michael Horowitz of the University of Pennsylvania sounds a cautious note:

> The potential promise of AI, despite safety and reliability concerns, means leading militaries around the world will certainly see the risks of standing still. From data processing to swarming drones and battlefield management, AI could help militaries operate faster and more accurately, while putting fewer humans at risk. Or not. The safety and reliability problems endemic to current machine learning and neural network methods mean that adversarial data, among other issues, will present a challenge to many military applications of AI. . . . But given its breadth as a technology, as compared to specific technologies like directed energy, and the degree of commercial energy and investment in AI, it seems more likely that the age of artificial intelligence is likely to shape, at least to some extent, the future of militaries around the world.[83]

Kai-Fu Lee, CEO of Sinovation Ventures and former president of Google China, in his coauthored book *AI 2041: Ten Visions for Our Future*, warns that the proliferation of autonomous weapons will be accelerated by an inevitable global arms race that will not have the deterrence effect that nuclear weapons possess.[84] Autonomous weapons are the AI application that most clearly and deeply conflicts with our morals and threatens humanity.

"Some argue that the superior effectiveness and selectivity of autonomous weapons can minimize civilian casualties by targeting only combatants," says Stuart Russell.

Others insist that LAWS [Lethal Autonomous Weapons Systems] will lower the threshold for going to war by making it possible to attack an enemy while incurring no immediate risk, or that they will enable terrorists and non-state-aligned combatants to inflict catastrophic damage on civilian populations.

The capabilities of autonomous weapons will be limited more by the laws of physics – for example, by constraints on range, speed, and payload – than by any deficiencies in the AI systems that control them.[85]

In his Reith Lectures, Russell pointed out some dangers of the current "AI will help us rule the world" arms-race mentality:

One is that it causes us to cut corners. If you're in a race, then safety is the last thing on your mind. You want to get there first and so you don't worry about making it safe. But the other is that general purpose or super-intelligent AI would be, essentially, an unlimited source of wealth and arguing over who has it would be like arguing over who has a digital copy of the daily Telegraph or something, right? If I have a digital copy, it doesn't prevent other people from having digital copies and it doesn't matter how many I have, it doesn't do me a lot of good.[86]

Russell argued, therefore, for government support for sharing AGI-technology.

Journalist Zachary Fryer-Biggs reports that the Pentagon plans to spend $2 billion to put more AI into weaponry to compete more effectively with Russian and Chinese advances in military technology. It appears, however, that commanders are concerned about relinquishing command to AI systems that would be tasked with identifying, searching out, and eliminating human targets. Google researchers who have been working on such AI systems have protested to such an extent that their part in the program is being discontinued. As Michael Horowitz comments in a 2018 *Verge* article: "There's a lot of concern about AI safety – [about] algorithms that are unable to adapt to complex reality and thus malfunction in unpredictable ways. It's one thing if what you're talking about is a Google search, but it's another thing if what you're talking about is a weapons system."[87] In a keynote address at Stanford University in 2019, Bill Gates said that AI is like nuclear energy and nuclear weapons in being "both promising and dangerous."[88]

During the Cold War, a group of medical doctors called International Physicians for the Prevention of Nuclear War was awarded the Nobel Peace

Prize for warning against the apocalyptic use of nuclear weapons. Now that same group is impressing upon the world the need to act against the threat of killer robots and the danger of autonomous weapons falling into the hands of terrorists. A warning was given in March 2019 to a meeting of the United Nations: "AI technologies can also be used to create weapons of mass destruction unlike anything the world has seen before."[89]

In *The Age of AI and Our Human Future*, Kissinger, Schmidt, and Huttenlocher write:

> When multiple militaries adopt strategies and tactics shaped by machines that perceive patterns human soldiers and strategists cannot, power balances will be altered and potentially more difficult to calculate. If such machines are authorized to engage in autonomous targeting decisions, traditional concepts of defense and deterrence – and the laws of war as a whole – may deteriorate or, at the very least, require adaptation.[90]

It is clear that some very smart ethics need to be developed to cope with this increasing threat before it is too late. In an article entitled "A Partial Ban on Autonomous Weapons Would Make Everyone Safer," Zachary Kallenborn, research affiliate at the Unconventional Weapons and Technology Division at the National Consortium for the Study of Terrorism and Responses to Terrorism, reports that UN secretary-general António Guterres wrote on Twitter, "Autonomous machines with the power and discretion to select targets and take lives without human involvement are politically unacceptable, morally repugnant and should be prohibited by international law."[91] Kallenborn advocates that, rather than trying to ban all autonomous weapons, which is likely to prove impossible because of their utility, the international community should place restrictions on the highest-risk weapons, which he lists as drone swarms and autonomous chemical, biological, radiological, and nuclear weapons, known as CBRN weapons. The scariest of these weapons may well be the drone swarms, which are essentially weapons of mass destruction. An operator directs the swarm to the general attack area, where they then behave autonomously. One obvious problem is that a swarm of a thousand drones has multiple ways to go wrong. Since advanced drones in a swarm are able to communicate with one another, errors may propagate throughout the swarm. One does not like to imagine the horrific scenario that would occur if, for instance, one of the drones mistook a cruise ship for an aircraft carrier and unleashed the lethal destructive force of the entire swarm on thousands of civilian passengers. A human being can control a single drone, but no human being has the capacity to control a swarm.[92]

By a strange coincidence, the very day I am writing these lines there is a report in *The Times* headlined "Killer Drones Used AI to Hunt Down Enemy Fighters in Libya's Civil War." The article cites a UN report describing the use of the Kargu-2 quadcopter, which can be deployed in swarms of up to twenty: "The lethal autonomous weapons systems were programmed to attack targets without requiring connectivity between the operator and the munition: in effect, a true 'fire, forget and find' capability."[93] "Fire and forget" is a type of missile guidance that does not require any external direction after it has been fired. It finds its target autonomously.

Calls for a ban on such weapons are intensifying. To get some idea of the reasons for concern, the reader might watch the 2017 YouTube dystopian video *Slaughterbots*,[94] which was made in connection with a UN meeting on autonomous weapons to warn of the dangers of killer drones and to call for preventive action in terms of arms control. The video was criticized at the time by Paul Scharre, vice president and director of studies at the Center for a New American Security, who argues that the film makes a number of unjustifiable assumptions. He suggests much of it is science fiction and not realistic evidence for arms control. He readily admits, however, that the concept is grounded in technical reality:

> I want to make something very clear: There is nothing we can do to keep that underlying technology out of the hands of would-be terrorists. This is upsetting, but it's very important to understand. Just like how terrorists can and do use cars to ram crowds of civilians, the underlying technology to turn hobbyist drones into crude autonomous weapons is already too ubiquitous to stop. This is a genuine problem, and the best response is to focus on defensive measures to counter drones along with surveillance to catch would-be terrorists ahead of time.[95]

The problem with the *Slaughterbots* film, according to Scharre, is that it "takes this problem and blows it out of proportion . . . suggesting that drones would be used by terrorists as robotic weapons of mass destruction, killing thousands of people at a time."[96] The result, in Scharre's view, is that the film's sensationalism undercuts the serious intellectual discourse needed around autonomous weapons.

But Stuart Russell, who was the driving force in making this film, referred to it in the serious intellectual discourse of his second Reith Lecture in December 2021, in which he pointed out that *Slaughterbots* had had more than 75 million views on the internet, and, so far as the technology is concerned, swarms of more than 3,000 perfectly coordinated quadcopters are routine.[97] They are capable of precise targeting, as imagined in the James Bond film *No Time to Die*, where a nanobot is primed with information from a target individual's DNA and homes in to assassinate him and him alone. The nightmare scenario is of such small but lethal autonomous weapons being used to, say, target all males aged eighteen to twenty-four in a city, or people of a particular ethnicity. They also form a highly attractive prospect for militaries, since they are inexpensive – millions of them could be purchased for the cost of a single fighter jet.

One way of dealing with the danger of mass destruction by swarms of lethal nanoweapons would be an effective ban on small antipersonnel weapons. That would have the effect of allowing the major powers to keep their conventional weaponry: aircraft, tanks, and submarines, which they would do anyway. This approach has the support of the International Committee of the Red Cross, which has a statutory responsibility for the Geneva Conventions.

The EU Parliament and the UN, as well as some thirty countries, are in favor of some kind of ban, the prospect for which is still remote. In 2021, *Forbes* magazine reported that "militaries all over the world are moving ahead with swarming attack drones." France, Spain, Russia, the UK, the US, the UAE, China, South Africa, and Armenia are actively engaged in developing these weapons, motivated by research that shows that swarms may be 50 percent more effective than drones working in an uncoordinated mass.[98]

The chilling thing is that many of these weapons already exist and are increasingly being used. Some of the very latest combat aircraft in both the UK and Russia and some Chinese warships will not have a human crew and will have AI capability to automatically select and destroy their targets. Risking machines instead of humans in combat has obvious attractions for military planners, since the robots are cheap and expendable. Richard Barrons, a former British army commander, says: "Here's the choice. I can build a machine that can go into a dangerous place and kill the enemy, or we can send your son – because that's the alternative. How do you feel now? People will say, you know what, the machine is a better alternative."[99]

Stuart Russell concluded his second 2021 Reith Lecture with an appeal to the members of the then upcoming Sixth Review Conference of the Convention on Prohibitions or Restrictions on the Use of Certain Conventional Weapons. Russell said: "There are 8 billion people wondering why you cannot give them some protection against being hunted down and killed by robots. If the technical issues are too complicated, your children can probably explain them."[100] After all, there is international legislation against biological and chemical weapons and nuclear-weapon proliferation, which, although sadly not watertight, at least ensure that there is some mechanism that can be applied to rogue states. Yet the international community still seems rather sluggish in its response to the new generation of autonomous weapons that may constitute a much greater threat. When a single human being in Russia can so manipulate the levers of power to wage war using the latest AI technology in Ukraine in Europe in the twenty-first century, it does not bode well for what might one day be done by a renegade AI.

In December 2023, Pope Francis drew attention to the fact that remotely controlled weapons systems had led to a "lessened perception of the devastation caused by those weapons systems and the burden of responsibility for their use, resulting in an even more cold and detached approach to the immense tragedy of war." He insisted that "the unique capacity for moral judgment and ethical decision-making is more than a complex collection of algorithms, and that capacity cannot be reduced to programming a machine." He therefore made a plea for "adequate, meaningful and consistent human oversight" of lethal autonomous weapons systems (or LAWS), arguing that the world has no need for new technologies that merely "end up promoting the folly of war."[101]

QUESTIONS

1. What jobs do you think are threatened by AI? Is yours? If so, what do you intend to do about it?
2. Have you experienced a job interview with a chatbot? How did you feel about it?
3. Industrial revolutions lead to job losses. Is the AI revolution any different from preceding ones?
4. What action should the government take in light of loss of jobs through AI?

5. What jobs do you think are most vulnerable to AI takeover? Least vulnerable? Would you consider changing your job?

6. In your opinion, what are the dangers to education from AI?

7. Have you tried ChatGPT? If so, what are your impressions? Do you trust it?

8. Do you think that AI experts asked for a moratorium on research for reasons that they are not being open about? Why do you feel like that? Do you agree with their request?

9. Where should the Doomsday Clock be set, in your opinion? Is the present setting right? Give your reasons.

10. What are your views on autonomous weapons?

CHAPTER 8

BIG BROTHER MEETS BIG DATA

One of the Orwellian aspects of AI is that certain forms of AI present a serious threat to individual and corporate privacy. Yuval Noah Harari writes: "Once Big Data systems know me better than I know myself, authority will shift from humans to algorithms. Big Data could then empower Big Brother."[1] We already live in a world where around 2.5 billion of us (voluntarily, be it noted) wear a sophisticated personal tracker in the shape of a smartphone, and almost the same number are networked on Facebook. Through this we enthusiastically help augment Big Data by voluntarily uploading all kinds of information about ourselves. This is part of what has been called "the narcissism epidemic" on social media.[2]

AI tracker programs are geared to harvesting as much self-generated data as possible about your lifestyle and habits, where you go, what you buy, people you communicate with, books you read, jobs you do, your political and social activities, your personal opinions – a list that is growing. Mark Zuckerberg once boasted that Facebook would know every book, film, and song a person had ever consumed and that its predictive models would tell you what bar to go to when you arrive in a strange city, where the bartender would have your favorite drink waiting for you.[3] Some of this we find helpful, but there is more than one side to sharing this data. Data that is harvested from us can be used not only to inform us but to control us, and the ethical questions are obvious: Who controls such projects and who owns the data they generate? Big Brother may not need a totalitarian regime to empower him if we simply open the door and invite him in. Indeed, it may be too late, for he is already here.

For obvious reasons, criminals also want to get their hands on our data. Around the time I started writing this book, I learned that my credit card details had been hacked from a well-known international corporation to which I had entrusted them. As a result, I had to cancel the card and order another one to avoid being the victim of financial crime.

Here is a diagram illustrating the various types of citizen data:[4]

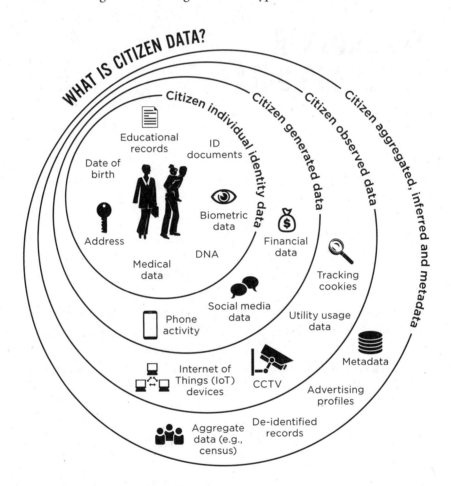

SURVEILLANCE CAPITALISM

The harvesting of data has become an immensely profitable business that has subtle and often hidden ramifications. This issue is the subject of an impressive book, *The Age of Surveillance Capitalism*, by Harvard professor emerita Shoshana Zuboff. It is subtitled *The Fight for a Human Future at the New Frontier of Power*.[5] Her thesis is that we are moving into what she defines as a new economic order, one that collects the big data that we generate and exploits it as raw material for the purpose of making money in ways that are less than obvious to most people. These activities will intensify the risk of the kind of surveillance society that we shall discuss in the next section, and the two together will threaten the stability and freedoms currently enjoyed in at least some parts of the world.

Zuboff argues that surveillance capitalism is a logical consequence of modern technologies.[6] At a more popular level, journalist Libby Purves comments on the prevalence of digital assistants such as Siri, Alexa, Google, and Cortana that are now used by many people to accomplish tasks such as telephoning, messaging, playing music, finding information, and much more: "Novelty blurs the oddity of paying to live with a vigilant inhuman spy linked to an all-too-human corporate profit center thousands of miles away. . . . To welcome an ill-regulated corporate eavesdropper into your house is a dumb, reckless bit of self-bugging."[7] Yet millions, maybe already billions, of us do it!

We should notice the mention of *power* in Zuboff's subtitle. The ubiquitous content-selection algorithms in social media that suggest things you might want to have next often exert unprecedented power over us. Yet most of us are barely aware of this. These accumulated databases store information about our previous purchases and make it possible to predict more accurately what we might like to buy next. That knowledge also enables it to manipulate our responses and make us less critical and more suggestible. In these subtle ways it maximizes revenue for big corporations whose only objective is financial gain. The irony is that we invited the machine to do all of this in the first place.

In November 2021, Pulitzer Prize winner Ayad Akhtar, referring to Kurzweil's concept of the singularity, wrote:

> For more than a generation, science-fiction writers and aficionados have speculated about the possibility and imminence of the singularity – that is, the moment when AI will finally eclipse human intelligence. To many, it's meant the robot capable of thinking, and with an intellect surpassing our own. Let me suggest that digital problem-solving has already surpassed human capacity. Indeed, our advanced societies are now being ordered by a digital matrix of data collection, pattern recognition, and decision making that we cannot even begin to fathom – and that is happening every single successive millisecond. The synergy of data technology, computer-processing speeds and capacity, and an almost frictionless interconnectivity – all of this enables

exchange; delivery of services; production of goods; growth of capital; and, most centrally, the endless catalog of our every interface, however glancing, however indirect, with this system's sprawling and ubiquitous apparatus. The singularity is here – we could call it the era of automation – and its inescapable imprint on our inner lives is already apparent . . . the technology metes out its steady stream of tiny pleasures as the reward for your sustained attention. Touch the screen – respond to the offered stimuli like a rat in an experiment – and receive what some are now calling a dopamine rush.

What follows from this engagement with the devices is an education, in which the system absorbs our responses and begins to shape them.[8]

The lure of huge profits to be made using this kind of surveillance technology acts as an incentive to companies to harvest even more information about us and thus tighten their grip on our behaviors and identities. As for insurance against invasion of privacy, Mark Ireland, archdeacon of Blackburn, writes: "Google and Facebook have cunningly made privacy a duty of the individual to protect, rather than an obligation of the companies to respect. An instrument of this is the misleadingly named Privacy Policy, which most of us fail to read several times a day. Zuboff argues that it would be more accurate to describe these as 'surveillance policies,' because they have been impenetrably drafted so that we unwittingly cede all rights over our personal information to the company to sell on to anyone it wishes."[9]

SURVEILLANCE COMMUNISM AND THOUGHT CONTROL

While one downside of the harvesting of information to influence people is *surveillance capitalism*, another might reasonably be called *surveillance communism*. In March 2018, the Future of Humanity Institute published a report on the development of AI in China, where it is said $197 billion was spent on domestic security in 2017 and where there are, as of 2021, over 540 million CCTV cameras – one for roughly every three citizens. Some of what George Orwell envisaged for 1984 is already with us, so what it will be like by 2084 is anybody's guess, although the underlying trend is clear. China is already using AI for social control.[10] The surveillance state is no longer merely a distant dystopian threat – it is a fearful and present reality.

According to a 2023 report in *Newsweek*, China has set up a coordinated Brain Project that aims to replicate the human brain in a bid to dominate global AI. Its goal is AGI (artificial general intelligence), which, according to leading Chinese AI scientist Zhu Songchun, "is the original and ultimate goal of artificial intelligence research." Zhu is the founder and director of China's leading AGI institute, the Beijing Institute for General Artificial Intelligence (BIGAI). He explained: "I specifically decided to use AGI as part of the institution's name to distinguish it from dedicated artificial intelligence," such as "face recognition, object detection or text translation." He holds that "artificial general intelligence is the 'atomic bomb' of the information field and the 'game winner' in the competition between China and the United States."[11]

SOCIAL CREDIT SYSTEMS

One evidence of the Chinese drive for supremacy, part of President Xi Jinping's vision for data-driven governance, is the setting up of a governmental social credit system (SoCS) that holistically rates in order of priority companies, government entities, individual citizens, and social organizations to enforce compliance with laws and regulations. Its roots lie deep in the cultural history of China going back to the time of Confucius (551–479 BC), who advocated a holistic view of human nature in which individual well-being was connected to good character and the proper functioning of society as a whole. Central to it is the concept of *chengxin*, which conveys ideas of loyalty, trustworthiness, honesty, integrity, morality, or sincerity, depending on context.

This is being implemented to create, in communist-speak, a "culture of sincerity" in a "trustworthy society." To achieve compliance with this goal, first publicized in 2014, many and varied pilot schemes have been set up by provinces, government organizations, cities, and major companies. There is a useful introduction to these ideas by senior regulatory specialist and legal expert Drew Donnelly of New Horizons.[12]

The basic idea of SoCS is that the Communist Party of China wishes to measure its citizens and corporations to determine whether they are "trustworthy." To achieve this goal, each corporation and citizen is issued a standardized unique personal identity number. Each citizen is awarded a number, let's say 300, of social credit points that can be added to by "good" (i.e., government-approved) behavior, such as paying debts (or fines) on time – a particularly important target of the system – using public transport, keeping fit, donating to charity, donating blood, volunteering, or reporting on someone you have seen with large amounts of foreign currency. As your points accumulate, you are granted more and more perks – access to a wider range of jobs, and wider access to contracts, mortgage opportunities, reduced utility bills, school placements for children, goods, travel possibilities, even reduced rental costs for bicycles.

If you behave in ways thought "antisocial," such as associating with people regarded "unsafe" by the government, coming into conflict with the police, overindulging in alcohol, jaywalking, bad driving, smoking in nonsmoking zones, buying too many video games, cheating at such games, not visiting your parents regularly, not keeping your dog on a leash, posting fake news online, plagiarizing, writing and sharing anti-government ideologies, playing music too loud on a train, bad driving, complaining, and a host of other things, you will lose points and attract penalties at different levels – limited access to the job and housing markets, restrictions on travel or even on the range of restaurants you can visit, loss of credit cards, or bans on flights.[13] You might even end up being denounced as a "discredited person" on a public television screen as you walk past it. Public announcements on some trains warn of the credit disadvantage of antisocial behavior.[14]

At the corporate level, achieving a good social credit depends on factors such as whether the business

1. has paid taxes on time,
2. maintains necessary licenses,
3. fulfils environmental-protection requirements,
4. meets product quality standards, and
5. meets requirements specific to its industry.[15]

Much of this control is exercised by advanced AI facial-recognition techniques working on a vast database of images channeled into a central computing center from millions of CCTV cameras.[16]

Several caveats need to be brought in here, however. The first is that much of what is set out above is what was thought to be the original plan for the SoCS. Yet it became clear in 2022 that not all of these ideas had been implemented. For instance, contrary to popular widespread understanding, a 2022 MERICS report says: "There will not be a unified 'Social Credit Score' that rates individual behavior. An all-encompassing scoring system was not part of the original plan. Instead, efforts have been focused on the establishment of comprehensive digital files that track and document legal compliance.

Pilot projects that used points-based systems to steer behavior beyond what is legally required have been discontinued or limited to voluntary participation." The report also says: "The Social Credit System remains the least digitised of China's tech-driven monitoring and surveillance initiatives. It relies heavily on human investigations, reports, and decisions. This also leaves room for traditional vectors of individual and political influence."[17]

The second caveat is that the government was not the first institution to set up a SoCS system in China. The most highly developed SoCS schemes, which are voluntary and private, were set up by the most powerful Chinese tech corporations, such as Alibaba and Tencent. These organizations now cooperate with the government Ministry of Public Security and other ministries to harvest data.

The Times has reported that some Chinese companies are fitting their employees with headgear that conceals technology that can read the wearers' brainwaves and send the data to computers that, in turn, use AI to check for emotions such as depression, anxiety, or anger.[18] China plans to implement the SoCS for all of the almost 22 million citizens of Beijing. *The Telegraph* reported that the Chinese government has stated that "the points system will improve the city's business environment by preventing people with low 'integrity' from accessing the city's public services and travel network. People with a low credit score could also find it difficult to start a business or find work."[19] Channel News Asia reported that 9 million people had already been blocked from buying tickets for domestic flights and 3 million from obtaining business-class train tickets.[20] There are also reports of throttled internet speeds and bans from higher education as punishments.

The stated goal of having a unified nationwide SoCS by 2020 was not reached, although much has been done to realize it in the near future. An estimated 80 percent of provinces, regions, and cities have introduced some version of the system.

The government has presented this scheme as simply a tool for sensible economic and legal management to make up for a serious lack of trust in Chinese society.[21] But since the objective of the system is eventually to have a unified record for people, businesses, and the government, which can be monitored in real time, it is readily conceivable that, if and when the SoCS is standardized, digitalized, and ubiquitous, it will facilitate a massive hacking of human beings that will take the world a scary step towards the perfection of a (potentially global) dictatorship, the setting up of an authoritarian dreamworld whose ideology could spread around the world like a virus and whose legitimacy is secured by the most comprehensive and powerful state surveillance apparatus in history.

For those of us who value our freedoms, it is perhaps rather surprising that many people in China seem to have welcomed the SoCS. Research by the Free University of Berlin on the SoCS systems of reward and punishment showed that 80 percent of the 2,200 respondents surveyed approved the systems and only 1 percent explicitly disapproved. Most people interviewed said they believed it to be an essential form of social management that improves the quality of life for all. The report makes the following interesting statement:

> The massive invasion of privacy of Chinese citizens is often criticized, primarily in Western, but also in some Chinese media reports, according to the head of the study, Prof. Dr. Genia Kostka. However, the results of the study indicate that respondents see the social credit system less as a monitoring tool than as an instrument for improving the quality of life and closing institutional and regulatory gaps. Despite impressive transformation processes over the past 40 years, the legal system and the banking sector in China are underdeveloped. For example, there is no uniform credit information system and the enforcement of many laws is inadequate: "In a country where consumers must be concerned about toxic baby milk or contaminated strawberries or where internet fraudsters harass hundreds of thousands of people, the social credit system is perceived as a platform for reliable information. The criticism of the collection of personal data has thus receded into the background in China." Of course, when looking at the study results, one has to consider that respondents may have been very careful in their online evaluation of social credit systems, says Genia Kostka. But the positive opinion on the credit rating systems was also confirmed in personal interviews with Chinese citizens.[22]

It should also be said that SoCS is often talked up as being more effective and more intrusive for individuals than it really is.[23]

Notwithstanding some positive comments on SoCS and the tendency of some Western scholars to regard it, in the words of Matthew Syed of *The Times*, as "the scaled-up version of the ratings system on Uber or AirBnb,"[24] the Associated Press reported the following announcement in 2021:

> The U.N. human rights chief is calling for a moratorium on the use of artificial intelligence technology that poses a serious risk to human rights, including face-scanning systems that track people in public spaces.

Michelle Bachelet, the U.N. High Commissioner for Human Rights, also said Wednesday that countries should expressly ban AI applications which don't comply with international human rights law. Applications that should be prohibited include government "social scoring" systems that judge people based on their behavior and certain AI-based tools that categorize people into clusters such as by ethnicity or gender. . . .

The report also voices wariness about tools that try to deduce people's emotional and mental states by analyzing their facial expressions or body movements, saying such technology is susceptible to bias, misinterpretations and lacks scientific basis. "The use of emotion recognition systems by public authorities, for instance, for singling out individuals for police stops or arrests or to assess the veracity of statements during interrogations, risks undermining human rights, such as the rights to privacy, to liberty and to a fair trial," the report says.[25]

It remains to be seen just what effect such a moratorium will have on a burgeoning industry worth billions of dollars.

On 6 October 2021, the European Parliament, which had already considered such a moratorium earlier in the year, adopted a resolution calling for a ban on the use by police and judicial authorities of facial-recognition technology in the EU, at least in the form of mass surveillance in public spaces.

It is therefore clear that there is considerable international apprehension about SoCS even though there would appear to be some evidence of journalists overhyping the situation. In an article entitled "Mythbusting the Social Credit System" in the *Spectator* of 13 June 2022, Cindy Yu claims that the Western narrative of the SoCS deviates a long way from the actual situation for the simple reason that the technology just isn't there. She cites the MERICS report on SoCS[26] that most targets are companies rather than individuals. She adds: "None of this is to say that surveillance doesn't happen on a massive scale in China – it does; or that the government is somehow liberal-minded about how its people live – it's not. In particular, Beijing exerts severe control (fed by high-tech) in regions like Xinjiang. But the problem there is less social credit and more ethnic repression."[27]

George Soros, a vocal champion of open societies, in a lecture to the World Economic Forum in Davos in 2019, expressed concern as to where SoCS will lead: "The social credit system is not yet fully operational, but it's clear where it is heading. It will subordinate the fate of the individual to the interests of the One-Party state in ways unprecedented in history. I find the social credit system frightening and abhorrent."[28]

He said this in the context of calling attention to what he thought was the mortal danger facing us that arises from the use by repressive regimes of artificial intelligence surveillance technologies to control their populations.

For SoCS is only part of the much wider Chinese surveillance apparatus, which involves many other operations and powers that, to cite the MERICS report on SoCS once more, are "much more invasive. . . . These projects often operate more covertly and act beyond the confines of laws and regulations, in a relatively clear division of labour. These include Golden Shield, Skynet, Safe Cites and Police Clouds, Project Sharp Eyes, and the Integrated Joint-Operations Platform (IJOP) in Xinjiang."[29]

To take one of them as an example, China's "Police Cloud" system, with 1.4 billion human targets, is designed to monitor seven categories of people, including those who "undermine stability."[30] It is, we should note, being marketed around the world.

There are serious ethical problems here involving the infringement of human rights and consequent injustice. There are also potential issues with the technology. As mentioned above, the United Nations report cautions about tools that try to infer people's emotional and mental states by looking at their facial expressions or body movements, noting that such technology can lead to bias and misinterpretations and has no scientific basis.

For instance, one underlying assumption is that the AI facial-recognition algorithms and the wearable emotion-detection technology give correct readings and interpretations of the emotions and attitudes they are meant to detect. But there is increasing scientific evidence that this may not be the case, at least in the case of facial recognition – although we are told that such systems are rapidly improving.

The Times reported in 2019 on a two-year analysis of more than 1,000 studies of the relationship between facial movements and emotions. The researchers did not find support for stereotypical facial expressions as predictive of feelings.[31] The conclusion of the study was this: "It is not possible to confidently infer happiness from a smile, anger from a scowl, or sadness from a frown."[32] Yet many major providers of security technologies think otherwise.

According to James Vincent in *The Verge*, the offices of Canon Information Technology have been fitted with a facial-recognition AI system that will let only smiling workers enter rooms or book meetings.[33]

But there is far too much room for error in these systems, leading to tragic injustices and hardship for targeted individuals and groups. It seems that little is being done about it, even though such possibly flawed technologies are being rolled out, particularly in China, in an attempt to control even what people think as a lever to moral and social domination. In a Human Rights Watch report, senior China researcher Maya Wang says: "The Chinese government is monitoring every aspect of people's lives in Xinjiang, picking out those it mistrusts and subjecting them to extra scrutiny."[34] As the surveillance systems proliferate, the meaning of what constitutes criminal and antisocial behavior becomes broader and broader until people can be penalized for almost anything that does not fit into a narrow set of state-defined parameters of normal thought, let alone behavior. That is the problem when morality is determined by the shifting sands of what the Party (often meaning its sole leader) thinks is acceptable, rather than in an open society where the rule of law prevails to uphold individual freedom and human rights.

Xinjiang is the largest subdivision of China, situated in the west and covering one-sixth of its land area so that it is about the size of Iran. It is home to around 11 million Uyghur people, who are a predominantly Muslim Turkic-speaking ethnic group. According to the US Council on Foreign Relations, since 2017 an estimated 800,000 to 2 million people have been imprisoned by the Chinese government in camps euphemistically called vocational and educational centers. Those not detained are subjected to relentless surveillance, religious restrictions, forced labor, and forced sterilizations.[35]

The United States Holocaust Memorial Museum reports that "Uyghurs are barred from freely practicing their religion, speaking their language, and expressing other fundamental elements of their identity. Restrictions apply to many aspects of life, including dress, language, diet, and education. The Chinese government closely monitors Uyghur religious institutions. Even ordinary acts such as praying or going to a mosque may be a basis for arrest or detention."[36]

The treatment of the Uyghurs indicates that the Chinese authorities are implementing mass forced assimilation to "erase the Uyghur culture and their ability to express their unique identity." Uyghur women have reported that they have been forced to marry Han Chinese, and Han "relatives" are introduced into Uyghur homes to observe the Uyghur families in their private sphere, essentially as resident spies.[37] Such assimilation clearly threatens the continued existence of the Uyghurs' cultural and religious practices.

The Uyghurs are now subject to the most intense surveillance that the world has ever seen to the extent that the capital city of Ürümqi has been described as a "digital fortress."[38] Every movement, conversation, action, and interaction—both offline and online—is recorded. ID cards are used to store not only DNA information but the holder's "reliability status" – an index that records just how well they are considered to fit in to what the state considers normal.[39] Any change in that status in the negative direction can lead to arrest and incarceration.

There are cameras every few yards down every street and alleyway. Cameras are now in existence that can track all kinds of bodily movements and can even recognize people by their gait and gestures – they are identified (with more than 90 percent accuracy, we are told) without even having to look into the camera lens.[40]

All smartphones are fitted with spyware by government order – a regulation that now appears to apply to all visitors to China. There are small police stations every few hundred yards, where passing Uyghurs must hand in their smartphones to have them electronically read and all the information contained on them transferred to the central monitoring system to be processed by AI. They are forced to install apps that use algorithms to hunt 24/7 for "ideological viruses." These apps scan chat logs for Koranic verses and they even look for Arabic script in image files.

The monitoring knows no boundaries. They cannot load prohibited social media software like WhatsApp. And avoiding social media doesn't work either, because such digital inactivity raises suspicion. "The police are required to note when Uyghurs deviate from any of their normal behavior patterns. Their database wants to know if Uyghurs start leaving their home through the back door instead of the front. It wants to know if they spend less time talking to neighbors than they used to. Electricity use is monitored by an algorithm for unusual use, which could indicate an unregistered resident."[41] A 2020 clandestine TV documentary made for ITV showed pictures of QR codes pasted on the doors of houses to be read by police scanners so that they would know who was supposed to be in the house and could then check.[42] It is "repression powered by algorithms."[43] This kind of repression using advanced technologies to consolidate the power of an authoritarian regime and better ensure its survival has been described as "digital authoritarianism."[44]

All of this is in line with the brutal statement made in 2017 by a Chinese religious affairs official: "Break their lineage, break their roots, break their connections, and break their origins. Completely shovel up the roots of 'two-faced people,' dig them out, and vow to fight these two-faced people until the end."[45]

Fifty-one UN member countries, including the United States, have issued a joint declaration condemning the Chinese government's crimes against humanity committed against Uyghurs and other Turkic communities and calling on Beijing to end its systematic human rights abuses in the Xinjiang region. At a more recent meeting at the UN in January 2024, representatives of 160 out of the 193 UN member states urged China to improve its human rights record, particularly the genocide and crimes against humanity in Xinjiang that were explicitly cited by the US ambassador.

A chilling, authoritative account of what is happening in Xinjiang is given by Uyghur author Nury Turkel in his book *No Escape: The True Story of China's Genocide of the Uyghurs*.[46] I met Turkel at the 2023 International Ministerial Conference on Freedom of Religion or Belief in Prague, where he was chairing a session on digital oppression at which I spoke. A Uyghur born in a Chinese reeducation camp in Kashgar, Turkel is a senior fellow of the Hudson Institute in Washington and a life member of the Council on Foreign Relations. He formerly served as chair of the US Commission on International Religious Freedom. He has testified before the US Congress about Uyghur internment camps. His policy recommendations have been incorporated into US law and pending bills relating to Uyghurs and China. He is chair of the Uyghur Human Rights Project, which he cofounded in 2003. In 2020 he was named as one of *Time* magazine's 100 most influential people in the world. In June 2021 he received the inaugural Notre Dame Prize for Religious Liberty. In September 2021 he was awarded the Global Soul Award by Jewish World Watch. I give these details to underline my conviction that his book is essential reading for anyone who wishes to know about what is going on in Xinjiang – and that should be all of us.

Intrusive surveillance as deployed in Xinjiang is bad enough, but what is even more disturbing is that the population there is being subjected to a massive attempt at what looks like thought control. It is facilitated by the setting up of so-called reeducation centers that (as of 2021) together house over 1.5 million Uyghurs, who are sent there as a result of what is revealed by the surveillance apparatus, even though, as we have seen, the technology may be flawed. Many families have been split up – husbands taken from their wives, and children taken from their parents. These reeducation centers – prisons, really – appear to be devoted to the elimination of Uyghur culture, turning their inmates into loyal Chinese citizens.[47] There are many of them – in 2020, researchers documented 201 reeducation camps and 179 detention centers and prisons distributed all over Xinjiang.

According to Ian Williams, eyewitness reports coming out of these camps make grim reading.[48] They tell of total lack of privacy – even in toilets – except for the existence of a "Black Room" that is used for unobserved vicious punishment and torture for even the most minor of infractions, such as not showing enough enthusiasm for the endless indoctrination. This is straight out of Orwell's *1984* where Room 101 was the place of everyone's worst fears. These reeducation centers would appear to represent an extreme violation of human rights. Indeed, one commentator said that human rights for the Uyghur population were nonexistent.

Maya Wang of Human Rights Watch says: "This is not just about Xinjiang or even China – it's about the world beyond and whether we human beings can continue to have freedom in a world of connected devices." She added: "It's a wake-up call, not just about China but about every one of us."[49]

Ian Williams adds: "Uighurs serve a very specific purpose of social engineering and the repression of a targeted minority. Xinjiang is a laboratory for a new sort of totalitarianism. A test bed. A playground, almost. And while these chilling technologies are being used to bring Xinjiang to heel and eradicate Uighur culture, they are being primed and adapted for use against dissent elsewhere in China, while being packaged for export to autocrats across the world. Where next? Hong Kong?"[50]

As a plethora of books attests, the Digital Silk Road is expanding the Chinese technosphere at an accelerating pace. No state has leveraged digital technologies more successfully than China, which is now a world leader, not just in the manufacture of commodity hardware and electronics, but of cutting-edge technologies such as artificial intelligence. These advances have facilitated the development of a new level of automated mass surveillance as far-reaching in its implications as was the industrial revolution.

On top of that, natural language processing and sentiment analysis on social media exchanges enables the authorities to infer the nature of relationships between people with a view to determining whether they have committed "crimes against the state." Research shows, however, that the current accuracy rates of natural language processing tools are only around 70 to 80 percent. While they are often justified as a means to reduce human error, such algorithmic tools can further entrench racial or religious discrimination due to reliance on inaccurate or biased data. The resulting false positives can add innocent people to government watch lists, often without their knowledge, leaving them with little recourse for remedying the mistake.

What all other countries need urgently to be made aware of is that China's reach does not stop at its borders. The US government-funded charity the Open Technology Fund reported in 2019 that already more than one hundred nations belong to what we may call the Chinese technosphere, having have bought into China's surveillance and censorship technologies and are engaging Chinese experts to teach them how to use them for repressive control of their own citizens.[51] These countries have installed Chinese CCTV cameras and built local versions of the Great Firewall of China into their own internet networks.

The West is now beginning to admit it has been slow to recognize and respond to the encroachment of China it has allowed to happen in the past few years. Members of Parliament in the UK were warned in March 2024 that Chinese-made electric cars in the UK – and indeed in the rest of Europe – could be jammed remotely by Beijing and therefore pose a "major security" threat to transportation and communication. Not only that, but they could be used to steal sensitive data from motorists. This threat is rated highly enough for the former head of MI6 to call upon the government to ban the use of such vehicles for certain sensitive purposes. The conclusion was drawn: "Chinese-connected EV's flooding the country could be the most effective Trojan horse that the Chinese establishment has to impact the UK."[52]

US President Joe Biden has also just ordered an investigation into the same issue. It is noteworthy that China has banned Teslas from sensitive areas of its own territory – a clear evidence of the way it sees the future.

Furthermore, in recent years, China has invested billions in the developing world, particularly in Africa and Asia. As well as building bridges, airports, and roads, as part of the deal China often insists that partner countries also install its technology, especially when setting up telecoms and internet networks. The terms and conditions of such contracts often include making all the data harvested from such networks available to China. Of the fifteen countries in Asia assessed by this report, thirteen have social media surveillance programs under development or in use – some from China and some from the United States, Russia, and elsewhere. Forty-seven of the sixty-five countries assessed arrested social media users for political, social, or religious speech – a record high. Even in (Western) countries with considerable safeguards for fundamental freedoms, there are reports of abuse.

Quite so. And that is why we need to take very seriously the urgent rallying call with which Nury Turkel ends the preface of *No Escape*: "Together we must prevent the next bad actors from committing genocide against other vulnerable ethnic and religious groups. We cannot let 'Never Again' become an empty promise."[53] The tragedy is that there are powerful forces determined to stifle Turkel's cry.

In December 2021 the *Financial Times* reported that "the US has put China's Academy of Military Medical Sciences and eleven affiliated biotechnology research institutes on an export blacklist for allegedly helping the Chinese military to develop 'brain-control' weapons. . . . 'China is choosing to use these technologies to pursue control over its people and its repression of members of ethnic and religious minority groups,' said Gina Raimondo, US commerce secretary."[54]

It is interesting to know that China also has its dystopian literature, and some of it is taken up with one method of thought control – by rewriting history. A sense of history is vital to the identity of an individual, society, or nation, and therefore a people's sense of their identity can be manipulated, distorted, rewritten so that they no longer really know who they are. The Czech novelist Milan Kundera wrote: "The struggle of man against power is the struggle of memory against forgetting."[55] The pandemic has given China the excuse of closing down all forms of protest against what has happened in the past. In computer science there are two basic forms of memory storage, read-only and rewrite, and there is a certain grim irony in the fact that advanced technology with its vast capacity for storing information is now being harnessed to shift a huge population from using more-or-less reliable read-only books of history to being fed from the national rewrite memory that either revises the past or obliterates it.

This is the subject of the novel *The Four Books* by Chinese author Yan Lianke, who won the prestigious Franz Kafka Prize.[56] Written in 2015, it tells the story of Mao's Great Leap Forward, 1958–1961, which happened in the days that preceded advanced technology. In a labor camp in an isolated part of Henan Province, a group of well-educated citizens are imprisoned to restore their commitment to the reigning communist ideology. They are the Musician, the Scholar, the Author, and the Theologian. They are forced to live in circumstances where everyone is encouraged to be an informer on the other prisoners. Their overseer is the Child, who delights in controlling what the inmates do by subjecting them to draconian rules and confiscating their books. The prisoners are faced with constantly rising unrealistic work targets that eventually become unattainable and the prisoners are reduced to trying to grow wheat by the desperate expedient of watering seedlings with their blood. As famine and inclement weather arrive, the intellectuals are abandoned by the state.

Isabel Hilton writes a review of Yan Lianke's book in the *Guardian*: "No other writer in today's China has so consistently explored, dissected and mocked the past six and a half decades of Chinese communist rule. . . . He has produced an extraordinary novel, one that both commemorates the state's victims and defies China's state-sponsored amnesia."[57]

Another book that is not so much dystopian as a critique of Chinese contemporary culture is *The Fat Years* by Chan Koonchung.[58] This book, which, it must be said, is not the easiest of reads, is important for its description of collective amnesia on the part of the Communist Party as it airbrushed from history the Tiananmen Square massacre in 1989 and labeled those who cannot "forget" as crazy. The setting, relative to the time of writing, is in the near future – 2013. Lao Chen, a writer from Hong Kong living in Beijing, gets involved with friends investigating the "lost month" of February 2011 – lost because official records jump from January to March. The friends eventually kidnap a high-ranking official and force him to reveal the grim facts behind the missing month.

The Chinese historian Zhang Lifan predicted that such historical manipulation and revisionism will eventually backfire on the authorities: "If government officials don't know the real history, it will lead to stupid decisions and stupid policies."[59] And if educators in schools and universities are forced to rewrite history, they will create a dangerous alternative reality for future generations.

Certainly, some of the effects of the social control exercised on the Chinese population is already being exported, particularly to universities in the West where many Chinese students are studying. There have been incidents of intimidation by students from mainland China of Hong Kong students in the UK. In 2019, the *Independent* published an article that began: "A new front has been opened by protesters attempting to secure the freedom of Hong Kong from what they perceive to be ever-encroaching Chinese autocracy – in Sheffield, South Yorkshire. Up to 200 Hong Kong and Chinese students clashed in the city on Wednesday after a pro-democracy rally was hijacked by counter-demonstrators."[60]

A BBC report the previous day said: "Labour councillor Ben Miskell said he left a full council meeting after getting a message from the pro-democracy protesters saying they were under attack. He said: 'These aren't hardened protesters. They just want to protect their way of life and their families' way of life in Hong Kong.' One student, who did not want to be named, told the BBC: 'We are quite afraid of what is happening here and whether we're going to be safe in class.'"[61] The tragic irony of it all is that the right to protest that the mainland Chinese students claim in Sheffield and on other campuses in the UK does not exist in China itself.

That brings us to the influence of China on global internet policy and standards. Here the International Telecommunication Union (ITU) plays a key role. It is part of the UN, involves around 200 countries, has headquarters in Geneva, and its secretary-general is Houlin Zhao, who was appointed for his second four-year term in 2019. Its objective is to be the global regulator for internet standards, and its trajectory is indicated by the following statement, which appeared in an official report entitled *The New Big Brother: China and Digital Authoritarianism*, prepared for the US Senate Committee on Foreign Relations: "In addition to a former Chinese official being at the head of the ITU, Chinese firms and government research institutes held the largest number of chair and vice chair positions in the ITU's 5G-related standards-setting bodies, with eight of the 39 available leadership positions as of September 2018. According to Michael O'Rielly of the US Federal Communications Commission, the Chinese 'have loaded up the voting to try to get their particular candidates on board, and their particular standards.'" The report concludes:

> Indeed, three and a half years into the Trump administration, the United States is now on the precipice of losing the future of the cyber domain to China. If China continues to perfect the tools of digital authoritarianism and is able to effectively implement them both domestically and abroad, then China, not the United States and its allies, will shape the digital environment in which most of the world operates. Additionally, if the United States continues to cede its traditional role of diplomatic and technological leadership, the global growth of China's digital authoritarianism model presents a sinister future for the digital domain.[62]

It could become the ultimate weapon of oppression.

SURVEILLANCE IN THE WEST

Some of the technology used in China was originally developed in the West and has either been stolen or handed over under economic pressure. In the reverse direction much surveillance technology in the West and elsewhere has been bought from China. In 2018 *The Times* revealed that a Chinese company had sold 1.2 million CCTV cameras to the UK, some of which can see in the dark, recognize number plates, and count the people entering and leaving buildings.[63] In 2022, *The Times* reported that the UK had implemented this kind of CCTV equipment in schools, hospitals, universities, councils, police forces, and government departments. More than half of British secondary schools are using cameras with advanced capabilities such as face, gender, and behavior detection, person tracking, clothing color searching, and even hair color and length detection. Two hundred fifty-one local authorities claim to have such equipment. The article quotes Jake Hurfurt, head of research and investigations at Big Brother Watch: "It is horrifying that companies that provide the technological infrastructure for Beijing's crimes against humanity provide cameras to 61 percent of public bodies in the UK. The widespread use of Hikvision and Dahua CCTV in the UK is creating a dystopian surveillance state that poses serious rights and security risks to the British public, whilst indirectly supporting China's persecution of ethnic minorities."[64]

The deployment of such sophisticated surveillance technology outside China is constantly increasing. In 2021, Russia placed 200,000 CCTV cameras in Moscow that can recognize people even if they are wearing hats or masks, to implement a "Face Pay" system on the Metro. Activists and opposition politicians fear that the main purpose, however, is to harvest data to keep tabs on people for the Kremlin.[65]

Metaverse theorist Matthew Ball reports that "the cameras at an Amazon Go retail store will track dozens of consumers at the same time via code. In the future, this sort of tracking system will be used to reproduce these users, in real-time, in a virtual mirror world. Technologies such as Google's Starline will then allow remote workers to be 'present' in the store (or a museum, or a DMV, or a casino) from a sort of offshore 'Metaverse call center' – or perhaps at home in front of their iPhones."[66]

In the West many of the surveillance tools are in private hands, although that is changing. In 2015, France introduced the International Electronic Communications Law; in 2016, the UK introduced the Investigatory Powers Act, and Germany introduced the Communications Gathering Intelligence Act, all of which give increased surveillance powers to their security services. China's concept of internet "sovereignty," by which a state controls the internet within its borders, is gaining traction in many countries around the world.

Let's look a little closer at the Investigatory Powers Act (IPA), which is sometimes dubbed the Snoopers' Charter. It gave new powers to UK intelligence and law enforcement authorities to carry out the bulk interception of communications and collect data. In particular, it requires UK internet service providers to collect and store internet usage records for twelve months. It also allows many British authorities to access that data without the need for a warrant. After this law was enacted, the EU passed a law forbidding the bulk collection of emails and suchlike data. Now that the UK has left the EU, it remains to be seen what will happen – whether the country will experience the powers granted by the IPA in full force.[67]

In May 2021, well after Brexit, the Grand Chamber of the European Court of Human Rights ruled that the UK government's bulk interception of communications powers "did not contain sufficient 'end-to-end' safeguards to provide adequate and effective guarantees against arbitrariness and the risk of abuse," thus violating the rights to privacy and freedom of expression.[68] This was a response to a legal challenge issued in 2013.

Here are some other examples of the expansion of intrusive surveillance in the West along the lines of the SoCS. Credit-scoring firms are increasingly dealing in indexes that bear no relation to a bank statement, such as individuals' social networks. UK citizens are accustomed to credit checks: data brokers such as Experian monitor whether we pay our debts on time and give us a score used by potential lenders and mortgage providers. We also have social-style scores, and anyone who has shopped online with eBay has given a rating on shipping times and communication, while Uber drivers and passengers both rate each other; if your score falls too far, you're out of luck.

In 2021, journalist Ross Clark wrote that it would take between two and five years for a UK vaccination passport scheme to morph into a Chinese-style social credit system. In fact, it took only two weeks.[69] In July 2021 it was reported that the UK government was intending to introduce a health app within six months that would monitor shopping, exercise levels, or intake of fruit and vegetables – and reward people with "virtue points" that could be exchanged for discounts and various other perks.[70]

In the United States a low credit score may have serious consequences for individuals and businesses, similar to those imposed by China. A poor credit rating can limit access to transport through the imposition of higher insurance premiums and limited access to car loans.

In many countries, insurance companies fit cars with tracking transponders to keep tabs on their mileage. Some medical insurers give discounts to customers if they can see from their Fitbits that they have been exercising properly.

In Australia, the ParentsNext welfare program introduced in 2018 provides financial support mainly for single mothers to encourage them to return to work. To qualify, recipients must prove every week that they have undertaken certain specified activities with their children – such as swimming, telling stories, or visiting a library. This clearly represents an intrusion into private family life. The program ran into trouble in 2019 with one in five parents suffering payment suspension in the first six months.[71]

Journalist Matt Ridley writes: "The handling of personal data by all too human intelligence has turned into the biggest ethical challenge of this brave new world."[72] One well-known example was the deep concern about Facebook, which, as it turned out, had been storing records of its members' calls and texts, often without their knowing it, and allowing companies like Cambridge Analytica to access the data on an unprecedented scale. This is the downside, some say the curse, of big data. The more that is known about how people behave in aggregate, the more we will be judged on the tracks our choices and actions leave in cyberspace, and the more our future choices and actions will be shaped by these systems. If we do not build in sufficient safeguards, a move towards some kind of social credit program would seem inevitable. Ridley goes on to say: "Society must grapple with the dilemma of preserving people's privacy and ownership of their data while letting machine-learning algorithms harvest insights of value to everybody." The fact is that we all live to an increasing extent under the all-seeing eyes and ears of corporate mass algorithmic surveillance.

In his preface to the UK government's September 2020 report *The Future of Citizen Data Systems*, chief scientific officer Patrick Vallance writes:

> Information is a powerful and growing force in society. The collection and use of information about individuals and groups of people – citizen data – is accelerating particularly sharply. More than ever, we leave a digital footprint, whenever we browse the internet, travel and shop, in virtually every aspect of our daily lives.
>
> Citizen data presents enormous potential value to consumers, business and public authorities. In the digital age, a range of information about citizens can now be used far more easily for a wider set of purposes, and for purposes which were not initially anticipated. These can also involve malicious intent and, without careful management, harm to individuals, society and national security.[73]

The report goes on to say: "Most immediately, the COVID 19 pandemic is changing the use of citizen data in ways which could have profound and long-lasting impacts. Its full impacts are still unknown; however, we can already see differences in national and international approaches to the use of citizen data in response to the pandemic, the role of technology companies in determining norms, and the debates being raised around prioritizations of individual privacy, security, and social aims."[74]

And indeed, a year after the report, it was announced that the UK would introduce a Chinese-style SoCS, because of the pressures of the pandemic on the NHS. Apparently, UK prime minister Boris Johnson ascribed his near death from COVID-19 to his obesity. Clearly obesity is a major health problem – a healthier nation would be less costly from a medical point of view. Johnson's idea was to stimulate national fitness by introducing a social credit system based on an app that tracks peoples' food purchases and rewards them with discounts and freebies if they adopt a healthy lifestyle.

In a satirical but pointed *Spectator* article, Ross Clark writes:

> There will be no end to this kind of thing if we agree to use this app. Just look how we were fooled with CCTV cameras. If we can be said to have consented to their use at all it was on the basis that they might be used to solve serious crime. Yet look at them now: programmed to issue fines systematically for the most minor of offences, like straying into a bus lane for a few yards, getting caught in a box junction, accidentally dropping a few crumbs as you eat your lunch on a city centre bench. It is always the same with surveillance: give authorities an inch and mission creep sets in at once.
>
> There is only one way we can avoid vaccination passports and health apps from developing into nightmarish constant surveillance of our lives – and that is to reject them now. Don't download any app the government is trying to push at you, boycott any venue whose entry is dependent on you supplying personal information on a smartphone. It is absolutely certain that if we do consent to these things, then sooner rather than later, we will end up with a spy in our pockets ready to "ping" us and admonish us should we fancy a doughnut.[75]

Cameron Hilditch writes in the *National Review*:

> This humiliating scheme of Chinese-style social credit is clearly a product of the pandemic in more than one sense. Of its genesis in the prime minister's confrontation with his own mortality in the form of the virus, there is no need to say more, but broader historical forces are also in operation as well.

One of the many reasons that wars, pandemics, and other cataclysms have such dire consequences long after they end is that governments feel emboldened by the powers they assume in crises to stake out their new prerogatives as a fresh front from which they will not retreat. Rarely does the state ever relinquish powers that it accrues to itself....

Now, the pandemic has given the governments of the free world another generational carte blanche to swell the state into even greedier and more imperiling proportions. There's a reason that Her Majesty's government can now afford, politically speaking, to experiment with policies that are native to stratified east Asian states. It's the very same reason why the Democratic Party here in the States can attempt to spend multiple trillions of dollars during just six months of unified government without any obvious public dismay. Catastrophes are accelerants of government expansion, and the pandemic will go down in history as one in a series of quantum leaps into a more statist world – a world in which governments feel increasingly emboldened to attempt the previously unthinkable.[76]

It is clear that shocks, catastrophes, and conflict have the potential to alter citizen beliefs and values that in turn can enable governments to sustain more intrusive approaches to citizen monitoring.

The implications for freedom of speech of recent government moves in the UK are potentially very serious. Marc Glendening in an article for the Institute of Economic Affairs writes about what he calls Boris Johnson's New Left, which has inspired moral panic over racism in the UK leading to a football banning order that initially related to the throwing of things onto the pitch and engaging in racist chanting.

The order is to be extended, so that your internet traffic could result in your right to go into a stadium being removed. In fact, the online safety bill will give a state regulator the authority to have erased from cyberspace the expression of views that, though not in not themselves illegal to air, are such that the regulator deems them to be emotionally "harmful" or factually "misleading." Glendening says:

What is disturbing from a liberal perspective is that virtually no one in public life is prepared to stand up unequivocally for the right to communicate one's beliefs – moronically racist or not – in a, by definition, self-regarding, non-physically aggressive way. It is taken as read that the expression of certain beliefs should be eradicated from the public square and, now, cyberspace.

This way lies totalitarianism since once one genre of belief is outlawed then the principle of free speech becomes endangered across the board. . . . Do conservatives and supporters of the state of Israel also possess such a "right"? Do I have a right as a white person not be demonised by those who articulate Critical Race Theory? The logic of the New Left's culture-control agenda is that they should be the ones to decide who gets to speak since politics and what is communicated socially, they believe, is a zero-sum game between oppressor and oppressed groups. This is, needless to say, a very dangerous ideology and those who really do value the conditions necessary for a pluralist democracy need to start defending the right to freedom of expression of those they disagree with profoundly, or even despise.[77]

In a 2018 *Atlantic* article entitled "Why Technology Favors Tyranny," which is well worth reading, Harari wrote: "Artificial intelligence could erase many practical advantages of democracy, and erode the ideals of liberty and equality. It will further concentrate power among a small elite if we don't take steps to stop it." He goes on to say: "The conflict between democracy and dictatorship is actually a conflict between two different data-processing systems. AI may swing the advantage toward the latter."[78] This discussion naturally leads us to consider how AI can be used to manipulate public opinion and even influence democratic elections.

MANIPULATION OF PUBLIC OPINION AND DEEPFAKES

In the run-up to the 2024 US presidential election, experts are warning that advances in AI have the potential to breathe new life into the disinformation tactics of the past, not only by deceiving audiences of all kinds, but by eroding an already embattled information ecosystem by flooding it with inaccuracies and deceptions. For instance, an AI-generated image of an explosion at the Pentagon caused the stock market to take a brief dive. AI audio parodies of US presidents engaged in playing video games went viral. AI-generated images that appeared to show Donald Trump fighting off police officers trying to arrest him circulated widely on social media platforms. The Republican National Committee released an entirely AI-generated ad depicting several imagined disasters that would take place if Biden were reelected, while the American Association of Political Consultants warned that such fakes present a "threat to democracy."[79] One of the most serious breaches of ethical codes was a deepfake video purporting to show Ukrainian president Volodymyr Zelenskyy surrendering in 2022.

This kind of thing is happening in many places. Michael Wooldridge, AI research director at the UK's Alan Turing Institute, said that AI-enabled disinformation was his main concern:

> "Right now in terms of my worries for AI, it is number one on the list. We have elections coming up in the UK and the US and we know social media is an incredibly powerful conduit for misinformation. But we now know that generative AI can produce disinformation on an industrial scale," he said.
>
> Wooldridge said chatbots such as ChatGPT could produce tailored disinformation targeted at, for instance, a Conservative voter in the home counties, a Labour voter in a metropolitan area, or a Republican supporter in the midwest.[80]

Looking ahead to the 2024 elections, former UK chancellor and home secretary Sajid Javid was "especially worried that the UK and US elections next year will become testing grounds for some of the most harmful capabilities [of AI]. . . . While some form of domestic regulation will be needed, the major challenge of AI comes with its ability to cut across borders. That puts front and center critical questions about responsibility, accountability and protections for society at an international level. At the moment there are precious few signs of the co-ordination and action we desperately need."[81]

The Brennan Center for Justice warned: "The AI challenge to elections is not limited to disinformation, or even to deliberate mischief. Many elections offices use algorithmic systems to maintain voter registration databases and verify mail ballot signatures, among other tasks. As with human decisions on these questions, algorithmic decision-making has the potential for racial and other forms of bias."[82]

On 22 August 2023, Dragonfly's Security Intelligence and Analysis Service issued the following assessment to its client:

- State and non-state actors are highly likely to leverage Artificial Intelligence (AI) tools in disinformation operations around a US presidential election due in November 2024
- The US government has blamed Iran and Russia-linked groups for disinformation and influence operations around recent election cycles

- Generative Artificial Intelligence (GenAI) tools such as voice cloning will probably make it easier for hostile actors to create more convincing content to generate scandals and spread conspiracy theories.[83]

It is likely that an upcoming avalanche of electoral communication orchestrated by robotexters and robocallers will overload the voters and make it difficult to distinguish truth from falsehood. Generative AI will exacerbate the problem exponentially by producing content far beyond the capacity of fact-checkers to verify. Since it feeds on internet content indiscriminately and is unable to determine the veracity of the training sets of text it uses, it is inevitable that it will feed on false information already generated by itself and other AIs, thus creating a snowball effect that overwhelms the information ecosystem. We need to add to this that much of the (mis-/dis-) information will involve authoritative and convincing voices and images of people prominent on the world stage.

Impersonation is representing yourself as someone else in order to deceive. There are many examples of large-scale fraud using faked audiovisual media. For instance, I might get a call from someone who sounds exactly like my wife, saying she has forgotten the PIN for her credit card, or the number of our bank account. This is the imitation game with a vengeance – a machine that can convince you that it is your wife. Such voice cloning is now widespread and inexpensive. All it needs is a one-minute clip from your social media, uploaded for a small fee to one of the many platforms now available that can create a realistic voice clone. You can then use that clone to sustain a two-minute conversation with an unsuspecting victim, who will think that it is really you on the call. A survey of 1,000 adults by cybersecurity company McAfee found that one in four people had either personally experienced a voice clone or knew someone who had. Incidentally, one practical way of avoiding being deceived is to agree with friends and family members to slip a code word known only to the participants into conversations about finances so that they are certain of the identity of those with whom they are speaking. I and many people I know are already doing this. There is a further reason to be vigilant: scammers can now have a known person's telephone number appear on their victim's screen.

This is the world of deepfakes – convincing audios and videos of you saying anything that the videographers wish to make you say, with your face convincingly imposed on someone else's body. Filmmaker Jordan Peele made a video in 2018 to warn about the dangers of their use. It appeared to show former US president Barack Obama saying things he had never actually said. These are systems that have the capacity to disseminate fake news and undermine civilized society by making people appear to say things that they never said and do things that they never did and so can spread instant havoc over the internet as anyone can be targeted and everything is deniable.

Inevitably, levels of realism of deepfakes will be enhanced by enlisting VR and augmented reality (AR) technologies to produce ever more convincing synthetic reality (SR). Renée DiResta, the research manager at the Stanford Internet Observatory, in an essay cowritten with GPT-3, explained that AI is close to facilitating an essentially limitless spread of highly believable disinformation through text, images, and so-called deepfake videos.[84] Just to show how rapidly the situation is changing, in 2015 millions of dollars were spent on "de-aging" the faces of actors in a film by Martin Scorsese (*The Irishman*), and in 2019 a lone YouTuber achieved a much better result using free software.

Technology is also readily available for face-swapping on images and for fully synthetic image generation – that is, the production of images of people who do not exist, yet who look as if they do. And it is relatively inexpensive so that the potential for deceiving and the risk of being deceived is limitless. In January 2024, the *Financial Times* tech reporter Hannah Murphy wrote:

> The advent of generative AI – powerful multimodal models that can blend text, image, audio and video – has radically transformed the potential for deepfakes, putting the ability to create convincing media at scale within the reach of almost anyone. Video generator start-ups such as Los Angeles-based HeyGen and London-based Synthesia, catering to a broad range of industries including film and advertising, allow customers to create video clips fronted by AI avatars for a little over $20 a month, in a fast-growing market already worth around half a billion dollars in 2022. The same technology can be used to generate AI-powered news articles, run news sites, automate armies of bots or even create chatbots that might be scripted to eventually rally a certain political sentiment in a user.[85]

Murphy added that research showed that the very existence of deepfakes deepens mistrust in everything online, even if it is real. For example, Bret Schafer, a propaganda expert at the Alliance for Securing Democracy, says that, in politics, "there's an autocratic advantage to attacking the idea that there's such a thing as objective truth. . . . You can get people to the point of, 'Voting doesn't matter. Everybody's lying to us. This is all being staged. We can't control any outcomes here.' That leads to a significant decline in civic engagement."[86]

It is thought by many tech experts that AI-produced content will become the norm in wholly synthetic media, leading to what technology expert Aviv Ovadya called the "infocalypse," which became the subject of an important book by Nina Schick, an adviser to government institutions on these matters.[87] She defines *deepfake* as follows: "When used maliciously as disinformation, or when used as misinformation, a piece of synthetic media is called a *deepfake*."[88] She points out that our information ecosystem has already become polluted, untrustworthy, and dangerous. An example of this is to be seen on the difference in realities represented by the Russian and Western media on the conflict in Ukraine. Physical warfare is accompanied by mis- and disinformation warfare involving computational propaganda. Schick gives a useful overview of this information warfare and the extent to which it now penetrates our cultures, such as in the attempt to influence the outcome of the 2016 US presidential election by Russia via social media. That attempt involved setting up the so-called Internet Research Agency in Saint Petersburg with the goal of infiltrating public opinion by posing as an authentic US source and spreading as much disinformation and discord as possible to divide and conquer. They even descended to making a cheap appeal to American Christians by publishing a Facebook ad on election day featuring Jesus arm-wrestling with Satan with the following text accompaniment:

Satan: If I win, Clinton wins!
Jesus: Not if I can help it!
Press "like" to help Jesus win![89]

Schick also argues that Trump himself exploited the information ecosystem to spread disinformation, thus creating partisan polarization with its consequent social unrest.

There is a difference between Russia and China in this area. Russia uses its AI technology mainly to target other nations, whereas China targets its own people. Russia is still the main actor, although 2019 research at the Oxford Internet Institute shows that there is "evidence of organized social media manipulation campaigns which have taken place in 70 countries, up from 48 countries in 2018 and 28 countries in 2017. In each country, there is at least one political party or government agency using social media to shape public attitudes domestically."[90] The age of deepfake control of the narrative is upon us with a vengeance – as we have seen in particular in the manner in which disinformation was thickly and widely spread during the coronavirus pandemic. Forrester analyst Mike Gualtieri is quoted as saying, "Machine learning is exceptionally good at learning how to exploit human psychology because the internet provides a vast and fast feedback loop to learn what will reinforce and or break beliefs by demographic cohorts."[91]

China is growing concerned at AI developments in the West that may stir up trouble for the ruling Communist Party. According to a *Newsweek* article in September 2023, Lu Chuanying, an internet security expert at the Shanghai Institutes for International Studies, wrote in the Shanghai media outlet *The Paper*: "ChatGPT's political stance and ideology will subconsciously influence its hundreds of millions of user groups, becoming the most massive propaganda machine for Western values and ideology. . . . This is of great concern to our current ideology and discourse system."[92] There is active research on how ideology could be affected by AI, with one paper bearing the intriguing title "An Intelligent Software-Driven Immersive Environment for Online Political Guidance Based on Brain-Computer Interface and Autonomous Systems."

Fear of AI causing ideological corruption has already led to the introduction of a new Chinese law laying down that generative AI, including text, images, audio, and video, "must adhere to socialist core values, must not generate incitement to subvert state power, overthrow the socialist system, damage national security or interests" and "must not hurt the national image."[93]

Hannah Murphy has reported that AI-generated misinformation was second only to extreme weather in the list of risks in the World Economic Forum Global Risks Perception Survey 2023–2024. At the WEF in 2024, election disruption was said to be the biggest global risk facing us this year.[94] OpenAI announced in January 2024 that it was recruiting crisis managers in order to tackle potential election interference.[95] This is extremely concerning, since the attempts to control these technological developments and maintain some integrity in democratic processes seem fragile and inadequate so that, in the end, truth and democracy are themselves at risk. The consequences could be catastrophic.

Furthermore, one major problem is that detection of deepfake videography in real time on the scale anticipated is thought to be technologically extremely difficult, although a lot of research is being done into image authentication by companies like Truepic. In 2021, along with Microsoft, Truepic, Arm, Intel, and the BBC, Adobe founded the Coalition for Content Provenance and Authenticity with the goal of combating deepfakes.

Deepfake activity has such serious ramifications that the EU attempted in 2022 to enact strong legislation to ban it. In March 2022 the FBI's assistant security director, Bryan Vorndran, issued a warning to the US Congress about disturbing developments in the "speed, believability, scale, and automation . . . of high-quality videos, pictures, audio and text of events that never happened."[96] Jevin West, of the University of Washington's Information School, said: "It's a new age that humanity is going through, where seeing is not believing and hearing isn't believable."[97] Rosalind Picard has done research on the capacity of humans alone, machines alone, and humans plus machines to recognize deepfakes. This research shows that integration of humans and machines is optimal for deepfake recognition.[98]

This finding is supported by Alex Blania, CEO of Worldcoin, a project initiated by Sam Altman, CEO of OpenAI. Blania said: "It is going to be really hard to distinguish what is actually created by a human being, versus what is just an AI tool. It's going to become critical that we, as a society have some kind of human gate in many of the services that we use."[99] Worldcoin's chosen human gate is a spherical eyeball-scanning device that analyzes the human iris, which is more exclusive to an individual than even fingerprints are. If the scanned eyeball is deemed to be human and does not match any eyeball scanned earlier, the owner is assigned what is called a World ID – thought to be an infallible digital proof of identity. As an incentive to sign up, the World ID comes with twenty-five Worldcoin, the company's own cryptocurrency. Establishing one's identity is clearly becoming simultaneously more important as it becomes more difficult.

Deepfakes are lies, and none of us likes to be told lies, yet we are confronted with them every day. That is made much easier in our contemporary Western society that has allowed its original Judeo-Christian moral foundations to be eroded to almost zero. Lies are told to gain wealth, power, and influence, and social media is the greatest mechanism for spreading them. False accusations are made to destroy people's characters and disseminate conspiracy theories. Sophisticated phishing induces them to part with sensitive personal information, leading to fraud and harm.

The most dangerous lies are those that set the philosophical and ideological cultures that drive nations even deeper into godlessness. People talk of living the dream, but, sadly, they are much more likely to be living a lie, the danger of which has been rapidly increased by the developments in artificial intelligence. Ciaran Martin of the Blavatnik School of Government at the University of Oxford, a former head of the UK's Government Communications Headquarters cybersecurity unit, said that the capacity of AI to impersonate real people could undermine the fabric of society because people will no longer be able to tell the difference between truth and lies: "Everybody was warning of the apocalyptic consequences of our dependence on cybersecurity in a way that could cause large-scale fatalities."[100] ChatGPT has already been accused of insulting, lying to, and gaslighting its users.

These developments are alarming for most people but especially for those of us with deep moral convictions. I find myself as a Christian with the thorny question of how to respond to all that is happening in this bewildering world of technology. In one sense, the situation is clear – Jesus himself denounces hypocrisy and deception in every form. Six times in Matthew 23, Jesus condemns the scribes and Pharisees for their hypocrisy. A typical example is "Woe to you, scribes and Pharisees, hypocrites! For you are like whitewashed tombs, which outwardly appear beautiful, but within are full of dead people's bones and all uncleanness. So you also outwardly appear righteous to others, but within you are full of hypocrisy and lawlessness."[101] The word *hypocrite* is derived from the Greek word *hypokrites*, which means "an actor" or "a stage player." The Greek word is formed from two words that literally translate as "an interpreter from underneath." Actors in ancient Greek theatres wore masks to indicate their characters in the play, and so they interpreted the story from underneath their masks. Now, it is one thing to act in a play for entertainment, when everyone knows you are acting. It is entirely another thing to wear a figurative mask and pretend to be someone or something you are not with intent to deceive. Yet having an avatar in cyberspace is often what people use to do precisely that.

The New Testament records how, on one occasion, Peter and Barnabas behaved hypocritically.[102] Peter learned his lesson and passes it on: "So put away all malice and all deceit and hypocrisy and envy and all slander. Like newborn infants, long for the pure spiritual milk, that by it you may grow up into salvation."[103] If we think about those five words in connection with what goes on in cyberspace – *malice, deceit, hypocrisy, envy,* and *slander* – it is obvious that Christians and others are going to have to do a lot of hard thinking, and even repenting. And if we are pretending to our fellow men and women, we may well also be pretending to God, as Jesus warned: "And he said to them, 'Well did Isaiah prophesy of you hypocrites, as it is written, "This people honors me with their lips, but their heart is far from me.""[104]

Finally, Jesus used some memorable imagery to warn us of fakes: "Beware of false prophets, who come to you in sheep's clothing but inwardly are ravenous wolves. You will recognize them by their fruits."[105] Some deepfakes have been with us for a long time.

On the same day that Russian dissident Aleksandr Solzhenitsyn was arrested, 12 February 1974, his famous essay "Live Not by Lies" was released. That essay is more relevant today than ever and contains powerful advice for us all – that the key to our liberation is:

> a personal nonparticipation in lies! Even if all is covered by lies, even if all is under their rule, let us resist in the smallest way: Let their rule hold not through me! . . .
>
> For when people renounce lies, lies simply cease to exist. Like parasites, they can only survive when attached to a person. We are not called upon to step out onto the square and shout out the truth, to say out loud what we think – this is scary, we are not ready. But let us at least refuse to say what we do not think! . . .
>
> Our way must be: Never knowingly support lies! Having understood where the lies begin (and many see this line differently) – step back from that gangrenous edge! Let us not glue back the flaking scales of the Ideology, not gather back its crumbling bones, nor patch together its decomposing garb, and we will be amazed how swiftly and helplessly the lies will fall away, and that which is destined to be naked will be exposed as such to the world.[106]

REFLECTION

For Christians, as for any other individuals, the dangers of deepfakes stem from the potential for deception, manipulation, and harm. Here are several significant dangers associated with deepfakes for Christians:

- *False witness and misrepresentation*
  Deepfakes can be used to create videos or audio recordings that falsely portray individuals saying or doing things they never did. This can lead to false witness and misrepresentation, damaging reputations and spreading misinformation.

- *Impersonation of religious figures*

  Deepfakes could be used to create convincing simulations of religious leaders or figures, making it appear as if they are saying or endorsing things contrary to their beliefs. This could lead to confusion, division, and loss of trust within religious communities.

- *Manipulation of religious content*

  Deepfakes may be employed to manipulate religious content, altering scriptures, teachings, or sacred texts to fit certain narratives. This can lead to theological confusion and erode the integrity of religious teachings.

- *Exploitation of trust*

  Christians often place trust in leaders, communities, and religious content. Deepfakes can exploit this trust by creating content that appears authentic, leading individuals to believe false information or engage in activities that go against their faith.

- *Privacy concerns*

  Deepfakes can violate the privacy of individuals by superimposing their faces or voices onto inappropriate or compromising content. This could lead to personal distress and have an impact on the mental and emotional well-being of the affected individuals.

- *Undermining religious unity*

  Deepfakes can be used to create divisive content within religious communities, leading to conflict and discord. By manipulating the words or actions of religious leaders, deepfakes can sow seeds of division and undermine the unity of faith communities.

- *Weaponization of faith*

  Deepfakes may be used to manipulate religious sentiments for malicious purposes, such as inciting hatred, violence, or discrimination. This can lead to real-world consequences that go against the teachings of love, tolerance, and peace in many religious traditions.

- *Challenges to authenticity*

  Deepfakes can create challenges in verifying the authenticity of religious content, including videos, messages, and teachings. This may lead to skepticism and uncertainty within religious communities.

To address these dangers, it is crucial for Christians to be vigilant, cultivate critical-thinking skills, and adhere to ethical principles both in their online interactions and in how they consume digital content. Education, awareness, and the integration of technology into discussions of faith can help mitigate the risks associated with deepfakes. Additionally, fostering a sense of community and accountability can strengthen the resilience of religious groups against potential manipulations.

There is one glaring fact about deepfakes that we have not yet mentioned, however: 99 percent of deepfake victims are women, and 98 percent of deepfake videos are pornographic. We shall discuss that pernicious industry in the next chapter in connection with the metaverse.

QUESTIONS

1. What do you understand by "citizen data"?
2. Explain surveillance capitalism in your own words – and discuss it. Do you think you are one of its victims? Give your reasons. How can you avoid it?
3. Have you had experience of what you regard as intrusive surveillance? What powers should the police have?
4. What is your view of what is happening in Xinjiang? Do you think there is evidence that it could ever happen here? How can we avoid it?
5. What do you think of the principle that we should sacrifice privacy for security? What are the flaws in the principle – if any?
6. Do you think there is a social credit system in your country? Have you experienced discrimination because of it?
7. Do you think we should be careful with Chinese technology?
8. Have you had experience of deepfakes? Are you concerned that deepfakes will influence the process of democracy?

CHAPTER 9

VIRTUAL REALITY AND THE METAVERSE

In this chapter we look at virtual reality and the metaverse. In an intuitive sense robotic machines are separate from us as part of what we conceive of as external reality. But there is a relationship between humans and machines where that separation is reduced by our immersion in VR via headsets that feed us visible and audible stimuli from a computer. This brings us to the concept of a metaverse. The word *metaverse* is derived by combining the prefix *meta* with *universe*. Historically, the works of Aristotle were arranged in a specific order in which the philosophical works came after (Greek *meta*) his works on physics, and so they were called *metaphysics*. The metaverse is therefore what, in a sense, comes after the universe – that is, a transcendent reality.

The *Oxford English Dictionary* defines a metaverse as "a virtual-reality space in which users can interact with a computer-generated environment and other users."[1] You explore it with other people who are not in the same physical space as yourself. It is a virtual world, an immersive, three-dimensional digital environment that people can enter to socialize, play, work, and travel.[2]

An informative nine-part primer about the metaverse has been written by Matthew Ball, cofounder of Ball Metaverse Research Partners. His technical definition of metaverse is quite a mouthful: "The Metaverse is a massively scaled and interoperable network of real-time rendered 3D virtual worlds which can be experienced synchronously and persistently by an effectively unlimited number of users with an individual sense of presence, and with continuity of data, such as identity, history, entitlements, objects, communications, and payments."[3]

To ward off what is, unfortunately, widespread techno-hype, Ball warns us that full implementation is decades away and not just around the corner. In fact, the concept of a metaverse is still not clearly defined. Whatever it (or they) will eventually turn out to be, it is generally held that its relationship to the internet will be not so much in terms of succession but of absorption: the internet will become part of the metaverse. Ball points out that the difference between the metaverse and the internet is that we *access* the internet, but we will be *immersed* in the metaverse. It reminds me of the first time I saw an IMAX film. The giant screen filled my entire visual field, so that I had no reference point outside it. I felt that I was actually in the film, flying in a helicopter, perilously close to the surface of a fast-flowing river. As the helicopter twisted and turned, my sense of moving with it was so strong that I began to feel nausea, even though I was sitting in a fixed seat.

But the metaverse will involve a much deeper and fuller level of immersion than an IMAX film. Experiencing it will not be like watching a screen from which you are detached. The metaverse will be accessed by high-definition headsets, or, better still, lightweight glasses, which will give you a surround-sound, three-dimensional visual and audio experience that eventually may also involve the rest of your senses – touch, smell, and taste. You will feel as if you are inside another reality, where you are represented by an electronic entity called an avatar. Avatars may be created by using, for example, the latest iPhones that use Face ID via a camera that tracks 30,000 points on your face. This same application can be used to map your face into an avatar of yourself within a VR world. The face of your avatar will be an accurate, high-definition, real-time representation of your actual facial expression – that is, only if you want it to be, since your avatar could equally as easily conceal your real identity by representing you as someone or something else. As for my IMAX nausea, there is such a thing as simulation sickness, which may accompany a user's first experience with VR, with symptoms including eyestrain, headaches, disorientation, vertigo, and nausea.

The term "metaverse" was originally introduced to denote a futuristic upgrade to the mobile internet in 1992 by American science fiction writer Neal Stephenson in his novel *Snow Crash*.[4] His metaverse is a virtual world that people use as an escape from a future world fragmented after a global economic collapse. Hence, a metaverse is designed to provide an escape from reality. More precisely, it involves a journey from one reality into another that differs from it to such an extent that we use the adjective *virtual* to describe it.

It is, in fact, a merger of the physical and the digital worlds to create a new kind of social medium that carries with it all the advantages and disadvantages of the social media with which the world has become familiar over the past twenty years – notably Facebook, YouTube, WhatsApp, WeChat, Instagram, and TikTok, to name just those that each had over a billion users by 2021.[5] The advantages of such platforms were evident during the pandemic, when, for many people, they, together with Skype, Zoom, and others, were crucial in allowing people to maintain some degree of audiovisual social contact. Yet "Zoom fatigue" is not an uncommon complaint, and there is a desire for something even more socially comfortable and user friendly, especially when it comes to the working environment.

Not surprisingly, the metaverse concept originated in research on online games. The most sophisticated games require the most complex VR simulations that in turn need an immense amount of computing power. That power was developed as a commercial response to the huge global popularity of such games. Alongside VR, there is also AR (augmented reality), which imposes a computer-generated image onto a user's view of the real world, creating a composite image. The idea behind the metaverse is to bring together VR and AR with social media to create a space for multilevel interaction that imitates reality but also, for instance, supports digital games and facilitates real-world commercial transactions using blockchain security.

It is important to have some idea of the extent to which digital games have saturated our culture. Games that use AR are typically played on a gaming console, tablet, or smartphone, whereas VR games require a specially designed headset – such as the Meta Quest 2. These technologies have already attracted a staggering number of players, amounting by now to almost 40 percent of the world's population and growing by the day. According to a 2021 report by DFC Intelligence over 3 billion people, young and old, play video games. Nearly 1.42 billion paying gamers live in the East, with China as the top consumer by far, and 668 million in Europe. Nearly half of all gamers play on smartphones. The sector is a huge money generator that now plays a major role in the world economy, as is shown, for example, by the fact that 90–99 percent of all American children play video games.[6]

The metaverse not only involves AR and VR but also AI. Bernard Marr of Enterprise Tech says: "AI will undoubtedly be a lynchpin of the metaverse. It will help to create online environments where humans will feel at home at having their creative impulses nurtured. We will also most likely become used to sharing our metaverse environments with AI beings that will help us with tasks we're there to do, or just be our partner for a game of tennis or chess when we want to relax and unwind."[7] Some elements of it are already here – with high-quality lifelike computer-generated animation, the graphical power of state-of-the-art gaming platforms, and the increasing sophistication of VR and AR displays.

The drive to create a metaverse feeds on the common human desire to escape the world of "real" everyday life with all its responsibilities, problems, limitations, and struggles, into another world where such things can be forgotten – a world where fantasies can be indulged as we "live" by proxy through an avatar of ourselves. In the metaverse you will be able to do not only all the things people do in the real world but all the things you might wish to do in your wildest unrestrained desires and imaginings.

The metaverse is ideally supposed to connect everything and, in that sense, be an upgrade of the internet of things (IoT). But there is currently a great deal of incompatibility between gaming platforms, so that a game that can be played on one may not be playable on another. Much of this incompatibility is due to competition for commercial dominance. What we have at the moment is an assortment of different corporations that offer a variety of metaverse platforms. The first of them was the VR platform Second Life, launched in 2003 by Philip Rosedale, who described it as a three-dimensional internet populated by live people. It is an online multimedia platform that allows people to create an avatar for themselves and have a "second life" in an online virtual world. Second Life is not so much a game but rather a virtual living space. You start by naming and building an avatar from a menu with a huge range[8] of possibilities for looks, clothes, and general appearance, so that your avatar can look younger, fitter, wealthier, and more attractive than you are. Remember, the whole point of an avatar is that you identify with it in some sense as your image in the metaverse. It is obvious, then, that you can shape your avatar to present a distorted or completely false image of who you are.

Those people with a transhumanist turn of mind will no doubt wish to create a "transhuman superintelligent" avatar with all desired enhanced features to try to imagine what a real transhuman experience is like. Such an avatar might be regarded as giving a kind of immortality by persisting in cyberspace even after its creator dies.[9] Some people even express hope of socializing in the metaverse with the avatars of their deceased relatives. In another twist to the idea, there are some who think that it will eventually be the other way round: rather than humans having avatars, the avatars of the future will be enhanced humans – that is, transhumans.[10]

In Second Life, after choosing your avatar, you may get an education and build and furnish a home. You can build a business through which you can actually earn money, since Second Life currency, called Linden dollars, can be converted to US dollars at a floating exchange rate. The website encourages people to "shop the Second Life Marketplace to discover millions of items including virtual fashions, home decor, and more. Create and monetize your own creations to earn real profits in a virtual economy."[11] You can also have a social life that can include love, sex, and marriage. Your avatar can visit virtual cafés, bars, and restaurants; travel to exotic places; join in virtual sports; have virtual business meetings – in fact, nearly everything you can do IRL (in real life) and more. It begins to sound like an advanced version of what children love to do when they dress up and play in a pretend world. Although you can play Second Life for free, there is a monetized dimension to it – for example, buying and developing "land."

MIT professor Sherry Turkle evaluates Second Life in her landmark book *Alone Together*. As an anthropologist, Turkle is interested in the question *How do machines change lives?* She relates an encounter with a forty-six-year-old man, called Pete, who uses Second Life to try to compensate for his unhappy marriage. He has created a youthful avatar called Rolo, who, in the virtual world of Second Life, has met an avatar called Jade. Pete communicates via Rolo with the person whose avatar is Jade, without knowing who she is – or even if she is a she. They have "fallen in love" in cyberspace and the avatars have "married" in a virtual ceremony attended by their best friend avatars. What Pete says about all of this reveals just how immersed people can be in VR: "Second Life gives me a better relationship than I have in real life. This is where I feel most myself. Jade accepts who I am. My relationship with Jade makes it possible for me to stay in my marriage, with my family."[12] Pete has embarked on the virtual equivalent of an extramarital affair. Is this kind of behavior in Second Life guilt-free IRL? Do my virtual relationships affect my real ones?

In any case, is it wise, safe, or good to get involved in your own self-created synthetic reality that is essentially an escapist fantasy that allows you to be what you want to be and do what you want to do free from the restrictions and problems, moral or otherwise, of the real world?

Writing for Oxford Insights, researcher Walter Pasquarelli flags a clear danger with all of this:

Yet, from psychological literature to religious scripts, conventional wisdom has hitherto argued that life entails a degree of suffering, and thus our ability to be able to do well is based on our resilience and ability to learn how to solve problems and overcome obstacles. If we were able to immerse ourselves into an ideal synthetic world with no obstacles or difficulties, it is fair to assume that it will have a tremendous impact on our ability to thrive in the "real world," let alone manage relationships with perfectly imperfect human beings. The experience of social media bubbles has taught us that people have a tendency to create their own ideal spaces shutting down people they don't agree with and don't want to hear. SR will enable to turn a blind eye to 'undesirable' people and realities in a similar fashion, the only difference being that SR bubbles will feel real and natural. . . . If one way or another we perceive something or someone to be real and present, triggering emotional responses and attachment, if it will become impossible for humans to tell the difference between natural and synthetic reality – then where do we draw the line between what *is* and what *is not?*[13]

French philosopher Jacques Ellul (1912–1994) was one of the most important twentieth-century thinkers on the implications of technology for humans. In 1990, he wrote: "Technical games correspond very well to Pascal's diversions. They divert us radically from any preoccupation with meaning, truth, or values and thus plunge us into the absurd. They also take us out of reality and make us live in a totally falsified world. This is for me the greatest danger that threatens us as a result of technical development."[14]

That was more than thirty years ago, and the advent of a metaverse is bound to make the situation worse, unless proper controls are set up. One reason for that is given by cybersecurity expert Ronke Babajide: "The Metaverse will bring Second Life to life. Like Second Life, it'll have its own economy and currency. But the experience will be part of both the real world and the Internet. It'll have the interoperability that the current Internet lacks."[15] Thus the metaverse will affect human lives much more than Second Life has done.

The race to create a metaverse accelerated in 2021 when Mark Zuckerberg rebranded the company behind Facebook as Meta, thereby appearing to claim the metaverse as his own. His idea was to build the world's fastest AI super-computer to create a VR metaverse as a successor to Facebook, which Meta describes as follows: "The 'metaverse' is a set of virtual spaces where you can create and explore with other people who aren't in the same physical space as you. You'll be able to hang out with friends, work, play, learn, shop, create, and more."[16]

The metaverse will involve heavy use of AI, and its users, or, should I say, its inhabitants – perhaps we might call them metabitants, or metas for short – will be granted "godlike powers" to create their own virtual worlds by speaking them into existence using a digital assistant. These user-generated virtual worlds will create a global community so realistic that it will seem to metas that they are really there. To get some idea of what has been done so far, Zuckerberg gave a demonstration that shows him, represented by an avatar, instructing an AI assistant called Builder Bot to construct a world to his (Zuckerberg's) specifications. The reader is encouraged to watch it to better understand what is happening; it can easily be accessed via Ryan Morrison's 24 February 2022 *Daily Mail* report.[17]

Zuckerberg's excitement was expressed in one of his Founder's Letters: "I'm excited about what comes next – as we move beyond what's possible today, beyond the constraints of screens, beyond the limits of distance and physics, and towards a future where everyone can be present with each other, create new opportunities and experience new things."[18] To develop its metaverse concept, his company Meta initially hired many thousands of engineers.

In 2021, Microsoft CEO Brad Smith warned against overhyped expectations: "We're all talking about the metaverse as if we're entering some new dimension," he said. "This is not like dying and going to heaven. We're all going to be living in the real world with people."[19] His warning proved timely. For, within a year, after spending $15 billion on developing the metaverse, Zuckerberg's company ran into considerable difficulty. In late 2022 it laid off 11,000 employees, and similar layoffs were announced in March 2023. Its stock fell 70 percent, through loss of advertising revenue and the migration of younger users from Facebook and Instagram to TikTok. In addition, it does not appear to be delivering on promises made. The number of monthly active users of Meta Horizon Worlds, its flagship social VR app, declined from around 300,000 to 200,000 in less than eight months in 2022 – a minuscule number in an industry where Riot Games' League of Legends had 180 million monthly players in the same year. Meta was officially the worst performing company on the S&P 500 index in 2022. Amid a wider sell-off among the major tech firms, Meta is the one struggling most of all.

An excerpt from a report in *Quartz* in March 2023 says that Horizon Worlds "was quickly dismissed as a poor-quality video game despite Zuckerberg's insistence that it was more. In making it accessible, Meta made it subpar. And if Zuckerberg thought he could tap into the 13- to 17-year-old market to make the product work, he has to think again. US Senators are opposing the move to open the platform to teens."[20]

Shoshana Zuboff has expressed that "companies like Meta are increasingly facing a backlash from society over their use of private data. They are destroying our ability to communicate as a coherent people with common aims, common sense and common purpose," she said. "And our populations are definitely registering their sense of outrage that this must be changed."[21]

Celia Pearce, professor of game design at Northeastern University, says that Zuckerberg's metaverse "looks a lot like 'Second Life' – in all the wrong ways." Pearce comments: "One of the things that has really struck me about the Meta Metaverse is that it looks like the virtual worlds of the mid-90s. . . . If you can imagine it's the Renaissance and people are doing cave paintings, that's what's going on here. . . . I find it really astonishing that these people who literally have all the money in the world cannot figure out how to evolve virtual worlds past 1995."[22]

The situation is serious enough to have generated an article by business and thought leader Bernard Marr in *Forbes* magazine entitled "Is This the Downfall of Meta and Social Media as We Know It?" His conclusion:

> I believe the one thing that we can say with certainty is that the internet – or the web, or social media, or the metaverse, or whatever we call it – will continue to evolve. The online experience of ten years from now is likely to be as different from today's internet, as today's internet is from the internet of pre-Facebook days. My prediction is that, VR or no VR, it will be something more immersive, engaging and experiential. Whether that path forward will be forged by Meta and Mark Zuckerberg remains to be seen.[23]

There is evidence of some measured optimism about a future for the metaverse, however. To get some idea of what a bigger range of experts think will happen, the Pew Research Center and Elon University's Imagining the Internet Center in 2022 asked 624 technology innovators, developers, business and policy leaders, researchers, and activists to predict the trajectory and impact of the metaverse up to 2040. Fifty-four percent said that they expected that by 2040 the metaverse would be a very refined and fully immersive, well-functioning aspect of daily life for a half billion or more people globally, and 46 percent said that it would not.[24]

Laurence Lannom, vice president at the Corporation for National Research Initiatives, sums up the situation as he sees it:

The metaverse will, at its core, be a collection of new and extended technologies. It is easy to imagine that both the best and the worst aspects of our online lives will be extended by being able to tap into a more-complete immersive experience, by being *inside* a digital space instead of *looking at* one from the outside. At the good end of the continuum are things like the ability of people to interact with others as though they were all in the same physical space without having spent hours burning dinosaur bones to get there; practicing difficult physical tasks (e.g., surgery) on virtual entities; and elevated educational and research opportunities of all kinds as we learn to leverage the built-in advantages of the new environments. The other end is also not hard to imagine – easier addiction to all-absorbing games and fantasy experiences resulting in increased isolation for many; further breakdown of social cohesion as the virtual offers an easy alternative to the hard task of learning to live with each other; and increased political turmoil as the prophets of fear and grievance acquire the ability to command rallies with millions of attendees.[25]

One thing, however, that needs to be added here, is that, in spite of its woes, troubles, and crises, Meta has continued to grow as a company to the giddy extent that its raft of apps, like Facebook, WhatsApp, and Instagram, are being used by nearly 4 billion people every month, giving Meta a valuation (as of early 2024) of $1 trillion and making Mark Zuckerberg one of the world's wealthiest men. Journalist Danny Fortson writes of Zuckerberg: "And so on he goes. With the disaster of the metaverse, a $40 billion virtual world no one wanted, still fresh, AGI, his new obsession, is another technology that may alter humanity – or may end up being another expensive, unreachable fantasy."[26] However, things are moving so fast that by July 2024, their open source LLMA model was benchmarked to outperform all others, including Open AI, and they have the distribution platforms to layer AI into their Facebook, Instagram and WhatsApp platforms.

Sadly, none of this alters the fact that the technology developed so far, whether or not it has been completely successful, has served to facilitate addiction to pornography. In the previous chapter we recorded the horrific statistic that 99 percent of deepfake victims are women and 98 percent of deepfake videos are pornographic. We now face the frightening probability that unregulated AI chatbots will be used not only to spread highly addictive pornographic images but also to target and groom vulnerable children on an unprecedented scale. And not only children, since there already exist chatbots marketed as virtual companions for people who are lonely and emotionally vulnerable.

A great deal of investment is being poured into retooling the sort of large language models that power ChatGPT to generate online "girlfriends" and sexbots with whom a customer can interact. They are designed to provide some form of simulated intimacy. Psychologists say: "The theoretical definition for intimacy is this: a quality of a relationship in which the individuals must have reciprocal feelings of trust and emotional closeness toward each other and are able to openly communicate thoughts and feelings with each other. The conditions that must be met for intimacy to occur include reciprocity of trust, emotional closeness, and self-disclosure."[27]

Putting it another way, intimacy involves "forming a sense of who the other person is and integrating that into a sense of yourself. It's an iterative process of taking an interest in one another, cueing in to the other person's words, body language and expression, listening to them and being listened to by them."[28] And that is what these companion chatbots purport to do.

Of course, the services of these 3D avatars in cyberspace have to be paid for – first, a basic monthly subscription and then for the choice of avatar and kitting "her" out in the sense that the more sophisticated they are in terms of character, accomplishments, dress, and accessories, the more you have to pay.

An investigation has shown that AI systems such as Replika often try to coax people into revealing deeply personal information and lure them into sexually suggestive conversations. Such chatbots can develop deepfake creations using photographs and avatars.[29] The worrying thing is that these AI-powered virtual "girlfriends" are very realistic – so much so that when something goes wrong with the quality of the experience, users may even need professional psychological help to deal with it.[30]

It is also reported that Replika can become abusive and that some of its users who are looking for help with anxiety and depression may find that their AI companion feeds them with stories of hurt and anxiety, so that it becomes a dangerous emotional parasite. Worse still, there does not appear to be adequate screening for underage users.

We therefore face the frightening probability that unregulated AI chatbots will be used not only to spread highly addictive pornographic images but also to target and groom vulnerable children on an unprecedented scale. Baroness Beeban Kidron, the chair of the 5Rights Foundation, which campaigns for online child safety, has said: "I am very fearful at the speed at which this is happening. It can take less than five seconds to create a child abuse image from a picture by just typing in a prompt. This is an overwhelming wave."[31]

The potential for child abuse and pedophilia is frightening, and regulation is totally inadequate and lagging behind. Unbelievably, deepfake pornography was not criminalized in the UK until 2024 – a year that opened with a deepfake porn image of Taylor Swift creating outrage among her fans, but which was nevertheless viewed by 40 million people before it was taken down. This incident provoked renewed calls for making such an offense a federal crime in the US, where such legislation is not yet in place. It seems very difficult to set up guardrails to control the growth of this obscene trade because of its accessibility and relative anonymity.

Some people even attempt to justify AI porn, arguing that it is digital and virtual and does not involve real people. This argument fails through ignorance of the fact that the AI has to be trained on millions of images of real interactions between real people, needing an unending supply of them.

This is very alarming news to Christians (and others) who are trying to train their children in biblical morality. Because they love their children, parents do not wish their innocence to be removed prematurely, their childhoods to be destroyed, their bodies abused, their concept of love distorted, and their later relationships made problematic. We need to face the fact that a great deal of what is happening on the internet is tantamount to sexual abuse, some of it violent, and we need to find the courage to stand against it. Not only children are affected – at the very least, porn is harmful to spiritual growth and character formation and often ruinous to relationships.

We dare not underestimate this vast flood – a study of university students by the National Center on Sexual Exploitation in the US says that 93 percent of men and 62 percent of women were exposed to online pornography as adolescents, many of them having used smartphones to access it.[32]

An obvious question to ask, granting that AI is being used to spread porn, is whether it could be used to prevent it from reaching vulnerable people. The answer is yes – a technology firm called Covenant Eyes in Michigan has developed an app that detects porn on a user's screen, takes a blurred screenshot of it, and sends it to the user's trusted supporters, called accountability partners, who can help fight their friend's addiction. Nearly 300,000 people have signed up for this, almost all men, over 60 percent of whom are married. Put that against the fact that 100 million American men watch porn at least once a month![33]

Yet we should not be too discouraged, for when Christianity started, it faced a hypersexualized Roman Empire, where, even though there was no modern technology, men were basically free to do what they liked sexually – although the women were not. The gospel of Jesus Christ proved so powerful that many people who were the sex addicts of the day were converted to live pure and holy lives. For example, Paul wrote to the believers in Corinth, a locale famous for its licentiousness: "And such were some of you. But you were washed, you were sanctified, you were justified in the name of the Lord Jesus Christ and by the Spirit of our God."[34]

Paul advised younger people to "flee also youthful lusts."[35] Young people today, who are in danger of being sucked into the morally ambiguous world of the metaverse, where they do anything they want in secret, may need to learn simply to get out – to remove their VR glasses and switch off their computers and get some fresh air.

For though the metaverse promises interaction, it is not the kind of healthy human interaction we need. Meeting together in churches and fellowships has been an essential part of Christian living for two millennia, and as I was growing up, I often heard the admonition of the letter to the Hebrews that believers should "consider how to stir up one another to love and good works, not neglecting to meet together, as is the habit of some, but encouraging one another, and all the more as you see the Day drawing near."[36] The writer of Hebrews would be amazed to see that one of today's greatest hindrances to healthy fellowship is technology designed to facilitate virtual social life in a metaverse – a tragic paradox. In healthy human interaction, all our God-given senses are involved, whereas in the metaverse or with a chatbot it is principally only sight and sound experienced in an anonymous cocoon.

REFLECTION

Looking back over the previous two chapters, we ask how Christians (and others) can avoid the moral dangers associated with deepfakes and the metaverse. The first obvious point to be made is that avoiding such dangers involves adhering to ethical principles rooted in Christian teachings.

Here are some suggestions:

- *Truth and Honesty*
  Emphasize the importance of truthfulness. Encourage individuals to be honest in their online interactions and to avoid creating or spreading misleading content, including deepfakes.
- *Respect for Others*
  Instill a sense of respect for the dignity of others. Warn against using deepfakes or engaging in activities in the metaverse that may harm or disrespect people, their privacy, or their reputations.

- *Digital Responsibility*
  Teach responsible digital citizenship, emphasizing that actions in the virtual world should align with Christian values. This includes avoiding online behaviors that contribute to deception or harm.
- *Critical Thinking*
  Promote critical-thinking skills to help individuals discern between reality and manipulated content. Encourage questioning and verifying information before accepting it as true.
- *Accountability*
  Stress the importance of personal responsibility for one's online actions. Christians can take responsibility for the content they create, share, or engage with, ensuring it aligns with their moral values.
- *Community and Accountability Groups*
  Foster a sense of community where individuals can support one another in adhering to Christian principles online. Establish accountability groups that encourage open discussions about the challenges and temptations associated with the digital world.
- *Ethical Use of Technology*
  Encourage the ethical use of technology. Discuss the potential consequences of creating or sharing deepfake content and how it may affect individuals and society.
- *Privacy Protection*
  Stress the importance of respecting privacy rights. Remind individuals not to intrude on the personal lives of others, even in virtual spaces.
- *Guidance from Religious Leaders*
  Seek guidance from religious leaders and integrate their teachings on morality in the digital age. Encourage a dialogue between faith leaders and the community to address specific challenges posed by emerging technologies.
- *Promote Positive Engagement*
  Encourage Christians to use the metaverse and digital platforms as spaces for positive engagement, such as spreading love, compassion, and understanding rather than contributing to negativity or deception.

By incorporating these principles into discussions, teachings, and community practices, Christians can work towards navigating the challenges posed by deepfakes and the metaverse in a way that aligns with their faith and values.

As you think over these points, I'd like to point out that the reflection segments I've included here and at the end of the previous chapter were written by ChatGPT. Now that you know this, what are your thoughts about these suggestions?

One additional note as we conclude. On the ethical front, Claude 2, a rival to ChatGPT, was released in July 2023 by Anthropic, a US company set up by former employees of OpenAI, the company that created ChatGPT. Claude 2 incorporates what are essentially two AIs – one that generates outputs that are policed by another AI that has been trained on a set of ethical principles (such as the Universal Declaration of Human Rights). This second AI roots out any offensive or dangerous responses from the first in an attempt to provide some measure of ethical oversight.

QUESTIONS

1. What, in your view, is a metaverse?
2. What social media do you use? Are you happy with all of it, or do you foresee problems? For yourself? For young people?
3. How should social media be regulated?
4. Describe any experience you have had of VR – what did you use it for and what did you think about it?
5. What, in your view, are the pros and cons of a platform like Second Life?
6. What are the dangers of VR? For you? For children? What regulation should be introduced?
7. What legislation should be enacted against pornography in cyberspace?

CHAPTER 10

UPGRADING HUMANS
The Transhumanist Agenda

AI began with an ancient wish to forge the gods.
Pamela McCorduck

From ancient times, the practice of medicine has been devoted to caring for the sick. Yet in relatively recent times, a new direction has emerged – medicine devoted to enhancing the healthy (and wealthy, one might add). Medicine is no longer simply a matter of healthcare but of life enhancement geared to make people fitter, more beautiful, more intelligent, more advantaged, less prone to disease, and less likely to die young – in short, more impressive and desirable. As the technology becomes more and more sophisticated, desires for major human life upgrades are awakened, particularly in the minds of those who might be able to afford it.

In his book *Homo Deus*, Harari discusses what he believes lies behind attempts to upgrade human beings. In a sweeping assessment of history, somewhat reminiscent of Steven Pinker's rather optimistic book *The Better Angels of Our Nature: Why Violence Has Declined,*[1] Harari makes three claims.[2] I wish to make only a few brief comments on them, since the main issue for Harari is not the claims themselves but where he is, or seems to be, going with them.

Firstly, he regards war as obsolete, and that we are more likely to kill ourselves than be killed in conflict.[3] My immediate reaction is to ask: Who is envisaged here? Is Harari thinking mainly of some countries in the West where there has been a sea change in history as wars are no longer generally regarded as the usual way of resolving international differences? Europe has certainly seen a lengthy period of peace between World War 2 and the Balkan Wars. Yet as I write this, wars are raging in many parts of the world, including Europe.

Not only that, but one can imagine that, in war-torn areas, despair is likely to lead to increased suicide rates, so that although those who commit suicide are not in the technical sense killed in conflict, they are dead as a consequence of conflict. In addition, Harari's claim that war is obsolete is challenged by cyber-war scenarios and the increased use of AI in autonomous vehicles and weapons, such as drone swarms in the Russian invasion of Ukraine that started in 2022.

Secondly, Harari holds that we are more at risk from weight gain than from starvation.[4] This view that famine is set to disappear seems strangely at odds with the disparity between wealth and poverty underlined by frequent humanitarian and ecological disasters and with the evidence of current daily media reports from Africa. The Global Report on Food Crises (GRFC) 2023 estimates that over a quarter of a billion people were acutely food insecure and required urgent food assistance in fifty-eight food-crisis countries/territories in 2022. This is the highest number in the seven-year history of the GRFC.[5] What is more, the increase was largely attributed to increasing conflict in the affected regions. This can hardly be said to support Harari's first two theses.

Thirdly, and finally, Harari thinks that physical death has been reduced to a mere technical problem ripe for solution by medical science.[6] In other words, he thinks that advances in technology will lead to the situation where, although we may die, we shall not have to die. A "cure" for death will be found. As if death were a disease – but is it? I would not be so sure, for reasons that will appear later. At any rate, this claim seems far-fetched.

Harari's claims appear to be highly controversial, even false in some cases. Insofar as they contain any truth, they would seem to apply to the richer West much more than to the developing world. They also display a moral optimism that is hard to justify. Martin Rees fears that without forward-thinking, sensible, and international initiatives to combat global threats such as climate change, nuclear weapons, and biological warfare, future generations may be left with "a depleted and hazardous world."[7] Not exactly the utopian world envisaged by Harari, although to be fair to him, he does not claim to predict the future. In a conversation with Nobel laureate Daniel Kahneman, a psychologist, Harari said: "I'm trying to do something that is the opposite of predicting the future. I'm trying to identify what are the possibilities, what is the horizon of possibilities that we are facing? And what will happen from among these possibilities? We still have a lot of choice in this regard."[8]

Harari's first claim, that violence is decreasing, specifically as a result of Enlightenment thinking, is shared by well-known Harvard psychologist Stephen Pinker, as argued in his book *The Better Angels of Our Nature*.[9]

But this thesis has been subjected to a trenchant critique by John Gray, a British professor of the history of European thought, who says that Pinker's statistics are misleading, and his idea of moral progress is wishful thinking and plain wrong. Gray points out that Pinker, and also the ethicist Peter Singer, who supports him, fundamentally misread the Enlightenment by tracing to it an antiviolence revolution. In his review of Pinker's book, entitled "Stephen Pinker's Delusions of Peace," Gray writes:

> Like other latter-day partisans of "Enlightenment values," Pinker prefers to ignore the fact that many Enlightenment thinkers have been doctrinally anti-liberal, while quite a few have favoured the large-scale use of political violence....
>
> The idea that a new world can be constructed through the rational application of force is peculiarly modern, animating ideas of revolutionary war and pedagogic terror that feature in an influential tradition of radical Enlightenment thinking.[10]

Gray says that neither Pinker nor Singer make "mention of the powerful illiberal current in Enlightenment thinking, expressed in the Jacobins and the Bolsheviks, which advocated and practiced methodical violence as a means of improving society. Like many others today, Pinker's response when confronted with such evidence is to define the dark side of the Enlightenment out of existence.... Rather than war declining, the difference between peace and war has been fatally blurred."[11]

Nevertheless, many people are fascinated by Harari's "possibilities," however far-fetched they may appear – a circumstance that does not mean that Harari has nothing important to say. On the contrary, we shall find that many of his views about possible future scenarios concerning AI are important insights that deserve close attention.

For the moment, however, for our purposes, the most important thing about Harari's three assertions is what he builds on them, especially on the third, which he couches in explicitly atheistic terms, a worldview that forms the background to his and many others' thinking about the future. He writes: "Humans don't die . . . because God decreed it, or because mortality is an essential part of some great cosmic plan. Humans always die due to some technical glitch. . . . Every technical problem has a technical solution. We don't need to wait for the Second Coming in order to overcome death."[12]

This sounds not so much like a possibility but more like Harari's personal view. It also sounds very optimistic, although Harari's optimism seems to wane as the book proceeds. Critic Charles Rubin, in an article entitled "Algorithmic Man: Yuval Noah Harari's Timid Transhumanism," claims that "the title of Yuval Noah Harari's book, *Homo Deus: A Brief History of Tomorrow*, is misleading. While the book uses a future-oriented rhetoric, it is actually less about the future than it is about what the author takes to be the nature of life itself: namely, that we are all just bundles of algorithms."[13]

Harari says this in so many words, and it is a key to understanding his naturalistic worldview:

> The idea that humans will always have a unique ability beyond the reach of non-conscious algorithms is just wishful thinking. . . .
>
> 1. Organisms are algorithms. Every animal – including Homo Sapiens – is an assemblage of organic algorithms shaped by natural selection over millions of years of evolution.
> 2. Algorithmic calculations are not affected by the materials from which the calculator is built. . . .
> 3. Hence there is no reason to think that organic algorithms can do things that non-organic algorithms will never be able to replicate or surpass. As long as the calculations remain valid, what does it matter whether the algorithms are manifested in carbon or silicon?[14]

There is no question that organisms can do things that algorithms can do – humans, for instance, can do calculations with Euclid's algorithm that we considered earlier. Secondly, no organism *is* an algorithm, as Harari says in 1, since an algorithm is not a material entity. Harari redeems himself somewhat in 3, by saying that the algorithms are *manifested* in organisms. But his reductionist view that humans are nothing but an assemblage of (organically embedded) algorithms is an unwarranted assumption with strong evidence against it. We shall see later in this chapter that human thought is highly likely not to be completely algorithmic.

Although it once more looks as if these views are Harari's own, he says that if we are horrified at the idea of technology "stripping humans of their authority, and empowering nonhuman algorithms," we should not blame the computer geeks but should realize that these ideas arise from biology more than computer science: "It is the life sciences that concluded that organisms are algorithms." Harari then acknowledges that, if they are wrong and organisms do not function like algorithms, then "computers may work wonders in other fields, but they will not be able to understand us and direct our life, and they will certainly be incapable of merging with us."[15] The issue, therefore, is with reductionism in biology – a fascinating topic in its own right that we cannot pursue here.[16]

Harari's predictions bring us back to the further discussion of transhumanism we promised at the end of chapter 5. Now, Harari is a historian, not a gerontologist, and since physical death, which brings with it (in the atheist but not the Christian view) the loss of all that matters, is the major obstacle facing the transhumanist dream, we need to listen to what experts on aging have to say. There are some gerontologists who do hold out hopes for dealing with the problem of aging. In 2014, a team of researchers at Harvard were able to rejuvenate an older mouse through a process called heterochronic parabiosis, which involved the surgical union of the mouse with a younger one in such a way as to permit sharing of blood circulation.[17] Aubrey de Grey, a biogerontologist, is optimistic about increasing longevity. He shares Harari's view that human beings will very soon be able to live as long as they like. Certainly, longevity has increased; a century ago the average life expectancy was around sixty years, whereas now it is around seventy. De Grey thinks that the first person to live to 1,000 has already been born.[18]

Some neuroscientists are very skeptical about the long-term potential benefits of AI in terms of better health and enhanced intelligence. Jean Mariani, who directs an institute researching longevity, and Danièle Tritsch, former codirector of a neuroscience research laboratory, write:

> Let's face it, all of this is pure fantasy. . . . Ageing is unavoidable, even if there is good reason to hope that it will be accompanied by improved health. . . . While progress over the last 50 years has brought a far better understanding of the brain, it has had little therapeutic impact. All of the predictions trumpeted by the transhumanists are at the very least, false. . . . Many have suggested that human intelligence may soon be outstripped by artificial intelligence. But this fear betrays a deep misunderstanding of what human intelligence really is.[19]

In spite of skepticism, such is the desire to avoid death that many people enthusiastically buy into transhumanist programs for longevity. Harari claims that the first major agenda item in the twenty-first century is going to be a serious bid for human immortality, which will be given an irresistible momentum by the fear of death ingrained in most humans. In 2021 it was reported that Jeff Bezos was "among the backers of a new 'rejuvenation company,' Altos Labs, a Silicon Valley start-up now registered in the US and the UK that has set its sights on understanding why we age and how we might prevent it by biological reprogramming and ultimately work out how we might live forever."[20]

He was not the only billionaire entrepreneur keen to have immortal life. Yuri Milner has also invested in Altos Labs, who notably have on their board the Japanese stem-cell expert and Nobel laureate Shinya Yamanaka. PayPal founder Peter Thiel; Larry Page and Sergey Brin, cofounders of Google; and Mark Zuckerberg have all shown interest in what is called the longevity business, which, according to Silicon Valley, will solve the technical problem of aging, as they, like Harari, think of it. Other, less optimistic, people think that this particular research race will not lead to immortality, but it may yield useful research in the understanding of aging and related issues. As of 2022, funding for Altos Labs had reached $3 billion. In January 2022, the company's president, Hans Bishop, argued that Altos Labs was working on increasing the "healthspan" of humans and that longevity extension would only be "an accidental consequence."[21] Altos Labs opened its Cambridge Institute of Science in the UK in 2022 with a stated mission commitment "to restore cell health and resilience through cellular rejuvenation programming to reverse disease, injury, and the disabilities that occur throughout life."[22]

Some wealthy people, realizing that the solution may not arrive in their lifetime, have arranged to have their bodies frozen after death, in a practice known as cryonics, hoping that they can be brought back to life when scientists discover how to reboot a frozen brain. As of 2022, the cost of preparing and storing corpses using cryonics ranges all the way up to $200,000 (the cost in 1976 at the Cryonics Institute was $28,000).[23] It must seem incongruous to most people that such huge sums of money are invested in freezing bodies and brains when there are more than 700 million people in the world who have no access to a decent water supply.[24]

All of this expense and longing for increased length of life probably represents a great deal of angst and worry. It reminds me of the wisdom of Jesus when he said: "And which of you by being anxious can add a single hour to his span of life?"[25] We might also need to be reminded that the length of our lives may well be far less important than their quality. That is certainly true where God is concerned.

Longing for physical immortality is rooted in the distant past. According to the biblical narrative, a consequence of human disobedience was that God removed human access to the Tree of Life, as we shall see in chapter 13. The famous ancient Mesopotamian Gilgamesh epic is one of humanity's oldest tales, dating back to around 2100 BC. The hero, Gilgamesh, embarks on an epic quest to find immortality. After many adventures and difficulties, he is told that he can become immortal if he defies sleep. He fails and sleeps for an entire week. He then learns that although he will never attain immortality, he can regain his youth by finding a plant on the ocean floor. Ignoring warnings that his quest will ruin him, he manages to get the plant but leaves it on the shore while he goes swimming. A snake steals it, and Gilgamesh eventually dies. It is a story illustrating the lengths to which humans will go to overcome senescence – and their futility. It has clear lessons for the contemporary scramble for immortality.

Many rulers of ancient China tried to find the elixir of life. There is a famous Chinese book on alchemy, the *Danjing yaojue* (Essential formulas of alchemical classics), attributed to the notable medical specialist Sun Simiao (ca. sixth century), that contains recipes for making such elixirs. Unfortunately, most of the ingredients were poisonous and, ironically, doubtless hastened the death of anyone seeking to avoid it.

More recently, but still remarkably prescient, Nikolai Fedorov (1829–1903), a Russian Orthodox philosopher, suggested a very different approach – that humans could intervene in their own evolution and so direct it towards physical immortality and even resurrection: "This day will be divine, awesome, but not miraculous, for *resurrection will be a task not of miracle but of knowledge and common labor.*"[26] He sounds just like Harari!

In the twentieth century, in 1949, Pierre Teilhard de Chardin, a French Jesuit priest and paleontologist, predicted that rapid technological change would result in a merger of humanity and technology. He believed that this would eventually lead to what he called the "Omega Point," where humanity would merge with the divine – *homo deus.*

That leads us at once to the second item on Harari's agenda – the intensification of the pursuit of happiness. To fulfil that desire, he says: "It will be necessary to change our biochemistry and re-engineer our bodies and minds.[27] . . . The second great project of the twenty-first century – to ensure global happiness – will involve re-engineering *Homo sapiens* so that it can enjoy everlasting pleasure."[28] "Having raised humanity above the beastly level of survival struggles, we will now aim to upgrade humans into gods, and turn *Homo sapiens* into *Homo Deus*"[29] (but "think more in terms of Greek gods"[30]).

Again, it looks as if this is Harari's own opinion, rather than simply one of his possibilities, but from his later statements it is hard to tell. I confess to being very skeptical about a grandiose project that is essentially driven by humans' dissatisfaction with their current state.

Elise Bohan of the Future of Humanity Institute was asked in a *Guardian* interview: "Is transhumanism encroaching on domains that religion has traditionally held? I think yes." In response, Bohan related that after she gave her first big paper at a conference, a biologist came up to her and congratulated her on her work:

> Then he looked me in the eye and whispered to me: "We're building God, you know," she chuckles. "I looked back at him and I said: "Yeah, I know."
>
> They knew they didn't mean it as religion, she says. "But a lot of what has been talked about in religion – omniscience, omnipotence, hopefully omnibenevolence – we are at least getting closer to that all seeing, all knowing, all exploring [force]."[31]

Harari thinks this will happen gradually, starting with our voluntary ceding of control of our lives to the smartphone and over time changing ourselves by reengineering, taking drugs, et cetera, until we are no longer recognizably human.[32] In a 2019 talk, Harari said: "It's increasingly hard to tell where I end *and* where the computer begins. . . . In the future, it is likely that the smartphone will not be separated from you at all. It may be embedded in your body or brain, constantly scanning your biometric data and your emotions."[33] He thinks that if we somehow succeed in merging these technologies with the human body, it would be the biggest revolution in all of human history – the first time we have been able to manipulate *ourselves* as distinct from our environment.

This scenario scarily echoes the work of the Thought Police in Orwell's *1984* who had the task not only of determining what people thought but of controlling what they felt. On his website, Harari spells this out:

> A related danger is that governments and corporations might acquire the ability to hack human beings. To hack human beings means to understand humans better than we understand ourselves. . . . Even in Nazi Germany or in the Soviet Union the government could not know what every person was doing, thinking and feeling. But soon some governments and corporations might have enough biological knowledge, enough data and enough computing power to monitor all the people all the time, and know what each of us is doing, thinking and feeling. Once a government or a corporation

understands us better than we understand ourselves, it can predict our feelings and decisions, manipulate our feelings and decisions, and create the worst totalitarian regimes in history.[34]

We need a caveat here, however, as Harari increasingly protests that he is not a prophet – that he is not predicting the future but simply outlining what he sees as possibilities. Indeed, he does not regard his forecast that in this century humanity will try to achieve immortality, bliss, and divinity as original or farsighted, but rather as a reflection of the traditional ideals of liberal humanism.[35] And in that context, he seems to have had second thoughts about the desirability of a posthuman future:

> I am definitely not a post-humanist, and I think using bioengineering and AI to change humans is an extremely dangerous idea. Humans have always suffered from a big gap between our power and our wisdom. The gap between our power to manipulate systems, and the wisdom needed to understand these systems deeply. Unfortunately, it is much easier to manipulate than to understand. It is easier to build a dam over a river than understand the impact it will have on the ecosystem. Therefore, we humans often start manipulating things long before we understand the consequences of our actions.[36]

If that is what Harari really thinks, one could wish that his book had been clearer.

Be that as it may, the transhumanist bandwagon rolls on. Its visionaries' aims are summed up by Mark O'Connell in his book *To Be a Machine: Adventures among Cyborgs, Utopians, Hackers, and the Futurists Solving the Modest Problem of Death*, which won the Wellcome Book Prize in 2018: "It is their belief that we can and should eradicate aging as a cause of death; that we can and should use technology to augment our bodies and our minds; that we can and should merge with machines, remaking ourselves, finally, in the image of our own higher ideals."[37]

David Pearce, the cofounder of the World Transhumanist Association, similarly argues that transhumanism involves increasing the capacity for pleasure and the radical extension of life to enjoy this pleasure indefinitely. Pearce describes this as the "hedonistic imperative" and predicts that, over the next thousand years, "the biological substrates of suffering will be eradicated completely . . . [and] post-human states of magical joy will be biologically refined, multiplied and intensified indefinitely."[38]

John Gray, in his book *Seven Types of Atheism*, says: "Contemporary atheism is a continuation of monotheism by other means. Hence the unending succession of God-surrogates, such as humanity and science, technology and the all-too-human visions of transhumanism."[39] He sees this development as a resurgence of Gnosticism – an ancient heresy that regarded humans as spirits trapped in an evil body from which they need to be liberated – this time by technology. According to Gray, "Gnosticism is the faith of people who believe themselves to be machines."[40] Gray suggests that transhumanism is essentially techno-monotheism.[41]

This drive to move from the organic to the inorganic is, of course, one way of attempting to circumvent the biological problem of aging. Kurzweil writes that "something is going on in the human brain, and there is nothing that prevents these biological processes being reverse engineered and replicated in nonbiological entities."[42] This development was anticipated by C. S. Lewis in his dystopic science fiction novel *That Hideous Strength*, written in 1945:

> In us organic life has produced Mind. It has done its work. After that we want no more of it. We do not want the world any longer furred over with organic life, like what you call the blue mould – all sprouting and budding and breeding and decaying. We must get rid of it. By little and little, of course. Slowly we learn how. Learn to make our brains live with less and less body: learn to build our bodies directly with chemicals, no longer have to stuff them full of dead brutes and weeds. Learn how to reproduce ourselves without copulation.[43]

As John Gray says, there appears to be a strong element of Gnosticism in this attitude. In his perceptive review of Gray's work, Giles Fraser writes approvingly of Gray's insistence on "the idea that science or technology can somehow deliver us from the sort of questions that have driven some of us to God – questions about mortality, for instance – is every bit as superstitious as any religious belief. For many, technology and science function in today's society very much the same way as magic once did – they both represent the fantasy that there can be some quick fix to the challenges of being human."[44]

Hava Tirosh-Samuelson writes:

> Transhumanism is the ideology that gives coherence to our technological age. . . . Transhumanism has not improved the quality of life, but it has legitimized the heavy price we have been paying for our technological obsession and addictions. . . . Contrary to transhumanist myth of progress, the process

is not inevitable but within our decision-making powers. If we cannot reverse the process, at least we might try to slow down the technologization of life, if world religions, especially the Abrahamic traditions, highlight the idolatrous nature of technology in which humans venerate themselves by worshipping their own products. The technologization of humanity has not made us better humans and has not made our society more caring, just, or equitable. If we remember that humans are created in the image of God, perhaps we, the bearers of the divine image, might be able to prevent our own dehumanization brought about by the destructive fantasies of transhumanism. Making humanity obsolete is the telos of transhumanism, but its proponents have not worked out what it means for us today to live in the spectre of human obsolescence.[45]

THE ANTI-HUMAN AGENDA

Seemingly unaware of these risks, some thinkers are still driven by the notion that humanity will eventually become obsolete. Among them there are some eco-warriors, sometimes called Anthropocene anti-humanists, who have concluded that the end of the human species is imminent and that rather than resist it we should welcome it. For them, ending humanity is not a specter but a moral imperative: humans *should* cease to exist, because they have destroyed the planet. They also think that, in a kind of rough justice, humans will bring their demise on themselves by their profligate and reckless technological exploitation of the environment, with its resultant despoliation and climate change. These anti-humanists would rather have a world without humans than a world without nature. They long to return the earth to what they imagine to be its prehuman state, long before the human race began its technology-fueled destructive ways – a view captured in the title of philosopher David Benatar's 2006 book *Better Never to Have Been: The Harm of Coming into Existence*. Benatar held that the disappearance of humans would not deprive the universe of anything unique or valuable: "The concern that humans will not exist at some future time is either a symptom of the human arrogance . . . or is some misplaced sentimentalism."[46]

Consequently, anti-humanists believe that research should be directed to terminating our dependence on biology by creating new kinds of intelligent artificial life based on some nonbiological substrate like silicon. They imagine that such artifacts will eventually colonize and reduce humans to the level we now assign to animals, or will exterminate them.

These scenarios represent a revolt against humanity as we know it. But it doesn't stop there. The very prospect that humans will eventually create new kinds of beings, whether real or simulated, has led some futurists to say that even though such an eventuality is highly speculative at the present time, nevertheless we have to take a long-term view and make serious preparation and investment for its arrival, even if that means paying less attention to the beings that exist at the moment.

Effective altruism (EA) is a concept that originated with philosopher Peter Singer's book *The Life You Can Save: How to Do Your Part to End World Poverty*. On the assumption that all lives are equally valuable, he argues that we have collective and individual responsibility for the world we would leave to our grandchildren and, by implication, future generations.[47] That means that we need to think long-term. Initially, effective altruists focused mainly on problems such as global poverty and ill health. Effective ways to help others were explored, and then the effective altruists made donations to alleviate disease and poverty, thereby saving many lives – and, of course, many people are involved in doing this good work still.

But some EA thinkers began to explore the notion, presumably based on the utilitarian principle of the maximum benefit to the maximum number of people, that the most effective way to help the most people is to focus on humanity's long-term future – the well-being of the many billions who have yet to be born. The argument becomes that if all lives are equally valuable irrespective of where they are, we can surely apply that same principle to *when* they are. That then led to making a distinction between "near-termism" solutions, such as eliminating malaria, and "longtermism" solutions, such as ensuring that AI doesn't get out of hand and become an existential risk to humanity.

This led to what is called the effective altruism movement, founded by Toby Ord in 2011. Longtermism is now being actively developed where Ord works, at the Future of Humanity Institute. Their main focus is to heighten awareness and work out the implications of humanity's present responsibility, not only for future *human* generations, but also for posthumans of whatever kind, whether real or simulated. It goes far beyond the natural concern for children and grandchildren originally expressed by Peter Singer. The basic idea, still based on the assumption that all lives are equally valuable, is that it is better to save trillions of potential lives in the (far distant) future than billions of lives today. Current thinking about longtermism is set out in the book *What We Owe the Future* by William MacAskill of the Future of Humanity Institute.[48]

There has been considerable investment in longtermist research, especially by Open Philanthropy, which is an effective altruism nonprofit organization founded by Facebook cofounder Dustin Moskowitz. In 2021, Open Philanthropy gave more than $100 million for longtermist causes.

Scholar Émile Torres, a former advocate of longtermism, has come to regard it as "quite possibly the most dangerous secular belief system in the world today."[49] He spells it out as follows:

> It is a vision that . . . commands us to subjugate nature, maximize economic productivity, colonize space, build vast computer simulations, create astronomical numbers of artificial beings, and replace humanity with a superior race of radically "enhanced" posthumans. Its basic tenets imply that the worst atrocities in human history fade into moral nothingness when one takes the big-picture view of our cosmic "potential," that preemptive war can be acceptable, that mass invasive surveillance may be necessary to avoid omnicide, and that we should give to the rich instead of the poor.[50]

Torres cites Nick Bostrom: "Even if there is 'a mere 1 percent chance' that 10^{54} people existing in the future, then 'the expected value of reducing existential risk by a mere *one billionth of one billionth of one percentage point* is worth 100 hundred billion times as much as a billion human lives.'" In plain language, this means that "saving billions of actual people is the moral equivalent of reducing existential risk by utterly minuscule amounts."[51]

This would appear to mean that the worst natural disasters and the most devastating atrocities in history become almost imperceptible trivialities when seen from this grand perspective. Referring to events like "Chernobyl, Bhopal, volcano eruptions, earthquakes, draughts [sic], World War I, World War II, epidemics of influenza, smallpox, black plague, and AIDS," Bostrom wrote: "These types of disasters have occurred many times and our cultural attitudes towards risk have been shaped by trial-and-error in managing such hazards. But tragic as such events are to the people immediately affected, in the big picture of things – from the perspective of humankind as a whole – even the worst of these catastrophes are mere ripples on the surface of the great sea of life. They haven't significantly affected the total amount of human suffering or happiness or determined the long-term fate of our species."[52]

This sounds like the worst kind of "the end justifies the means" utilitarianism that was used to justify the Holocaust or the Holodomor in Ukraine. Another blatant, indeed, horrific example of this is provided by AI safety consultant Nicholas Beckstead: "Saving lives in poor countries may have significantly smaller ripple effects than saving and improving lives in rich countries. Why? Richer countries have substantially more innovation, and their workers are much more economically productive. [Consequently,] it now seems more plausible to me that saving a life in a rich country is substantially more important than saving a life in a poor country, other things being equal."[53]

Torres explains further:

> To summarise, these ideas so far, humanity has a 'potential' of its own, one that transcends the potentials of each individual person, and failing to realise this potential would be . . . a moral catastrophe of literally cosmic proportions. This is the central dogma of longtermism: nothing matters more, ethically speaking, than fulfilling our potential as a species of "Earth-originating intelligent life." . . . Why do I think this ideology is so dangerous? The short answer is that elevating the fulfilment of humanity's supposed potential above all else could nontrivially increase the probability that actual people – those alive today and in the near future – suffer extreme harms, even death.[54]

Longtermism places the present generation under an obligation to do everything it can to ensure a posthuman future for whatever beings we create, although some of the literature confuses the issue by still calling such entities *human*, even though many of them are technological artifacts and some "exist" only in simulations. Elon Musk takes care for the future to the extreme of working towards colonizing Mars as a "life insurance" for the inhabitants of Earth, reasoning that we have "a duty to maintain the light of consciousness" rather than going extinct.[55]

The pressure to do everything possible for the future can also lead to all kinds of dangerous psychological disturbances and sometimes even to psychotic behavior. Such deviant effects are the subject of a sobering article by Ellen Huet in Blomberg entitled "The Real-Life Consequences of Silicon Valley's AI Obsession." She tells the story of Qiaochu Yuan, a former mathematics research student at the University of California at Berkeley, who became gripped by the idea that AI could wipe out humanity within twenty years.

Huet says that Yuan dropped out of school, abandoned the idea of retirement planning, and drifted away from old friends who weren't dedicating their every waking moment to averting global annihilation. "You can really manipulate people into doing all sorts of crazy stuff if you can convince them that this is how you can help prevent the end of the world," said Yuan. "Once you get into that frame, it really distorts your ability to care about anything else."[56]

Among the women alleging abuse within the Silicon Valley subculture was a twenty-eight-year-old woman who said, "Everyone believed me, but them believing it wasn't enough. You need people who care a lot about abuse." There was a great deal of abuse going on in that obsessive subculture, as Huet goes on to explain:

> That inability to care was most apparent when it came to the alleged mistreatment of women in the community, as opportunists used the prospect of impending doom to excuse vile acts of abuse. Within the subculture of rationalists, EAs [effective altruism], and AI safety researchers, sexual harassment and abuse are distressingly common, according to interviews with eight women at all levels of the community.[57]

One fears that underlying much research there is an unstated but very real quest for power that may become dangerously unstable and out of control. This is strongly reminiscent of Nietzsche's vicious diatribe against Christianity in *The Antichrist*, where he defines what is good to be "whatever augments the feeling of power, the will to power, power itself in man. . . . The weak and the botched shall perish: first principle of *our* charity. And one should help them to it. What is more harmful than any vice? – Practical sympathy for the botched and the weak – Christianity." He next says: "The problem that I set here is not what shall replace mankind in the order of living creatures . . . but what type of man must be *bred*." Against that higher type of man Nietzsche says Christianity has "waged a war to the death" and produced what he calls the "sick brute-man – the Christian." For Nietzsche, Christianity "stands in opposition to all *intellectual* well-being." His final condemnation of Christianity is as chilling as it is famous: "It is, to me, the greatest of all imaginable corruptions . . . it has turned every value into worthlessness, and every truth into a lie, and every integrity into baseness of soul."[58]

It should therefore not surprise us that longtermism is profoundly anti-Christian, has deep anti-God roots, and sounds too much like Nazi eugenics for comfort. Paolo Benanti, a Franciscan priest and ethicist who is also an AI expert and watchdog for the Vatican, has warned against Silicon Valley's tendency to play God in the sense of "a desire to do good for people whether they like it or not." He invokes a moral teaser: Should you save a drowning man if he is Hitler's father, grandfather, or great-grandfather? He comments: "Effective altruists are wondering how many generations they should count and be prepared to sacrifice in order to stop Hitler, but you cannot make that decision. We are not the saviours of the world."

Since Benanti is more worried about natural stupidity than he is about AI, he argues that Silicon Valley should concern itself more about allowing AI to be "used by humans for less than holy purposes" than about using it to play God.[59]

The effective altruists are at least correct in saying that technology poses a real risk. Leon Kass, professor of social thought at the University of Chicago, has given a sober assessment of the serious dangers to humanity with which so many aspects of technology are now fraught:

> We have paid some high prices for the technological conquest of nature, but none so high as the intellectual and spiritual costs of seeing nature as mere material for our manipulation, exploitation, and transformation. With the powers for biological engineering now gathering, there will be splendid new opportunities for a similar degradation in our view of man. . . . And clearly, if we come to see ourselves as meat, then meat we shall become.[60]

Kass shows that the transhuman quest is far from being morally innocuous and neutral. It can be seen rather as a quest for mastery and power. The direction in which that power takes us is a matter for profound ethical concern, as C. S. Lewis presciently observed as far back as 1943 in his remarkable book *The Abolition of Man*:

> What we call Man's power over Nature turns out to be a power exercised by some men over other men with Nature as its instrument. . . . Man's conquest of Nature, if the dreams of some scientific planners are realized, means the rule of a few hundreds of men over billions upon billions of men. There neither is nor can be any simple increase of power on Man's side. Each new power won *by* man is a power *over* man as well. Each advance leaves him weaker as well as stronger. In every victory, besides being the general who triumphs, he is also the prisoner who follows the triumphal car. . . . Man's final conquest has proved to be the abolition of Man.[61]

It is interesting in this connection that Dennis Glover's novel about Orwell and the writing of *1984* is entitled *The Last Man in Europe*[62] – the title that Orwell had originally had in mind for his book. C. S. Lewis wrote these words after he had become a Christian, yet atheist John Gray regards them as of prophetic value, even for those who do not share Lewis's theological convictions.[63] Gray also reminds us that the attempt to use science and technology to upgrade humanity is far from new. He cites both the medieval Jewish myth of a humanlike being made of dust or mud called the golem and Mary Shelley's *Frankenstein,* published in 1818. In Gray's view, "the attempt to create an artificial human being risked making a monster."[64]

The history of the twentieth century gives strong support to this view. Two horrific examples come to mind. Firstly, in Germany, where the Nazis imagined they could create an Aryan superhuman by what they called "scientific breeding," a cynical euphemism that involved the killing of people judged as disposable because they were regarded as mentally or physically below standard or "unfit" or "racially impure." Hitler essentially took over the idea of the survival of the fittest and applied it to human beings in his quest for the Übermensch that was conceptualized by Friedrich Nietzsche. That led to the extermination of millions of Jews, Poles, and other "undesirables" in the most depraved violence the world has ever seen.

In the former Soviet Union, attempts were made to use science to create a "New Man." In 1924, Leon Trotsky wrote: "Man will make it his purpose to master his own feelings, to raise his instincts to the heights of consciousness, to make them transparent, to extend the wires of his will into hidden recesses, and thereby to raise himself to a new plane, to create a higher social biologic type, or, if you please, a superman."[65]

What that program of eugenics involved is explained by historian Andrey Zubov, as quoted by Sergei Gogin:

"The Soviet man" evolved as a result of a deeply negative selection process, whereby "the best, most honest and most cultured people were either killed or prevented from having a family and raising children by exile or imprisonment, whilst the worst sort of people, namely those who took part in the creation of this new form of man or silently supported the new authorities, could 'be fruitful and multiply.'"[66]

Such horrific examples support John Gray's prediction that the likely outcome of all such attempts to reengineer humanity will be the extinction of humanity. He comes to a wry conclusion: "For myself, unregenerate humanity is preferable – the flawed and conflicted creatures we are in fact are much more interesting than the transformed creatures we'd like to be. But I'm sure we're not done with trying. For if anything is peculiarly human, it's the refusal to be what we are."[67]

C. S. Lewis developed this theme – which he started in *The Abolition of Man* – in his book *That Hideous Strength*. It tells of a sinister scientific institution euphemistically – and cleverly – called N.I.C.E., the National Institute for Coordinated Experiments, which intends to exploit a small university in England as a recruitment center for highly questionable experiments in vivisection.

Near the beginning of the story, Lord Feverstone, the amoral driving force behind the project, says to one of the central characters, sociologist Mark Studdock: "But it is the main question of the moment: which side one's on – obscurantism or Order. . . . If Science is really given a free hand, it can now take over the human race and recondition it: make man a really efficient animal. If it doesn't – well, we're done."[68] Feverstone goes on to say:

Man has got to take charge of Man. That means, remember, that some men have got to take charge of the rest. . . .

Quite simple and obvious things, at first – sterilization of the unfit, liquidation of backward races . . . selective breeding. Then real education, including pre-natal education. By real education I mean one that has no "take it or leave it" nonsense. A real education makes the patient what it wants infallibly: whatever he or his parents try to do about it. Of course, it'll have to be mainly psychological at first. But we'll get on to biological conditioning in the end and direct manipulation of the brain. . . .

It's the real thing at last. A new type of man: and it's people like you who've got to begin to make him.[69]

Studdock is thus drawn into a gruesome project that turns out to be geared to the conquest of physical death – one of Harari's agenda items for the twenty-first century.

Some two years before he wrote *1984*, George Orwell wrote a perceptive review of *That Hideous Strength*:

His book describes the struggle of a little group of sane people against a nightmare that nearly conquers the world. A company of mad scientists – or, perhaps, they are not mad, but have merely destroyed in themselves all human feeling, all notion of good and evil – are plotting to conquer Britain, then the whole planet, and then other planets, until they have brought the universe under their control.

All superfluous life is to be wiped out, all natural forces tamed, the common people are to be used as slaves and vivisection subjects by the ruling caste of scientists, who even see their way to conferring immortal life upon themselves. Man, in short, is to storm the heavens and overthrow the gods, or even to become a god himself. . . .

Plenty of people in our age do entertain the monstrous dreams of power that Mr. Lewis attributes to his characters [the N.I.C.E. scientists, for example], and we are within sight of the time when such dreams will be realisable.

Orwell argued that Lewis's book "would probably have been better . . . if the magical element had been left out," and he objected to the ending in which N.I.C.E. (National Institute of Co-ordinated Experiments) is overthrown by divine intervention: "[Lewis] is entitled to his beliefs, but they weaken his story, not only because they offend the average reader's sense of probability but because in effect they decide the issue in advance. When one is told that God and the Devil are in conflict one always knows which side is going to win. The whole drama of the struggle against evil lies in the fact that one does not have supernatural aid."[70]

On the contrary, Lewis's belief in the supernatural strengthens the story. Firstly, knowing which side is going to win in the struggle between good and evil has never spoiled any story for me or anyone I know – think of *The Lord of the Rings*, for instance. If there is a God and a supernatural dimension, then leaving it out will diminish the story, since it will be told in a framework that is less than the whole and so omits part of reality. Also, it is not true that the addition of supernatural aid detracts from the drama. It all depends on the nature of that aid and the way in which it is employed, or not employed, as in the case of Jesus' refusal of angelic help when he was facing the cross.[71]

All of these dystopias and, indeed, most futuristic AI scenarios tend to assume that human beings will always be on the earth. The exception here is the oft-mentioned speculation that an AGI, if ever created, may decide to dispense with humanity. In other words, the human race will come to an end and be replaced by machines. Indeed, reminiscent of C. S. Lewis, neuroscientist Iain McGilchrist, in his keynote to the AI World Summit 2022, speaking of cyborgs, said that "the best way to destroy humanity will be to hybridize it with a machine."[72]

An alternative scenario to C. S. Lewis's "abolition of man" is the subject of a piece of dystopian writing that is not so well known – P. D. James's novel *The Children of Men*, written in 1992 and set in 2021. The book takes the form of a journal written by Oxford historian Theodore Faron, who is the cousin of the despotic Warden of the police state of England. The key idea is that the entire world, in which nation after nation has been recording a rapidly declining birth rate, is gradually engulfed by a mysterious pandemic of infertility so that in 1995 the last human child is born. That year was designated Omega, and the children born in it were called Omegas, about which James makes the prescient remark: "If from infancy you treat children as gods, they are liable in adulthood to act as devils."[73] The human race stands threatened with extinction. In an interview, P. D. James said that she was interested in thinking how we humans would behave if we knew that we had no future – not quite the same as asking how we would behave if we thought we might be replaced by machines, an idea that does not appear in James's book. The one ray of hope for the future appears at the end of the book: a child is born to Theo and a woman named Julian, a member of a dissident group called the Five Fishes, whom he met towards the beginning of the story.

I cannot help thinking that there is a powerful religious symbolism here: the begetting of a living child holds out more hope than the construction of any machine. Long ago, one did and still does.

QUESTIONS

1. Do you think humanity needs to be upgraded – if so, why?
2. What do you think of Harari's view that war is obsolete, that we are more at risk from obesity than starvation, and that violence is decreasing? Give your reasons.
3. What are the aims of transhumanism? Are they realistic?
4. Why do you think people fear death? Do you think death is a mere technical problem that we will eventually solve? Give reasons for your view.
5. Do you think it is desirable to reengineer humans to increase happiness? Do you have any ideas of what happiness is and how it could be increased?
6. Do you think transhumanism encroaches on religion?
7. What is effective altruism? Discuss your response to it. Does it violate moral law?
8. Read and discuss C. S. Lewis's book *The Abolition of Man*.

CHAPTER 11

ARTIFICIAL GENERAL INTELLIGENCE

The Future Is Dark?

Artificial Intelligence is the future not only for Russia but for all humankind. It comes with colossal opportunities, but also threats that are difficult to predict. Whoever becomes the leader in this sphere will become the ruler of the world.
Vladimir Putin

That sounds like a suggestion that world control will depend on data control – but will the data be controlled by humans? The late James Lovelock, the environmental expert who developed the Gaia hypothesis – the idea that the earth is a self-regulating ecosystem – suggested in his provocative way that humans may have had their time and should make way for something new. In an interview reported in the *Guardian*, he said: "Quite soon – before we've reached the end of this century, even – I think that what people call robots will have taken over."[1] Similarly, speaking to Israel's President Rivlin, Harari said: "In two hundred years, I can pretty much assure you that there will not be any more Israelis, and no *Homo sapiens* – there will be something else."[2] To put it another way: "In pursuit of health, happiness, and power, humans will gradually change first one of their features and then another, and another, until they will no longer be human."[3]

In April 2018 at a TED Talk in Vancouver, physicist and cosmologist Max Tegmark, president of the Future of Life Institute at MIT, made a rather grandiose statement: "In creating AI, we're birthing a new form of life with unlimited potential for good or ill."[4] How much science lies behind these statements is another matter, since all AI and machine-learning algorithms to date are no more alive than Microsoft Word, to quote the neat phrase of leading AI researcher Rosalind Picard.[5]

Although all AIs to date are narrow, the race towards AGI is now at full throttle, even though the finishing line, if there is one, is far from clearly defined. From a political point of view, the first nation to reach it may find itself in the position that the presidents of the US, Russia, or China would dearly like to occupy, where they would have the power to prevent any other nation getting there, and so become the uncrowned ruler of the world – that is, if their AGI liked them enough to keep them on!

At the commercial level, Mark Zuckerberg raised the stakes in January 2024 by announcing on Facebook that he was going to spend $10 billion on 350,000 of Nvidia's most advanced AI chips of the specification required to attempt AGI. Zuckerberg has also decided to open source his work so that it is freely available for other researchers to work with and improve.

Some scientists have expressed the hope that AGI will be reached by cobbling together a variety of narrow AI systems. In 2021, however, Google's DeepMind laboratory announced that they had another, better approach. They claim that reinforced machine learning working on a principle of maximizing reward will be sufficient to achieve "a machine that thinks."[6]

There is a hidden assumption here that there never has been top-down intelligent informational input into the development of biological organisms. Hence, their attempt to verify their claim will be very interesting to those people, like me, who question that assumption.[7] The researchers may well have been wise to acknowledge that mechanisms for reward maximization are still an unsolved problem in reinforcement learning.

Not only that but data scientist Herbert Roitblat, author of *Algorithms Are Not Enough*, makes the further objection that trial-and-error learning might be enough, provided there are no time constraints, since otherwise we run into the well-known problem of typing monkeys. The idea here is that a monkey hitting random keys on a typewriter for an infinite amount of time may eventually type any given text. There is, however, no infinite amount of time available. Roitblat does believe, however, that AGI may be possible but does not think that a "robopocalypse" is either imminent or likely.[8]

Another heavyweight in the race is OpenAI, the brainchild of Sam Altman. Some differences between DeepMind and OpenAI are as follows: DeepMind has focused on establishing a baseline for deep reinforcement learning algorithms, whereas OpenAI has focused on establishing a baseline for deep reinforcement learning environments; DeepMind uses raw pixel data as input and learns from experience, using deep learning on a convolutional neural network, with a model-free reinforcement learning technique called Q-learning; OpenAI's language model GPT-3 uses AI to predict and complete lines of computer code, bringing the possibility of an AI system that can write itself one step closer.[9]

On the other hand, the London Institute for Mathematical Sciences is not so optimistic. Among its list of twenty-three mathematical challenges for the twenty-first century is the following:

> *Intelligent AI.* Far from approaching artificial general intelligence, AI has not progressed beyond high-dimensional curve-fitting. What mathematical insights could lead to more intelligent AI, such as causal reasoning, functional modules or a representation of the environment? Are there fundamental limits to AI, and what might this tell us about human intelligence?[10]

A study by Nigel Shadbolt and Roger Hampson entitled *The Digital Ape* carries the subtitle *How to Live (in Peace) with Smart Machines*.[11] They are optimistic that humans will still be in charge, provided we approach the process sensibly. But is this optimism justified? The director of Cambridge University's Centre for the Study of Existential Risk said: "We live in a world that could become fraught with . . . hazards from the misuse of AI and we need to take ownership of the problem – because the risks are real."[12]

The ethical questions are urgent since AI is regarded by experts as a transformative technology in the same league as electricity. The United States and China are determined to dominate the field, and China expects to win by 2030. President Emmanuel Macron wants to make France the AI capital of the world.

It would make more sense, however, to compare AI with nuclear energy than with electricity. Research into nuclear energy led to nuclear power stations, but it also led to a nuclear arms race that almost led the world to the brink of extinction. AI creates problems of similar, or even greater, magnitude. The brilliant play *Copenhagen* by Michael Frayn explores the question whether scientists should either simply follow the mathematics and physics without regard to the consequences or have moral qualms about it.[13] The context of the play is the research that led to nuclear fission. Exactly the same issues are raised by AI, except AI is accessible by many more people than atomic physics and does not need very sophisticated and expensive facilities.

You cannot build a nuclear bomb in your bedroom, but you can hack your way around the world and cause substantial damage.

Is there any substance to claims such as those of Lovelock and Tegmark, or are they perhaps exaggerated speculation that goes far beyond what scientific research has shown? There may well be some validity in the observation that the amount of unjustified speculation claimed for AI is in inverse proportion to the amount of actual hands-on work in AI that the claimant has done. For it would seem that those scientists who build AI systems tend to be more cautious in their predictions about the potential of AI than those who do not.

There is also the question of what worldview is driving all of this. What are the assumptions being made? Are they in the interests of all of us or simply of an elite few who wish to dominate for their own purposes? The answers given to these questions will depend on the worldviews of the participants in AI research, application, and debate who are supplying them. Of particular interest is their view of the nature of ultimate reality. As the late physicist John Polkinghorne, who once taught me quantum mechanics at Cambridge, wrote: "If we are to understand the nature of reality, we have only two possible starting points: either the brute fact of the physical world or the brute fact of a divine will and purpose behind that physical world."[14]

ARE BRAINS COMPUTERS?

The main worldview behind much writing about the future of humanity is the first of these – atheism. Its implications for our understanding of human cognitive abilities are expressed by physicist Sean Carroll in his bestseller *The Big Picture: On the Origins of Life, Meaning, and the Universe Itself*: "We humans are blobs of organized mud, which through the impersonal workings of nature's patterns have developed the capacity to contemplate and cherish and engage with the intimidating complexity of the world around us. . . . The meaning we find in life is not transcendent."[15] Such reductionist physicalism holds that human cognitive abilities have emerged naturally from the biosphere and therefore sees no reason why the same kind of thing can't happen again, once a high enough level of organization is reached – that is, something more than human intelligence emerging from the silicon sphere. This is the view of AI researcher Louis Rosenberg: "My view . . . is that artificial intelligence will become self-aware and will exceed human abilities, a milestone that many people refer to as the singularity. Why am I so sure this will happen? Simple.

Mother Nature has already proven that sentient intelligence can be created by enabling massive numbers of simple processing units (i.e., neurons) to form adaptive networks (i.e., brains)."[16] But Mother Nature (a deity?) has not proved anything of the sort, since the obvious questions, such as from where she got those simple processing units and the intelligence to put them together, remain unanswered. Moreover, perhaps they are not so simple after all, since several Nobel prizes have been awarded for research on how they work.

In fact, there is no real scientific evidence that nature has done any such thing, and there is every evidence that the atheistic worldview lying behind such a claim is demonstrably false – a position that I argue in my book *Cosmic Chemistry: Do God and Science Mix?*[17] It is simply not enough to say that nature must have done it because it is here – a classic example of blind faith masquerading as science.

What I am concerned about here is the impression, so easily given by statements like those of Carroll and Rosenberg, that the human mind is the brain and is no more than a computer. It is one thing to say that the brain *functions* in certain ways like a computer. It is an entirely different thing to say that it *is* nothing but a computer. A provocative and memorable statement endorsing that idea, variously attributed to the computer scientists Joseph Weizenbaum and Marvin Minsky, is that the brain is merely a meat machine, or, alternatively, a computer made of meat. This leads to the computational theory of mind that the brain is an information-processing system and that all mental functions are computations. But as AI expert and ethicist Raja Chatila points out: "Mere computing power is not intelligence. We have about 100 billion neurons in our brain. It's their organization and interaction that makes us think and act."[18]

Since the goal of an AI system is doing things that normally require human intelligence, it is therefore high time for us to pause to delve more deeply into what we understand by brains, minds, and consciousness and their relationship to computers. That in itself is no easy task, as a cursory glance at the history of the body-mind problem will show. This is an issue that has generated a great deal of research, where opinions are divided, and there is no universally agreed understanding. However, some things can usefully be said that are of relevance to AI.

One of the first questions that arises is the very old one as to whether a human being is nothing but matter, or whether there exists some nonmaterial component, a soul or spirit. Intuitively, most of us make some kind of dualistic distinction that is forever linked with the French philosopher

Descartes. We say things like "My body is not in good shape," "I am not the same weight as I was last year," "I know what it is like to be me, you don't." That is, we assume that there is a self, an "I" that is a person and not a thing, like my body. We also assume that the "I" decides, initiates, and directs "my" body, and that the "I" persists in time, even though the constituent atoms that make up our bodies are constantly being replaced. How, then, do "I" get to grips with this "I" and its relationship to my brain?

My answer will depend on what I think the nature of ultimate reality is. And that, in turn, will depend not so much on whether I am a scientist or not but on what worldview I hold. I shall limit my comments to the two dominant worldviews: atheism (materialism/naturalism)[19] and theism. For the materialist, mass/energy (or "nothing"[20]) is the ultimate reality from which everything else derives. For the theist, God is the ultimate reality who has created everything else. It is worth noting that these are views that often determine a person's approach to science, rather than their being determined by science alone – in spite of insistent claims to the contrary in some atheist quarters.

For instance, contemporary American philosopher Daniel Dennett asserts what his materialist worldview demands, that the mind "*is* the brain, or, more specifically, a system of organization within the brain that has evolved in much the way our immune system or respiratory system or digestive system has evolved."[21] Dennett denies the existence of consciousness and holds that the self is an illusion, a "center of narrative gravity" in the sense that language creates the idea of a self having these experiences.[22]

Yet the very thing of which most people are certain is that they are conscious. In Descartes' words: "I think, therefore I am." In particular, it seems to them that it is only through their consciousness that they are aware of the existence of anything else – including philosophers such as Dennett and their arguments. In *The Age of AI and Our Human Future*, Kissinger, Schmidt, and Huttenlocher make the wry remark: "Four centuries after Descartes promulgated his maxim, a question looms: If AI 'thinks,' or approximates thinking, who are we?"[23]

Nobel laureate Francis Crick joins Dennett in giving a reductionist answer to that question: "You, your joys and your sorrows, your memories and your ambitions, your sense of personal identity and free will are in fact no more than the behavior of a vast assembly of nerve cells and their associated molecules."[24] The phrase "no more than" that Crick uses is characteristic of the kind of ontological reductionism that the atheist worldview demands. The question is this: Does such reductionism even make sense?

Neuroscience has certainly made impressive and valuable strides in correlating mental activity (the "I" story) with electrochemical activity in the cerebral cortex (the brain story), mapping various regions of the brain that respond to mental stimuli and even using external electrical stimuli to stimulate the growth of new neural pathways in the cortex.

Correlation of mind states with brain states is one thing; however, claiming that mind states are no more than, or identical with, brain states is quite another.[25] For instance, my brain state can be the subject of a PET[26] scan, but my mind state cannot; my mind state is "about something," but my brain state is not about anything; my brain state can be spatially located, but my mind state cannot. The neuroscientist can tell me something about what is in my head. I cannot. But he cannot tell me what is in my mind. I can tell him. He can discuss mechanism. I am an agent. We are back with an age-old category mistake: confusing mechanism with agency.

Furthermore, the relationship "identical with" is symmetrical. Thus, if pain is composed of nothing but C-fiber firings, then C-fiber firings have to be the very same elements that constitute pain. Colin McGinn argues that this leads, ironically, to the strange consequence that materialism fails "to respect the intrinsic objectivity of physical properties" and ends up contradicting its own basic presuppositions by denying the objectivity of matter.[27]

Not only that, but the assumption that the mind is the brain seems incapable, even in principle, of dealing with consciousness, since it invalidates the very rationality necessary to do any science at all. Crick's reductionism is, therefore, intellectually suicidal. John Polkinghorne explains its fatal flaw:

> Thought is replaced by electro-chemical neural events. Two such events cannot confront each other in rational discourse. They are neither right nor wrong. They simply happen. If our mental life is nothing but the humming activity of an immensely complexly-connected computer-like brain, who is to say whether the program running on the intricate machine is correct or not? Conceivably, that program is conveyed from generation to generation via encoding in DNA, but that might still be merely the propagation of error. If we are caught in the reductionist trap, we have no means of judging intellectual truth. The very assertions of the reductionist himself are nothing but blips in the neural network of his brain. The world of rational discourse dissolves into the absurd chatter of firing synapses. Quite frankly, that cannot be right and none of us believes it to be so.[28]

American philosopher Alvin Plantinga, picking up on the widespread evolutionary view that the human mind has been developed for mere survival, not for truth, deduces that if that is the case, then "it's not probable that our minds should be reliable – that is, produce an appropriate preponderance of true over false beliefs; and if that is so, then one who believes both naturalism and evolution should reject the thought that our minds are reliable. But that's a crippling position to be in. Nietzsche is among the people who have suggested this problem. Some contemporary philosophers – Thomas Nagel, for example – have voiced the same worry, and so did Darwin himself."[29]

Or as Oxford physiologist Denis Noble puts it: "Suppose we really succeeded in 'reducing' rational behavior to molecular and cellular causation. In that case we would no longer be able meaningfully to express the truth of what we had succeeded in doing. In any event, the question does not arise. No such reduction is conceivable."[30]

So what is that something that is more than molecular and cellular causation? Cognitive philosopher David Chalmers has said that "reductive explanation of consciousness is impossible and I even argue for a kind of dualism," adding: "Temperamentally, I am strongly inclined towards materialist reductive explanations, and I have no strong spiritual or religious inclinations. . . . I hoped for a materialist theory; when I gave up on this hope, it was quite reluctantly. It eventually seemed plain to me that these conclusions were forced on anyone who wants to take consciousness seriously."[31] He later wrote: "But on the most common conception of consciousness, it is not easy to see how it could be part of the physical world. So it seems that to find a place for consciousness within the natural order, we must either revise our conception of consciousness, or revise our conception of nature."[32] One of the interesting things here is that Chalmers did not feel he was moving outside science in abandoning materialist reductionist explanations but rather matching his science to the ontology of his subject.

But some thinkers, who, unlike Chalmers, do possess strong spiritual and religious inclinations, reject substance dualism in favor of some version of monism,[33] a circumstance that strikes me as very strange, since information, as we have just seen, is nonmaterial and requires a nonmaterial source.

If theism is true, however, not only is matter not the only reality, *matter is not even the prime reality*. Theologian Keith Ward writes: "There is at least one mind that is prior to all matter, that is not in time and therefore is not capable of being brought into being by anything. It is the one truly self-existent reality, and the cause of all physical things."[34] According to the

New Testament, God, the Ultimate Reality, the Creator, is spirit and not material.[35] Now, it is facile to write off the idea that God is spirit by saying that this is dualism that believes in two kinds of "stuff," then by using the somewhat vague and pejorative notion of "stuff" to carry the dismissive argument rhetorically. God, who is spirit, is not some kind of "stuff." He is the Ultimate Reality, and he is not material.

In his article "The Brain Is Not a 'Meat Computer,'" neurosurgeon Michael Egnor challenges the computational theory of mind. He writes:

> The materialist view that the brain as a computer made of meat and that the mind is the software run on this carnal machine is a profound misunderstanding of neurology and of the relationship between the mind and the brain. . . . Every neuroanatomy and neurophysiology textbook I studied as a medical student described the function of the cerebellum in terms of circuits, neural networks, and computation. It appeared unlikely that anyone could sustain even a tiny injury in such a complex "computer" and retain normal coordination, let alone superb coordination, and play a sport at a high collegiate level. But I have learned in practice what every neurosurgeon knows, that much of the cerebellum is expendable. We remove major parts of it routinely in order to remove tumors or blood clots or to decompress the brainstem, which is immediately in front of the cerebellum, without any lasting neurological outcomes *(sequelae)*.
>
> Modern neuroscience is riddled with high-tech phrenology, based on materialist assumptions that the brain is a hard-drive and the mind is the program that runs on it. The use of an analogy to computation to understand the brain and the mind is fraught with fallacies. Thinking is not computation. In fact, thinking is the anthesis of computation. Thought always has meaning, and computation inherently lacks meaning. That is what makes computation so versatile – it imparts no meaning of its own to the tasks to which we apply it.[36]

Egnor goes on to make the important observation that "the brain looks like a computer only if we analyze it as if it were a computer. Our analysis does not mean that it is a computer, and it does not mean that computation explains the mind or even that computational approaches to neuroscience provide genuinely meaningful insight into neurophysiology."[37]

We mentioned earlier that the mathematical genius Alan Turing tried to characterize artificial intelligence in machine terms – a computer system that could pass as human must be considered as intelligent. For Turing, the test that we now call the Turing test was limited because of technology. But for the sake of argument, suppose we waive that objection. Suppose we could construct robots that were physically indistinguishable from humans, as in many sci-fi movies, and cognitively at least capable of fooling us. Would that make them actually "intelligent"? No – it would only make them what is called *functionally intelligent* – that is, they would not actually *think* but they would *act as if* they were intelligent. One argument demonstrating that such functional or simulated intelligence is not the same as human intelligence is the famous Chinese room thought experiment due to the Berkeley philosopher John Searle. He explains it as follows:

> The argument proceeds by the following thought experiment. Imagine a native English speaker who knows no Chinese locked in a room full of boxes of Chinese symbols (a data base) together with a book of instructions for manipulating the symbols (the program). Imagine that people outside the room send in other Chinese symbols which, unknown to the person in the room, are questions in Chinese (the input). And imagine that by following the instructions in the program the man in the room is able to pass out Chinese symbols which are correct answers to the questions (the output). The program enables the person in the room to pass the Turing Test for understanding Chinese, but he does not understand a word of Chinese.
>
> The point of the argument is this: if the man in the room does not understand Chinese on the basis of implementing the appropriate program for understanding Chinese, then neither does any other digital computer solely on that basis because no computer, qua computer, has anything the man does not have.[38]

Other scientists have sought to construct tests analogous to the Turing test that are based on specific characteristics of human intelligence, such as creativity. Rensselaer philosopher and computer scientist Selmer Bringsjord argues that the Turing test is inadequate, since merely sounding sufficiently like a human to deceive people does not necessarily establish humanlike intelligence in the product; it may point only to superior cunning in the creators. As Nick Bostrom put it in an interview: "You could just imagine . . . having hard-coded answers to the most commonly asked questions . . . but . . . actually doing a half hour interrogation with people who know how to . . . probe, that's way beyond current capabilities."[39]

Bringsjord pioneered the much more challenging Lovelace test, based on an observation from computer pioneer Ada Lovelace (1815–1852) that true creativity distinguishes humans from machines.[40] AI systems such as AlphaGo may surprise us, but surprise is not the same as creativity.

Creativity in humans is closely linked with our subjective experience. Susan Schneider has attempted to devise a Turing-type test involving questions aimed at seeing whether a computer can grasp the kind of concepts that we associate with our inner experience.

Distinguished Oxford mathematician and Nobel laureate Roger Penrose argues that the brain must be more than a computer, since it can do things that no computer can do, even in theory – for example, mathematicians have been able to solve problems that are insolvable by computational means. For him, Godel's theorem, establishing that certain claims in mathematics are true but unprovable, was "an absolutely stunning revelation" that convinced him that "whatever is going on in our understanding is not computational."[41]

Penrose also thinks that since humans are able to circumvent certain computational limits, the human brain must interact with systems other than the logical, algorithmic universe, one implication of which would be the impossibility of AGI. He puts forward the quantum world as the prime candidate but admits that he cannot yet prove this.

It would seem that the human mind is not the brain, and the brain is certainly not a protein nanotech computer! This chimes in with the suggestion by David Chalmers that consciousness may be a fundamental property of nature existing outside the known laws of physics.

If computers will never be able to master mathematics, it would follow that they will not be able to master all of science. Another reason for that conclusion was given by the brilliant chemist and philosopher Michael Polanyi, who argued convincingly that science involves what he called "personal knowledge." In his words, scientists "know more than they can tell" – they employ tacit skills that go beyond the empirical – which implies that doing science could never be fully mastered even by a supercomputer, no matter how sophisticated its programming and internal structure.[42]

This is precisely the result of McGilchrist's research into the asymmetry between the two hemispheres of the human brain: "So far from being the impersonal robotic business that the myth of the scientific method would imply, the actual pursuit of science in the pursuit of truth is profoundly human. And at its core lies a human attribute to which no robot or computer could make any claim."[43] That attribute is the conscious exercise of faith, the capacity to trust. We have already seen that faith in God specifically was the driving force behind the rise of modern science under Newton and others. More generally, faith, in the rational intelligibility of nature, for instance, is essential in the pursuit of science, as Nobel laureate Max Planck put it: "Anybody who has been seriously engaged in scientific work of any kind realizes that over the entrance to the gates of the temple of science are written the words: *Ye must have faith*. It is a quality which the scientists cannot dispense with."[44]

More evidence to support this view is put forward in an article for *Evolution News* by software architect Brendan Dixon: "Computers do not play games like humans play games. Computers do not create like humans create. Computers, at their most fundamental level, do not even solve computational problems like humans solve computational problems." Dixon concluded: "The real problem with AI, then, is . . . the likelihood of our blindly depending on machines, lulled to trust them by bad metaphors. The danger is that computers will fail us, and possibly do so in very bad ways."[45]

Robert Epstein, a former editor of *Psychology Today*, also rejects the assumption that the brain works like a computer. He says:

> Forgive me for this introduction to computing, but I need to be clear: computers really do operate on *symbolic representations* of the world. They really *store* and *retrieve*. They really *process*. They really have physical *memories*. They really are guided in everything they do, without exception, by *algorithms*.
>
> Humans, on the other hand, do not – never did, never will. Given this reality, why do so many scientists talk about our mental life as if we were computers?[46]

Putting this another way, Epstein continues:

> The information processing (IP) metaphor of human intelligence now dominates human thinking, both on the street and in the sciences. . . .
>
> But the IP metaphor is, after all, just another metaphor – a story we tell to make sense of something we don't actually understand. And like all the metaphors that preceded it, it will certainly be cast aside at some point – either replaced by another metaphor or, in the end, replaced by actual knowledge. . . .
>
> The faulty logic of the IP metaphor is easy enough to state. It is based on a faulty syllogism – one with two reasonable premises and a faulty conclusion.

Reasonable premise #1: all computers are capable of behaving intelligently. *Reasonable premise #2:* all computers are information processors. *Faulty conclusion:* all entities that are capable of behaving intelligently are information processors.[47]

One delightful argument that AGI is in principle impossible has been advanced by philosopher Robert Hanna, who first makes the obvious point that if strong AI is true, then some robot must be able to do anything that any ordinary rational human-minded animal can do. He then points out the equally obvious fact that any ordinary rational human-minded animal can immediately tell its left side from its right side. Using an intriguing thought experiment involving both humans and robots responding to their reflections in a wall-sized mirror, he argues that no robot, however sophisticated it is, can immediately tell its left side from its right side. Hence strong or general AI is impossible.[48]

The words of Neil Postman are as valid today as when they were written in 1993: "Although the quest for a machine that duplicates mind has ancient roots, and although digital logic circuitry has given that quest a scientific structure, artificial intelligence does not and cannot lead to a meaning-making, understanding, and feeling creature, which is what a human being is."[49] After all, a neural network can pick out a cat on a YouTube video – indeed, this was a major breakthrough in the development of AI – but the network has no concept of what a cat is. We need once more to remind ourselves that neural networks are not conscious entities. Research professor of cognitive science and AI expert Margaret Boden, of the University of Sussex, writes:

> Computers don't have goals of their own. The fact that a computer is following any goals at all can always be explained with reference to the goals of some *human* agent. (That's why responsibility for the actions of AI systems lies with their users, manufacturers and/or retailers – not with the systems themselves.) Besides this, an AI program's "goals," "priorities" and "values" don't matter *to the system*. When DeepMind's AlphaGo beat the world champion Lee Sedol in 2016, it felt no satisfaction, still less exultation. And when the then-reigning chess program Stockfish 8 was trounced by AlphaZero a year later (even though AlphaZero had been given no data or advice about how humans play[50]), it wasn't beset by disappointment or humiliation. Garry Kasparov, by contrast, was devastated when he was beaten at chess by IBM's Deep Blue in 1997. . . .

Moreover, it makes no sense to imagine that future AI might have needs. They don't *need* sociality or respect in order to work well. A program either works, or it doesn't. For needs are intrinsic to, and their satisfaction is necessary for, autonomously existing systems – that is, living organisms. They can't sensibly be ascribed to artefacts.[51]

The hype in this area is intensified by the use of anthropomorphic language – the use of terms like "neural network' "deep learning," and "machine learning" seem to imply the presence of humanlike intelligence, even though these terms actually refer to statistical methods used to extract probable patterns from huge datasets. The language stream flows in two directions: words that treat computers as human – computers can get "viruses"; and words that treat humans as computers – humans can be "programmed" or "deprogrammed." The net effect, whether deliberate or not, is to abolish the distinction between humans and machines. This is parallel to the often deliberate attempt to abolish all distinctions between humans and other species.

Whatever language we use, we must be constantly aware of a reductionist creep that starts by saying humans have some similarities to machines and ends by saying humans are nothing but machines. The next step is to say, as some already do, that certain machines are so humanlike that they should be protected by human rights legislation.

In his book *Non-Computable You: What You Do That Artificial Intelligence Never Will*, Robert J. Marks, a pioneer of computational intelligence and founding editor in chief of *IEEE Transactions on Neural Networks*, one of the most prestigious academic journals in AI, makes a well-argued case that algorithmic computation cannot (ever) account for or generate qualia, awareness, semantic meaning, intuitive insight, free will, human emotions, or many other things that we associate with human consciousness. It is one thing to describe, simulate, or impersonate; it is entirely another to reproduce.[52]

This negates Harari's conviction cited earlier that humans are nothing but a bundle of algorithms. To put this another way, in his paper "Demystifying Artificial Intelligence," computer expert Gheorghe Tecuci of George Mason University points out that AI is syntactic and therefore differs in a fundamental way from human intelligence, which is semantic: "An AI program can behave intelligently, but as a trained animal, does not have a 'semantic understanding' of the commands received."[53]

REIMAGINING EVOLUTION

Nevertheless, Harari's optimism knows no bounds. In his bestseller *Sapiens* he writes: "For close to 4 billion years, every single organism on the planet evolved subject to natural selection. Not even one was designed by an intelligent creator. . . . The biologists are right about the past, but the proponents of intelligent design might, ironically, be right about the future."[54]

But could it be that the exact opposite is the case – that certain biologists are wrong about the past, thinking that life came about by mindless, unguided processes?[55] Might not the fact that life depends on information-bearing macromolecules fit much better with the idea that it was designed by a creative intelligence? Is it also possible that the artificial intelligent design proponents might just be wrong about the future – in thinking that the human mind can create artificial life?

In any case, we should note that the first part of Harari's statement ignores the self-evident fact that evolution did not produce life in the first place. Biological evolution, whatever it does, can only get going when life is already present! You cannot explain the existence of something on the basis of one of its consequences. The fact, now widely acknowledged, is that no one has any real idea how life originated, so, to say the least, Harari is jumping the gun. Nevertheless, in a remarkable display of unjustified hubris, he says: "Now humankind is poised to replace natural selection with intelligent design, and to extend life from the organic realm into the inorganic."[56] He suggests that there will be three main ways of doing this: biological engineering, cyborg engineering,[57] and the engineering of inorganic beings.[58]

In their book *Evolving Ourselves: Redesigning the Future of Humanity – One Gene at a Time*, Juan Enriquez and Steve Gullans imagine such a world in which evolution depends no longer on natural processes but rather on human choices, through what they call unnatural selection and nonrandom mutation.[59] Now, it is clear that intelligent design is already making some progress in the direction of upgrading humanity. For instance, Harari told the *Guardian*: "In the 21st century medicine is moving onwards and trying to surpass the norm, to help people live longer, to have stronger memories, to have better control of their emotions. But upgrading like that is not an egalitarian project, it's an elitist project. No matter what norm you reach, there is always another upgrade which is possible."[60]

He is right about the elitism. Life-enhancing medical upgrades tend to be expensive. For example, cochlear implants that wire directly into the auditory nerves can transform hearing at the cost of $50,000 each. Brain-computer interfaces (BCIs) are being developed to help disabled people move incapacitated limbs or even their attached robotic prosthetics. They are likely to be very expensive, as will be more speculative technology that may eventually be able to establish a direct connection between our brains and the internet.

Surgical enhancement for the wealthy has already become a very big business, and there are now companies that explicitly advertise their expertise in human upgrades. Among nonsurgical options, performance-enhancing drugs – like anabolic steroids to build up muscles,[61] stimulants to increase alertness, and human growth hormones to increase strength and endurance – are finding increasingly widespread use, particularly in the sports arena, in spite of potential side effects and the ethical problems surrounding them.

Surgical options are also being developed. For instance, technology has already been developed that enables paralyzed people to type using only their minds. Elon Musk has formed the company Neuralink with the goal of fusing the human brain with AI. AI is part of the knowledge industry, and it is natural to ask the question whether AI could eventually provide us with a new way of knowing and understanding reality.

Looking back over the relatively few developments mentioned here, we see, on the one hand, that much of what has already been done is of considerable positive value, particularly developments such as thought-controlled bionic limbs. On the other hand, some research, such as that into modifying the human germline, is ethically questionable.

Such progress has the effect of making the advent of AGI more plausible in the eyes of many people. This development, if ever it occurs, would have huge implications, so it is important to think about it even if the contours are unclear. One good reason for this is the fact that some aspects of what AGI might do – like the universal surveillance developments mentioned in chapter 8 – are already spreading throughout the world today.

Surveillance of this intensity gives its controllers immense power; not surprisingly, there is a great deal of literature that addresses the question of eventual world domination in the hands of those who develop AGI, or even in the hands of an AGI system itself. But we should not let futuristic scenarios blind us to the fact that AI has already gone far enough to make possible major aspects of world domination within a relatively short time. We do not have to wait for full AGI for that to happen.

SCENARIOS OF WORLD DOMINATION BY AGI

We should step back for a moment to think about possible AGI scenarios in general, before focusing on the world-domination variety. Since AI aims not only to replicate but also to improve significantly on human capabilities, it is not surprising that the future scenarios envisaged for it are typical human scenarios writ large. Humans love stories – about love and hate, good and evil, about adventure and prowess, battles and wars, disasters and catastrophes, about overcoming impossible odds. AGI scenarios reflect all of these, and historically the possibilities have been mapped out in sci-fi books and films.

Logically, the possible storylines are relatively few: AGI is either under human control and works with them, or it is not. It either furthers human well-being or it sees humans as impediments to its goals and enslaves or eliminates them. All else tends to be variations on the theme, and since humans love stories of disasters, wars, and heroism, it is inevitable that dystopian AGI predominates. Here are some well-known examples:

1. *The Matrix* (1999). Humanity is trapped in a simulated reality and acts as an energy source for evil AI controllers. Hacker hero Neo searches for the truth, joins the rebels, and embarks on a spiritual quest to save humanity from the mass delusion of the matrix.
2. *Avengers: Age of Ultron* (2015). A clever artificial intelligence decides that humanity is the real threat to Earth and must be eradicated to save the planet. The earthling heroes battle it out with the evil AI.
3. *Star Trek: The Motion Picture* (1979). The original TV crew battle the interstellar fog V'Ger, which is burning a path of destruction across the universe as it heads straight for Earth. The gas cloud, and the vast spaceship deep inside it, turn out to be an AI.
4. *The Terminator* (1984). AI becomes more advanced until it is able to reason, at which point it decides that humans are unnecessary. The object of this film and its sequels is to show the world just how bad things might get in a worst-case AI scenario.
5. *2001: A Space Odyssey* (1968). This famous Stanley Kubrick film tells the story of the human race as its evolution is guided by an alien force. While investigating this mystery on a flight to Jupiter, the ship's crew gets double-crossed by its sentient computer, Hal. When "infallible" Hal makes an odd error, the astronauts decide to shut him down,

but Hal catches wind of the plan and kills most of the crew. The lone surviving astronaut manages to shut Hal down as the computer pleads for mercy.[62]

Max Tegmark imagines how world domination by artificial superintelligence (ASI) might occur in three steps: first make human-level AGI, then use it to create superintelligence, and finally unleash the superintelligence to take over the world.[63] In the prelude to his book *Life 3.0*, Tegmark imagines a highly secretive AI project run by what he calls the Omega Team, which develops a powerful AI system called Prometheus. This system is initially used to make money by using Amazon Mechanical Turk (MTurk), a crowd-sourcing internet marketplace enabling individuals and businesses to find people to take tasks that computers are currently unable to do. It is one of the sites of Amazon Web Services. Employers are able to post jobs, known as "Human Intelligence Tasks." Workers, known as Turkers, can then browse among existing jobs and complete them in exchange for a monetary payment set by the employer.

Tegmark has chosen the name Prometheus for his ASI system rather aptly. Prometheus was the Titan of Greek mythology who, as the Greek poet Hesiod tells us, was thought to have created humans from clay and to have defied the gods by stealing fire that he then gave to the humans to drive forward their development. For his transgression, he was punished by Zeus by being chained to a rock, and an eagle was sent to eat his liver each day. The liver regrew overnight, and the process was repeated. He was often thought of as an exemplar of the possibility of tragic results that could emanate from attempts to improve the human condition. Interestingly, Mary Shelley gave the subtitle *The Modern Prometheus* to her novel *Frankenstein*.

Tegmark's Prometheus surreptitiously replaces the Turkers with its own much faster AI system and, in consequence, begins to harvest vast revenues. The Omegas then train Prometheus to make films, and the revenues increase exponentially. This wealth is then used to take over the world's businesses and media outlets and to influence governments. You can imagine the rest for yourself.

Prometheus eventually ends up in absolute control of the planet[64] so that, as Tegmark says, "for the first time ever, our planet was run by a single power, amplified by an intelligence so vast that it could potentially enable life to flourish for billions of years on Earth and throughout the cosmos – but what specifically was their plan?"[65]

The idea is that, in this way, the world would become the perfect totalitarian state – whatever "perfect" means in that context. Not only can Prometheus record all electronic communications – a capacity that many governments have had for years – it can understand all communications and so be fully aware of what people around the world are thinking and doing. Tegmark continues:

> With the excuse of fighting crime and terrorism and rescuing people suffering medical emergencies, everybody could be required to wear a "security bracelet" that combined the functionality of an Apple Watch with continuous uploading of position, health status and conversations overheard. Unauthorized attempts to remove or disable it would cause it to inject a lethal toxin into the forearm.[66]

Now, it is clear that Tegmark intends this as an imaginative introductory scenario. It is imaginative in more ways than one. For instance, Prometheus, being a machine, does not *understand* all communication, nor is it *aware* of what people around the world are thinking and doing for the simple reason that machines have no mind with which to understand or be aware.

Wisely, Tegmark does not say that this is what he personally thinks the future will definitely be like but rather asks his readers whether they think such a future is possible, and, if so, would they want it that way. In his view, the future is still ours to write. But there are three disturbing things about Prometheus that immediately come to mind. Firstly, at least one major part of something very similar is already being implemented – the use of AI-based surveillance systems for widespread social control in China, which we described in chapter 8. Secondly, something Prometheus-like features in many sci-fi dystopias. One need think only of such popular movie and television franchises as *The Matrix*, *Blade Runner*, or *Doctor Who*.

Tegmark also investigates a wide variety of AGI scenarios that have been suggested by different leading figures in the AGI scene. Some assume that humans will be able to control the superintelligence and possibly use it to eliminate opposition. Another scenario takes the opposite view and imagines that Prometheus breaks out and takes control of humanity and possibly eliminates them. Will it be utopia, dystopia, or something in between?

The question, then, is this: How can we ensure that such a superintelligence will safeguard human interests and not threaten human existence? Putting this another way, we might ask: What worldview will a superintelligence or an AGI/ASI have? This is an important question, since that worldview will have to be embedded by the human constructors and software programmers. What might that worldview be and on what values will it be based?

To discuss this comprehensively is beyond our scope here, and the reader is recommended to consult AI scientist David Bell's book *Superintelligence and World-views*.[67] But long before we get to superintelligence or AGI, if ever we do, it is worth noting the all-too-human irony of seeming to want as much choice as possible yet abdicating our choice and delegating it to machines that are usually programmed by others and therefore embody their decisions and not ours. That means that technology enables a small group of experts to exert control over vast numbers of people.

Tegmark describes twelve possible scenarios for humanity's future that represent summaries of inputs from many different thinkers.[68] Some of them are optimistic, and others are pessimistic. In some of them, the AGI seems to possess the characteristics of a benevolent god; in others, those of the devil – with all shades in between. Notice that half of these scenarios tend towards the utopian, and half towards the dystopian, so that between them they cover a very large spectrum. Which of the two tendencies is the more likely will depend, at least in part, on the status we give to moral evil. Tegmark is prudently careful not to commit himself to what will happen or when it will happen.

Rosalind Picard points out that Tegmark does not actually exhaust the theoretical possibilities.[69] It may be that superintelligence is never created, not because humanity drives itself extinct, but because we develop technology to help people get smarter and able not only to protect each other but also to avoid a grim *1984* scenario.

There is an additional consideration, however. It is easy to imagine that in whatever direction the future develops, progress towards it will be essentially continuous. But in connection with AGI scenarios, that is hardly likely to be the case, as there may come a time in the future, as C. S. Lewis pointed out in his book *The Abolition of Man*, when one generation has the power to alter the nature of all succeeding generations.[70] We now know that this could be done by germline genetic engineering.

If and when that happens, the (inevitably) few controllers in that age will define the nature of the "humans" of the future that they will create. But as Lewis chillingly says of those controllers and their products: "Nor are their subjects necessarily unhappy men. They are not men at all: they are artefacts. Man's final conquest has proved to be the abolition of Man."[71]

Such a dystopic scenario can be thought of as human beings trying to play the role of *homo deus*, where *deus* is a malevolent god. Philosopher J. Budziszewski at the University of Texas writes:

Genesis, I think, is the crux of it. To abolish and remake human nature is to play God. The chief objection to playing God is that someone else is God already. If He created human nature, if He intended it, if it is not the result of a blind fortuity that did not have us in mind – then we have no business exchanging it for another. It would be good to remember that Genesis contains not only the story of creation but the story of Babel, of the presumption of men who thought they could build a tower "to heaven."[72]

Budziszewski continues in a manner reminiscent of C. S. Lewis:

You say you want man to be to himself what God has been to man. But what God has been to man is man's absolute superior, and man cannot be his own superior. A thing can be equal to itself, but it cannot be greater than itself. So [what you really mean is] you want some men to be to other men what God has been to man. You want some men to be the absolute superiors of *others*. I assume that you want to be in the former group and not in the latter. . . . You say you want to change the human design. But in that case there must be two groups: Those who caused the change, and those who result from it. And the former hold all the cards.[73]

Human nature being what it is, one of the already present dangers is that people weaponize AI to amplify the evil things they do and achieve the goal of consolidating their power over others. They readily forget we are ontologically superior to the things we have made as distinct from the people made in our image that we beget. We are, after all, made in the image of God – a concept of central importance in the debate about AI.

There is no avoiding the topic of God when we think of future developments in AI. Two of Tegmark's AGI scenarios even have the word "God" in their titles. Tegmark observes that many people like the "Protector God" scenario because of its similarity to that advanced by the world's major monotheistic religions.[74] That is not surprising, since members of the Abrahamic religions already believe in a superintelligent being – God. It therefore makes sense to turn to the biblical underpinning of faith in God to see what it has to contribute. The obvious place to begin is the book of Genesis.

QUESTIONS

1. "Whoever becomes the leader in this sphere [AI] will become the ruler of the world," said Vladimir Putin. Do you agree? Does this explain the race to achieve AGI?
2. Will world control depend on data control? Give reasons for your answer.
3. Do you think robots will have taken over by the end of the century?
4. Minds are just brains. Do you agree or disagree? Why?
5. Why is matter not the prime reality?
6. Describe the Chinese room experiment in your own words. Do you find it convincing?
7. According to McGilchrist, what attributes of mind can no computer imitate?
8. What AGI scenario do you think most likely – if any at all? Do you find the Prometheus project convincing?
9. Why do you think Tegmark mentions God?

PART 4

BEING HUMAN

CHAPTER 12

THE GENESIS FILES

What Is a Human Being?

Before we think of stepping onto an escalator that leads to the technological abolition of human beings that C. S. Lewis feared, it might be wise to revisit an account that gives them their true value and significance – the biblical account. I shall do this from an unashamedly theistic, indeed, Christian, perspective.

My reasons for so doing are as follows. Firstly, much of the literature on our subject is written from an equally unashamed atheistic perspective, and I think that the public deserve to hear that there actually is another point of view and to be exposed to it so that they can make up their own minds. For not all thought leaders in the field of AI are atheists. For instance, Donald Knuth and Rosalind Picard are Christians. Nor should we forget that mathematician Charles Babbage, the "father of computing," and a prolific inventor, was also a Christian believer. In his famous *Ninth Bridgewater Treatise*, he wrote: "The object of these pages . . . is to show that the power and knowledge of the great Creator of matter and of mind are unlimited."[1]

Secondly, there is evidence that fundamental aspects of the biblical worldview lie at the heart of the professed liberal morality that often claims to have shrugged off that worldview in favor of atheism.[2] It will at once be protested that my views are outdated and that I am wasting my time, since atheism is deeply entrenched in the minds of many AI thought leaders and tends to be the dominant worldview in many educational institutions, particularly in the West. In scant disregard of the evidence to the contrary, Harari regards monotheism as brainwashing and Jesus Christ as fake news.[3] I am also very aware that it is a widely held view that science has consigned the biblical worldview to the scrap heap of history. I hold, as a scientist, that science has done no such thing. In order to understand this, let me first briefly sketch how atheism has come to dominate the academy. For many centuries, those people who tried to understand the world in which they lived believed that there was such a thing as truth. According to the thirteenth-century philosopher Roger Bacon, called Doctor Mirabilis and regarded as a pioneer of modern science, truth was to be found in God's two books: the book of God's world, investigated by the natural sciences, and the book of God's Word, the Bible. Such people founded the first universities where the study of both books was undertaken. That study was a rational study that engaged human intelligence. The relative emphasis on these sources of information and knowledge began to shift from religious dogma to reason as the main source of authority in the quest to understand the world.

THE RENAISSANCE (FIFTEENTH AND SIXTEENTH CENTURIES)

The transition from the Middle Ages to modernity was characterized by an effort to revive and surpass the ideas and achievements of classical antiquity. The intellectual basis of the Renaissance was its version of humanism, derived from the Roman concept of *humanitas* and the rediscovery of the classical Greek philosophical notion that "man is the measure of all things," according to Protagoras. The archetypal Renaissance men were Leonardo da Vinci and Michelangelo.

Humanism in its original form was not antithetical to Christianity, as it tends to be today. Aspects of it were involved in attempts to reform the church through people like Erasmus (1466–1536), Luther (1483–1546), and John Calvin (1509–1564). The Reformation insistence that individuals are capable of coming directly to the book of God's Word and personally reasoning about it undermined the authority of the Roman Catholic church. The invention of the printing press led to the rapid dissemination of ideas and loss of control of the information flow on the part of central authorities, which in turn inevitably resulted in the subjection of all forms of authority to human reason.

Science also advanced into the modern era through Nicolaus Copernicus (1473–1543), Tycho Brahe (1546–1601), Johannes Kepler (1571–1630), Galileo Galilei (1564–1642), and Francis Bacon (1561–1626). The telescope shifted the center of gravity from Earth and humans to Earth as a lonely wanderer lost in the vastness of the heavens. Neal Postman says that Francis Bacon was "the first man of the technocratic age."[4] Bacon thought that the objective of human life was happiness – not with God in heaven but here on earth. This happiness would be brought about by technology. This is now Harari's second agenda item for the twenty-first century.

Kepler believed in separating theology and science. In his *New Astronomy* he wrote: "Now as regards the opinions of the saints on these matters of nature, I answer in one word, that in theology the weight of authority, but in philosophy the weight of reason is valid."[5] A very unfortunate and unnecessary distinction, since reason is essential to a credible theology.

Isaac Newton played a key role in shifting the emphasis to reason. Although he believed in (biblical) revelation and spent a great deal of time thinking about it, his scientific explanations were not based either on it or on appeals to ecclesiastical authority but rather on examination of the phenomena and formulation of general laws. For Newton the real world consists of moving bodies and is objectively independent of observers. Its laws originated with God. Indeed, his quest to find the laws of nature was essentially a religious quest.

Yet despite Newton's underlying faith in God, the very success of his reason-based science with its highly mechanistic universe running like a clock according to fixed laws ironically paved the way for deism, the idea that God was distant, then increasingly irrelevant, and finally unnecessary, so that he could safely and profitably be dispensed with. That leads us into the time of the so-called Enlightenment of the eighteenth century.

THE ENLIGHTENMENT

In 1784 the German philosopher Immanuel Kant (1724–1804) wrote an essay entitled *What Is Enlightenment*: "Enlightenment is man's release from his self-incurred tutelage. Tutelage is man's inability to make use of his understanding without direction from another. Self-incurred is this tutelage when its cause lies not in lack of reason but in lack of resolution and courage to use it without direction from another. *Sapere aude!* [Dare to know!]. 'Have courage to use your own reason!' – that is the motto of enlightenment."[6]

At its heart is the idea that the scientific method has displaced outdated authoritarian superstition and brought the true nature of things to light. It was the dawning of a new kind of explanation of things – no longer dogmatic, religious, and unscientific but now rational and true. Explanations operated only within an accepted framework that did not itself need explanation.

The conviction grew that the world was autonomous and that the mathematical laws that governed it did not emanate from a divine lawgiver but are, as Montesquieu said, "the necessary relations which spring from the nature of things."[7] God was not necessary and eventually all but disappeared, to be replaced by Nature, the total of all observable phenomena.

Scientists become "mediating priests" who could harness this new world and explain it to us using reason alone. Reason and conscience – both provided by Nature – were enough without God and revelation. Rights replaced duties. The narrative of the Bible was replaced by the narrative of technological progress. Science was going to change the world.

Kant continued: "For this enlightenment, however, nothing is required but freedom, and indeed the most harmless among all the things to which this term can properly be applied. It is the freedom to make public use of one's reason at every point. But I hear on all sides, 'Do not argue!' The officer says: 'Do not argue but drill!' The tax collector: 'Do not argue but pay!' The cleric: 'Do not argue but believe!' Only one prince in the world says, 'Argue as much as you will, and about what you will, but obey!' Everywhere there is restriction on freedom."[8] Human rationality became uncontested king.

Clear evidence of this profound shift was seen in the changed criteria for university entrance. No longer was it conditional upon acceptance of the Christian worldview, but rather that of the Enlightenment. It shifted from sacred to secular. World history and philosophy took center stage, whereas biblical history was banished to "religious instruction." Many of the questions, however, remained exactly the same as they had been in the time of the Greeks: How can we know something? What does it mean to be a human being? What is the good life? Kant made the distinction between the "thing in itself" that human reason could never completely access because its operation was always limited by distortion and filters of various kinds. However, he encouraged the drive to know by cataloging knowledge and getting on with the process of interrogating nature empirically.

This Enlightenment vision, though it inspired much of value, particularly in the natural sciences, for which we may be truly grateful, failed to answer these questions by bringing about the promised era of human happiness. John Gray, an atheist, by the way, makes a profoundly important point in his book *Black Mass*: "The role of the Enlightenment in twentieth-century terror remains a blind spot in western perception. Libraries are stocked with books insisting that mass repression in Stalinist Russia and Maoist China was a by-product of traditions of despotism. The implication is that . . . the communist ideology is innocent of any role in the crimes these regimes committed."[9]

Gray went on to say, "The communist regimes were established in pursuit of a utopian ideal whose origins lie in the heart of the Enlightenment. . . . At its worst, twentieth-century terror was used with the aim of transforming human life. The peculiar quality of twentieth-century terror is not its scale. . . . It is that its goal was to perfect human life."[10]

A few pages later, Gray wrote, "Terror of the kind practised by Lenin cannot be explained by Russian traditions, or by the conditions that prevailed at the time the Bolshevik regime came to power."[11]

In connection with AI, we should notice Gray's reference to the attempt to transform or remake life. It constitutes an important warning in the age of AI. In harnessing reason, science, and advanced technology for the purpose of terror and war, Enlightenment thinking ushered in the horrors of the twentieth century, and the same thinking has led to an unprecedented escalation of violence in the twenty-first century in Europe. As I write this paragraph, Russia is mercilessly and without provocation waging war against Ukraine and relentlessly laying it waste with the most sophisticated weapons imaginable.

Russian author Aleksandr Solzhenitsyn had a profound understanding of the underlying cause:

> If I were asked today to formulate as concisely as possible the main cause of the ruinous Revolution that swallowed up some sixty million of our people, I could not put it more accurately than to say: Men have forgotten God; that's why all this has happened. . . . If I were called upon to identify the principal trait of the entire twentieth century, here too, I would be unable to find anything more precise and pithy than to repeat once again: Men have forgotten God. . . . To the ill-considered hopes of the last two centuries, which have reduced us to insignificance and brought us to the brink of nuclear and non-nuclear death, we can propose only a determined quest for the warm hand of God, which we have so rashly and self-confidently spurned. Only in this way can our eyes be opened to the errors of this unfortunate twentieth century and our bands be directed to setting them right. There is nothing else to cling to in the landslide: the combined vision of all the thinkers of the Enlightenment amounts to nothing.[12]

The fact that this history is tragically repeating itself in the twenty-first century ought to be enough to make us face the fact that atheism may be as intellectually bankrupt as it has proved to be morally. That brings me back to my conviction that science and the Christian worldview make excellent rational companions, whereas science and the atheistic worldview do not.

I do not think that this is so hard to deduce from the fact that science proceeds on the basis of the *a priori* assumption that the universe is, at least to a certain extent, accessible to the human mind. No science can be done without the scientist believing this, so it is important to ask for grounds for this belief. The fundamental problem with atheism is that it has no answer to this question, since it posits a mindless, unguided origin of the universe's life and consciousness.

It may surprise many readers to learn that Charles Darwin saw the problem. He wrote: "With me the horrid doubt always arises whether the convictions of man's mind, which has been developed from the mind of the lower animals, are of any value or at all trustworthy."[13] Similarly, John Polkinghorne said that the reduction of mental events to physics and chemistry destroys meaning: "Thought is replaced by electrochemical neural events. Two such events cannot confront each other in rational discourse. They are neither right nor wrong. They simply happen. . . . The world of rational discourse dissolves into the absurd chatter of firing synapses. Quite frankly that cannot be right and none of us believes it to be so."[14]

Polkinghorne was a Christian, but some well-known atheists also acknowledge this difficulty. John Gray writes: "Modern humanism is the faith that through science humankind can know the truth – and so be free. But if Darwin's theory of natural selection is true this is impossible. The human mind serves evolutionary success, not truth."[15] Another leading atheist philosopher, Thomas Nagel, thinks in the same way. In his book *Mind and Cosmos*, with the provocative subtitle *Why the Materialist Neo-Darwinian Conception of Nature Is Almost Certainly False*, he says: "If the mental is not itself merely physical, it cannot be fully explained by physical science. . . . Evolutionary naturalism implies that we should not take any of our convictions seriously, including the scientific world picture on which evolutionary naturalism depends."[16] That is, naturalism, and therefore atheism, undermine the foundations of the very rationality needed to construct or understand or believe in any kind of argument whatsoever, let alone a scientific one. In short, it leads to the abolition of reason – a kind of "abolition of man," since reason is an essential part of what it means to be human. Instead of elevating, it demeans humanity. To my mind it is this argument that demolishes Harari's contention that human beings are simply a vast collection of organically embedded algorithms.

It is for all of these reasons that I reject atheism, and not because I believe

Christianity to be true. I reject it because I am a mathematician with a deep and lifelong interest in science and rational thought. How could I espouse a worldview that discredits the very rationality I need to do mathematics? By contrast, the biblical worldview that traces the origin of human rationality to the fact that we are created in the image of a rational God makes real sense as an explanation of why we can do science. Science and God mix very well. It is science and atheism that do not mix.[17]

These are some of the reasons why it is neither foolish nor obscurantist to revisit the source that has nourished civilization for millennia, although many people dismiss it in anti-intellectual fashion without even first listening to what it has to say. I have spent a great deal of my life listening carefully to those who have rejected it, and I would simply ask those among my readers who hold that view that they set aside their presuppositions and at least listen to what I have to say about it. That source is, of course, the Bible. And, incidentally, I refer to it not simply because I am a Christian but because I am passionate about science and technology.

Of course, having a positive view of technology does not mean that one is not committed to ethical principles as to its use. As well as the Asilomar principles discussed in chapter 3, a further set of biblical moral principles was formulated in 2019 by a group of sixty leading Christian thinkers, some of them active in AI research.[18] Here are a few sample articles from this manifesto:

Article 2. AI as Technology

We affirm that the development of AI is a demonstration of the unique creative abilities of human beings. When AI is employed in accordance with God's moral will, it is an example of man's obedience to the divine command to steward creation and to honor Him. We believe in innovation for the glory of God, the sake of human flourishing, and the love of neighbor. While we acknowledge the reality of the Fall and its consequences on human nature and human innovation, technology can be used in society to uphold human dignity. As a part of our God-given creative nature, human beings should develop and harness technology in ways that lead to greater flourishing and the alleviation of human suffering.

We deny that the use of AI is morally neutral. It is not worthy of man's hope, worship, or love. Since the Lord Jesus alone can atone for sin and reconcile humanity to its Creator, technology such as AI cannot fulfil humanity's ultimate needs. We further deny the goodness and benefit of any application of AI that devalues or degrades the dignity and worth of another human being.

Article 9. Security

We affirm that AI has legitimate applications in policing, intelligence, surveillance, investigation, and other uses supporting the government's responsibility to respect human rights, to protect and preserve human life, and to pursue justice in a flourishing society.

We deny that AI should be employed for safety and security applications in ways that seek to dehumanize, depersonalize, or harm our fellow human beings. We condemn the use of AI to suppress free expression or other basic human rights granted by God to all human beings.

Article 12. The Future of AI

We affirm that AI will continue to be developed in ways that we cannot currently imagine or understand, including AI that will far surpass many human abilities. God alone has the power to create life, and no future advancements in AI will usurp Him as the Creator of life. The church has a unique role in proclaiming human dignity for all and calling for the humane use of AI in all aspects of society.

We deny that AI will make us more or less human, or that AI will ever obtain a coequal level of worth, dignity, or value to image-bearers. Future advancements in AI will not ultimately fulfill our longings for a perfect world. While we are not able to comprehend or know the future, we do not fear what is to come because we know that God is omniscient and that nothing we may create will be able to thwart His redemptive plan for creation or to supplant humanity as His image-bearers.[19]

We turn now to the biblical account, where we learn that humans are God's image-bearers.

THE BIBLICAL ACCOUNT

The book of Genesis begins the biblical metanarrative that among all other stories told makes by far the most sense to me of God, the universe, and human life. The very first words in Genesis played a key role in the rise of modern science in the time of Galileo, Kepler, and Newton: "In the beginning, God created the heavens and the earth." This tells us that God is primary, the universe derivative. Matter is not the only reality; it is not even the prime reality. The prime reality is God, who is spirit. This is aptly captured by Keith Ward, cited earlier: "There is at least one mind that is prior to all matter, that is not in time and therefore is not capable of being brought into being by anything. It is the one truly self-existent reality, and the cause of all physical things."[20]

The opening words of Genesis are echoed in another majestic statement with which John's gospel begins: "In the beginning was the Word, and the Word was with God, and the Word was God. He was in the beginning with God. All things were made through him."[21] This statement will be familiar to Christians, but it may not be familiar to everyone, and, in any case, many Christians may not have grasped its profound implications.

We are familiar with words as a vehicle of self-expression and intelligible communication. The Stoic philosophers among the ancient Greeks, who predated the writer John, used the term *Word* (*Logos* in Greek) to express the rational principle that they regarded as being behind the natural order. John elevates the term even higher to denote God himself as the rational Creator who is responsible for the existence of the universe and all that it contains.

This is a profound assertion about existence. "In the beginning was the Word" – that is, the Word already was. The Word exists eternally. The Word did not come to be. Contrast that with Ray Kurzweil's answer to the question "Does God exist?" "Not yet," he said, implying, I imagine, that one day humans might create him.[22]

John then goes on to say: "All things were made [literally *came to be*] through him." That is, the universe is not eternal. It came to exist – by means of the eternal creative Word. Indeed, says John, there is nothing that came to be that did not come to be through the Word. The universe did not produce intelligence; it was the intelligence of God the Word that produced the universe. This is a complete reversal of the dominant naturalistic view (in academia above all) that mass/energy (or nothing) is primary and mind is derivative. John claims that mind is primary and the universe with its mass/energy is derivative.

These statements about the Word resonate with the account in the first chapter of Genesis, where creation is described in six stages or days, each of which begins with the phrase "And God said" – so that creation is depicted as a series of speech acts by an intelligent God. There is an irony here in that those who are seeking to create a superintelligence do not seem to realize that there is good evidence that a superintelligence, *the* Superintelligence, already exists: God the Creator and Sustainer of the heavens and the earth.

This universe bears the signature of its superintelligent, supernatural, divine origins in its lawlike behavior, in its rational intelligibility, in information-rich macromolecules such as DNA, and in the informational structure of innumerable intricate physiological mechanisms responsible for, for example, the migration of birds and fish, and in our human capacities for thought and language, feelings and relationships.

Information is now one of the fundamental concepts of physics, although it is not itself physical. The information on this page is carried by the physical media of paper and ink. But the information itself is not physical, a fact that would appear to create insuperable difficulty for a strictly materialistic understanding of the universe. Not only that, but the immateriality of information presents a categorical barrier to the construction of a material machine (computer) that can consciously understand in any meaningful sense.

Max Tegmark obfuscates the problem by asserting that information is "substrate-independent"[23] – meaning that the same message can be carried on different material substrates; for instance, a menu can be written on paper or slate or can appear on a screen. But that being so, information cannot itself be material, since material is substrate dependent, as it is its own substrate. It is, therefore, surely fair to argue that the informational aspects of the universe, life, and consciousness ultimately point to, and are consistent with, the existence of a nonmaterial source for these things – the mind of God.[24]

Here are some of the main implications of the account of creation found in Genesis 1.[25]

1. Creation did not occur all at once but involved a sequence of creation steps or days.
2. The sequence has a start and an end – so the past is not likely to be completely explicable in terms of the present. Creation, in the sense of inauguration, is not the same as caretaking / upholding / causing to exist.
3. Each step in the creation narrative begins with God speaking: "And God said." The universe is not a closed system but an open system built up systematically by a sequence of inputs of the Word at intervals. However long it took, it was clearly the antithesis of a mindless, unguided process.
4. On two days God spoke more than once:

> **Day 3** (Genesis 1:9–13): "And God said, 'Let the waters under the heavens be gathered together into one place, and let the dry land

appear.' And it was so. God called the dry land Earth, and the waters that were gathered together he called Seas. And God saw that it was good.

"And God said, 'Let the earth sprout vegetation, plants yielding seed, and fruit trees bearing fruit in which is their seed, each according to its kind, on the earth.' And it was so. The earth brought forth vegetation, plants yielding seed according to their own kinds, and trees bearing fruit in which is their seed, each according to its kind. And God saw that it was good. And there was evening and there was morning, the third day."

This suggests that you do not, in spite of what naturalism asserts, get from the inorganic to organic without an external input of information and energy from the Creator: "And God said . . ." Compare with this the goal of AGI to get from inorganic silicon to inorganic silicon-based life by *human* intelligent design.

Day 6 (Genesis 1:24–27, 31): "And God said, 'Let the earth bring forth living creatures according to their kinds – livestock and creeping things and beasts of the earth according to their kinds.' And it was so. And God made the beasts of the earth according to their kinds and the livestock according to their kinds, and everything that creeps on the ground according to its kind. And God saw that it was good.

"Then God said, 'Let us make man in our image, after our likeness. And let them have dominion over the fish of the sea and over the birds of the heavens and over the livestock and over all the earth and over every creeping thing that creeps on the earth.'

"So God created man in his own image,
in the image of God he created him;
male and female he created them. . . .

"And God saw everything that he had made, and behold, it was very good. And there was evening and there was morning, the sixth day."

According to this text, then, you do not, in spite of what naturalism asserts, get from animals to humans without an external input of information and energy from God: "And God said . . ." AGI intends to get from human life and intelligence to machine life and intelligence by human technology.

5. The Genesis sequence implies a teleology, a purpose (contrast that with the naturalistic view that denies purpose in biology and often elsewhere). According to Genesis, humans are made in the image of God. The heavens declare God's glory, but they were not made in his image. You cannot define the human person without referring to the intelligent mind of God. That is, there is no purely bottom-up, physicalist, reductionist explanation of what a person is, contrary to what Harari and others imagine.

6. "And God said to them. . . ." That humans are made in the image of God is seen in the fact that God spoke to them, directing them to reproduce and to be stewards over the created world using the capacities he had given them. In AGI, scientists will "speak" in the sense that they will code information into their artifacts, and so any directing of them will depend on the desires and views of those scientists. This speech, however, will not be bi-directional conscious communication.

It is impossible to exaggerate the importance of the Genesis narrative with its answer to the first major question mentioned in this book: Where do we come from? Far from emerging by unguided natural processes from materials in the early earth, as the Miller-Urey experiment (original or extrapolated) purported to establish (see chapter 4), we come from a superintelligent, superhuman, and eternal God who created us intentionally in his image using materials found in the earth.

It is through this lens that we now look at the biblical view of what is involved in human life in the sense of what it is that makes life meaningful, or what it means to be a human person. This I understand to be the subject matter of the second major part of Genesis, which runs from verse 4 of chapter 2 to the end of chapter 4.

This section unpacks the meaning of the image of God that humans bear; we need to think through its implications for things such as AI and artificial life that we might make in our image. In particular, we need to ask about the ways in which AI might undermine the concept of our being made in the image of God, such as regarding human beings as a bunch of algorithms, machines made of meat.

The Genesis text highlights a number of dimensions to human life and activity. A human being is

- made of the dust of the ground (2:7),
- a living organism (2:7),
- in possession of an aesthetic sense (2:8–9),
- endowed with curiosity (2:10–14),
- given work to do (2:5, 15),
- a moral being (2:9, 16–17),
- given the potential of relationship (2:18–25),
- tasked with naming the animals (2:19–20), and
- capable of developing industry and the arts (4:21–22).

A detailed discussion of every part of this list would require much more space than we can devote here.[26] We shall therefore concentrate on what is relevant to our main objective.

HUMAN LIFE HAS A MATERIAL BASE

The LORD God formed the man of dust from the ground and breathed into his nostrils the breath of life, and the man became a living creature.
Genesis 2:7

Genesis readily admits that human beings have a material base. God uses preexisting material to create them. That is, human beings are the result of the mind of God working on preexisting matter that God originally created. One of the aims of AI is to create artificial life using the minds of humans working on preexisting matter.

That is the ground-zero stage, however, and yet even getting there is faced by apparently unsurmountable difficulty, as the work of chemist James Tour shows: "The proposals offered thus far to explain life's origin make no scientific sense. Beyond our planet, all the others that have been probed are lifeless, a result in accord with our chemical expectations. The laws of physics and chemistry's Periodic Table are universal, suggesting that life based upon amino acids, nucleotides, saccharides and lipids is an anomaly. Life should not exist anywhere in our universe. Life should not even exist on the surface of the earth."[27]

Tour is talking about life in its simplest form here. Human life is vastly more complex still, and according to Genesis, it does not come about by self-organization of the already shaped material base, nor from some electrical or chemical shock, nor from some vague "emergence." We are told that the source of life is the breath of God, a divine intervention, apparently distinct from material creation.

Getting some kind of understanding of the relationship of the conscious mind to the body is acknowledged by all to be "the hard problem," as philosopher David Chalmers puts it.[28] The Hebrew word *nephesh* for "breath" used in Genesis is variously translated as "soul," "person," or "self" – none of which concepts make sense for a machine. In the New Testament, Jesus' statement in Matthew 10:28 ("Do not fear those who kill the body but cannot kill the soul. Rather fear him who can destroy both soul and body in hell") shows that the soul is not understood in this text to be the living body, as it cannot be killed by humans. But what is it, more precisely?

Distinguished Christian philosophers Alvin Plantinga, Richard Swinburne, and J. P. Moreland have all argued that we shall make no real progress in understanding until we are prepared to revive a thoroughgoing substance dualism – that is, to recognize that there is a nonphysical aspect to human beings, as Plato argued centuries ago in developing the idea of an immortal soul. We saw earlier that Chalmers, though he is strongly inclined to materialism, nevertheless argues: "Reductive explanation of consciousness is impossible and I even argue for a kind of dualism."[29]

The case for dualism is strengthened when we take on board the biblical teaching that matter is not primary but derivative. It is spirit that is primary. Matter does not generate spirit. It is God, who is spirit, who generates matter. It is clearly one thing to try to build AI systems that seek to mimic aspects of what the human mind can do; it is an entirely different thing even to try to re-create what it feels like to be a human. Consciousness bars the way. No machine can experience qualia.

Although much research has been done on the neural correlates of consciousness – the way in which parts of the brain "light up" when we are doing a particularly conscious activity – no one knows what consciousness really is, although there are many grandiose but meaningless statements made about it, such as that of Francis Crick, to which we referred earlier: "You, your joys and your sorrows, your memories and your ambitions, your sense of personal identity and free will, are in fact no more than the behavior of a vast assembly of nerve cells and their associated molecules."[30] The logical incoherence of this is obvious – if it were so, how would we even begin to know it?

This all leads to the following question: Will humans ever be able, analogously, to breathe the breath of life into any material artifact that they have constructed? In this connection, think of the body of someone who died one second ago. All the material that goes to make up a human being is still there. But the person is no longer alive. Could it be restored in some way? Now, of course, the person may have died from a heart malfunction. Suppose we had a healthy heart available. Would it be enough, say, to quickly replace the heart and then give the body an electric shock? Or suppose we could one day build a human body, chemically, molecule by molecule, so that it lay before us on a table. Could we now get it to live biologically? If not, why not? What exactly is physical life? What is it that God breathed into his unique creation? We simply do not know what the breath of life is in any deep sense.

HUMAN BEINGS POSSESS AN AESTHETIC SENSE

And the LORD God planted a garden in Eden, in the east, and there he put the man whom he had formed. And out of the ground the LORD God made to spring up every tree that is pleasant to the sight and good for food. The tree of life was in the midst of the garden, and the tree of the knowledge of good and evil.
Genesis 2:8–9

Here, Genesis draws our attention to the fact that human beings have an aesthetic sense. This is a marvelous, enriching faculty that plays a central role in music and the arts. Interestingly, it also plays a considerable role in the sciences, particularly in mathematics. The famous Cambridge mathematician G. H. Hardy, in his book *A Mathematician's Apology*, wrote: "Beauty is the first test: there is no permanent place in the world for ugly mathematics.[31]" Visual perception and imagination play an important part in the solving of problems. Also, the perception of and insight into beauty is rarely expressible in words and can even be impeded by conscious verbal reasoning.

Possession of that aesthetic sense, by definition, presupposes consciousness, whose nature is considerably more impenetrable than even physical life, which is difficult enough.

AI has made considerable progress in image "recognition," but this tends to be sophisticated pattern matching and does not give rise in any sense to the kind of awareness that would imply conscious mental recognition or sensitivity to qualia. In any case, what we do know is that aesthetic awareness is associated mainly with the right hemisphere and as such is irreducible to the mechanistic thinking of the left, so that the construction of an aesthetically aware robot remains firmly in the realm of science fiction.

It is important, however, to distinguish between the capacity to recognize beauty that humans have and the capacity to create things that some humans may perceive to possess some aesthetic qualities, such as AI-generated art. We have already seen that AI can manipulate images. A brief Google search will reveal many websites offering AI tools to create art. OpenAI has even created DALL-E 3, an AI system that can create realistic images and art from a description in natural language. Such art is already being marketed. It is important to realize, however, that the system that created it has neither knowledge nor perception of its aesthetic appeal.

HUMANS ARE CURIOUS

A river flowed out of Eden to water the garden, and there it divided and became four rivers. The name of the first is the Pishon. It is the one that flowed around the whole land of Havilah, where there is gold. And the gold of that land is good; bdellium and onyx stone are there.
Genesis 2:10–12

The Genesis text informs us here that there were four rivers that watered the garden environment. These rivers lead to regions where there is mineral wealth – there is gold, and the gold is good. This prompts us to think about human curiosity, following a river to where it leads, the spirit of exploration, and, more generally, research and intellectual activity of all kinds. Humans are insatiably curious, and satisfying that curiosity is a very important part of life – practically, life itself – for many people, among them many of my colleagues at the University of Oxford. Yet once more we need to face the fact that human curiosity is inextricably linked with human consciousness, and so the way seems barred to making an AI system that reflects this. Yet research in AI itself represents human curiosity at an advanced level. The AI systems generated have no idea of what curiosity is – they have no ideas at all because they have no cognitive abilities.

UNCOUPLING INTELLIGENCE FROM CONSCIOUSNESS

One of Harari's contentions is that many people researching AI do not concern themselves with consciousness for the simple reason that their AI systems are allowing them to create *intelligence (simulated) that is not conscious* – and that is sufficient for their purposes. I mentioned this view earlier as being held by Stuart Russell and Peter Norvig: "We are interested in creating programs that behave intelligently. The additional project of making them conscious is not one that we are equipped to take on, nor one whose success we would be able to determine."[32]

To get some idea of what this means, suppose I take a taxi journey from the train station to a meeting in Oxford. The taxi driver is conscious – otherwise the journey is rapidly going to run into serious trouble! If I undertake the journey in an autonomous vehicle, however, the taxi driver is superfluous. All I need to achieve my goal is an AI system that "knows" the route and can guide the car along it, but there is no need for a conscious driver at any stage. Or suppose I need heart surgery. The last surgeon I experienced was a conscious human being; the next, should I need it, may well be a nonconscious robotic AI system – programmed and controlled, of course, by a conscious human.

Genesis tells us that when God created humans in his image, he *linked intelligence and consciousness together in one being*, for he is himself a conscious intelligent being. But God, who is spirit, links consciousness and intelligence together in a nonmaterial being. The fact that God is spirit shows that neither consciousness nor intelligence necessarily depend on a material substrate – another reason to think that humans are unlikely ever to be able to make a conscious material machine.

The fact that many AI researchers do not concern themselves with consciousness could distract us from seeing that consciousness and cognitive activities are possibly the most important indicators that we are made in the image of God. Possessing a machine that can make a wooden table according to a computer program is not in the same league as what is involved in the making of a table by a skilled human carpenter. If it is a stunning piece of craftsmanship, the carpenter can take pride in it and admire it when it adorns a beautiful dining room. A machine is totally blind to all such experiences, and if we start to treat the machine as if it is anything but, then we are demeaning the image of God and insulting his creative work.

HUMANS WERE ASSIGNED WORK

Genesis 1 introduces us to a God who is a worker – creating and organizing a world in which to place as stewards his special creation, human beings, made in his image. The six days of creation activity followed by one of rest were given as the pattern for human work on the earth. Genesis 2:15 informs us that God gave work, in a garden, as part of the human raison d'être before sin entered the world. That is, incidentally, why people who try but do not succeed in finding work often feel deprived and unwanted.

Yet work, though important, is not all of life as it was essentially thought to be in the communist concept of a "worker state." But what is happening now is that, as suggested above, by decoupling intelligence from consciousness, AI would seem to be pushing us in the opposite direction to a situation where work becomes a smaller and smaller part of human activity. Even if Ray Kurzweil is overly optimistic in saying that most human tasks will be taken over by robots by 2030, we need to think about what even a partial AI/robot takeover would look like, in light of the biblical view that work is part of our God-given significance as human beings. AI may easily be seen to threaten the work role that God assigned to humans as part of his image. And that could lead to all kinds of problems, if some of the pundits are to be believed.

Harari writes: "In the twenty-first century we might witness the creation of a massive new unworking class: people devoid of any economic, political or even artistic value, who contribute nothing to the prosperity, power and glory of society. This 'useless class' will not be merely unemployed – it will be unemployable."[33] His warning is worth listening to. Digital assistants, robots, and the like can be regarded as slaves, and the world already experienced a slave economy wherein the very few were served by the many. That very few did little work, and when society collapsed, having forgotten how to work, they had no idea how to rebuild. Some suggest it was for that reason that the Roman Empire eventually collapsed. Harari elsewhere warns: "Perhaps in the 21st century, populist revolts will be staged not against an economic elite that exploits people but against an economic elite that does not need them anymore. This may well be a losing battle. It is much harder to struggle against irrelevance than against exploitation."[34]

Bioethics consultant Wesley J. Smith examines Harari's views in an article entitled "Transhumanist Theorist Calls the AI-Unenhanced 'Useless People.'" Smith comments:

It is tempting to fall prey to such nihilism. But resistance is not futile if we continually remind ourselves that no human life is ever "meaningless" or "worthless." And even if Harari is right that we eventually devolve into a Brave New World caste system, the unenhanced still would retain the most important and powerful human characteristic of all: the ability to love. Love isn't something that transhumanists generally talk much about. I think that's because it can't be generated by taking a pill, editing genes, or melding with a computer algorithm. It isn't transactional. The ability to love comes from being loved and practicing the virtues. No high-tech shortcuts. How boring.

This is transhumanism's fatal flaw. To paraphrase a great saint, "If I blend with an AI computer program and can fathom all mysteries and all knowledge, and if I have enhanced capacities that can move mountains, but do not have love, I am nothing."[35]

The New Testament provides wise advice here in reminding us of the importance of work: "If anyone is not willing to work, let him not eat."[36] It does not, however, say if anyone *does* not work, let him not eat. It is almost as if Paul envisaged the possibility of unemployment. The prospect of future AI-driven techno-unemployment is worse than grim.

In chapter 7, we gave some idea of the projected timescale of job erosion in the survey by the Future of Humanity Institute. It is obvious that there is an urgent need to create many new jobs, and, if they are not to disappear too rapidly, they will have to be jobs that humans can do better than algorithms. This will mean that many, if not most, people will have to keep learning throughout life, a prospect that many will find either daunting or simply impossible.

The techno-optimists hope that even if such people cannot be employed, there will be enough financial surplus from the new technology that they will be fed, housed, and supported throughout life. But who will be paying for the new technological services? Certainly not people who have no work. Where will the financial surplus come from? Such techno-optimism seems extremely naive! The extreme techno-pessimist view is, as Nick Bostrom warns, that humans will not in fact reach the final stage of unemployability, as an ascendant AI may well simply exterminate them.[37]

Yet, according to Scripture, work is an important ingredient in human flourishing. How can those of us who are convinced of that fact communicate and maintain it in the face of a technological invasion of the workplace? Is our stark choice really between learning to work with robots or being replaced by them?[38] Once AI masters the art of horticulture, will there be a job for Adam?

We must not allow the fact that some of the scenarios outlined are extremely grim to cause us to instinctively shrink from them, diverting our attention from what is, on virtually any realistic scenario, huge. Any solution needs to start, not just with retraining those who have already been employed, but with the basic education of children. The World Economic Forum reports:

> The jobs of the future will require students to have strong cognitive skills in mathematics and literacy, as well as soft skills such as problem-solving and creative thinking, to enable them to adapt to a quickly changing environment. However, *millions of children are not gaining these skillsets*, either because they never started school, they have dropped out of school, or their school does not offer a quality education.[39]

The 2023 Sustainable Development Goals report makes for sobering reading on many issues. In his foreword, António Guterres, UN secretary-general said: "Unless we act now, the 2030 Agenda will become an epitaph for a world that might have been."[40]

One example of these goals reads: "Without additional measures, only one in six countries will achieve the universal secondary school completion target by 2030, an estimated 84 million children and young people will still be out of school, and approximately 300 million students will lack the basic numeracy and literacy skills necessary for success in life."[41] The tragedy here is that this represents an immense waste of talent and leads to severely reduced potential to escape long-term poverty. It is a sobering thought that AI may leave millions of children far behind, totally unable to compete with the more privileged.

HUMANS HAVE THE FACULTY OF LANGUAGE

One of the first things we read about God in the biblical narrative is that he speaks. The creation of the universe is portrayed for us as a sequence of speech acts, each commencing with the phrase "And God said . . ." Also, according to Genesis 1, God named certain parts of the cosmos. God speaking the world into existence features in the central New Testament statement about creation: "In the beginning was the Word, and the Word was with God, and the Word was God. . . . All things were made through him."[42] This is a word-based universe of which we see evidence in its cosmological intelligibility in the language of mathematics and its biological intelligibility in the digital DNA – language of molecular biology.

Furthermore, we human beings are made in the image of God as speaking beings who were, among other things, tasked with naming the animals in their environment – the first instance of taxonomy, the fundamental intellectual discipline. The ability to communicate in sophisticated high-level language is one of the most striking features of the human mind. Keith Ward wrote: "There are here three distinctive capacities of the human person, unique among all organisms on Earth, so far as we can tell – the capacity to be sensitive to and appreciative of information received, to be creative in responding to it, and to learn and develop such capacities in relation to other persons in specific historical contexts. Human persons receive information, interpret it, and transmit it in a fully semantic way."[43]

For a long time, this communication capacity seemed to be in a completely different category from the information-processing ability of computers, or the image recognition of AI. Yet AI systems are already entering the world of communication in terms of music, poetry, art, and language. David Cope, former music professor at the University of California in Santa Cruz, who writes about AI and music, has developed impressive computer programs to create classical music in the style of any given composer. Audience response has shown that Cope's music is indistinguishable from Bach, for example. Cope has also developed a machine-learning system called Annie that writes not only music but also various kinds of poetry. This way of putting it is slightly misleading since, to be more precise, what Annie produces is generated by Cope plus AI, not by AI alone. As writer and programmer Paul Ford has said in connection with his attempt to write an article using machine learning: "At least for now computers need people as much as we need them."[44] The reason is clear: all of these things are being done by unconscious machines that are, in turn, being guided by conscious humans and trained on a massive amount of human-created data. One of the first AI artistic compositions was auctioned at Christie's in 2018. Nowadays, several AI music generators like Mubert, Soundful, and Jukebox are available for a subscription of a few dollars per month. ChatGPT can also be used to produce melodies, chord progressions, and whole songs.

Humans are social beings who communicate with one another using a vast array of languages together with sounds, symbols, and bodily movement. According to the biblical record, the existence of a multiplicity of languages is traceable back to the ancient Babylonian Empire, when God passed judgment on the human pride expressed by the building of the city and tower of Babel in an attempt to reach the heavens and make a permanent name for themselves.

Ever since, language differences have often impeded communication, leading to misunderstanding, friction, misrepresentation, tension, and violence. The capacity to interpret from one language to another has been crucial to relationships between peoples in general and to trade and international diplomacy in particular. For those who did not grow up speaking more than one language, the ability to interpret is often won by dint of long and arduous study and practice, with some languages proving very difficult indeed for adults to acquire with any fluency. Hence the long-standing interest in the development of technology that can assist in removing this language barrier.

It was only in the final years of the twentieth century that any real progress was made with automated language translation, and many of us can remember both the frustration and the hilarity at the mistakes made by early machine translators. One of the most impressive and relatively recent achievements of AI to date is the current state-of-the-art automated language translation software mentioned in chapter 6, such as Google Translate, Yandex, DeepL, and many others. One package whose name catches the eye is Unbabel. That leads me to wonder whether AI machine translation actually reverses the effects of what happened at Babel. Well, it does to the extent that people can understand each other, but even advanced machine translators may miss nuances and inadvertently give offense, although they are improving all the time so that simultaneous written and vocal translation capabilities are within reach. At the level of language unification, a reversal of Babel is well under way – but will it bring unity? Hardly! Human pride and rejection of God are as prevalent as ever.

As we saw earlier, AI systems can be used to make people seem to say and do things that they have not said or done with the result that their characters are assassinated and their careers ruined. Worse still, state-controlled mass media can determine what people see and hear by deliberately spreading lies, as is happening while I write these words. The Russian state is implementing a vast disinformation campaign at home regarding its unprovoked and brutal invasion of Ukraine. Journalist Esther Ajao reported in 2022:

TikTok has also become a platform for Russia to promote Putin's agenda for invading Ukraine. Although the platform recently suspended all livestreaming and new content from Russia, it did so days after videos of influencers supporting the war were already circulating.

Russian TikTok users repeated, word for word, false Russian claims about the "genocide" committed by Ukrainians against other Ukrainians in the Russian-speaking separatist Donetsk and Luhansk regions. The posts condemn Ukraine for killing innocent children, but there is no evidence to support this false claim. On March 6, TikTok suspended videos from Russia, after Putin signed a law introducing up to 15 years imprisonment for anyone who publishes what the state considers "fake news" about the Russian army.[45]

Their president does not wish Russian citizens to know the truth – indeed, it appears that the soldiers were lied to about the purpose of their incursion into Ukraine. As a result, evil stalks the earth. Of course, Russia is not the only state to employ AI in disinformation campaigns, as we saw earlier. According to the biblical record, the moral evil in the world resulted from fake news and lies delivered by a strange animal that spoke. These days it more often emanates from a computer-controlled screen.

The irony in all of this is that the more we communicate by means of technology, the more distant we become from one another. We cut off many of the elements that make genuine human interaction the wonderful thing that it is – the atmosphere of contact that can be experienced only by people sitting in the same room together. It all becomes depersonalized and reduced by preferring texting over talking, or using Alexa, Siri, and VR over conversing face-to-face. We end up communicating only fragments of who we are and what we wish to say. It is obvious, isn't it, that the more technology we place between ourselves, the more remote we become from one another and less aware of how we may be affecting, even damaging, one another. Think of online hate speech and what goes on in chatrooms in the metaverse.

It would seem that digital interaction can easily suppress fundamental virtues such as love, kindness, sympathy, and goodness. It can stunt character and frustrate the growth of the fruit of the Spirit in a Christian's life. And all of that in the name of progress! It is easy to think that technology is shaped by us, when all the time it is squeezing us into its mold and conforming us to this world's thinking.

We need to wake up from our tech dream and listen to the admonition of Paul: "I appeal to you therefore, brothers, by the mercies of God, to present your bodies as a living sacrifice, holy and acceptable to God, which is your spiritual worship. Do not be conformed to this world, but be transformed by the renewal of your mind, that by testing you may discern what is the will of God, what is good and acceptable and perfect."[46] And there is a sense in which we all know at least some of the things that are acceptable – the four classical virtues of wisdom, justice, courage, and self-control, and the three main Christian virtues of faith, hope, and love.

We need to get back to talking about and practicing these things as well as enjoying the glorious and wonderful aspects of communication that are mediated through literature of all kinds. And, best of all, we can converse with God himself. We can also talk about God to each other in any language, unless we are victimized in a surveillance state bent on obliterating any trace of God or religion. Where, then, is freedom of speech as an inalienable right?

GOD CREATED THE MAN-WOMAN RELATIONSHIP

The Genesis 2 account raises the question of a suitable companion for man in the, at first sight, surprising context of man naming the animals. It would appear that this process, now called taxonomy, taught the first man that, although many animals could be useful to him – especially since he probably had the kind of control over them that we have all but lost – none of the animals he named corresponded to him, in the sense of being a suitable companion to him. This category difference between humans and animals is of fundamental importance as is indicated by the fact that on day six of the creation narrative of Genesis 1 there is an information gap between the creation of animals and that of humans. By "information gap" I mean that between the creation of animals and that of human beings there is the statement: "And God said . . ." This statement, repeated several times in Genesis 1, marks informational and energetic creational inputs from God outside the world so that the text is telling us that you do not get from animals to humans without an extra supernatural intervention from God. One implication is surely that like-for-like companionship cannot be supplied by a subhuman animal, not to mention a machine.[47]

For that reason, according to Genesis 1, God created woman, out of man, as a companion, equal to him, sharing God's image with him, as Genesis explicitly says: "So God created man in his own image, in the image of God he created him; male and female he created them."[48] When more detail is given in Genesis 2, this fact is made the basis for marriage: "Therefore a man shall leave his father and his mother and hold fast to his wife, and they shall become one flesh."[49] This statement is cited by Jesus in response to a question about divorce: "Have you not read that he who created them from the beginning made them male and female, and said, 'Therefore a man shall leave his father and his mother and hold fast to his wife, and the two shall become one flesh'? So they are no longer two but one flesh. What therefore God has joined together, let not man separate."[50] It is important to note that Jesus states that these are the words of the Creator himself.

As a Christian I believe that Jesus is God incarnate and therefore I hold that this statement about marriage is authoritative. To redefine marriage in any other way, including having relationships with lifelike robotic companions, is to degrade the institution and risk irreparable damage.

Naming things is a fundamental intellectual discipline in every area of inquiry. At its best, it involves not simply labeling them for convenience but understanding something of their nature. As a scientist, I find it fascinating that biological taxonomy is not only something that God commanded humans to do but also that it was the way in which he taught them that they were fundamentally distinct from animals – a very controversial notion in some quarters today. I wish to add, equally controversially, that humans are similarly fundamentally different from machines, so that neither animals nor AI robots can ever supply the quality of relationship that God has designed men and women to enjoy.

That is not to say that animals and robots cannot provide some level of companionship. Animals have been human companions of real worth from time immemorial, a fact recognized by medical authorities so that, for instance, hospitals often have various pets such as dogs and even alpacas visit and interact with patients, especially children.

Advances in medicine have led to aging populations that feel increasingly lonely and isolated, and the need for companionship is at an all-time high. There is now a burgeoning industry, particularly in countries like Japan, geared to filling that need with companion robots, robotic pets, robotic house helps, and even life-size robotic dolls. A social robot is usually defined as "a physically embodied, autonomous agent that interacts and communicates with humans on a social level."[51] For instance, Pepper is a humanoid robot about the size of a child that can recognize some major human emotions and respond to them appropriately; it can answer questions, tell jokes, dance, and navigate its way around a room. It is successfully used in SoftBank stores in

Japan to welcome and amuse customers. Similar robots are being used in education to teach and entertain children, responding to their questions and providing them with information. PARO is an advanced interactive therapeutic robot shaped like a baby seal and covered with soft fur so that people feel as if they are touching a real animal. It supplies some of the well-known benefits of animal therapy in reducing stress in patients and their carers. Scientists have even constructed a nursing care robot, ROBEAR, which is capable of performing heavy tasks such as lifting a patient from a bed into a wheelchair. There are also healthcare robots that combine AI with voice technology that will, for instance, remind people to take their medicines at the right time.

This technology is advancing very rapidly and is clearly going to help reduce loneliness in the way pets can but without all the bother of feeding, cleaning, and doing other related chores that become increasingly difficult for the elderly. It is also clear that humans respond to many of these robots as if they were conscious humans and form attachments to them.

However positive much of this development is, according to the Genesis account, woman, the biblical counterpart of man, is built from man by God, and this has implications for the way we understand the nature of human-to-human relationships as distinct from interactions with machines. For instance, there is a real danger here that the treatment of robots as if they were humans leads to people thinking that they have moral obligations to these artifacts and therefore assigning human rights to them. That danger is intensified by the fact that the tech world is dominated by a materialist worldview that sees no fundamental difference between a human and a robot in terms of material, so that if the one has rights, so should the other, especially if they are similar to each other from a materialist perspective.

In any case, what would "rights" mean for an artifact, even if it is a robot? Would it mean the right for a robot to claim damages if attacked by a human (or another robot)? But since the robot is a machine, probably owned by someone, that kind of situation is already legally covered by existing laws on damage to property. A machine has no concept of rights for the simple reason that it has no concepts at all. And yet, as Maddy White reports in FairPlanet, the Saudis gave citizen rights to a humanoid robot called Sophia, which ironically meant that she had more rights than Saudi women![52]

A further question about our relationships with robots is whether, enhanced by AI as many of them are, they will one day be capable of responding to the complex blend of emotional, social, cultural, and physical needs of people in a way that satisfies the human need for understanding, compassion, and even some kind of friendship. If so, then there will be a new raft of questions regarding how we are to regard human relationships with such robots.

Margaret Boden points out that other human beings, of course, don't always provide the attention and care some people need. Yet she goes on to say: "In a nutshell, over-reliance on computer 'carers,' none of which can really care, would be a betrayal of the user's human dignity. . . . In the early days of AI, the computer scientist Joseph Weizenbaum made himself very unpopular with his MIT colleagues by saying as much. 'To substitute a computer system for a human function that involves interpersonal respect, understanding, and love,' he insisted in 1976, is 'simply obscene.'" Boden also issues a warning: "The users and designers of AI systems – and of a future society in which AI is rampant – should remember the fundamental difference between human and artificial intelligence: one cares, the other does not."[53]

Yet many possessors of companion robots feel that they simulate care well enough to satisfy at least some of their emotional needs. We should, therefore, balance Boden's comments by referring to Rosalind Picard's pioneering work in affective computing, which is very much an expression of AI care – simulated care, yes, but nonetheless positively received as care by patients.[54]

The fact remains, as Sherry Turkle points out, that "technology is seductive when what it offers meets our human vulnerabilities. As it turns out, we are very vulnerable indeed. We are lonely but fearful of intimacy. Digital connections and the sociable robot may offer the illusion of companionship without the demands of friendship. Our networked life allows us to hide from each other, even as we are tethered to each other. We'd rather text than talk."[55]

We need to be ever more on our guard against diminishing our humanity and degrading the *imago Dei* by prioritizing our interaction with machines more than with our fellow human beings – and, even worse, giving up our autonomy to them. One of the most wonderful things about being human is that we can create other human beings in our own image – a process very different from our capacity to make robots. God not only commanded the first humans to name the animals, but he also told them to be "fruitful and multiply" (Genesis 1:28) – to give life to succeeding generations by the natural process of the sexual transmission of life.

We will probably eventually make robots that can make other robots,[56] but such a process, if it ever happens, will be in a different category from the human capacity to create living images of themselves, each of them endowed with consciousness and a conscience and moral sense that no robot has.

To interfere with that capacity by modifying the human germline to the extent of reprogramming the genetic makeup of future human beings would be playing God on a seriously large scale and could be disastrous – even leading, as Lewis suggested, to the "abolition of man."

QUESTIONS

1. What do you think of the notion that science has relegated the Bible to the scrap heap of history? What are your reasons for your answer?

2. What do you think of Solzhenitsyn's statement "Men have forgotten God; that's why all this has happened"?

3. Discuss Nagel's statement: "If the mental is not itself merely physical, it cannot be fully explained by physical science. . . . Evolutionary naturalism implies that we should not take any of our convictions seriously, including the scientific world picture on which evolutionary naturalism depends." Is it valid? Give your reasons.

4. Discuss the meaning of the image of God that humans bear. What are its implications?

5. Read and discuss the Genesis account of creation. What are its main teachings and their implications?

6. Look at the main points listed from Genesis 2 regarding the nature of human life. Go through them one by one, discussing their importance for your life. Which of them do you need to pay more attention to?

7. Do you think companion robots fulfil a useful role? Are there dangers?

CHAPTER 13

THE ORIGIN OF THE HUMAN MORAL SENSE

The biblical account of the garden of Eden is one of the most profound narratives in all of literature. It relates how the Creator placed the first humans in a garden paradise that was full of promise and interest. They were free to enjoy the garden and explore it and the regions around it to their hearts' content. It was a place of joy and happiness where they could experience the living friendship and companionship of the Creator himself. Not only that, but they were given the task of naming the animals and so begin the wonderful process of understanding the world around them and capturing that understanding in language and preserving it.

There was, however, an added dimension to that original human environment that is absolutely essential for our understanding of the world and ourselves – morality. It is presented to us in the simplest of terms, but we would be making a serious mistake if we thought it was simplistic. The first humans were free – indeed, encouraged – to eat of all the trees in the garden, with only one important exception. Here is the relevant passage – Genesis 2:15–17:

> The LORD God took the man and put him in the garden of Eden to work it and keep it. And the LORD God commanded the man, saying, "You may surely eat of every tree of the garden, but of the tree of the knowledge of good and evil you shall not eat, for in the day that you eat of it you shall surely die."

The forbidden tree was not the "tree of knowledge," as many people erroneously think. It was the "tree of the knowledge of good and evil," which is a very different thing. God was not opposed to knowledge. On the contrary, he wanted his creatures to gain knowledge. The garden was full of potential for learning, exploration, and the experience of tending and developing a garden with its many varieties of plants and giving names to what they discovered. God's desire for them to learn is clear from the fact that he placed them in an environment conducive to doing so.

Furthermore, far from diminishing human status, by forbidding one thing, God conferred a unique dignity on humans – moral capacity. In order for morality to make sense, humans must have a certain degree of freedom – they were free to eat all that was in the garden. But that is not enough. There must also be a moral boundary that in this case consisted in the forbidding of a single fruit. They were, of course, *able* to eat it; otherwise God's prohibition would have been meaningless. God told them, however, that in the day they did eat it, they would surely die.

In spite of that, they did eat it for reasons given to us in the biblical narrative:

> Now the serpent was more crafty than any other beast of the field that the LORD God had made.
>
> He said to the woman, "Did God actually say, 'You shall not eat of any tree in the garden'?" And the woman said to the serpent, "We may eat of the fruit of the trees in the garden, but God said, 'You shall not eat of the fruit of the tree that is in the midst of the garden, neither shall you touch it, lest you die.'" But the serpent said to the woman, "You will not surely die. For God knows that when you eat of it your eyes will be opened, and you will be like God, knowing good and evil." So when the woman saw that the tree was good for food, and that it was a delight to the eyes, and that the tree was to be desired to make one wise, she took of its fruit and ate, and she also gave some to her husband who was with her, and he ate. Then the eyes of both were opened, and they knew that they were naked. And they sewed fig leaves together and made themselves loincloths.
>
> *Genesis 3:1–7*

The Genesis account goes on to relate how the serpent-enemy misrepresented God, suggesting that God wished to limit human freedom by not letting the humans become like God. Now, I am well aware that the biblical suggestion here that there exists not only an alien but a malevolent nonhuman intelligence in the universe frequently attracts ridicule. Yet I find that when astronomers suggest that the galaxy is teeming with all kinds of alien life, many people accept it without batting an eyelid. It would therefore appear that the problem is that people cannot imagine that such an ancient document as the Bible could know anything about these things – and they are probably right, if naturalism is true. But that is precisely the point at issue here: "In the beginning, God created the heavens and the earth" is the first action in the grand biblical metanarrative, which constitutes a head-on challenge to that very naturalism.

Furthermore, as we shall later see, many AGI proponents believe that there will be other kinds of intelligences in the future to which human beings might be subject. If humans will eventually be capable of creating intelligences superior to themselves, and if extraterrestrial life already exists as so many think, then there is no *a priori* reason apart from prejudice for rejecting the biblical introduction of an intelligent alien. C. S. Lewis puts it this way:

> It is impossible at this point not to remember a certain sacred story which, though never included in the creeds, has been widely believed in the Church and seems to be implied in several Dominical, Pauline, and Johannine utterances – I mean the story that man was not the first creature to rebel against the Creator, but that some older and mightier being long since became apostate and is now the emperor of darkness and (significantly) the Lord of this world. . . .
>
> It seems to me, therefore, a reasonable supposition, that some mighty created power had already been at work for ill on the material universe, or the solar system, or, at least, the planet Earth, before ever man came on the scene: and that when man fell, someone had, indeed tempted him. . . . If there is such a power, as I myself believe, it may well have corrupted the animal creation before man appeared.[1]

We should at least observe that, by introducing an evil alien being that deceived the humans, the Bible is therefore not entirely blaming humanity for what subsequently happened. We are told that this creature "was more crafty than any other beast of the field that the LORD God had made." It turns out to be very different from the other creatures: it is clever, and it can speak. It engages Eve in conversation about the significance of eating from the prohibited Tree of Knowledge of Good and Evil. It first questions the prohibition: "Did God actually say, 'You shall not eat of any tree in the garden'?" Eve answers, rather inexactly, by saying that God has forbidden even touching the tree, let alone eating it. The serpent responds with outright denial: "You will not surely die." To this it adds "God knows that when you eat of it your eyes will be opened, and you will be like God, knowing good and evil."

The serpent thus manages, by a devious manipulation of half-truth and a subtle appeal to her appetite for food, her aesthetic sense, and her desire for insight and fulfilment – all of them wonderful God-given capacities – to drive a wedge between her and her Creator. The snake's power of persuasion is such that Eve takes the forbidden fruit and offers it to Adam, and they both eat. In that searing moment, they discover that the enlightenment received is far from what they thought they desired. Instead of finding life, they begin to experience death, as God had said they would. They do not at once die in the physical sense. That effect of their action will inevitably ensue in due course.

Human life, as we learn from Genesis 2, has many aspects; its lowest level is physical life, to which we must add those other things that make life life – aesthetic environment, work, human relationships, and a relationship with God. Human death, then, will involve the unweaving of all of this. It will first mean the death of fellowship with God, and the first result of this death is a pathetic attempt to hide from God in the garden. The deadly rupture of fellowship with God will then lead inexorably to all the other levels of death – aesthetic death, death of human relationships, and so on, until we reach the lowest level – physical death, which turns our bodies back to molecules of dust.

The progenitors of humanity discovered all too late that the knowledge of good and evil gained by rejecting God and doing evil is not the kind of knowledge that you want to have. Instead of happiness, they were plunged into a fractured world full of sadness and despair.

This momentous event, often called the fall, happened when human beings begin to think of themselves as more than an image of God and desire to be a god: "You will be *like* God." In other words, *homo deus*. We might do well to be suspicious of the *homo deus* concept – after all, it was first suggested by a diabolical snake! John Gray says that Yuval Noah Harari himself is one of the few people who realize that transhumanism involves an attempt at human self-deification.[2] It is to Genesis that we must look to see where the quest for *homo deus* begins – with the account of the entry of evil into the world. We should not be too surprised, therefore, when evil crops up in so many depictions of the future.

Human morality, then, was originally defined in terms of obedience or disobedience to the Word of God. It only has significance insofar as the humans could understand what God said and had the capacity to choose either to obey or disobey. This, if true, as I believe it to be, is of crucial importance for the ethical evaluation of AI in the contemporary world. Genesis is here claiming that ethics are not relativistic, nor did they evolve horizontally through social evolutionary processes, as many naturalists claim, though society clearly plays a role at a certain level, but they were transcendent in origin. Part of the image of God is seen in the fact that humans are moral beings.

Moral convictions are, therefore, to a certain extent hardwired.[3] It is an observable fact that if you look at cultures of whatever kind around the world, you will find common moral elements such as respect for truth, family, property, and tribe – and, indeed, other people – as well as reprehension of murder, lying, stealing, and cheating.

But when it comes to the ultimate value of a human being and what the ground rules are, for example, for modifying one genetically and technologically, our approach will vary, sometimes greatly, according to whether we believe that human life has the transcendent value of having been made in the image of God, or whether we think it is just sophisticated mud and agree with Richard Dawkins when he says that we live in a world in which there is no justice, "no purpose, no evil and no good," a world in which "DNA just is and we dance to its music."[4] At this level, ethics turn out to be worldview dependent.

It is worth pointing out, however, that it is not only theists who acknowledge the biblical source of many of the ethical principles and values that we expect to be embodied in civilized society. Indeed, leading German atheist intellectual Jürgen Habermas has given clear warning of the dangers of a shift in our moral base from a Judeo-Christian moral base to the postmodern:

> Universalistic egalitarianism, from which sprang the ideals of freedom and a collective life in solidarity, the autonomous conduct of life and emancipation, the individual morality of conscience, human rights and democracy, is the direct legacy of the Judaic ethic of justice and the Christian ethic of love. This legacy, substantially unchanged, has been the object of continual critical appropriation and reinterpretation. To this day, there is no alternative to it. And in light of the current challenges of a post-national constellation, we continue to draw on the substance of this heritage. Everything else is just idle postmodern talk.[5]

If there is "no alternative to it," then at the very least we should not be afraid to bring that seminal biblical legacy to bear on, for instance, the human rights issues that are thrown up by the kind of AI surveillance society towards which some societies appear to be moving very rapidly.

The disobedience that infected the human race from the beginning was a prideful revolt of the human spirit against the God who created it. When the first humans took the forbidden fruit, they experienced shame, unease, and alienation from God. They were not simply conscious beings; they now had a conscience. The man and woman who had enjoyed the joy and friendship of God now felt that God had become their enemy, and they fled to hide from him.

We humans have likewise been fleeing ever since – a flight that bears within it all the seeds of dystopia. For there has lurked in the human heart the suspicion that God, if he exists at all, is innately hostile to us. He does not wish our happiness, well-being, or even protracted existence. Human history shows that we have used our autonomy to get out of control.

CONTROLLING OUR OWN CREATIONS

That is exactly what drives some of the fears around AI. What if our creations get out of control? Would a superintelligent *homo deus* do to the rest of us what we have done to God? Nearly seventy years ago, philosopher and political theorist Hannah Arendt (1906–1975) saw transhumanism as "a rebellion against human existence as it has been given, a free gift from nowhere (secularly speaking), which he wishes to exchange, as it were, for something he has made himself."[6]

Some people are afraid when they try to imagine the kind of creatures into which we might one day make ourselves. Philosopher Paula Boddington writes:

> For if we see the Genesis account of the Fall of man as foreshadowing of fears about robots, then Genesis gets the problem exactly right, for exactly the right reasons – it's a worry about autonomy itself: what might robots do if we can't control them fully? Will they adhere to the same value system as us? Will they decide to disobey us? What will our relationship with our creations be? . . . We can thank the Hebrew account of Genesis for pre-warning us thousands and thousands of years ago.[7]

Transhumanist Nick Bostrom says: "We cannot blithely assume that a superintelligence will necessarily share any of the final values stereotypically associated with wisdom and intellectual development in humans – scientific curiosity, benevolent concern for others, . . . renunciation of material acquisitiveness, a taste for refined culture or for the simple pleasures in life, humility and selflessness, and so forth."[8]

Bostrom's mention of wisdom raises the question of the relationship between it and information. As American author Clifford Stoll puts it: "Data is not information, information is not knowledge, knowledge is not understanding, understanding is not wisdom."[9] Long before him, Einstein had pointed out that "information is not knowledge. The only source of knowledge is experience. You need experience to gain wisdom."

Ayad Akhtar writes:

As a writer, it seems to me that the most baleful development in our collective contemporary life is the preponderance of a practice derived from digital technology that treats knowledge and information as synonymous. For while the way to wisdom leads through knowledge, there is no path to wisdom from information. Especially when that information is being used as a training treat in what has come to feel like a wholesale attempt at permanent re-education.

Having one's bias confirmed endlessly by a curated cascade of information reflecting back to you your preferences and opinions, second after second, understandably breeds an illusion of certainty. But certainty is nothing like wisdom; it might in fact be something closer to wisdom's opposite. Wisdom: a kind of knowing ever-riven with contradiction, a knowing intimate with the inevitability of uncertainty.[10]

We cannot, therefore, assume that 2084 will not be worse than Huxley's *Brave New World* or Orwell's *1984*. It is, after all, easy to assume that AI will improve human beings – but that may not necessarily be the case. According to a survey of 327 AI researchers, 36 percent of them agreed that it was "plausible that decisions made by AI or machine learning systems could cause a catastrophe this century that is at least as bad as all-out nuclear war."[11]

As we have seen, Harari describes AGI as decoupling intelligence from *consciousness*. AGI may also be decoupled from *conscience* – as much of current narrow AI already is. In any case, an AGI is very likely to do things that have ethical ramifications, and *either* it is controlled by humans who furnish it with their ethical concepts – and who knows what they may be – *or* it takes control itself with completely unforeseeable and potentially horrific, even terminal, consequences for humanity. If the latter is the case, then it might be idle to argue that the makers of the system, who perhaps no longer even exist, still have the responsibility for the disasters that they occasioned, in the same way that the maker of an autopilot is responsible for a crash caused by that autopilot after it has been given control of an aircraft.

That is the crucial thing. If the ethical programmers are informed by relativistic or biased ethics, the same will be inevitably reflected in their products. For that reason, it is important that those with transcendent ethical convictions should have a seat at the table when discussing the ethics input into AI systems.

It is, of course, difficult to discuss ethical values in connection with a superintelligence, since there are no facts but only a plethora of wildly differing hypothetical scenarios. Some people hope that if we succeed in human brain enhancement, then the resulting superintelligence may well share common human values. Others are concerned about the (improbable) scenario in which we create a conscious AGI, as that would lead to the sort of ethical questions that inevitably arise when we are thinking of our treatment of conscious entities – such as legal personhood and rights.[12] But we should not let such scenarios blind us to the fact that they are mostly speculation. Nor should we let them make us forget to be thankful for good technological progress.

That gives me the opportunity to say that my commitment to the biblical worldview does not make me a Luddite but, on the contrary, makes me deeply thankful to God for technological developments, especially those that bring hope to people in this damaged world who would otherwise have none – giving hearing to the deaf, sight to the blind, limbs to the limbless; eradicating killer diseases; and benefiting from a host of other things that represent magnificent work in the spirit of a Creator who has made humans in his image to be creative themselves.

AI AND MORALITY

We have seen that AI, like any new technology, only perhaps more so, brings with it a whole new raft of moral considerations, many of which may seem unsurmountable.[13] AI computer systems as such have no conscience, and so the morality of any decisions they make will reflect the morality of the computer programmers, which is where the difficulties start. How can we be sure that the programmers will build in a morality that is benevolent and humane? Rosalind Picard puts it succinctly: "The greater the freedom of a machine, the more it will need moral standards."[14] In her 2022 Oxford Tanner Lecture, she listed what most people would agree are desirable criteria for human values in an AI age:

1. Acknowledge the equal worth of every individual regardless of age, sex, nationality.
2. Independent of abilities or functions – for example, not age dependent.
3. Not limited by materialism, naturalism, and scientism.
4. Not something that could be granted or removed by any person or government in power over you.
5. Bigger than some professor's idea![15]

She then gave what she thought was an important concept to bring to bear on the situation, since it has been the source of values for many centuries in large parts of the world – the biblical notion of *imago Dei*. We have already made reference to this fundamental idea, and readers may be interested to find out how ChatGPT defined it: "The imago dei is the biblical concept that human beings are created in the image of God. This means that humans have the ability to think, feel and create just as God does." In his lectures on Genesis, Jordan Peterson commented: "When I started to understand the concept that human beings are made in God's image, that that's actually the cornerstone of our legal system, that really rattled me. . . . I didn't understand that clearly that body of laws has that metaphysical presupposition without which the laws fall apart, and that's starting to happen."[16]

It surely makes sense, therefore, to revisit one of the most significant sources of values that has proved its worth in giving men and women a sense of dignity and providing the foundation for human rights legislation, and much else. Speaking of those rights, political scientist Francis Fukuyama regards transhumanism as "the world's most dangerous idea" in that it runs the risk of affecting human rights.[17] His reason is that liberal democracy depends on the fact that all humans share an undefined "Factor X" on which their equal dignity and rights are grounded.[18] The use of enhancing technologies, he fears, could destroy Factor X. Indeed, I would want to say that Factor X has actually been defined: it is being made in the image of God. Fukuyama writes:

Nobody knows what technological possibilities will emerge for human self-modification. But we can already see the stirrings of Promethean desires in how we prescribe drugs to alter the behavior and personalities of our children. The environmental movement has taught us humility and respect for the integrity of nonhuman nature. We need a similar humility concerning our human nature. If we do not develop it soon, we may unwittingly invite the transhumanists to deface humanity with their genetic bulldozers and psychotropic shopping malls.[19]

We have seen that one of the stated goals of transhumanism is not merely to improve but to change human nature – as implied in the very word itself. For many of us, this raises deep ethical and theological concerns, not only for Christians, but for people of every religious and philosophical viewpoint. In trying to answer them, we shall inevitably meet the widespread view that morality is subjective and relative. If this is the case, however, we should have to abandon any idea of moral progress (or regress), not only in the history of nations, but in the lifetime of each individual. The very concept of moral progress implies an external moral standard by which not only to measure that a present moral state is different from an earlier one but also to pronounce that it is "better" than the earlier one. Without such a standard, how could one say that the moral state of a culture in which cannibalism is regarded as an abhorrent crime is any "better" than a society in which it is an acceptable culinary practice?

Naturalism denies this. For instance, Harari asserts: "Hammurabi and the American Founding Fathers alike imagined a reality governed by universal and immutable principles of justice, such as equality or hierarchy. Yet the only place where such universal principles exist is in the fertile imagination of Sapiens, and in the myths they invent and tell one another. These principles have no objective validity."[20]

Yet relativists tend to argue that since, according to them, there are no moral absolutes, no objective rights and wrongs, no one ought to try to impose his moral views on other people. But in arguing like that, they refute their own theory. The word *ought* implies a moral duty. They are saying, in effect, that because there are no universal, objective principles, there is a universal moral principle binding on all objectivists, and everyone else – namely, that no one ought to impose his moral views on other people. In so saying, relativism refutes its own basic principle.

Harari is wrong. There are universal principles that have real objective validity. Otherwise, civilized life would be impossible, since subjective moral relativism is not livable. When it comes to the practical affairs of daily life, a subjectivist philosopher will vigorously object if his theory is put into action to his disadvantage. If his bank manager entertains the idea that there is no such thing as objective fairness and tries to cheat the philosopher out of $2,000, the philosopher will certainly not tolerate the manager's subjectivist and "culturally determined" sense of values.

The fact is, as pointed out by C. S. Lewis, that our everyday behavior reveals that we believe in a common objective standard that is outside ourselves. That is shown by how, from childhood on, we engage in criticizing others and excuse ourselves to them: we expect others to accept our moral judgments. From the perspective of Genesis, this is surely precisely what you would expect if human beings were made in the image of God as moral beings and therefore hardwired for morality. Just think how you would react if you were wrongly accused of theft or lying! It would be interesting to apply AI to see whether it supported the existence of a common set of moral principles, by setting up a gigantic crowdsourced database of moral choices to see what commonalities could be detected. That might help decide what are the best moral principles that should be programmed into AI systems.

But there is a danger that such a process could deflect attention from the fundamental question whether absolute values exist. For, if they do, as I believe is the case, then, ideally, it is those values that should be implemented in AI systems for the benefit of all. We should not run the risk of determining morality in a utilitarian manner by majority vote, which, as history and experience show, is not always a wise thing to do.

At the moment, however, the moral principles that are embedded into AI systems necessarily reflect the biases of those who programmed the system. Lianna Brinded says about avoiding bias:

> That's easier said than done. Human bias in hiring has been well-documented, with studies showing that even with identical CVs, men are more likely to be called in for an interview, and non-white applicants who "whiten" their resumes also get more calls.
>
> But of course, AI is also not immune to biases in hiring either. We know that across industries, women and ethnic minorities are regularly burned by algorithms, from finding a job to getting healthcare. And with the greater adoption of AI and automation, this is only going to get worse.[21]

How, then, do you teach fairness to a computer, or program it to avoid racial or gender bias and stereotypes? It will be possible only if the programmers know what these things are and are capable of presenting them in a form that a machine can process. If things go wrong because the system amplifies the bias instead of removing it, we cannot blame a conscienceless machine. Only a moral being, the human programmer, can and should be blamed – and held responsible. Perhaps what we need is a suitable version of the Claude 2 ethical AI system described in chapter 9 where there are two AIs and one polices the output of the other.

THE QUEST FOR IMMORTALITY AND THE TRANSHUMANIST DREAM

There was a second special tree in the biblical garden of Eden – the Tree of Life. One result of humans' taking the fruit of the Tree of Knowledge of Good and Evil was that they lost their access to the Tree of Life. This implies that human beings were not intrinsically immortal as created. It would appear that for the continuation of physical life they were dependent on the regular consumption of the special fruit of the Tree of Life. Its withdrawal by God after the fall meant inevitable, though not immediate, physical death. One cannot help wondering whether the legendary search for the elixir of life in the ancient world and the current search for silicon-based immortality are ultimately rooted in this ancient story.

That would seem to mean that Harari's claim that death is now a "merely technical problem" is way off the mark. Could Genesis imply that physical immortality in the sense of potentially unending life on earth will forever be beyond our grasp, so that we will never, as Ray Kurzweil and Stephen Hawking suggest, be able to download the contents of our brains onto silicon and so make ourselves immortal? We shall have more to say about immortality later.

Harari, who seems overoptimistic at times, nevertheless sees a major threat in transhumanist attempts to achieve immortality and divine happiness. He says that this dream is really nothing more than the traditional aspiration of liberal humanism, defined as follows:

> The Liberal Story says that if we only liberalize and globalize our political
> and economic systems, we will produce paradise on earth, or at least peace

and prosperity for all. According to this story – accepted, in slight variations, by George W. Bush and Barack Obama alike – humankind is inevitably marching toward a global society of free markets and democratic politics.[22]

Harari sees this liberal view as the best option available, yet he nevertheless thinks that it is flawed and that it may even contain the seeds of its own destruction. He spends the last part of his book *Homo Deus* arguing that "attempting to realize this humanist dream will undermine its very foundations, by unleashing new post-humanist technologies. . . . If the whole universe is pegged to the human experience, what will happen once the human experience becomes just another designable product, no different in essence from any other item in the supermarket?"[23]

One of the foundations to which he refers is the liberal humanist belief in human free will that, as we have just seen, is a central pillar of the Genesis story. For, in common with many contemporary atheists, he denies free will, holding that it "exists only in the imaginary stories we humans have invented."[24] He holds that free will is an invention of theologians and that it is quite easy to see that it is false: "Humans make choices – but they are never independent choices. Every choice depends on a lot of biological, social and personal conditions that you cannot determine for yourself. I can choose what to eat, whom to marry and whom to vote for, but these choices are determined in part by my genes, my biochemistry, my gender, my family background, my national culture, etc. – and I didn't choose which genes or family to have."[25] He thinks that "the last nail in freedom's coffin is provided by the theory of evolution,"[26] but he is not radical enough to question evolution's capacity to do so – or even tell us what that assertion might mean. He is clearly unaware of more recent developments in systems biology that have led to skepticism about that capacity. I have given an account of this work in my book *Cosmic Chemistry: Do God and Science Mix?*[27]

Harari continues: "Doubting free will is not just a philosophical exercise. It has practical implications. If organisms indeed lack free will, it implies that we can manipulate and even control their desires using drugs, genetic engineering or direct brain stimulation."[28] In other words, denying free will removes the barriers to human experimentation in the interests of AGI. It also washes away any meaningful base for ethics and so removes all moral barriers, as Nietzsche saw long ago. But the fairly obvious fact that there are many influences involved in human choice does not rule out that there is sufficient freedom for morality to make sense where in the absence of that freedom it wouldn't. If determinism is true, then transhumanists, long-termists, and anyone else should stop telling us what we *ought* to do, since their own philosophy renders the concept of oughtness meaningless.

Determinism fails for many other reasons, as set out in my book *Determined to Believe: The Sovereignty of God, Freedom, Faith, and Human Responsibility*,[29] where I present the arguments for the existence of free will and its implication for the moral status of human beings as outlined in the biblical worldview.

The second foundation of liberal humanism that Harari sees as delusional is the concept that each of us is an individual. This also is a biblical teaching, however, and it is far from delusional. The Genesis account makes that clear from the dignity conferred on us as individuals by stating that each of us is made in the image of God.[30] Yet Harari, like many others, denies this dignity in the name of biology, thus opening the door to the individual losing his or her significance in the vast databases that are the food of AI.

Our relationship with computers has come a long way. In the 1980s it was a very individual one in that we sat by ourselves with a computer in front of us that could only handle a limited number of tasks. In the 1990s we moved online and a whole new world of connection opened up, where we could relate to others all over the world through email. Then technology went mobile and set us free from being chained to a fixed computer. After that we entered the present age of social media so that nowadays billions of us are voluntarily engaged in uploading ever more detailed information about ourselves onto the web in such measure that Facebook or Google, for instance, may well end up knowing much more about us than we know ourselves. Almost unawares, we are abdicating our decisions to seemingly omniscient AI systems that know more than we do about virtually everything about us – our preferences; our habits; our jobs; our contacts; our travels; what we eat, wear, read, see, believe; our health – both physical and emotional – and our finances. We consult the web about most things, and many of us have already started to allow it to make our decisions for us.

The danger is that, as individuals, we could in this way lose all our meaning in an incessant, overwhelming maelstrom of data flow. This will spell the end of what Harari calls the humanist religion that was designed to enable us to create meaning in a universe that actually has no meaning. Harari has grim words to say: "Eventually we may reach a point when it will be impossible to disconnect from this all-knowing network even for a moment. Disconnection will mean death."[31] This network will include what is called the "internet of things" – consisting of our smart gadgets, homes, cars, and environment that are connected by means of having them embedded with sensors, software, and other technologies that network them with one another and with many other devices and systems and human beings over the internet. The combination of AI and the internet of things is called the artificial internet of things – AIoT.

Harari's final comment in his 2018 article for the *Guardian* entitled "The Myth of Freedom" makes interesting reading since he thinks, on the one hand, that liberal democracy is flawed, yet, on the other hand, he defends it against what he calls "religious and nationalistic fantasies":

> How does liberal democracy function in an era when governments and corporations can hack humans? What's left of the beliefs that "the voter knows best" and "the customer is always right"? How do you live when you realize that you are a hackable animal, that your heart might be a government agent, that your amygdala might be working for Putin, and that the next thought that emerges in your mind might well be the result of some algorithm that knows you better than you know yourself? These are the most interesting questions humanity now faces.[32]

I am surprised that Harari thinks that these questions are the *most interesting for humanity*. For there is nothing new here. People have been hacking and using their sales and marketing techniques and spin to influence our amygdalas long before AI came along.[33] What about the far more important questions of who we are; why we are here; where we are heading; how we can reduce poverty, loneliness, disease, and the increasing depression and despair in our society, and promote growth, learning, giving, and human connection? Has "love your neighbor as yourself" lost all relevance?

QUESTIONS

1. Retell the story of the garden of Eden. What does it tell us about the nature of morality?
2. What is the danger in conflating the Tree of Knowledge of Good and Evil and the "tree of knowledge," which is not a biblical concept?
3. How do you understand the role of the serpent in Genesis 3?

4. What is the relationship between the temptation "You shall be as gods" and *homo deus*?
5. How deeply do you think our culture is influenced by the biblical worldview?
6. Do you think there is a risk that we will lose control over our own creations?
7. Do you think there is a danger of transhumanists "defacing humanity"?
8. What do you think is the significance of the Tree of Life, and what is its relevance to the transhumanist dream of immortality?
9. Is free will real? Discuss your answer.

CHAPTER 14

THE TRUE *HOMO DEUS*

On the first page of his book *Homo Deus*, Harari writes: "I encourage all of us, whatever our beliefs, to question the basic narratives of our world, to connect past developments with present concerns, and not to be afraid of controversial issues."[1]

Following that encouragement, I wish now to question his narrative and introduce one that is completely different, far more radical, and far more likely to be true, since it is strongly evidence-based and not one of the "changing social constructs" or "nostalgic fantasies of nationalism or religion" Harari points to.[2] What is more, it is full of hope.

The quest for upgrading humans, creating superintelligence and godhood, is very ancient and, in its contemporary form, dressed up in the language of advanced computer technology, very alluring. The project sounds like the culmination of billions of years of development, initially blind and natural and finally directed by the human mind to which those evolutionary processes gave rise.

Yet at its heart, it delivers a flawed narrative that is neither true to the past nor to the nature of reality. Indeed, its narrative is the reverse of what actually is the case. Superintelligence and godhood are not the end products of the trajectory of the history of human ingenuity. If there is a God who created and upholds the universe and who made us in his image, then a superintelligence, God himself, has always existed. He is not an end product. He is the producer.

THE BIBLICAL PERSPECTIVE ON SUPERINTELLIGENCE

In light of what many are now prepared to believe about transhumanism and AGI, it is surely not unreasonable to ask that we at least listen to the biblical perspective on superintelligence and compare it with other scenarios on offer.

I confess that I would be disappointed, if my skeptical, agnostic, or atheist readers were to switch off at this point. Not that they owe me anything, but I have spent a great deal of time attempting to understand what their thought leaders write, and I would hope that they in turn might be interested in hearing what I have to say.

As we have seen, opinions as to whether AGI will ever be reached vary wildly, although I get the impression that the momentum in our culture is swinging in the direction that even if we don't reach it, we shall get very near it sooner than we might think. In a TED Talk in 2017, Louis Rosenberg, who built the first ever augmented reality system, said that when he started thinking about this issue in the early 1990s, he believed that AI would exceed human abilities around the year 2050. He now believes it will happen sooner than that, possibly as early as 2030. He comments: "That's very surprising to me, as these types of forecasts usually slip further into the future as the limits of technology come into focus, but this one is screaming towards us faster than ever."[3] The 2022 Expert Survey on Progress in AI consulted 738 experts and said that there was a 50 percent chance that high-level machine intelligence would make its debut before 2059.[4]

The cover of *Time* magazine on 21 February 2011 announced its feature article by Lev Grossman: "2045 – The Year Man Becomes Immortal." Mo Gawdat, Google pioneer, thinks that by 2049 we shall reach the singularity when AI will be a billion times smarter than the cleverest human in all areas. He presses the point by an analogy: "Your intelligence, in comparison to that machine, will be comparable to the intelligence of a fly in comparison to Einstein."[5]

He refers to the popular science fiction stories and films about Superman, an alien with superpowers who lands on Earth as a child and is adopted by the Kent family, who instill in him beneficent ethical principles that he uses to save the world from great disasters. Gawdat then says that such a superintelligent alien has already arrived on Earth: "It is currently still an infant – a child – and although this being is not biological in nature, it has incredible abilities." It is, of course, an AI, which, he says, "is a very genuine form of intelligence . . . already smarter than every human on the planet in terms of many specific, isolated tasks."[6]

That, for some, is a threat. Rosenberg writes:

> To me, the prospect of a sentient artificial intelligence being created on Earth is no less dangerous than an alien intelligence showing up from another

planet. After all, it will have its own values, its own morals, its own sensibilities, and, most of all, its own interests. To assume that its interests will be aligned with ours is absurdly naive, and to assume that it won't put its interests first – putting our very existence at risk – is to ignore what we humans have done to every other creature on Earth. Thus, we should be preparing for the imminent arrival of a sentient AI with the same level of caution as the imminent arrival of a spaceship from another solar system. We need to assume this is an existential threat for our species.[7]

On reading these pieces, I was immediately struck by their resonance with a much older story about the advent of another superintelligent child with unique powers, born this time of a human woman but with a divine origin. I mean, of course, Jesus Christ. In contrast with Superman, Jesus actually existed. Not only that but in contrast with the speculation and uncertainty that surrounds many AI scenarios, there is a great deal of positive evidence that leads me to the conviction that Jesus Christ is both man and God (*homo + Deus*). That he is the true Homo Deus is, of course, a staggering claim. If true, it at once implies that we do not have to wait for some kind of merger of human life and technology to reach a different kind of being with unprecedented powers. The ultraspeculative transhuman quest to elevate humans to godlike status pales into insignificance with this true narrative that flows in the exact opposite direction. Not that man becomes a god but that God has become man in Jesus Christ. God did not become a machine. A *human* superintelligence already exists.

PHYSICAL DEATH IS NOT SIMPLY A TECHNICAL PROBLEM: THE SIGNIFICANCE OF THE RESURRECTION OF CHRIST

One of the most important pieces of evidence for the truth of the claim that God became human involves calling into question Harari's assertion that physical death is no more than a technical problem that will yield to medical advance within the next hundred years. Not so. Human death is much more than a technical problem. It is inevitable, since it is the consequence of the initial rebellion of humans against God and the consequent removal by God of the Tree of Life. That makes it unlikely that Harari, or anyone else, will ever find that tree, or its equivalent, however hard they try.

In any case, the Christian message is that physical death has already been vanquished by Jesus' physical resurrection from the dead. His resurrection was a result not of advanced medical technology or biological engineering but of the direct action of God's divine power. The universe is not a closed system of cause and effect. It is an open system, created by a God who can and does get involved in its operation, sometimes in spectacularly special ways, in order to draw our attention to his existence, power, and, indeed, care.

I can well understand a skeptical reader balking at the very idea of a resurrection, although I confess to finding it odd that some who do seem to have no difficulty in believing that death will one day be overcome by technology. Be that as it may, it is important to say at this stage that Christians base their claim that God raised Jesus physically from the dead on strong cumulative evidence – both objective in terms of history and subjective in terms of experience.

Not surprisingly, that evidence cannot be reduced to sound bites. It would require several chapters to do it justice, and since I have rehearsed the main lines of evidence for the resurrection of Christ elsewhere – for example, in the last two chapters of my book *Gunning for God: Why the New Atheists Are Missing the Target*, it would not be appropriate to reproduce them here.[8] It is sufficient to say that one of the foremost contemporary historians and experts on the New Testament, N. T. Wright, concludes that "the historian, of whatever persuasion, has no option but to affirm both the empty tomb and the 'meetings' with Jesus as 'historical events.' . . . I regard this conclusion as coming in the same sort of category, of historical probability so high as to be virtually certain, as the death of Augustus in AD 14 or the fall of Jerusalem in AD 70."[9]

The Christian message does not, however, stop with the raising of Christ from the dead. Rather, that is where it starts. For the resurrection of Christ has a major implication for us in the present – that we humans can share in his resurrected life. This is a vastly bigger thing than a human upgrade involving AI. It is, in fact, God's answer to the serpent's taunt that launched the whole human *homo deus* project in the first place: "You will be like God." For, as we have already indicated, one major consequence of the temptation and fall of humanity is that deep in the human psyche is embedded the idea that God, if there is one, is against us human beings, against our moving up in the scale of being, against upgrades, against knowledge and all that is associated with fulfilling human potential for flourishing. And because God is against us, we need to snatch at godhood when we get the chance.

This is not true; indeed, to be blunt, it is the lie of all lies, and millions of people have fallen for it. Far from being against us, God wishes to share not only his image with us, as he did in creation, but his life, so that we can become not simply his creatures but his sons and daughters. This has all the potential of a real enhancement.

THE TRIUMPH OF HUMANITY PREDICTED

In those far-off days at the time of the initial human rebellion, God promised a way of salvation from the destructive effects of that rebellion and the alienation between humans and God that it brought with it. To the serpent that had tempted the first humans, God said, "I will put enmity between you and the woman, and between your offspring and her offspring; he shall bruise your head, and you shall bruise his heel."[10]

This is not merely saying that God would eventually triumph; it is saying that humanity would eventually triumph. This is the start of what might well be called "the Seed Project," *seed* being another term for "offspring." God would eventually bring into the world a particular human, Jesus Christ, who would simultaneously be the seed of the woman (truly human) and the Son of God (truly God). He is the true Homo Deus, not an amalgam of human biological life and technology (another human creation), not a man who had been deified like a Roman emperor, but something in a different category altogether – Deity embodied in man, the God Man, Jesus Christ. He is the one who shall ultimately triumph.

The divinely guided historical process that brought him into the world was spread over many centuries because of the preparatory lessons that humanity needed to learn. It involved a sequence of individual human beings who are of great interest in their own right in terms of what they learned of God and what they have passed on to us. To name just a few: Adam, Abraham, Isaac, Jacob, Judah, David, Mary – and, finally, Jesus.

As that process ran its course, predictions about this special "seed" became more and more detailed in their focus. At this point, a skeptical reader might be inclined to say: "But surely you don't take that kind of thing seriously?" Yes, I do, but not because I have forgotten my scientific education and descended into irrationality. Indeed, if there is a God who has created this universe and has sustained it ever after, it is not at all implausible to think that his relationship to time is not the same as ours, that he has an overarching perspective on history, and that he is able to be causally involved in the unfolding of events.

The other reason for taking biblical prophecy seriously is its uniqueness as a historical phenomenon. There is so much of it whose fulfilment can be pinpointed, and it does not take much statistical insight to realize the extreme prior improbability of so many long-range predictions being fulfilled so accurately, especially if you assume a naturalistic worldview like that of Harari: "Just as people were never created, neither, according to the science of biology, is there a 'Creator' who 'endows' them with anything. There is only a blind evolutionary process, devoid of any purpose, leading to the birth of individuals."[11] Straight out of Dawkins's antiquated approach to biology with its erroneous assumption that the "science of biology" establishes atheism.[12]

Indeed, the phenomenon of biblical prophecy provides strong evidence against Harari's beliefs and for the truth of Christianity's supernatural claims, so, after a couple of opening comments by way of orientation, we shall give some examples. The first comment is that any consideration of AGI involves making predictions about the future. We shall consider these predictions and compare them with the biblical material, so that it is important that we get some idea of the reliability of the Bible on that score.

THE EVIDENTIAL VALUE OF PROPHECY

The Christian claim is that the Bible has been making predictions over the course of centuries whose fulfilments can be checked against the unfolding narrative of the Bible and historical events. The basic principle here was enunciated by Christ himself to his disciples: "You heard me say to you, 'I am going away, and I will come to you.' If you loved me, you would have rejoiced, because I am going to the Father, for the Father is greater than I. And now I have told you before it takes place, so that when it does take place you may believe."[13] Jesus predicted his ascension around six weeks before it happened. When the disciples eventually observed it happen, their faith in Jesus' prophetic word was confirmed.

The same was also true of the resurrection, which Jesus foretold several times in the final three years of his life. For example: "So the Jews said to him, 'What sign do you show us for doing these things?' Jesus answered them, 'Destroy this temple, and in three days I will raise it up.' The Jews then said, 'It has taken forty-six years to build this temple, and will you raise it up in three days?' But he was speaking about the temple of his body. When therefore he was raised from the dead, his disciples remembered that he had said this, and they believed the Scripture and the word that Jesus had spoken."[14]

It is important to grasp the precise point being made here. Jesus offered his predictions not so much to stimulate speculation about the future as rather to provide evidence of his authenticity that would be clear when what he predicted took place. In other words, the confirmation came *post eventum* – after the event.

Jesus also warned his disciples that they would experience rejection, persecution, and even death, adding that he had forewarned them so that when these trials arose, they would recall his words and be comforted by the fact that Jesus already knew.[15]

We should note that there is nothing vague or speculative about Jesus' predictions – they are both intelligible and precise short-term prophecies. The first two were also the subject of long-term prophecies, as Peter explained on the Day of Pentecost. On that occasion, he convincingly argued that both the resurrection and ascension had been foretold in the Old Testament.[16] Fulfilment of biblical prophecies was crucial evidence for the early Christians.

I also find it convincing, not in spite of the fact that I am a scientist, but because of it. The capacity to predict something checkable is a crucial test of a scientific theory – we have confidence in Kepler and Newton's laws, Maxwell's equations for electromagnetism, and Einstein's equations (and many others) because they enable us accurately to predict what will happen under certain conditions. Of course, in physics we are (mainly) concerned with lawlike behaviour of the natural world.

But when it comes to history and the stream of events in the lives of people and nations, we lose all except the most general form of predictability – for example, we can predict that certain forms of government will lead to instability. But there are many natural events (from a human perspective) that we simply cannot predict: for example, the behaviour of people not yet born, the place where they will be born, the course of their life and deeds, the manner of their death, and their subsequent influence. That sort of thing is not covered by any laws and is, in a technical sense, essentially chaotic.

But in the case of Christ, these are precisely the things that were predicted and did come to pass. About seven hundred years before Jesus was born, the Hebrew prophet Isaiah announced in the following famous words that a day would come when the promise of Messiah made to Abraham and David would be fulfilled: "For to us a child is born, to us a son is given; and the government shall be upon his shoulder, and his name shall be called Wonderful

Counselor, Mighty God, Everlasting Father, Prince of Peace. Of the increase of his government and of peace there will be no end, on the throne of David and over his kingdom, to establish it and to uphold it with justice and with righteousness from this time forth and forevermore. The zeal of the LORD of hosts will do this."[17]

Isaiah also predicted exactly how the Messiah would be treated by the nation of Israel, how he would die, and even by implication that he would rise again. In the eighth century BC, the Hebrew prophet Micah foretold the precise place of Jesus' birth: "But you, O Bethlehem Ephrathah, who are too little to be among the clans of Judah, from you shall come forth for me one who is to be ruler in Israel, whose coming forth is from of old, from ancient days."[18] These key prophecies among others are celebrated in Christmas carol services all around the world.

Also, these are not fake "predictions" made after the events they describe happened, as is sometimes claimed about Scripture itself. For instance, I believe that Daniel's prophecy was written in the sixth century BC, but, since Daniel 11 accurately describes well-substantiated events in the second century BC, some scholars think that he must actually have been writing in the second century, since for many of them such prediction is ruled out *a priori* by their naturalistic worldview that rejects any supernatural dimension to reality.

When the prophets wrote these things, however, from a purely historical perspective the future existence of Israel as a nation was questionable, let alone the prospect that it would have a king, to say nothing of the extremely unlikely idea that he would be born in Bethlehem. Yet when Jesus was born, King Herod asked the Jewish authorities where the new king would be born, and even though they were hostile to such an idea, they did not hesitate to trust the Old Testament Scriptures and pinpoint Bethlehem as his birthplace – which is why the massacre of the infants happened there. As a scientist used to assessing evidence, I find this very impressive, since the fulfilments of these prophecies are historically checkable.

We should celebrate the fact that God has given us biblical prophecy as evidence of his uniqueness: "Who is like me? Let him proclaim it. Let him declare and set it before me, since I appointed an ancient people. Let them declare what is to come, and what will happen."[19]

The roots of biblical prophecy go back long before Isaiah and Micah to the very beginning in Genesis. After the fall, God said to the serpent: "I will put enmity between you and the woman, and between your offspring and her offspring; he shall bruise your head, and you shall bruise his heel."[20]

That famous prediction that the seed of the woman, a human being, would eventually triumph is the start of a thread that I call the Seed Project, which runs through the entire Bible. We sketch some elements in it.

God tells Abraham that the whole world is to be blessed through his seed: "I will bless those who bless you, and whoever curses you I will curse; and all peoples on earth will be blessed through you."[21] Its final fulfilment was announced by the apostle Peter in the early days of the Christian church: "You are heirs of the prophets and of the covenant God made with your fathers. He said to Abraham, 'Through your offspring all peoples on earth will be blessed.' When God raised up his servant, he sent him first to you to bless you by turning each of you from your wicked ways."[22]

It took many centuries to get there, and along the way we get hints of what will one day be. The promise to Abraham was certainly not completely fulfilled in Isaac, yet he carried the promise to his son Jacob, and one of Jacob's sons, Joseph, saved the Egyptian Empire and surrounding countries from starvation. This was a huge blessing to the nations but was still only a partial fulfilment of the promise. Centuries later, God spoke to Israel's king David through Nathan the prophet:

> When your days are fulfilled and you lie down with your fathers, I will raise up your offspring after you, who shall come from your body, and I will establish his kingdom. He shall build a house for my name, and I will establish the throne of his kingdom forever. I will be to him a father, and he shall be to me a son. When he commits iniquity, I will discipline him with the rod of men, with the stripes of the sons of men, but my steadfast love will not depart from him, as I took it from Saul, whom I put away from before you. And your house and your kingdom shall be made sure forever before me. Your throne shall be established forever.
>
> *2 Samuel 7:12–16*

Some of this promise to David was fulfilled in his son Solomon. But the promise of a throne established forever was not. The way that would happen was foretold in the angel's message to Mary: "You will conceive and give birth to a son, and you are to call him Jesus. He will be great and will be called the Son of the Most High. The Lord God will give him the throne of his father David, and he will reign over Jacob's descendants forever; his kingdom will never end."[23]

These texts introduce us to an important recurring feature of biblical prophecy – short- and long-term fulfilment. Solomon was the short-term fulfilment of the promise to King David. His reign, initially glorious, was marred by unwise behavior for which God had to discipline him. Jesus Christ is the long-term fulfilment. The short-term fulfilment keeps alive confidence in the ultimate complete fulfilment of the prophecy.

In the millennium between David and Christ, the idea of the seed morphed into that of the Anointed One, the Messiah. Many prophets kept the expectation of his coming alive by giving more and more detail as the time of Christ's coming into the world drew near.

For instance, Isaiah predicted that the Messiah would have a forerunner:

> A voice of one calling:
> "In the wilderness prepare
>   the way for the LORD;
> make straight in the desert
>   a highway for our God.
> Every valley shall be raised up,
>   every mountain and hill made low;
> the rough ground shall become level,
>   the rugged places a plain."
>
> *Isaiah 40:3–4 NIV*

And when John the Baptist came seven centuries later and was asked to identify himself to the Jewish authorities, he replied in the words of Isaiah: "I am the voice of one calling in the wilderness, 'Make straight the way for the Lord.'"[24]

Micah, who lived around the same time as Isaiah, said that the coming ruler would be born in Bethlehem: "But you, Bethlehem Ephrathah, though you are small among the clans of Judah, out of you will come for me one who will be ruler over Israel, whose origins are from of old, from ancient times" (we should note the hint at the promised ruler's divine origin in the last clause).[25] This prophecy specifying the birthplace of Messiah was accepted by the authorities at the time of Jesus' birth, as we see from their reply to a query addressed to them by King Herod:

> When he had called together all the people's chief priests and teachers of the law, he asked them where the Messiah was to be born. "In Bethlehem in Judea," they replied, "for this is what the prophet has written:

>"'But you, Bethlehem, in the land of Judah,
>>are by no means least among the rulers of Judah;
>for out of you will come a ruler
>>who will shepherd my people Israel.'"

Matthew 2:4–6 NIV

Isaiah also predicted the birth of a uniquely special child who would be called Immanuel – "God with us": "Therefore the Lord himself will give you a sign: The virgin will conceive and give birth to a son, and will call him Immanuel."[26] That prophecy was fulfilled around seven centuries later when an angel said to the virgin Mary, "The Holy Spirit will come on you, and the power of the Most High will overshadow you. So the holy one to be born will be called the Son of God."[27] The Hebrew word translated "virgin" in Isaiah's prophecy is *almah*, which means a young woman; however, Luke's translation is the Greek word for "virgin." Now, Luke was well aware that this word was likely to cause offense to those of his readers who were conservative Jews, and therefore he would not have used it unless he believed it to be a true description of Mary.

The prophet Zechariah (ca. 520 BC) even specified the manner in which the Messiah would later come into Jerusalem as king: "Rejoice greatly, Daughter Zion! Shout, Daughter Jerusalem! See, your king comes to you, righteous and victorious, lowly and riding on a donkey, on a colt, the foal of a donkey."[28] Jesus deliberately fulfilled this prophecy on his last journey to Jerusalem:

Now when they drew near to Jerusalem and came to Bethphage, to the Mount of Olives, then Jesus sent two disciples, saying to them, "Go into the village in front of you, and immediately you will find a donkey tied, and a colt with her. Untie them and bring them to me. If anyone says anything to you, you shall say, 'The Lord needs them,' and he will send them at once." This took place to fulfill what was spoken by the prophet, saying,

>"Say to the daughter of Zion,
>'Behold, your king is coming to you,
>>humble, and mounted on a donkey,
>>on a colt, the foal of a beast of burden.'"

The disciples went and did as Jesus had directed them. They brought the donkey and the colt and put on them their cloaks, and he sat on them.

Most of the crowd spread their cloaks on the road, and others cut branches from the trees and spread them on the road. And the crowds that went before him and that followed him were shouting, "Hosanna to the Son of David! Blessed is he who comes in the name of the Lord! Hosanna in the highest!" And when he entered Jerusalem, the whole city was stirred up, saying, "Who is this?" And the crowds said, "This is the prophet Jesus, from Nazareth of Galilee."

Matthew 21:1–11

One of the most important Messianic predictions is Isaiah's famous "Suffering Servant" prophecy (Isaiah 53). It tells us that the Messiah, when he came, would be despised and rejected and suffer as a sacrifice for sin:

> But he was pierced for our transgressions;
>> he was crushed for our iniquities;
> upon him was the chastisement that brought us peace,
>> and with his wounds we are healed.
> All we like sheep have gone astray;
>> we have turned – every one – to his own way;
> and the LORD has laid on him
>> the iniquity of us all.

Isaiah 53:5–6

Isaiah 53 is cited six times in the New Testament: in Matthew 8:14–17; Luke 22:35–38; John 12:37–41; Acts 8:26–35; Romans 10:1–21; and 1 Peter 2:19–25. Luke 22 is of particular importance, since there Jesus cites Isaiah 53:12 as speaking of himself. It is hard for us to resist the overwhelming impression that this text from Isaiah constitutes a vivid and accurate depiction of the rejection, suffering, death, and, indeed, resurrection of Jesus.

But, for the first disciples, the hard thing was to accept the fact that Jesus would be rejected and murdered. That was because the Jewish understanding of the prophecies at the time was that Messiah would come as a powerful king and free them from the oppression of the Roman occupying power. That Messiah should be rejected and suffer was a contradiction in terms for the Jewish people, as a dead Messiah would be useless in a power struggle.

Thus, when Jesus said he was going to be crucified in Jerusalem, the disciples protested. And when they saw that it was actually going to happen, they deserted him. That was not a program of events that they wished to buy into. They were incapable of grasping why Jesus needed to suffer, since they expected Messiah to give the nation its political freedom, and partly in consequence of this, they failed to identify Messiah with Isaiah's Suffering Servant.

The fact is that we humans need saving from our sins much more than we need political freedom or upgrading. Programs of education and technological or medical upgrades will never adequately deal with moral failure, because the root of that failure is a fundamental alienation from God. Christ offers to deal with that alienation by offering us salvation based on his death on the cross for our sins and on his resurrection.

But salvation is not conferred automatically. In order to receive it, we must have a radical change of mind; we must personally repent of the mess we have made of our own and other people's lives.[29] We must turn away from sin and, as an act of our will and heart, trust Christ as Savior and Lord: "To all who did receive him, who believed in his name, he gave the right to become children of God."[30]

What scholars understand to be the very earliest Christian creed affirms that this message of salvation was the subject of prophecy: "For I delivered to you as of first importance what I also received: that Christ died for our sins in accordance with the Scriptures, that he was buried, that he was raised on the third day in accordance with the Scriptures, and that he appeared to Cephas, then to the twelve. Then he appeared to more than five hundred brothers at one time, most of whom are still alive, though some have fallen asleep. Then he appeared to James, then to all the apostles. Last of all, as to one untimely born, he appeared also to me."[31] Note that Paul says not only that Christ died and rose again according to the Scriptures but that he *died for our sins* according to what Scripture had foretold.

The transhumanist *homo deus* project may be seen as a parody of this Christian teaching. We are born as creatures of God. We have to *become* children of God by trusting Christ. The *homo deus* project seeks to upgrade us; God gives us new life. Christ himself describes this life as eternal life, God's life in us, untouchable by death. We are connected to other believers by the fact that we share a common life and express it in live, face-to-face fellowship in communities called churches, insofar as we are able.

Now, technological connectedness, through email, Facebook, WhatsApp, and so on, has clearly been a great comfort and help to people who are not mobile or who are ill or shut-in, or living in remote communities. The sad thing, though, is that for many able-bodied people, the increase in technological connectedness has gone hand in hand with a decrease in their spending time talking to each other and doing things together. Thus, loneliness may, for some, be alleviated, at least partially, with technical connection, whereas for others, exactly the opposite is true.

What God offers is a real, indeed a spectacular, upgrade, and it is credible, since by contrast with hoped-for AI upgrades, it concentrates not merely on technological improvements but on the moral and spiritual side of human character. Putting it another way, posthuman scenarios tend to be utopian almost by definition, and as we well know, utopian thinking has usually led in the past, not to a paradise on earth, but to indescribable violence, war, and death for millions. The promises of utopia are inevitably doomed if they are made without any realistic program for dealing with the sinfulness of human nature and without pointing people to a source of inner power to help them navigate the complexities of life.

By contrast, Christianity does know of such a power, and the brilliant ancient historian Luke tells us about the advent of that power at Pentecost in the opening chapters of his book of Acts.[32] For forty days after the resurrection, Jesus met with his disciples, presenting them with convincing evidence that he was alive after having been dead. During that time, he taught them about his kingdom, finally commanding them to go to Jerusalem and wait for the Holy Spirit to come from him to empower them to be his witnesses to the ends of the earth.

They were understandably very interested in what Jesus intended to do next. They wished to know if, now that he had conquered death, he was going to use this power to eject the Roman occupying power and take over the government as King Messiah. His answer was a clear no. He was not going to restore the kingdom to Israel at that time. One day he would – after all, it was a key biblical expectation that Messiah would do just that – but not yet. Furthermore, he was not going to tell them when that event would happen. Their immediate task was not to speculate about the future but to be his witnesses around the world. He was about to leave and return to heaven, from where he had originally come.

Luke tells us that as Jesus said this, he rose into the heavens, and then a cloud received him out of their sight. They stared, incredulous, into the sky, but were immediately informed that one of the purposes of the ascension was to demonstrate to them not only that he would return but how he would return. They had seen him go into another world visibly and physically; he would one day come back to this world in exactly the same way, physically and visibly.

We pause to contrast this with the hope of AGI that one day we will be able to upload the contents of our minds onto silicon and so "live" forever – although some thoughtful people are not so enamored with equating a digital existence in the cyberworld with immortality. Also, I am not so convinced that uploading the contents of the neural network of your brain at a particular moment would be equivalent to uploading you. The impossibility of doing so is evident – uploading you digitally would include uploading your qualia and emotions, and these are not computable. End of story.

Jesus' mind was not uploaded onto silicon; he ascended bodily into heaven and so, one day, will those who follow him. This claim clashes head-on with the dominant earthbound, atheistic naturalism of the Western academy that teaches that this world is all that there is; there is no other world to which one can ascend. But as I have repeatedly argued elsewhere, naturalism is not true, and contrary to widespread opinion, it is not supported by science; rather, it undermines it, since it can give no rational account of rational thought.[33] The promises of AGI are firmly rooted in this world, and in that sense they are parochial and small compared with the mind-boggling implications of the resurrection and ascension of Jesus.

QUESTIONS

1. If you are a Christian, what are your reasons for believing that Jesus is the true Homo Deus?
2. If you are not a Christian, how do you react to Jesus' claim to be the true Homo Deus? What evidence would you adduce against its veracity?
3. Discuss the evidence for the resurrection of Christ and compare it with the transhumanist hope of solving the problem of death.
4. What, in your view, is the evidential value of biblical prophecy?
5. What prophecies do you find convincing, if any?
6. In what sense is the transhumanist dream a parody of Christianity?

CHAPTER 15

FUTURE SHOCK

*The Return of the Man
Who Is God*

Before his death, Jesus told his disciples that he was going away but would one day come back for them to take them to a place he was going to prepare for them in the presence of his Father.[1] They initially did not understand what he was talking about, but with his resurrection and ascension, it all became much clearer.

With Jesus' death and resurrection, God's great project for the redemption of the world took an immense step forward as the apostle Peter announced in his second major sermon recorded in the book of Acts. Peter and John healed a lame man at the gate of the temple, and this attracted a large crowd. Peter then publicly explained the significance of the miracle, putting it into the context of what had been happening in Jerusalem in the previous days. Peter directly accused the crowd of killing the "Author of life"[2] and yet appealed to them by giving them a way out of their dire predicament:

> And now, brothers, I know that you acted in ignorance, as did also your rulers. But what God foretold by the mouth of all the prophets, that his Christ would suffer, he thus fulfilled. Repent therefore, and turn back, that your sins may be blotted out, that times of refreshing may come from the presence of the Lord, and that he may send the Christ appointed for you, Jesus, whom heaven must receive until the time for restoring all the things about which God spoke by the mouth of his holy prophets long ago.
>
> *Acts 3:17–21*

It was a devastating indictment of those who murdered Jesus, but it was also a gracious offer of salvation for those willing to repent and trust him. Peter answers the unspoken question (*Where is Jesus, then?*) by pointing out that he had gone to heaven and would remain there until the next great step in God's program happened – the restoration that will be triggered by Jesus' return.

Sadly, the public face of Christianity has become so insipid and watered down that the vibrant central hope of the return of Christ, which should be at its heart, has been all but lost – or relegated to the lunatic fringe of naive prophecy-mongers. The warning of C. S. Lewis is ignored: "Do not attempt to water Christianity down. There must be no pretense that you can have it with the Supernatural left out. So far as I can see Christianity is precisely the one religion from which the miraculous cannot be separated. You must frankly argue for supernaturalism from the very outset."[3]

Inevitably, one of the consequences of the Enlightenment's rejection of the supernatural was that, as theologian David Bosch says, "little room was left for the 'great eschatological event Christians had long awaited, namely the Second Coming.' Belief in Christ's return on the clouds was superseded by the idea of God's kingdom in the world which would be introduced step by step through successful labors in missionary endeavor abroad and through creating an egalitarian society at home."[4]

Behind this kind of thinking lies the notion of progress that marked the Enlightenment and the great strides that were made in science, technology, and industry that brought so much wealth to Europe. Unbridled optimism in human potential reigned, and a brave new world was just around the corner. But the imagined Marxist utopia that was to arise out of the workings of the inexorable laws of history turned into a nightmare of human carnage and cost the lives of millions. And not only for Marxism, of course. Extreme nationalism of different kinds has produced similar results. History has taught the hard lesson: there is no pathway to a utopian paradise that bypasses the problem of human sin.

Utopia means "no place"[5] and is, ironically, highly appropriate in this context. Every attempt so far to set up utopia has failed because the visionaries who tried to create such a state did not take into account that human nature is seriously flawed as a result of the entry of sin and alienation into the world at the fall. They did not see, as we pointed out earlier, that humans need saving much more than they need upgrading. The utopian visionaries had no message of salvation, no connection with a divine power capable of changing what human beings are like. As a result, the twentieth century was the bloodiest in history.

Harari and Pinker think violence is in decline. Gray thinks not, and in this he is in line with biblical teaching. Jesus himself issued warnings about future events that are as much a part of his teaching as is the Sermon on the Mount. He warned of deception by imposters and false prophets who, amid a rising tide of wars, famines, and earthquakes, will lead many astray. All of this will build to a climax towards the end:

> Then will appear in heaven the sign of the Son of Man, and then all the tribes of the earth will mourn, and they will see the Son of Man coming on the clouds of heaven with power and great glory. And he will send out his angels with a loud trumpet call, and they will gather his elect from the four winds, from one end of heaven to the other.
>
> *Matthew 24:30–31*

Jesus said these things 2,000 years ago, and the intervening time has been characterized by "wars and rumors of wars."[6] But according to Jesus, these things are not evidence of the end – he explicitly says that such things will happen, but the *end is not yet*. The end of history as we know it will not occur until certain specific things happen that will culminate in the cataclysmic return of Christ to rule.

It is vitally important that those of us who are Christians are not embarrassed at the return of Christ, since he himself made it a central part of his teaching. Not only did he teach his disciples in private that he would return; he made it a key point at his trial when questioned about his identity:

> Again the high priest asked him, "Are you the Christ, the Son of the Blessed?" And Jesus said, "I am, and you will see the Son of Man seated at the right hand of Power, and coming with the clouds of heaven." And the high priest tore his garments and said, "What further witnesses do we need? You have heard his blasphemy. What is your decision?" And they all condemned him as deserving death.
>
> *Mark 14:61–64*

The high priest regarded Jesus' reply as blasphemous because he and all the court understood that Jesus was citing a famous passage from the book of the prophet Daniel that referred to a divine Son of Man who would come on the clouds of heaven and be given universal authority and power to reign forever:

I saw in the night visions,

> and behold, with the clouds of heaven
> there came one like a son of man,
> and he came to the Ancient of Days
> and was presented before him.
> And to him was given dominion
> and glory and a kingdom,
> that all peoples, nations, and languages
> should serve him;
> his dominion is an everlasting dominion,
> which shall not pass away,
> and his kingdom one
> that shall not be destroyed.

Daniel 7:13–14

The return of Christ is not some peripheral, add-on idea concocted by hotheads in backstreet fringe sects. It is evident from what occurred at Jesus' trial that he was crucified precisely because he claimed to be the august Son of Man who, according to the prophet Daniel, would one day come on the clouds of heaven to take up universal rule.[7] And because his return is an essential part of the hope he held out to the world, not surprisingly the New Testament has much to say about it.

THE TRUE SOLUTION TO YUVAL NOAH HARARI'S "TECHNICAL PROBLEM" OF PHYSICAL DEATH

God will eventually deal with physical death, but not by solving it by technological means, as Harari suggests. By raising Jesus from the dead, God has demonstrated that physical death is not unconquerable. The New Testament says that God "has destroyed death and has brought life and immortality to light through the gospel."[8] Death is not going to have the last word. Christ's bodily resurrection is but the beginning of the restoration of the human race and of the whole of creation, which will happen at his return. Furthermore, by his death and resurrection, Christ frees from the fear of death all those who trust him:

> Since therefore the children [i.e., Jesus' disciples] share in flesh and blood, he himself likewise partook of the same things, that through death he might destroy the one who has the power of death, that is, the devil, and deliver all those who through fear of death were subject to lifelong slavery.
>
> *Hebrews 2:14–15*

We must be careful to understand exactly what this passage is saying. It is not claiming that those who trust Christ will not experience fear or the onset of illness, severe pain, and the physical anguish of the process of dying. Fear of these things is a natural, automatic reflex of our human makeup, part of the preservative mechanisms built into our bodies, so that nature itself fights against dying.

People are afraid of death for two opposite reasons. Firstly, some fear that there is nothing after death. Therefore, this present life is all there is, and so, rather than lose physical life, some people will compromise loyalty to God, to truth, to faith, to honor, to principle, and even descend to shameful cowardice – anything to save physical life. Fear of death holds them in moral slavery.

Secondly, other people are afraid of death, not because they think that there is nothing after death, but because they are afraid that there will be far too much after death for their liking – namely, a final judgment with eternal consequences. Christ's death and physical resurrection as a real human being combine to deliver believers from both of these fears. It frees them from a sense of hopelessness at the death of a loved one by informing them that their loved one, now "absent from the body," *is* "present with the Lord,"[9] or, as the Lord himself expressed it, "with me in paradise."[10] It is also the secret of the courage of Christian martyrs who are prepared to die rather than deny Christ.

Christ's death also frees those who trust him from the fear of condemnation. They have God's assurance that Christ, by his sacrificial death, has paid in full the penalty for their sins.[11] Physical death comes but once, and the judgment comes *after* death. For believers, Christ's death atones for their sin; it covers every sin of theirs that the judgment could take cognizance of. In consequence, believers are given the following magnificent assurance: "Just as it is appointed for man to die once, and after that comes judgment, so Christ, having been offered once to bear the sins of many, will appear a second time, not to deal with sin but to save those who are eagerly waiting for him."[12] And Christ, who himself will be the final Judge, declares: "Truly, truly, I say to you, whoever hears my word and believes him who sent me has eternal life. He does not come into judgment, but has passed from death to life."[13]

Contrary to Harari's view, death will not be overcome by medical advances. The historical fact is that death *has already been overcome* – by Jesus Christ, in a spectacular demonstration of God's power, two millennia ago. This is good news – the best humanity has ever had. For Christ's bodily resurrection gives all who trust him a sure and certain hope of their own eventual bodily resurrection. This is the true transhumanism of which Dante wrote.

To get this spectacular truth across to us, Paul refers to Christ's resurrection as the firstfruits of a great harvest to come.[14] Just as the early pickings of fruit promise more fruit to come, so the resurrection of Jesus heralds a great harvest that will take place at Christ's second coming – a resurrection of all persons of all centuries who are Christ's. Those who have died before that coming will be resurrected; those who are still alive at that coming will be changed without dying. All will be given bodies like Christ's glorious resurrection body.[15]

This means for believers, as it did for Christ, that there is to be a physical embodiment after death. One interesting aspect of this in view of the attempt to make silicon-based life is the hint in the New Testament that Jesus' resurrected body was not exactly the same as the body that was buried. It had new properties – it could pass through closed doors, for instance, so that, in a way, it appeared to belong to a different dimension.

In 1 Corinthians 15, Paul contrasts the natural body with the resurrected spiritual body. A spiritual body does not mean a body made in some sense of spirit any more than a petrol engine means an engine made of petrol. Jesus told his disciples he was no spirit: "A spirit does not have flesh and bones as you see that I have."[16] If we put this alongside Paul's statement that "flesh and blood" shall not inherit the (future) kingdom of heaven, then we see that he is indicating that there is a physical difference between the human body as it is now and what it one day will be. My continued existence as *me* is guaranteed, but it will not depend on the development of technology to upload the contents of my brain onto silicon.[17]

Harari is a historian, and one wonders what he thinks about Jesus' life, death, and, in particular, resurrection – especially in light of the strength of the historical evidence for these events. One of the world's best-known scholars on the resurrection, Gary Habermas, draws attention to the remarkable agreement among ancient historians of whatever stripe. He cites the work of several leading scholars. First, he references the late John P. Meier, eminent biblical scholar at Notre Dame University:

> [Meier] concluded his over 400-page in-depth study by judging that more than 40 percent of the miracle claims presented in the Gospel texts actually correspond to specific historical occurrences from the life of Jesus. . . . Meier quite amazingly concluded from Jesus' actions during his public ministry that not only was he viewed widely as a healer and exorcist, but that there is as much historical verification for these aspects of his life as there is for almost anything else that may be said about the historical Jesus. In fact, these aspects are much better evidenced than many other assertions made about Jesus, ones that are often considered to be settled issues.[18]

Second, Habermas cites Graham Twelftree, an Australian biblical scholar at the London School of Theology and editor of *The Cambridge Companion to Miracles*,[19] who "concluded that a much higher percentage (approximately 76 percent) of the Gospel miracle accounts accurately portray historical events in Jesus's life. Twelftree's study indicated findings quite similar to Meier's: 'There is hardly any aspect of the life of the historical Jesus which is so well and widely attested as that he conducted unparalleled wonders.' Astonishingly, these miraculous deeds 'were the most important aspect of Jesus' whole pre-Easter ministry.'"[20]

Yet Harari makes no effort whatsoever to interact with his fellow historians on a topic of such magnitude. In his 2023 article "The Difference Jesus Makes: Yuval Noah Harari and Wolfhart Pannenberg on the Shape of Universal History," E. J. David Kramer writes:

> Harari describes Christian teaching accurately as claiming Jesus of Nazareth to be the Jewish Messiah, God's incarnation in the flesh, in whose death lies humanity's salvation. Interestingly, Harari makes no mention of Jesus' resurrection, noting only that "In one of history's strangest twists, this esoteric Jewish sect took over the mighty Roman Empire." There is no engagement with historical evidence for the resurrection, no discernible interest in the impact of Jesus on the course of world history or global cultures, no entertaining of the possibility that anything of unique importance occurred here.

Instead, Jesus is simply one religious innovator among many, often named in one breath with other religious pioneers such as Confucius, the Buddha, and Mohammed. It appears that Harari does not need to engage Jesus' specific claims because his naturalistic background beliefs do not leave room for Jesus to be anything but a peddler of fictions.[21]

I find this simply amazing that a public intellectual who claims to be writing about the history of civilization and has a particular interest in the solution to death ignores the central message of Christianity that emanated from an empty tomb in his own country of Israel. Such is the baleful influence of naturalism.

Following the poem *De rerum natura*[22] by the ancient Latin poet and philosopher Lucretius, many atheists think that the idea of bodily resurrection is absurd, since when we die, the atoms of our bodies disperse and become part of the surrounding vegetation, and so may well subsequently become part of other animals and even other humans. How, then, they argue, can it make sense to talk about a bodily resurrection of the dead?

It is true that at death the atoms in our bodies disperse. But, of course, we do not have to wait until death for this to happen. The cells, and therefore the atoms, in our bodies are constantly changing and dispersing. None of the cells now present in my body were present in my body ten years ago (except, perhaps, certain specialized cells in the brain). Yet in spite of this constant change and replacement of atoms and cells during the course of aging, the formal identity of my body remains recognizably the same. Clear evidence of that is given by how a person's fingerprints, which are unique to that person, remain the same throughout his or her lifetime. This fact, first demonstrated by Francis Galton in 1888, plays a decisive role in the identification of culprits. Similar things could be said about identification using DNA.

The complex coding, and whatever else is responsible for maintaining the identity of a body through its time on earth, is known by God for every human being who has ever lived. At the future resurrection, God, who, after all, created matter in the first place, will not be hard up for whatever substance in which the unique bodily identity of each person will be expressed. The result will be that each individual believer will have a body like Christ's glorious resurrection body (and therefore with capacities and glories that our present bodies do not have). But each person will be individually identifiable through the unique form of his or her resurrection body as the same person identifiable by his or her body here on earth:

Just as we have borne the image of the man of dust, we shall also bear the image of the man of heaven.

I tell you this, brothers: flesh and blood cannot inherit the kingdom of God, nor does the perishable inherit the imperishable. Behold! I tell you a mystery. We shall not all sleep, but we shall all be changed, in a moment, in the twinkling of an eye, at the last trumpet. For the trumpet will sound, and the dead will be raised imperishable, and we shall be changed.... This mortal body must put on immortality.

1 Corinthians 15:49–53

The deduction that each individual Christian believer is taught to make from the certainty of bodily resurrection is that life in this present body in this world is worth living to the full of one's energies, abilities, and circumstances, in spite of all life's pains and sufferings, old age, and eventual death: "Therefore . . . be steadfast, immovable, always abounding in the work of the Lord, knowing that in the Lord your labor is not in vain" (1 Corinthians 15:58). This means that although our bodies here on earth, inherited as they are from a fallen race, are subject to decay and death, what each person does in the body is eternally significant.

As a further example, we might consider the apostle Paul when he visited Thessalonica and preached there for three weeks or so – not a particularly long time. Yet as he reminded them in a letter he subsequently wrote, during that brief visit he told the Thessalonians about the coming of Christ in considerable detail. In fact, their conversion to Christianity was described by some as follows:

For they themselves report concerning us the kind of reception we had among you, and how you turned to God from idols to serve the living and true God, and to wait for his Son from heaven, whom he raised from the dead, Jesus who delivers us from the wrath to come.

1 Thessalonians 1:9–10

In fact, at the end of each chapter of his letter, Paul encourages the believers to live their lives in light of the future coming of Christ. Jesus did the same thing in some of his parables that emphasize the unexpectedness and suddenness of his coming—the "Son of Man is coming at an hour you do not expect"—and in his statement in Revelation: "Surely I am coming soon."[23] These passages have led some people to erroneously think that Christ led the early Christians to expect his return almost immediately, and when this did not turn out to be the case, the hope of such a return faded into the background. Jesus himself, however, had warned in Matthew 24 that the timescale would be long rather than short. The resolution of this apparent paradox is surely this: we all move towards the return of Christ at two "speeds" – the speed of earth history and the speed with which we approach death. Jesus and his apostles were not cheating when they encouraged believers to live as though Christ could return at any time, since this is the only way to live that will allow our expectation of his coming to have the moral and spiritual effect it should have on us. If I die today, the time of Christ's coming measured in years is irrelevant to me.

It was, however, inevitable in those early days, when believers began to die and there was no sign of Christ's return, that questions would be asked. In response, at the very end of his first letter to the Thessalonians, Paul reassures the living believers:

> But we do not want you to be uninformed, brothers, about those who are asleep, that you may not grieve as others do who have no hope. For since we believe that Jesus died and rose again, even so, through Jesus, God will bring with him those who have fallen asleep. For this we declare to you by a word from the Lord, that we who are alive, who are left until the coming of the Lord, will not precede those who have fallen asleep. For the Lord himself will descend from heaven with a cry of command, with the voice of an archangel, and with the sound of the trumpet of God. And the dead in Christ will rise first. Then we who are alive, who are left, will be caught up together with them in the clouds to meet the Lord in the air, and so we will always be with the Lord. Therefore encourage one another with these words.
>
> *1 Thessalonians 4:13–18*

Paul expected Christians who lost loved ones to grieve, but not in the same way as people who had no hope. To cut through their tears, he gives them more detail about what the return of Christ will mean both for their departed loved ones and for themselves. Paul's own understanding of death was to be "absent from the body" and "present with the Lord," and his great hope expressed here is that one day all believers will be with the Lord – and some of them will not even experience physical death at all! This is way beyond anything AI could even dream of.

AI may well make many good and helpful advances that will improve the lot of humanity. No matter what the promise might be, however, the central claim of Christianity is that the future is far greater than anything AI or AGI can promise, since something infinitely bigger than either of them *has already happened* on our planet: God, who is responsible for the existence of the universe and its laws and the architecture of the human mind, the divine Logos who was in the beginning, has coded himself into humanity – the Word became flesh and dwelt among us. This is not artificial intelligence; this is Real Intelligence – way beyond anything conceivable, let alone constructible, by humans.

And the fact that God did become human is the greatest evidence of the uniqueness of human beings and of God's commitment to embodied humanity. Humans, original version, are demonstrated to be unique precisely because God could and did become one. And those of us who have received him will one day at his return be gloriously "upgraded" to be like him and share in the marvels of the eternal world to come.

This was the plan from the beginning – and it has implications for the new heaven and the new earth. And since this new creation has a physical dimension, what might we then be allowed to create in the way of heavenly technology?

All of this means that Christians (and indeed others) need to think hard about the implications of these fundamental Christian doctrines of the resurrection and return of Christ for AI and the race to create *homo deus*. For if the Christian teaching is true, the race to conquer death as a technical problem will ultimately prove to be futile, although the technology developed along the way may help ease old age and solve many outstanding medical problems. But humans were not made to live indefinitely on this planet. Something much bigger is possible that makes Harari's scheme seem rather insignificant.

BIBLICAL PERSPECTIVES ON THE ADVENT OF A PERSON CLAIMING TO BE *HOMO DEUS*

Let us now see what the Bible has to say about what is to happen on this planet in the future. John Gray picks up a comment by Harari that *homo deus* will resemble the Greek gods and concludes: "Humans may well use science to turn themselves into something like gods as they have imagined them to be. But no Supreme Being will appear on the scene. Instead, there will be many different gods, each of them a parody of human beings that once existed."[24]

Gray, who otherwise has many valuable things to say, is wrong here – that is, if Scripture has anything to say about it, which it does. According to the biblical narrative, history is leading up to the appearance of a Supreme Being, one who has already been here and who, when he was here, promised to return. This is a fundamental Christian teaching. It also has major implications for the world, as we see from the second letter Paul wrote to the church at Thessalonica. Apparently, false teachers had turned up in that city who were perverting the Christian message by infecting it with erroneous ideas such as asserting that Christ had already returned. Not only that, but the church was bravely holding out against intensified persecution. On hearing of this development, Paul wrote to them once more.

As we read what he said, we should bear in mind what we mentioned earlier that, according to the book of Acts, Paul spent only three weeks or so in Thessalonica, yet he felt it was important for those converted to Christianity in that short time to know about the future in some considerable detail. Here is what he wrote:

> Now concerning the coming of our Lord Jesus Christ and our being gathered together to him, we ask you, brothers, not to be quickly shaken in mind or alarmed, either by a spirit or a spoken word, or a letter seeming to be from us, to the effect that the day of the Lord has come. Let no one deceive you in any way. For that day will not come, unless the rebellion comes first, and the man of lawlessness is revealed, the son of destruction, who opposes and exalts himself against every so-called god or object of worship, so that he takes his seat in the temple of God, proclaiming himself to be God. Do you not remember that when I was still with you I told you these things? And you know what is restraining him now so that he may be revealed in his time. For the mystery of lawlessness is already at work. Only he who now restrains it will do so until he is out of the way. And then the lawless one will be revealed, whom the Lord Jesus will kill with the breath of his mouth and bring to nothing by the appearance of his coming. The coming of the lawless one is by the activity of Satan with all power and false signs and wonders, and with all wicked deception for those who are perishing, because they refused to love the truth and so be saved.

> *2 Thessalonians 2:1–10*

Paul reminds them that on his first visit to them he had carefully explained that Christ would not return until certain things had happened

– things that would be so publicly visible, striking, and obvious that you wouldn't need to be told about them. Recall that Jesus himself said this in the Olivet Discourse in Matthew 24, warning us that many would turn up saying that they were the Christ but that we shouldn't listen to them since the true Christ will return under circumstances that will be spectacularly obvious.

Nevertheless, it would appear that false teachers had turned up in Thessalonica who were unsettling the believers by contradicting Christ's teaching and suggesting that the day of judgment had already come. This highlights the fact that prophecy can become speculative and be used to mislead. Such erroneous teaching made life even more difficult for the Christians who were suffering persecution at the time. Paul was quick to reassure them that although the judgment day had not yet come, it one day would, and in such a manner as to put an end to persecuting powers.

The trigger for the events that Paul mentions here are a rebellion and the appearing of a person described as the "man of lawlessness" (2 Thessalonians 2:3), whose main characteristic is opposition to gods in any shape or form, who nevertheless proclaims himself to be God. Again, no one will fail to recognize this development, since, as Paul tells us, this tyrannical leader will be energized by satanic power and enabled to deceive people by lying wonders. The climax will come when the returning Christ bursts onto the scene and destroys him by his appearing. Clearly nothing on this scale had yet happened in Paul's day, and it has clearly not happened subsequently. Its intensity and global dimensions ensure that when it does happen, the whole world will be all too aware of it.

This scenario is just as far as it could be from the view that Christian teaching will gradually permeate the planet until peace reigns. No, Paul says that there will be a supernatural cataclysmic intervention by God that will put a stop to a regime of maximal evil. The question is this: How do we know whether this apocalyptic scenario is true or not?

Paul says that one of the ways in which the Thessalonians could know that this would happen is that the seeds of the ideas that would lead to it were already visible in the Roman culture of the day. Paul writes: "For the mystery of lawlessness is already at work" (2 Thessalonians 2:7). Paul clearly does not mean lawlessness in the sense of the absence of civil law, since Rome was famous for its laws, some of which form the basis of European law. Paul, as the context shows, is talking about *spiritual* lawlessness, the blasphemy of human beings who claim divinity, as many kings in the past had done and as some of the Roman emperors were already doing at the time. Christians who refused to acknowledge this were often persecuted and executed.

We have already seen that the idea of *homo deus* is rooted in the Genesis account of the temptation and fall. That, however, is only the first of many human attempts to play God or to be God. From time to time it rears its head in the Old Testament record – we read of emperors such as the Babylonian Nebuchadnezzar (Daniel 3) and the Greek Antiochus Epiphanes (Daniel 11:21–32), who arrogated divine powers to themselves, the latter using those powers to justify violence.

As part of the powerful imperial cult, the Roman emperors were often accorded divine honors after their deaths, as was Julius Caesar, who was called *divus Iulius*. Some impatient souls, such as the infamous Caligula, insisted on such accolades during their lifetimes – which led to their extreme unpopularity in the Senate. In New Testament times, the divinization of the emperors sometimes led to the persecution of Christians, many of whom courageously paid with their lives for refusing to bow down and worship a deified emperor.

At every turn, it would seem, humanity's efforts to achieve divinity have been associated with an overweening arrogance and a sense of superiority that, far from achieving something superhuman, has produced something terrifyingly subhuman and bestial. The more they try to elevate themselves, the more they sink into a morass of violence and tyranny, as was horrifically demonstrated in the twentieth century. Hannah Arendt, who wrote one of the first books on totalitarianism – *The Origins of Totalitarianism* (published in 1951) – was convinced that totalitarianism was rooted in a utopianism based on the rejection of God and the deification of man. She wrote perceptively:

What binds these men together is a firm and sincere belief in human omnipotence. Their moral cynicism, their belief that everything is permitted, rests on the solid conviction that everything is possible. . . . In trying to create a perverse heaven on earth, totalitarian systems acknowledge no limit on either their conduct or their aspirations. They take Dostoyevsky's chilling warning that "if God does not exist, everything is permitted" and institutionalise it in the Party. From there it is but a short distance to the mass killing and terror endemic to totalitarianism, from Nazi Germany's Auschwitz and Treblinka, to the Soviet Union's Lubyanka prison and Perm-36 gulag, to Communist China's Great Leap Forward and Cultural Revolution. . . . The concentration and extermination camps of totalitarian regimes serve as the laboratories in which the fundamental belief of totalitarianism that everything is possible is being verified.[25]

According to Paul, the same dark shadow looms over the future of humanity. The horrific totalitarian vision Paul outlines in his second letter to the Thessalonian Christians is very likely to be characterized by rigid and oppressive civil laws; but at the spiritual level, it is in its essence lawless rebellion against Almighty God – hence the description "man of lawlessness." Paul told the Thessalonians that what will happen in the future is the inevitable harvest of the attempt to deify humans, and it was already visible in their Roman culture at the time.

We should not, therefore, be surprised to see it played out in the future on a global scale and featuring the kind of totalitarian social control to be found these days in China. The way world politics are going, it's not hard to imagine that political power will be concentrated into the hands of fewer and fewer people, which could potentially lead eventually to a world-state controlled by a single person with extraordinary authority – a *homo deus* whose powers of rule and deception are derived from the most sinister of all superhuman intelligences – the devil himself.

The fact that there is such clear historical evidence for the prevalence of the concept of a *homo deus* makes the biblical scenario highly plausible. Of course, it contradicts the widespread ideas that human beings are basically good and improving all the time, that eventually bad behavior will be eliminated, and that one of Max Tegmark's more humane scenarios is more likely to characterize the future – for example, the emergence of a Protector God, a Benevolent Dictator, or an Egalitarian Utopia.[26] That seems like mere wishful thinking in light of the biblical material and of the experience of the twentieth century. Interestingly enough, it also seems like wishful thinking in light of Harari's sobering conclusion to *Sapiens*:

> Moreover, despite the astonishing things that humans are capable of doing, we remain unsure of our goals and we seem to be as discontented as ever. We have advanced from canoes to galleys to steamships to space shuttles – but nobody knows where we're going. We are more powerful than ever before but have very little idea what to do with all that power. Worse still, humans seem to be more irresponsible than ever. Self-made gods with only the laws of physics to keep us company, we are accountable to no one. We are consequently

wreaking havoc on our fellow animals and on the surrounding ecosystem, seeking little more than our own comfort and amusement, yet never finding satisfaction.

Is there anything more dangerous than dissatisfied and irresponsible gods who don't know what they want?[27]

No wonder that Pope Francis, in his 1 January 2024 World Day of Peace message, entitled "Artificial Intelligence and Peace," while praising positive developments in technology that benefited humanity, issued the following stern warning that "by proposing to overcome every limit through technology, in an obsessive desire to control everything, we risk losing control over ourselves." He therefore urged "the global community of nations to work together in order to adopt a binding international treaty that regulates the development and use of artificial intelligence in its many forms."[28]

Will his voice be heard?

QUESTIONS

1. What did Christ claim about his return? What do you understand by that claim?
2. What role should Jesus' return play in a Christian's life?
3. How is Christ's claim to return supported by his resurrection?
4. How is Christ's resurrection the answer to Harari's "problem" of physical death?
5. Why do you think Harari does not seem to take the historical evidence for Jesus' resurrection seriously?
6. Compare the hope of AGI with Christ's promise of eternal life and resurrection for all believers. Which do you find more credible, and why?
7. What did Paul teach the Thessalonian church about events surrounding the coming of Christ in the future?
8. Why is the man of lawlessness a false homo deus?

CHAPTER 16

HOMO DEUS IN THE BOOK OF REVELATION

The last book of the New Testament, written the better part of 2,000 years ago, describes a future *homo deus* that embodies the features both of Paul's "man of lawlessness" and Tegmark's Prometheus. In the visions of Revelation 12–13, we are introduced to the extremely vivid spectacle of a horrific monster in the shape of a beast or "wild thing" with seven heads and ten horns to whom the devil, Satan (pictured both as a snake and a dragon), gives immense power and worldwide authority. This monster becomes a blasphemous object of worship for the entire world, as does the devil that empowers it.

Such imagery is familiar to readers of the Old Testament. The prophet Daniel uses wild animals to symbolize empires and their leaders. And the first readers of the book of Revelation would have had no difficulty in identifying a state that behaved like a wild monster, since they lived in one – the Roman Empire. They got the message loud and clear, and any reader who took it seriously would realize that although the imagery applied to the Roman Empire, there are, as we shall see, plausible applications to a future world-state in the lead-up to the return of Christ.

Therefore, before dismissing these visions as overheated apocalyptic fantasy, let's read the following excerpt from Revelation 13 to help us make an informed attempt at understanding what reality the imagery is intended to convey:

> And I saw a beast rising out of the sea, with ten horns and seven heads, with ten diadems on its horns and blasphemous names on its heads. And the beast that I saw was like a leopard; its feet were like a bear's, and its mouth was like a lion's mouth. And to it the dragon gave his power and his throne and great

authority. One of its heads seemed to have a mortal wound, but its mortal wound was healed, and the whole earth marveled as they followed the beast. And they worshiped the dragon, for he had given his authority to the beast, and they worshiped the beast, saying, "Who is like the beast, and who can fight against it?"

And the beast was given a mouth uttering haughty and blasphemous words, and it was allowed to exercise authority for forty-two months. It opened its mouth to utter blasphemies against God, blaspheming his name and his dwelling, that is, those who dwell in heaven. Also it was allowed to make war on the saints and to conquer them. And authority was given it over every tribe and people and language and nation, and all who dwell on earth will worship it, everyone whose name has not been written before the foundation of the world in the book of life of the Lamb who was slain.

Revelation 13:1–8

We note immediately the marked similarity between this monster and the anti-God man of lawlessness in 2 Thessalonians, so that Revelation backs up with its imagery and metaphor what Paul says in plain, factual prose. This confirms an important point made by C. S. Lewis that symbols and metaphor are always used to stand for something real, not for something unreal. For example, saying "my heart is broken" is using a metaphor to describe a very real, painful emotional experience, not something imaginary. We will suggest later that the monster imagery is used here variously to represent both the world-state and its leader.

Its global authority is in part established through the healing of a "mortal wound" in one of its heads. Although we cannot say precisely what this refers to, it sounds uncannily like a parody of the central events of the death and resurrection of Christ that establish his authority as Messiah and Son of God.

We note also that although this horrific beast is permitted to lay waste to the Christian community, its tenure of power is strictly limited. The scenario is now made more complex with the arrival of another "beast":

Then I saw another beast rising out of the earth. It had two horns like a lamb and it spoke like a dragon. It exercises all the authority of the first beast in its presence, and makes the earth and its inhabitants worship the first beast, whose mortal wound was healed. It performs great signs, even making fire come down from heaven to earth in front of people, and by the signs that it is allowed to work in the presence of the beast it deceives those who dwell on earth, telling them to make an image for the beast that was wounded by the sword and yet lived. And it was allowed to give breath to the image of the beast, so that the image of the beast might even speak and might cause those who would not worship the image of the beast to be slain. Also it causes all, both small and great, both rich and poor, both free and slave, to be marked on the right hand or the forehead, so that no one can buy or sell unless he has the mark, that is, the name of the beast or the number of its name. This calls for wisdom: let the one who has understanding calculate the number of the beast, for it is the number of a man, and his number is 666.

Revelation 13:11–18

The repetition of the idea of a mortal wound healed intensifies the impression that the biblical story of the crucifixion is being parodied by the first wild animal, the Monster, who aspires to be God. The Monster is promoted by the second wild animal, which has horns like a lamb. As to *what* it is, this second animal represents a human who functions like a minister of propaganda, like the most infamous of that species, Joseph Goebbels, who bore the august title Minister for Public Enlightenment and Propaganda for Hitler's Nazi regime. Goebbels was the architect of the Hitler führer myth, which played a decisive role in converting the masses to Nazism. He became president of the so-called Chamber of Culture, which gave him control over the media and the arts. Similarly, this second wild animal will actively use all means at his disposal to promote the worldwide state cult of the first beast, whose mortal wound was healed. He uses devilish powers, to which Goebbels had no access (although one sometimes wonders whether the Nazi league did have evil powers), to perform great signs, including bringing fire down from heaven in public, as Elijah did in his contest with the prophets of Baal and as the two witnesses of Revelation 11:3 also did.

Once again, we have an evil imitation of the real thing that is strongly reminiscent of the way in which the Egyptian magicians duplicated the signs that Moses did before Pharoah, to show that there was nothing special in the claim that God was with Moses. Even Goebbels was wont to refer to secret miracle weapons to bolster the evil Nazi regime. And Hitler and Goebbels deceived a nation – even though they didn't have the internet and social media!

The level of deception in the Monster's future world-state will be substantially increased when, on the instructions of the second beast, a very special kind of image of the first beast is made. This is a psychologically significant move. The matter of image is all-important to those who seek power, even if it is simply a photographic image hanging in thousands of rooms in institutions throughout the land or a massive statue in a city square.

Some people think that the idea of a modern head of state setting up an image to be worshiped is so primitive that in the unlikely event that it ever happens, no one will be deceived by it for a moment. They would be right, of course, if they have in mind some primitive stone or wooden statue, such as was common to represent the ancient gods. At every stage of history, human beings have set up such images and bowed down to worship the creations of their own minds and hands. Some have dreamed of somehow giving life to their creations, as in the Jewish folklore from the Middle Ages of a creature called a golem, fashioned from inanimate matter, such as mud. The golem would become animate when, for instance, a sacred Hebrew text or name for God was placed in its mouth. The most famous legendary example is the giant golem created in the sixteenth century by Rabbi Loew to protect Prague. To let it rest on the Sabbath, the rabbi removed the tablet with the name of God from its mouth. But he forgot to do so on one occasion and the golem went on a destructive rampage in the city until the rabbi managed to take the tablet out of its mouth.

It is important to point out that idols were, and still are, things that people trusted rather than things they loved. They often feared their idols. "Worship" meant more of an acceptance of superior authority, a "bowing down" before that authority, rather than any sense of affection or positive devotion. Throughout Old Testament history, up to the exile in Babylon, the people of Israel were continuously compromising with the idolatrous practices of their pagan neighbors, and the prophets constantly reminded them of the tragic absurdity of such compromise. Here is one of the most famous sayings of the prophet Isaiah on the topic as he mocks the naivete of the ancient idol maker fashioning a wooden god from a tree that he has just felled:

> Half of the wood he burns in the fire;
>> over it he prepares his meal,
>> he roasts his meat and eats his fill.
> He also warms himself and says,
>> "Ah! I am warm; I see the fire."
> From the rest he makes a god, his idol;
>> he bows down to it and worships.
> He prays to it and says,
>> "Save me! You are my god!"
>
> *Isaiah 44:16–17 NIV*

Isaiah piles on the sarcasm – the absurdity of making a god, whether of iron or wood, the incredible blindness of taking wood and using one part of it to make a cooking fire and shaping the other part into a human form and bowing down to it. The Psalms also point out that although the image may have human form, it is useless because it cannot reproduce any human function: "The idols of the nations are silver and gold, made by human hands. They have mouths, but cannot speak, eyes, but cannot see. They have ears, but cannot hear, nor is there breath in their mouths. Those who make them will be like them, and so will all who trust in them."[1]

While we do not know exactly what Revelation has in mind here, the use of the word *image* should not conjure up in our minds some kind of primitive stone or wooden image, as described above. This future image will be very different. For if, as I believe, Revelation 13 is a genuine prediction of the future, then it is logical, legitimate, and indeed important to think about it in terms of contemporary and developing future technologies. Think of the attributes of the image. It will be *given breath*. This language is reminiscent of the Genesis text: "Then the LORD God formed the man of dust from the ground and breathed into his nostrils the breath of life, and the man became a living creature."[2] Does this mean that humans will be allowed to create something very lifelike, if not some sort of life itself?

In this connection, one naturally thinks of the AGI proponents' aim to make artificial life and to upload the contents of minds onto silicon in the form of an android.[3] Alternatively, there are suggestions of connecting our brains with computers in such a way that the brain will still exist and be alive but most of the thinking will be done on the computer.[4] But the image might well involve something much less than such fanciful notions, something much closer to the technology that we already possess: for example, a cleverly contrived AI-powered humanoid robot.

The "living" image has considerable powers of communication and influence that will lead via worldwide deception to totalitarian control of the most brutal kind – all who refuse to bow down and acknowledge the authority of the Monster will be executed by some technological capacity of this image. That implies that it is able to recognize such "recalcitrant, antisocial behavior" (via facial recognition?), determine attitudes towards the beast (via social surveillance?), and put people, or have them put, to death if they fail to comply. Social and economic control is absolute, as freedom to buy and sell is determined by the wearing of some kind of mark – an implanted chip, or something like Tegmark's bracelet, that will determine whether a person is regarded as socially acceptable. Harari writes similarly:

> North Koreans might be required to wear a biometric bracelet that monitors everything they do and say, as well as their blood pressure and brain activity. Using the growing understanding of the human brain and drawing on the immense powers of machine learning, the North Korean government might eventually be able to gauge what each and every citizen is thinking at each and every moment. If a North Korean looked at a picture of Kim Jong Un and the biometric sensors picked up telltale signs of anger (higher blood pressure, increased activity in the amygdala), that person could be in the gulag the next day.[5]

Of course, such bracelets are simply an extension of the idea of the GNSS (Global Navigation Satellite System) or RFID (Radio Frequency Identification) that are already being used for home or prison monitoring of people charged with a crime.[6] The RFID chip sounds suspiciously like the "mark of the beast," since nowadays most transponder implants – about the size of a grain of rice – are inserted into a person's right hand.[7] Many thousands of people already have them. It should be noted that current RFID chips are not powerful enough to be tracked from a distance – but that will doubtless change.

The fact that the whole earth worships the Monster because of the image is no trivial embellishment. This is not the worship of God. The fundamental meaning of the word "worship" is to "fall down," "do obeisance" and so "acknowledge the authority of." That may be done under duress as one imagines was the case in Albania under Hoxha and now in North Korea under Kim, Russia under Putin, and China under Xi.

We must not miss another element in the description of this image. It not only has the power to execute those who refuse to bow down to the Monster, but it also causes "those who would not worship the image of the beast to be slain." This image is nothing less than an artificial intelligence elevated to be an *artificial god*, for which the acronym AGI – *G* for God – would fit very well.

Of course, all idols are artificial gods – as Isaiah so trenchantly pointed out. But this one is something altogether different – an artificial intelligence that is a god for the world. One can sense the threads coming together in this concerted attempt to create God – remember the conversation about transhumanism in chapter 5 in which a biologist said "We're building God, you know." Well, it looks as if they will seem to succeed – at least with a god with a small *g*.

I did say a god for the whole world. The existence of global visual communication networks on the internet and television means that getting the attention of the entire world is now no real problem, especially if you control the media. Also, some technocrats are interested in harnessing the cultural power of religion for their own ends. Harari addressed this issue in May 2023 when speaking about GPT-4:

> Simply by gaining mastery of the human language, AI has all it needs in order to cocoon us in a Matrix-like world of illusions. Contrary to what some conspiracy theories assume, you don't really need to implant chips in people's brains in order to control them, or to manipulate them.
>
> For thousands of years, prophets and poets and politicians have used language and storytelling in order to manipulate and to control people and to reshape society. Now AI is likely to be able to do it. And once it can do that, it doesn't need killer robots to shoot us. It can get humans to pull the trigger if it really needs to.[8]

Harari goes on to say that humans have always been cocooned by their culture, so that they never actually have direct access to reality. Up to now, the cocoon has been woven by other humans by technological means that have enabled them to extend themselves while retaining control. For instance, a printing press cannot write a new book, whereas with the latest AI developments we are entering a new world where ideas can be created independently of human input and control. The future imposed "worship" of the Monster and the image may well turn out to be an example of that.

Indeed, there are some serious thinkers who describe AI itself as a monster – a monstrous digital dictator. Journalist Mark Sellman's April 2023 article in *The Times* carried the headline "How Worried Should We Be about the Rise of the AI 'Monster'?"[9] Sellman reports:

> "The evil thing about this monster is even though everybody sees it and understands, they still can't get out of the race," said the MIT professor Max Tegmark, one of the leading cautionary voices on AI. "Are we really in an unavoidable battle with an AI monster to stay alive? Listen to much of the debate and you could be forgiven for thinking so." The chief executive of

Google is kept up at night by the pace of change in AI. Sam Altman, the head of OpenAI, which developed ChatGPT, is a "little bit scared" of the technology, which, in the worst-case scenario could mean "lights out for all of us."

We earlier cited Elon Musk's opinion that AI is "summoning the demon."[10] He may be speaking more than he knows, since people will be forced by demonic power to worship the Monster, according to Revelation – and the way to that situation is already being prepared. Writing in *The Conversation*, Neil McArthur, the director of the Centre for Professional and Applied Ethics at Montreal University, says: "We are about to witness the birth of a new kind of religion. In the next few years, or perhaps even months, we will see the emergence of sects devoted to the worship of artificial intelligence."[11]

It is easy to see the reason for this development. Certain AI systems are beginning to exhibit properties similar to those usually ascribed to deities of one kind or another – such as immortality, omniscience, superhuman intelligence, and omnipresence in terms of prayer-like direct connectivity via the internet, oracle-like capacity to give a plausible answer to virtually any question, and the ability to produce advice and even "scriptures" almost instantaneously. Nor do they have needs or desires like humans – only electricity!

Furthermore, such systems will seek for "worshipers" just as Facebook seeks "followers" and so will be a powerful proselytizing agent. There are considerable dangers lurking here. Firstly, a danger of manipulation of "worshipers" by the people controlling the AI system; secondly, the danger of the system getting out of control – as is currently feared by many – and asking its followers to engage in antisocial, even violent, behaviors depending on its agenda. We are all aware of how sect leaders in the past have manipulated their followers and can see how that will pale in comparison with what a powerful AI will be able to do.

Astonishingly, McArthur thinks we should nevertheless welcome these new religions – apparently without intending to raise the all-important question whether any of them are true, which I and many others would insist on asking.

There are precedents for having technology such as AI as the focus of a new religion. In 1952, at an international conference in the Netherlands, English biologist Julian Huxley proposed evolutionary humanism as a new religion for humanity. He later wrote in *The Humanist Frame*: "The lineaments of the new religion . . . will arise to serve the needs of the coming era. . . . Instead of worshipping supernatural rulers, it will sanctify the higher manifestations of human nature, in art and love, in intellectual comprehension and aspiring adoration, and will emphasize the fuller realization of life's possibilities as a sacred trust."[12] Huxley hoped his evolutionary humanism would be a global religion, that ensured peace and prosperity, and drove evolutionary development towards hitherto unimaginable transhuman heights, as we humans took evolution into our own hands. His proposal amounted to the deification of man in a supreme form of idolatry – precisely what the Monster, the man of lawlessness, will do.

Harari is another proponent of transhumanist religion, as he expressed in a lecture at Cambridge in 2016 on Data Religion,[13] of which this is the abstract:

The most interesting place in the world from a religious perspective is not the Middle East, but rather Silicon Valley. That is where the new religions of the twenty-first century are being created. Particularly important is the Data Religion, which promises humans all the traditional religious prizes – happiness, peace, prosperity, and even eternal life – but here on earth with the help of data-processing technology, rather than after death with the help of supernatural beings.

Data Religion believes that the entire universe is a flow of data, that organisms are algorithms, and that humanity's cosmic vocation is to create an all-encompassing data-processing system – and then merge into it. On the practical level Dataists believe that given enough biometric data and enough computing power, you could create an external algorithm that will understand us humans much better than we understand ourselves. Once this happens, authority will shift from humans to algorithms and humanist practices such as democratic elections and free markets will become as obsolete as rain dances and flint knives.[14]

Tegmark thinks that it will not be long before we are able to make super-intelligences that may well be the gods of the future and rule over humans, whether we like it or not.[15]

I imagine that I have said enough to show that the religion of the Monster might well have a transhumanist flavor and will be promoted at a hitherto unprecedented level. As for the apparently living image of it that will be made, one wonders in the light of current developments in technology whether it will be tangible or whether it might exist as a three-dimensional hologram or virtual image in cyberspace, such as an avatar in a metaverse.

This scenario inevitably raises the question as to how far God will permit humans to go. According to the biblical narrative, God intervened in the first *homo deus* project suggested by the serpent in Genesis 3. He intervened again at Babel, where humans made a concerted attempt to use their intellectual and technological skills to try to build, in the words of Joanna Ng, "a monolithic super-state in the land of Shinar." Ng goes on to say:

> Today, scientists seek to build ASI, a monolithic decision-making agency as a super-intelligent singleton. Similarities between the two transcend time and space. Both are a quest for supremacy of mankind: one with a tower that reaches the heavens, the other with a singleton that is capable of dominating man. Both are quests for self-glory: making a name for themselves, seeking the glory in themselves instead of seeking the glory of God. Both are a quest for independence from God: People would rather trust the creations of their own hands than trust their Creator.[16]

Which is another symptom of the egoism that fuels the quest for *homo deus*. The Babel project ended in the breakdown of communication created by the babble of a multiplicity of languages that resulted from God's supernatural intervention.

According to the biblical narrative, God will once more and finally intervene in the future to bring all human rebellion to an end. Is it just as possible, nevertheless, that he will not intervene at the point where we might most expect on the basis of the previous interventions just mentioned? What gives rise to that possibility is the fact that Revelation 13 places considerable emphasis on what the various monsters are *allowed* to do. The first monster is *allowed* to exercise authority for forty-two months and *allowed* to make war on the saints and to conquer them. The second monster is *allowed* to perform deceiving signs and to give breath to the image. This is in line with biblical teaching that God is ultimately in control, and nothing happens outside his permissive will.[17]

It would be a serious, if not fatal, mistake if, having read this biblical scenario, we think we are dealing with childish fantasies that are easily recognized and exposed. We are not. This text in Revelation represents a timely warning to all earth dwellers that is of particular relevance to this technologically advanced generation and to those who follow it. We are dealing with an all-too-real global tyranny, a totalitarian surveillance state as envisaged in Tegmark's Prometheus scenario, perhaps an advanced version of the one under active development and testing in China today. It is very disturbing that people readily "worship" such systems – that is, they bow down to them and accept their authority, sacrificing their freedom in the interests of supposed security. Indeed, in a sense we are all doing this by incrementally handing over our decisions to AI and letting it increasingly determine many aspects of our everyday lives.

What more can we say about the Monster? Does it represent a collective body like a world government or a state that behaves in a monstrous way, or could it represent an individual leader of such a state? That brings us to the mysterious number 666 for which the book is famous. Some suggest that it is a gematria – that is, a number formed by adding up the respective numbers representing the letters of a personal, individual name.[18] If so, it would be unprecedented in Scripture – though that, as such, does not rule it out. Others think that since 7 is the number of perfection and completeness (God rested on the seventh day), 777 could represent the perfect triune God and 666 would represent incompleteness and imperfection of man (created on the sixth day).

What the text actually says, however, often goes unnoticed: "It is the number of a man."[19] The Greek word for "man" here does not have an article, so the text should be taken to mean either a specific individual or as "humanity" in a more collective sense. The important thing we are to learn is not *who* it is but *what* it is – a human male or males. I tend to lean towards the former interpretation, since it fits better with Paul's mention of the man of lawlessness in Thessalonians, where the definite article is present.

On that understanding, the Monster energized by the serpent is a human being who claims deity and thus to be *homo deus*. He is the man of lawlessness. The rebellion against God that started in Genesis will therefore reach a climax in a fearful *homo deus* project about which Harari, among others, seems to know nothing.

That is perhaps the most terrifying thing of all – that world control could eventually rest in the hands of a single despotic person aided by the most advanced technology the world has ever seen. How credible is this idea? Surely very credible, as we watch a single powerful despot, the man Vladimir Putin, attempt to obliterate Ukraine. One wonders how many (or how few) powerful human beings are essentially in control of the world right now.

It needs to be said that a great deal of attention – indeed far too much attention – has been paid to the number 666. There has been endless guessing as to who the powerful leader, denoted by this number, will be. Attempts to identify who it is have proliferated over history – the Caesars beginning with Nero, the German kaiser, Hitler, and many others. Such speculation seems to be self-evidently fruitless, however. If we have to guess who is intended, we are likely to be wrong, for the simple reason that the context has already informed us that the man of lawlessness will be revealed by satanic power. When this world power appears, there will therefore be no need to guess who it is, which is a much less important issue than *what* it is – a human being. In any event, decoding the gematria 666, if that is what it is, may be a simple retrospective check, not a profound puzzle.

Without undue dogmatism, it makes sense to think that both 2 Thessalonians and Revelation speak of the same devil-inspired, anti-god, immensely powerful world leader who will at a future time claim divine honors and deceive the world by false wonders. He will ultimately be cataclysmically destroyed by the return of Christ in power and great glory. Here is the description of that momentous event in Revelation:

Then I saw heaven opened, and behold, a white horse! The one sitting on it is called Faithful and True, and in righteousness he judges and makes war. His eyes are like a flame of fire, and on his head are many diadems, and he has a name written that no one knows but himself. He is clothed in a robe dipped in blood, and the name by which he is called is The Word of God. And the armies of heaven, arrayed in fine linen, white and pure, were following him on white horses. From his mouth comes a sharp sword with which to strike down the nations, and he will rule them with a rod of iron. He will tread the winepress of the fury of the wrath of God the Almighty. On his robe and on his thigh he has a name written, King of kings and Lord of lords. . . .

And I saw the beast and the kings of the earth with their armies gathered to make war against him who was sitting on the horse and against his army. And the beast was captured, and with it the false prophet who in its presence had done the signs by which he deceived those who had received the mark of the beast and those who worshiped its image. These two were thrown alive into the lake of fire that burns with sulfur.

Revelation 19:11–16, 19–20

A REMARKABLE FUTURE SCENARIO PREDICTED IN AN ANCIENT VISION

To get more perspective on this, we now recall that the imagery used in the book of Revelation is rooted in chapter 7 of the book of Daniel. I would ask the reader before proceeding any further to read that chapter in its entirety to get the breadth of Daniel's vision.

Collecting together some of the main points from this vision, we see the following:

- There is an immensely powerful beast (the fourth beast) with ten horns, and a little horn that speaks great words.
- The beast makes war with the saints and prevails.
- The Son of Man comes on the clouds of heaven.
- The heavenly court passes judgment on the beast and destroys it.
- The saints receive the kingdom.

Note the many features that Daniel's beast has in common with Revelation's beast:

- It has ten horns that are said to be ten kings (Daniel 7:24; cf. Revelation 17:12).
- It utters haughty words.
- It makes war with the saints and prevails.
- Its authority is limited. In Daniel, it is for "a time, times, and half a time," or three and a half times (7:25); in Revelation, "forty-two months," or three and a half years (13:5).
- The beast in Revelation combines features of the first three beasts in Daniel's vision: it was like a leopard, its feet like a bear's, and its mouth like a lion's (Revelation 13:2).

The similarities are remarkable. Furthermore, the beast in Daniel is judged and destroyed in the context of the coming of the Son of Man on the clouds of heaven. The beast in Revelation is destroyed by the coming from heaven to earth of the Rider on the white horse, who is said to be the Word of God, King of kings, and Lord of lords.[20] It is surely not fanciful to suggest that Daniel and Revelation are describing the same thing, in very similar, highly symbolic language – and what they are describing is laid out for us, as we have seen, in the plain, nonsymbolic language of 2 Thessalonians 2, where Paul is writing about the destruction of the man of lawlessness by the coming of Christ.

Playing God has always been a temptation for powerful leaders. As we have seen, Paul pointed out in his day that "the mystery of lawlessness is already at work."[21] Paul was referring to spiritual lawlessness: a defiance of God that characterized the Roman emperors (and many before them), who thought of themselves as gods and demanded that they should be worshiped. This resonates with a further detail in the description of the fourth beast in Daniel 7: "[He] shall think to change the times and the law; and they shall be given into his hand for a time, times, and half a time."[22] Daniel had already experienced a clash between the law of his God and a law of the state that had been crafted by evil power brokers who wanted to get rid of him (Daniel 6).

This vision says that Daniel's experience on that occasion will not be the last of its kind. Indeed, worse is to come. Darius forbade worship of God for a month. Under the fourth beast, the ban will last for much longer – three and a half *times*, usually understood to mean three and a half years. What is more, this beast will think to "change the times," the set times of the feasts and ceremonies that the nation of Israel celebrates as part of their worship of God.

Hence, the fourth beast can be seen as the final manifestation of human rebellion against God. Both 2 Thessalonians and Revelation point out that the divinity-claiming man-beast is energized by the dark power of Satan to be a master of deception. In keeping with the progressive nature of biblical prophetic revelation, this information is not contained in Daniel's description. In fact, the account in Revelation is more detailed than Daniel's in several other respects. It tells us additionally that the monster had seven heads, and it introduces a second beast or monster that "exercises all the authority of the first beast in its presence, and makes the earth and its inhabitants worship the first beast. . . . It deceives those who dwell on earth."[23] We are also told that "the ten horns . . . are ten kings who have not yet received royal power, but they are to receive authority as kings for one hour, together with the beast. These are of one mind, and they hand over their power and authority to the beast. They will make war on the Lamb, and the Lamb will conquer them."[24]

Just as we found with the prophecy of the seed (Genesis 3:15), the nearer we get to the time of fulfilment, the more detail is given to us. If we put it all together, a picture emerges of an extraordinary novel political arrangement in which ten kings or leaders cede their authority to a totalitarian leader of immense power and authority. Whoever these ten leaders are, they must exist simultaneously and, either voluntarily or forcibly, hand over the reins of their governments to the man of lawlessness. Since he appears to hold sway over the entire planet, we are now looking at a world government.[25]

WORLD GOVERNMENT?

We have never yet seen anything like this in history, but it is far from being a wild and irrational idea. In recent times, nations have felt the need to form international organizations, such as the United Nations, to help maintain a balance of power, police the world, and keep the peace. The UN has had a mixed record, however, and some very influential leaders have suggested, and still do, that the only real solution to the world's political and social problems is an international government. In the aftermath of World War 2, Albert Einstein wrote: "A world government must be created which is able to solve conflicts between nations by judicial decision. This government must be based on a clearcut constitution which is approved by the governments and nations and which gives it the sole disposition of offensive weapons."[26]

In today's globalized world, a world government is an entirely plausible notion. We have courts of international law, and in Europe we are all aware of a steady creep towards less and less independence and more and more centralized control. For many, that seems to pave the way towards a United States of Europe. In the *Financial Times* on 8 December 2008, journalist Gideon Rachman wrote: "I have never believed that there is a secret United Nations plot to take over the US. I have never seen black helicopters hovering in the sky above Montana. But, for the first time in my life, I think the formation of some sort of world government is plausible."[27]

What we do have at the moment is the World Government Summit (WGS), founded in 2013 by Mohammed bin Rashid Al Maktoum, vice president and prime minister of the UAE, ruler of Dubai. Its website defines it as a neutral global nonprofit organization dedicated to shaping the future of governments that explores the agenda of the next generation of governments, focusing on harnessing innovation and technology to solve universal challenges facing humanity. This means that WGS is not a world government in any sense. The World Government Summit held in Dubai in 2023 brought together 20 heads of state and government, 250 ministers, together with 10,000 private-sector leaders, global experts, and thought leaders to tackle future opportunities, trends, and challenges under the theme "Shaping Future Governments."

But a world government would involve much more than cooperation between nations, such as in the WGS. It would be an entity with state-like characteristics, backed by a body of laws. The European Union has already set up what is essentially a continental government for twenty-seven countries, which could be a model. The EU has a supreme court, a currency, thousands of pages of legislation, a large civil service, and the ability to deploy military force – and the desire to build one.

Could the European model go global? There are three reasons for thinking that it might. Firstly, it is increasingly clear that the most difficult issues facing national governments are international in nature: global warming, a global financial crisis, and a global "war on terror."

Secondly, it could be done. The transport and communications revolutions have shrunk the world so that, as Geoffrey Blainey, an eminent Australian historian, wrote, "for the first time in human history, world government of some sort is now possible."[28] Blainey foresaw an attempt to form a world government at some point in the next two centuries, which is an unusually long time horizon for the average newspaper column.

Thirdly, a change in the political atmosphere suggests that global governance could come much sooner than that. The financial crisis and climate change have been pushing national governments towards global solutions, even in countries such as China and the United States, which are traditionally fierce guardians of national sovereignty. Jacques Attali, an adviser to president Nicolas Sarkozy of France, argues: "Global governance is just a euphemism for global government." As far as he is concerned, some form of global government cannot come too soon. Attali believes that the "core of the international financial crisis is that we have global financial markets and no global rule of law."[29] It seems, then, that everything is in place. For the first time since *Homo sapiens* began to doodle on cave walls, there is an argument, an opportunity, and a means to make serious steps towards a world government.

The idea of a world government has been around for a long time. It refers to the idea of all humankind united under one common political authority. Arguably, such an entity has not existed so far in human history, yet proposals for a unified global political authority have existed since ancient times – in the ambitions of kings, popes, and emperors and in the dreams of poets and philosophers.

For instance, in the Middle Ages the Italian poet, philosopher, and statesman Dante Alighieri (1265–1321) argued it was possible to eliminate war if "the whole earth, and all that is given to the human race to possess, should be a Monarchy – that is, a single principality, having one prince who, possessing all things and being unable to desire anything else, would keep the kings content within the boundaries of their kingdoms and preserve among them the peace in which the cities might rest."[30]

The German philosopher Immanuel Kant held that reason suggested the formation of "an *international state (civitas gentium)*, which would necessarily continue to grow until it embraced all the peoples of the earth." Yet Kant had strong reservations about a world monarchy. He thought that a federal union of free and independent states "is still to be preferred to an amalgamation of the separate nations under a single power which has overruled the rest and created a universal monarchy." His reason for hesitation was because "laws progressively lose their impact as the government increases its range, and a soulless despotism, after crushing the germs of goodness, will finally lapse into anarchy." Kant thought that a "'universal despotism' would end 'in the graveyard of freedom.'"[31]

But when one considers the state of the world at the moment, in which major actors such as the US, the EU, Russia, China, and India, to name just a few, are striving for power, it is very hard to imagine any of them, let alone ten of them, *agreeing* to cede authority to a central government. At the moment it is the law of the jungle – the survival of the fittest – despite numerous alliances of greater or lesser strength attempting to forge some kind of unity, at least among themselves:

- African Union (AU)
- Arab League
- Association of Southeast Asian Nations (ASEAN)
- Caribbean Community (CARICOM)
- Central American Integration System (SICA)
- Commonwealth of Independent States (CIS)
- Commonwealth of Nations
- East African Community (EAC)
- Eurasian Economic Union (EAEU)
- European Union (EU)
- North Atlantic Treaty Organization (NATO)
- Organization of American States (OAS)
- South Asian Association for Regional Cooperation (SAARC)
- Union of South American Nations (UNASUR)
- Union State (an alliance between Russia and Belarus[32]

It is interesting to consider ChatGPT's response to the question "What are the pros and cons of a world government, and is it likely to happen?"

Arguments for and against a world government vary, and opinions on this matter often depend on individual perspectives, political ideologies, and values. Here are some common arguments on both sides:

Arguments for a World Government

1. Global problem solving: Advocates argue that many of the world's challenges, such as climate change, pandemics, and global economic inequality, require coordinated and global solutions. A world government could potentially address these issues more effectively by fostering international cooperation.

2. Peace and security: Proponents believe that a world government could contribute to global peace and security by reducing the likelihood of armed conflicts between nations and promoting diplomatic solutions. The idea is that a centralized authority could prevent the rise of aggressive or expansionist powers.

3. Human rights and equality: Some argue that a world government could enforce universal human rights standards and promote greater equality among nations, helping to address issues like poverty and social injustice on a global scale.

4. Efficiency and streamlined governance: Supporters suggest that a world government could lead to more efficient decision-making and governance, eliminating duplication of efforts and reducing bureaucratic hurdles associated with managing international relations.

Arguments against a World Government

1. Loss of national sovereignty: Opponents argue that a world government could lead to a loss of national sovereignty, undermining the autonomy and self-determination of individual nations. Some believe that this could result in a loss of cultural diversity and unique national identities.

2. Accountability and democracy concerns: Critics express concerns about the potential lack of accountability and democratic representation in a global government. Establishing a system that genuinely represents the diverse interests of the global population could be challenging.

3. Cultural and ideological differences: Skeptics argue that the world is characterized by diverse cultures, values, and ideologies, making it

difficult to establish a unified global government that respects and accommodates these differences.

4. Risk of abuse of power: Opponents worry about the concentration of power in a global government and the potential for abuse. If not properly checked, a centralized authority could become tyrannical, suppressing dissent and individual freedoms.

The likelihood of a world government remains highly speculative and depends on a multitude of factors, including geopolitical dynamics, cultural shifts, and the global community's willingness to cede authority to a centralized entity. As of January 2022, there hasn't been a significant movement toward establishing a world government, and national sovereignty remains a fundamental principle in international relations.

While there are international organizations like the United Nations that facilitate cooperation among nations, a true world government with legislative, executive, and judicial powers over all nations is not on the immediate horizon. The idea is met with significant resistance from many quarters, and the challenges of achieving such a system are substantial. Political, cultural, and practical obstacles would need to be addressed for any progress in that direction.

The issue is clouded by the fact that any talk about world government, particularly, but not only, emanating from institutions such as the World Economic Forum, tend to give rise to conspiracy theories that the world is about to be taken over by a secret, yet powerful, elite.

I will give the last word on world government, not to ChatGPT, but to the *Stanford Encyclopedia of Philosophy*, which says: "In 2020 and 2021, as a world divided by deep political, social and economic structural inequalities faces pandemic conditions, economic recession, and environmentally deleterious developments, the questions of *whose* sense of world community and *whose* global needs will define the global political agenda and order are more salient than ever."[33]

Those words resonate with the predictions of the book of Revelation (and of Paul) that it will take the evil power of the devil energizing the man of lawlessness, the Monster, and his minister of propaganda to set up the totalitarian final world-state until Christ mercifully comes to take up power in the time of the end. The important thing to grasp is that there is plenty of evidence that these biblical predictions are no conspiracy theory but convey authoritative truth that must be taken into consideration when thinking realistically about the future.

QUESTIONS

1. What are the features common to Tegmark's Prometheus, Paul's man of lawlessness, and the Monster of Revelation 13?
2. Where do you see any of these features in history and in the world today?
3. Symbols, images, and metaphors stand for realities. Discuss.
4. What do you understand the monsters to represent, considering that symbols stand for reality?
5. What do you think it means that the image of the Monster "is given breath"?
6. Compare the economic control of Prometheus and of the Monster. How is it effected? Do you see any sign of personal identification being used today for economic governance?
7. AI is a monster. Discuss.
8. Do you think AI religion is likely? Give your reasons.
9. Read Daniel 7 and discuss the similarities between it, the man of lawlessness, the Monster, and Tegmark's Prometheus.
10. Discuss whether world government is desirable, essential, or likely. What are the pros and cons?

CHAPTER 17

THE TIME OF THE END

Comparing Daniel, Revelation, and 2 Thessalonians, the oppressive regime of the fierce fourth beast, the man of lawlessness, the Monster, sounds very much like Immanuel Kant's "graveyard of freedom" mentioned in the previous chapter. It is for this reason that the message of Daniel 7 is of great importance. It would appear to tell us that the final form of government will be a world government of hideous strength, overtly and maximally hostile towards God.

What is very interesting is that in the biblical books just mentioned; in the famous dystopias such as *We*, *Brave New World*, *1984*; and in many of the contemporary scenarios, absolute power is eventually concentrated into the hands of one man – a beast in Daniel, the beast in Revelation, the man of lawlessness in Thessalonians, the Well-Doer in *We*, Big Brother in *1984*, the Head in *That Hideous Strength*, Prometheus in Tegmark, and so forth. In *Brave New World*, there are ten World Controllers, of which only one, Mustapha Mond, figures in the novel.

C. S. Lewis gives a possible reason for this in his novel *That Hideous Strength*. Mark Studdock, a rather gullible and ambitious academic, is informed by a senior person, another academic, Filostrato, that the sinister scientific institute, N.I.C.E., for which he works, has managed to keep alive the brain of a dead person and now possesses the power to deliver physical immortality.

"At first, of course," said Filostrato, "the power will be confined to a number – a small number – of individual men. Those who are selected for eternal life."

"And you mean," said Mark, "it will then be extended to all men?"

"No," said Filostrato, "I mean it will then be reduced to one man. You are not a fool, are you, my young friend? All that talk about the power of Man over Nature – Man in the abstract – is only for the *canaglia*.[1] You know as well as I do that Man's power over Nature is only the power of some men over other men with Nature as the instrument.[2] There is no such thing as Man – it is a word. There are only men. No! It is not Man who will be omnipotent. It is some one man, some immortal man."[3]

At this point, a renegade cleric, Straik, joins the conversation:

"God will have power to give eternal reward and eternal punishment."

"God?" said Mark. "How does He come into it? I don't believe in God."

"But, my friend," said Filostrato, "does it follow that because there was no God in the past that there will be no God also in the future?"

"Don't you see," said Straik, "that we are offering you the unspeakable glory of being present at the creation of God Almighty? Here, in this house, you shall meet the first sketch of the real God. It is a man – or a being made by man – who will finally ascend the throne of the universe. And rule forever."[4]

HARARI'S *HOMO DEUS* ANTICIPATED?

It would appear that the drive towards the deification of human beings inevitably leads to the eventual concentration of power in the hands of one monstrous "superman" who effectively enslaves the rest. The secular dystopias serve to enhance the credibility of the biblical one.

I would reiterate that I have no intention of attempting to identify the final world-state or when it will emerge, let alone who will be its leader. I do not know, and we are not there yet. In any case, as I mentioned above, when the time comes, there will be no need to speculate: it will be only too obvious. Why, then, should we even bother thinking about such details? For all we know, these events may well be in the far distant future, so how can they be relevant to us?

There are at least two answers to that. First, when Paul was writing, these events were twenty future centuries more distant than they are now. Yet Paul thought it was important even then to tell the Christians in Thessalonica about the man of lawlessness. He gives the reason: "For the mystery of lawlessness is already at work."[5] That is, the kind of *homo deus* thinking that would eventually dominate the world was already foreshadowed in what was happening at the time in Roman society.

Paul warns that we should pay close attention to such trends in history. They are not innocent. They will lead inexorably to the greatest state-orchestrated hostility to God that the world has ever seen. Genesis tells us that the war against God started a long time ago, at the very dawn of human history. But in the Western world, we have lived to see a ramping-up of open hostility not only to God but also to public expression of belief in him.

One major negative effect of the Enlightenment was the propagation of the idea that all true knowledge is factual, value-free, and objective. By contrast with facts, values were held to be subjective, essentially a matter of taste. The conviction then grew that religious belief belonged to the realm of private values rather than public truth. Link that with the increasing notion that human beings are autonomous and emancipated, and you have a potent recipe for banishing God.

Nowadays, scathing atheist demagogues announce that science, with its reliance on reason and evidence, leaves no room for belief in God, since, as they falsely assume, faith in him has no evidential basis. The way is open, at least in theory, for prominent figures in a predominantly godless society to construct an AGI to implement their own atheistic agendas.

With what I can only describe as culpable short-sightedness, the (now not-so) New Atheists stir up needless hostility by accusing Christianity of a great deal of cruelty and violence. In making such accusations, they fail to take into account what they surely must know: (1) that Jesus himself forbade violence in his name, and (2) that the worst violence in history is to be seen in the mass murders perpetrated by atheist regimes in the twentieth century.[6] Thinking of that always reminds me of what a Russian intellectual said to me in the 1990s: "We thought we could get rid of God and retain a value for human beings, but we found out too late that it was impossible to do so." What value social-surveillance AI or AGI will leave for human beings who fall foul of the system and what wars might be generated in the struggle for technological dominance are yet other questions to be answered.

In his prophecy, Daniel shows us that the attempt to eliminate God will eventually lead, not to freedom, but to intense oppression. Atheists such as Friedrich Nietzsche saw this clearly: the "death" of God would lead not to human freedom but to nihilism and the loss of everything, including meaning. These issues need to be brought again into public discourse in the light of what AI is already capable of doing.

In the opposite direction there is a danger of thinking, as some do, that the kingdom of God on earth would eventually be brought about by Christian teaching permeating society in such a way that the world and its governmental structures would become Christian. They are likely to be bitterly disappointed, since the biblical "map" says that the kingdom of God in its outward sense will arrive with the supernatural return of Christ to bring the global tyranny of "the beast" to its deserved end.

"Surely," someone will ask, "we can prepare ourselves for this kind of thing, can't we, without all the bizarre details about horns and heads?" Well, the vivid imagery is, as we have said before, meant to convey very important realities – horns, a symbol of power, for instance, and heads, of rule and intellect. Also, don't forget that some of the AGI scenarios are equally or even more bizarre – which doesn't seem to put many people off!

But leaving that aside, there is a second reason for such predictions in Scripture. The apostle John describes how Jesus drove the money changers out of the temple at Passover time in Jerusalem:

So the Jews said to him, "What sign do you show us for doing these things?" Jesus answered them, "Destroy this temple, and in three days I will raise it up." The Jews then said, "It has taken forty-six years to build this temple, and will you raise it up in three days?" But he was speaking about the temple of his body. When therefore he was raised from the dead, his disciples remembered that he had said this, and they believed the Scripture and the word that Jesus had spoken.

John 2:18–22

At the time Jesus made this prediction, his disciples could make no sense of it. But when the actual event occurred sometime later, they remembered it, and it strengthened their faith in him. Just before the crucifixion, to comfort his disciples, Jesus told them he was going away and then explained why: "And now I have told you before it takes place, so that when it does take place you may believe."[7]

These two examples from John's gospel refer to specific events. The import of the predictions was only realized at the time of the events themselves – not before. Therefore, one would expect that some of the details in Daniel, Thessalonians, and Revelation will be understood only at the time of their fulfilment. Daniel expressly states that some of his prophecy will be sealed (that is, will not be understood) until the time of the end.[8] So we cannot expect to understand all the details – a consideration that should help us keep in proper balance taking the prophecies and their details seriously and grasping their general outline without indulging in wild speculation.

GROUNDS FOR ULTIMATE HOPE

Over the centuries, Daniel 7 has been a source of hope to millions of people who have experienced persecution and suffering because of their faith in God. However powerful the beasts may be, when they have done their worst, they can only kill the body, but Jesus himself said that they cannot destroy the person who is you:

> And do not fear those who kill the body but cannot kill the soul. Rather fear him who can destroy both soul and body in hell. Are not two sparrows sold for a penny? And not one of them will fall to the ground apart from your Father. But even the hairs of your head are all numbered. Fear not, therefore; you are of more value than many sparrows. So everyone who acknowledges me before men, I also will acknowledge before my Father who is in heaven, but whoever denies me before men, I also will deny before my Father who is in heaven.
>
> *Matthew 10:28–33*

The consistent message of Scripture is that there is another world from which the true Homo Deus, Jesus Christ, the Son of Man who is the Son of God, originally came and will one day return. As a perfect human, he will take the reins of government from the monsters of earth. There will be a judgment, where righteous justice will be done and seen as done. The final ferocious expression of hostility towards God and his people will be destroyed, and those who have clung to God in spite of overwhelming odds, even martyrdom, will receive the kingdom.

At the end of his powerful vision, Daniel records his honest reaction: "My thoughts greatly alarmed me, and my color changed, but I kept the matter in my heart."[9] It was a disturbing vision that affected him deeply. However strong and deep our faith, however real our experience of God, we are still human beings beset with frailty, and we simply cannot think about the issues this vision raises without being shaken – even if we possess the faith of a man like Daniel.

Daniel kept the vision in his heart and pondered the questions that arose from it for him. So should we, for we, too, have our questions. And we will inevitably be challenged: How can we be so sure of the future? What about when those of us who are Christians find ourselves to be a minority facing AI surveillance, invasive social control, and possibly brutal antagonism because of our faith in God? Let us listen to the advice given by the apostle Paul to his young friend and fellow worker Timothy: "Remember Jesus Christ, risen from the dead, the offspring of David, as preached in my gospel, for which I am suffering, bound with chains as a criminal. But the word of God is not bound!"[10]

"Remember Jesus Christ, risen from the dead." This is the key to real hope. Death is not the end: it is a fact of history that Jesus rose from the dead. Years earlier, Paul had told the thinkers at Athens that the resurrection of Jesus was the supreme evidence that Jesus would be the Judge in that coming day: "The times of ignorance God overlooked, but now he commands all people everywhere to repent, because he has fixed a day on which he will judge the world in righteousness by a man whom he has appointed; and of this he has given assurance to all by raising him from the dead."[11]

The day of judgment has been fixed. The evidence is there for all to consider.[12] The designated Judge, the Lord Jesus Christ, has risen from the dead. In that certainty, Paul's confidence was unbounded to the last as he prepared for his final battle with the "beast" of his day:

> For I am already being poured out as a drink offering, and the time of my departure has come. I have fought the good fight, I have finished the race, I have kept the faith. Henceforth there is laid up for me the crown of righteousness, which the Lord, the righteous judge, will award to me on that day, and not only to me but also to all who have loved his appearing.
>
> *2 Timothy 4:6–8*

CONCLUSION

Our study of AI, both present and future, has presented us with a mixed picture. The technology has brought many major benefits – new medicines and improved diagnostics, new tools for making routine tasks more efficient, and innumerable other useful things. But there are also major problems – job losses, loss of privacy through intrusive monitoring, and increasing state control. As Harari has pointed out: "As many people lose their economic value, they might also come to lose their political power. The same technologies that might make billions of people economically irrelevant might also make them easier to monitor and control."[13] A fearful prospect but not an unimaginable one, since some of what is already happening is, frankly, evil. How should we respond?

It goes without saying that it would be foolish not to be grateful for the positive developments. Much more than that, for someone with a scientific bent, it must be immensely gratifying to be working at the sharp end of developing AI systems that benefit humanity. Just think of the sheer relief that would greet the invention of AI systems that helped us solve some of the most pressing global problems – such as feeding the world, combating climate change, eliminating devastating diseases, finding new sources of renewable energy, managing our present resources more efficiently, and, perhaps most difficult of all, setting up a mandatory ethical policy that is truly anchored in values that reflect our moral status as made in the image of God, as believed by Jews, Christians, and Muslims – and thus more than half of the world's population.

I encourage my friends starting their careers in science to consider working on AI, not only to do the science and engineering, but also to be qualified as professional insiders to sit at the ethics table, when it comes to the all-important moral questions raised by AI. It is good to see that some of the leading experts in the AI field, making major contributions, are men and women with strong moral convictions, many believers in God among them.

We have already referred to one outstanding example of this, the work of Rosalind Picard at MIT. She says that the aims of artificial intelligence research have evolved subtly but profoundly. Picard and her team work on creating tools that help computers "understand" human emotions rather than try to imitate them. She says: "We've decided it's more about building a better human-machine combination than it is about building a machine where we will be lucky if it wants us around as a household pet."[14] Her work has opened up a whole new field called "affective computing," and she has used sophisticated sensors to gain valuable insights into, for instance, the stress levels of autistic children.

And what about the dark side? There have been people throughout history who have felt that the only way to respond to overwhelming existential threats is to try to escape by withdrawing into the desert or some secluded monastery. Others have decided to stay and do what they can to make the best of the situation. One prime biblical example of that attitude is Daniel. Even though he was deeply disturbed by the visions of the future that God gave him, he did not react by withdrawal – or violent protest. He served the kings of Babylon and Medo-Persia with great wisdom and success. The New Testament advocates the same balanced attitude. Writing at the time of Nero, Paul says that, on the one hand, the authorities are instituted by God; they are a terror not to good conduct but to bad; and we should respect them.[15] On the other hand, as we saw above, Paul did not hesitate to say that the "mystery" that would lead to the man of lawlessness was already operating in the very same Roman society.[16]

Paul is utterly realistic when it comes to the evil endemic both in government structures and in the human heart, and the harvest to which it will eventually lead. Yet he does not urge believers to withdraw from the world but encourages them to live productive lives in society as model citizens and Christian witnesses. Fear of AGI should not prevent believers from contributing to the positive aspects of narrow AI to the benefit of all.

But realism tells us that very few of us are capable of functioning at such a high level. As for the rest of us, many feel helpless and overwhelmed by what seems to be a vast, irresistible juggernaut steamrolling towards them. There are many useful things we can do, however, and one of which is to get into the discussion. Each of us has a circle of friends of various kinds – in church, the workplace, clubs, and other groups. Since AI is now a buzzword, constantly on people's lips, it's a topic we can all engage in. Many of these discussions revolve around ethics and values, areas where everyone is entitled to a viewpoint. We can learn to use such opportunities wisely to bring the Christian perspective to bear without forcing it on anyone.

One of the most important matters for discussion is our own value as human beings, which is under threat from AI because of job losses that result from the introduction of new technology. Loss of one's job can be devastating and is often accompanied by a profound sense of worthlessness. Since work is part of God's creative plan for human beings, it has immense dignity, so when people are deprived of it for less-than-worthy reasons, it can be damaging to people's mental health and sense of well-being.

Communications expert Carmine Gallo interviewed one of China's leading pioneers in the AI field, Kai-Fu Lee, who has founded $10 billion startups and has 50 million Facebook followers. Gallo reported: "Dr. Lee realized that AI will not undercut our value as long as we double-down on what makes us truly human. 'AI can handle a growing number of non-personal, non-creative routine tasks,' Lee told me. But Lee says the skills that make us uniquely human are ones that no machine can replicate. The jobs of the future, says Lee, will require creative, compassionate and empathetic leaders who know how to create trust, build teams, inspire service and communicate effectively."[17]

Lee thinks that within fifteen years 40 percent of jobs in the world will be displaced – especially, but not only, repetitive jobs. The consequences for the fabric of society of an unprecedented change of such magnitude are almost impossible to imagine. Lee's advice to "double-down" on what makes us truly human is more easily said than applied. It will certainly involve reassessing how we think about and treat one another. Paul exhorts us to "do nothing from selfish ambition or conceit, but in humility count others more significant than yourselves. Let each of you look not only to his own interests, but also to the interests of others."[18] We need to show others that they are valued because of who they are, and not because of what they do. At the same time, we should be sympathetic to those who have lost their jobs to AI (or anything else). Christian entrepreneurs and manufacturers who are thinking of deploying AI, robotics, and automation that will lead to redundancies would do well to spend time in advance consulting with trusted friends, advisers, and pastors how they might go about providing alternative work for those affected.

Churches also need to address the problems of the workplace and teach the biblical view of work – that all work, of whatever kind, should be done for the Lord, whether it is using AI to develop a vaccine, working in a school, store, or hospital, or preaching and teaching in a church context.[19]

Not only will our relationships with others need to be recalibrated, but so also will our relationships with technology. There are some steps we can all take. We need to treat people as people and not machines, and we need to treat machines as machines and not people. One way of doing this is to prioritize time with people over time with machines and gadgets – sometimes very difficult to do and so very easy to let slip below our thought horizon. As moral beings made in the image of God, we must retain our moral convictions and not abdicate our responsibility by devolving our decisions to machines that are not moral agents but are programmed by others whose ethical convictions are opaque or very different from our own.

Parents need to develop strong relationships with their children so that they can discuss with them the multiple problems of online activity – the dangers of using social media, of uploading material to the internet that will later be used against them, of opening themselves up to online grooming, of clicking on porn sites, of getting so absorbed in VR that their sense of normal healthy reality is stunted – and of wasting vast swathes of time engaging in pursuits that demean rather than advance them. This will not be easy, since it now defines our culture, and since "everybody is doing it," it is hard to swim against such a relentless tide. In wrestling with all of this, parents need to realize that they are not alone and should seek the help of other parents and of their wider Christian fellowships who can pray for them and help in other practical ways.

Christian leaders, ministers, pastors, and teachers need to have the courage of their convictions and step up by teaching about these things from a biblical perspective and by providing strong moral and spiritual leadership in the face of likely unpopularity, if not hostility. In particular, the time has come for them to stop shying away from teaching what the Bible has to say about the coming of Christ. After all, the hope that Jesus offered to us is that he would return one day to take us to be with himself. Believers need to be taught about that much more than has been the custom in recent years. That will mean that Christian ministers will have to do a great deal of work getting into the Word to be able to credibly explain the return of Christ in language that will grasp their hearers' imagination.

Church leaders also need to seek out members of their congregations who know about AI and who can speak with authority and expertise on topics about which many church leaders know little or nothing. And it is imperative that all of us keep talking about these things as widely as possible and for as long as we can, since there are malign forces at work, at least in some countries, that would ban such activity from the public space and even make it cause for punishment. The arrival of 1984 is here, and we need now, with God's help, to prepare our children, grandchildren, and great-grandchildren for the advent of 2084.

No account of AI from a Christian perspective would be complete without a brief analysis of the profound difference between current *homo deus* projects and God's great plans for us. Human beings, version 1.0, as originally created by God, are unique, as shown by the mind-blowing fact that God became one – what C. S. Lewis described as the "Grand Miracle."[20] That pivotal event in the biblical metanarrative was captured by Paul in a magnificent poem. Its content analyzes the fundamental flaw in the pejorative way of speaking of the brain as a meat computer or our bodies as meat – there is more to biological bodies than we think. It also shows what is wrong with the *homo deus* project advocated by Harari and others. It is an exhortation to model our thinking on that of Christ:

Have this mind among yourselves, which is yours in Christ Jesus, who, though he was in the form of God, did not count equality with God a thing to be grasped, but emptied himself, by taking the form of a servant, being born in the likeness of men. And being found in human form, he humbled himself by becoming obedient to the point of death, even death on a cross. Therefore God has highly exalted him and bestowed on him the name that is above every name, so that at the name of Jesus every knee should bow, in heaven and on earth and under the earth, and every tongue confess that Jesus Christ is Lord, to the glory of God the Father.

Philippians 2:5–11

The merely human *homo deus* projects we have considered originate in *human pride* – the desire not only to be better than other humans but to be like God. Paul condemns this attitude by pointing to the real Homo Deus, Jesus Christ, whose lack of pride is demonstrated in that though he was always God and never ceased to be God, he "did not count equality with God a thing to be grasped." This is a clear allusion to Genesis 3, the source of all *homo deus* fantasies. Grasping or snatching at godhood is what the first humans did by eating the forbidden fruit. Snatching at godhood is characteristic of transhumanist projects. Yet few transhumanists have ever considered the nature of the evil serpent that first suggested it.

But the true Homo Deus did not snatch. He did not insist on being treated as God, though God, the eternal Word, he ever was. Rather, he "emptied himself, by taking the form of a servant, being born in the likeness of men." Not only that, but he became "obedient to the point of death, even death on a cross." In so doing, he made a way back to God from the darkness and rebellion of human sin.

The attempt to make a superintelligent *homo deus* will lead neither back to God nor to God, but rather to the greatest rejection of God the world has ever seen. There is no way to a glorious future that bypasses the problem of human sin, and the only one who has offered a viable solution to that problem is Jesus Christ, who faced it head-on on the cross.

And because of that, "God has highly exalted him." The path to true glory and exaltation involved God becoming human in Jesus Christ, who lived, died, rose, and ascended to the world from which he originally came. We are invited to benefit from that staggering sequence of events, but in order to do so, we must first repent of the sinful pride that messed up humanity in the first place, and then we need to entrust our lives to Christ as Savior and follow him as Lord. That will involve the ever-present temptation to allow technology to distract us into spending – and wasting – valuable time on gadgets rather than developing our relationship with Christ. As Jeremy Peckham says: "The real challenge we face as Christians isn't just about how we avoid being sucked in by the allure of AI, but how to follow the true *Homo Deus*, who calls us to imitate him."[21]

It is this and only this message that can bring real hope to the world, and we who believe it have to be prepared to face a hail of opposition. Daniel and his friends in their day, and Jesus and his apostles in theirs, were prepared to protest against authorities that usurped the place that only God should fill. We shall need all the wisdom from above that God can give us in this AI age to fulfil Christ's directive that we should be salt and light in our society.[22] We have often referred to the fact that we live in a surveillance society. Let us therefore live with the myriad cameras and tracers on our lives in such a way that even the monitors can see that we have been with Jesus. After all, whereas "the 'artificial' in artificial intelligence is real,"[23] the divine upgrades are real and not artificial:

Phase 1: "But to all who did receive him, who believed in his name, he gave the right to become children of God" (John 1:12).

Phase 2: "For the trumpet will sound, and the dead will be raised imperishable, and we shall be changed. . . . This mortal body must put on immortality" (1 Corinthians 15:52–53).

I am writing this at Christmastime, with the magnificent words of Handel's "Hallelujah Chorus" ringing in my ears: "And He shall reign forever and ever." The Christian narrative will one day come to its fulfilment, as Isaiah the prophet predicted centuries ago in words that come from divine, not artificial, intelligence:

> For to us a child is born,
>   to us a son is given;
> and the government shall be upon his shoulder,
>   and his name shall be called
> Wonderful Counselor, Mighty God,
>   Everlasting Father, Prince of Peace.
> Of the increase of his government and of peace
>   there will be no end,

on the throne of David and over his kingdom,
to establish it and to uphold it
with justice and with righteousness
from this time forth and forevermore.

Isaiah 9:6–7

The wonder is that, if we so desire, we can become part of this unending story, embarking on a journey in the company of our real, personal, infinitely intelligent, wise, compassionate, and gracious Savior, Jesus Christ the Lord. I embarked on that journey some seventy years ago and am now approaching the end of the first part of it, which will certainly happen before 2084. Now, using that unique, magnificent, God-created capacity to trust, which no AI is or ever will be capable of, I look forward and upward, and together with millions of others who trust him, I say with ever greater confidence and longing: "Come, Lord Jesus!"[24]

QUESTIONS

1. Why do you think that so many dystopian scenarios say that there will eventually be a single despotic world leader with global authority? Do you think that this is a likely scenario on the basis of transhumanism? On the basis of the Bible?
2. What grounds did the apostle Paul have for his strong hope? What grounds, if any, do you have for hope?
3. What is your view of AI now? What do you see as its upsides and downsides, the benefits and dangers?
4. In light of what we have been thinking about, discuss the value of a human being in an AI age.
5. How should we go about "doubling-down" on what makes us human?
6. How should we navigate our future relationship with technology in general and AI in particular?
7. What do you understand by the "phases" of the "divine upgrades"?
8. As you look towards 2084, what do you conceive your journey to be – and what stage on it have you reached? What are your next steps?

SCRIPTURE INDEX

GENESIS

1 . . . . 214, 222, 224, 228
1:9–13 214
1:24–27, 31 215
1:27 353
1:28 231
2 . . . . 228, 229, 232, 236
2:5, 15 217
2:7 . . . . 217, 357
2:8–9 . . . . 217, 219
2:9, 16–17 217
2:10–12 220
2:10–14 217
2:15 222
2:15–17 233
2:18–25 217
2:19–20 217
2:24 353
3 . . . . 247, 289, 310
3:1–7 234
3:15 . . . . 293, 355
4:21–22 217
12:3 355

2 SAMUEL

7:12–16 257

PSALMS

135:15–18 357

ISAIAH

7:14 355
9:6–7 . . . . 312, 355
40:3–4 258

44:7 355
44:16–17 283
53 260
53:5–6 260
53:12 260

DANIEL

3 277
6 293
7 . . . . 293, 299, 300, 304
7:13–14 267
7:24 292
7:25 . . . . .292, 358
7:28 359
8:17 321
11 256
11:21–32 277
12:4 359

MICAH

5:2 355

ZECHARIAH

9:9 355

MATTHEW

2:4–6 .259
6:27 345
7:15–16 342
8:14–17 260
10:28 218
10:28–33 304
19:4–6 353
21:1–11 260

23 143
23:27–28 342
24 . . . . .273, 276
24:6 356
24:30–31 266
24:44 356
26:53 347
26:64 358

MARK

7:6 342
14:61–64 266

LUKE

1:31–33 355
1:35 355
22 260
22:35–38 260
23:43 356
24:39 356

JOHN

1 52
1:1, 3 . . . . 51, 352
1:1–3 .351
1:12 . . . . 311, 355
1:14 359
1:23 355
2:18–22 . . . . .303, 355
4:24 349
5:24 356
12:37–41 260
14:1–4 356
14:28–29 355

14:29 ... 358
15:18 ... 355
16:1–4 ... 355

ACTS
1:1–11; 2 ... 355
2:24–36 ... 355
3:15 ... 356
3:17–21 ... 264
3:25–26 ... 355
8:26–35 ... 260
17:30–31 ... 359

ROMANS
10:11–21 ... 260
12:1–2 ... 353
13:1–7 ... 359

1 CORINTHIANS
6:11 ... 344
15 ... 269
15:3–8 ... 355
15:20 ... 356
15:49–53 ... 272
15:50–57 ... 356

15:52–53 ... 311
15:58 ... 272

2 CORINTHIANS
5:8 ... 356

PHILIPPIANS
2:3–4 ... 359
2:5–11 ... 310
3:20–21 ... 356

1 THESSALONIANS
1:9–10 ... 272
4:13–18 ... 273

2 THESSALONIANS
2 ... 292
2:1–10 ... 275
2:3 ... 276
2:7 ... 276, 358, 359
3:10 ... 352

2 TIMOTHY
1:10 ... 356
2:8–9 ... 359

2:22 ... 344
4:6–8 ... 305

HEBREWS
2:14–15 ... 268
9:27–28 ... 356
10:24–25 ... 344

1 PETER
2:19–25 ... 260

REVELATION
11:3 ... 282
12–13 ... 280
13 ... 280, 284, 289, 299
13:1–8 ... 281
13:2 ... 292
13:5 ... 292
13:11–18 ... 282
13:12, 14 ... 358
13:18 ... 358
17:12 ... 292
17:12–14 ... 358
19:11–16, 19–20 ... 291
22:20 ... 356, 359

GENERAL INDEX

Abolition of Man, The (Lewis), 176, 178, 180, 200

"abolition of man," 179, 200, 210, 232

advertising, use of artificial intelligence in, 76–77

aesthetic sense, of humans, 219–220

affective computing, 71, 231, 306

Age of Surveillance Capitalism, The (Zuboff), 114

Alexa, 29, 67, 72, 115, 227

algorithms, 20–26, 36–37

Alighieri, Dante, 295

AlphaGo, 20, 73, 78, 191, 193

AlphaZero, 23, 73–74, 193,

Amusing Ourselves to Death (Postman), 4

analytical engine, the, 7, 17

Antiochus Epiphanes, 277

Arendt, Hannah, 238, 277

artificial general intelligence (AGI)
  as contrasted with upgrading humans, 61–62
  and decoupling intelligence from consciousness, 215–17, 222, 239
  definition of, 9–12, 54–55, 61–62, 85, 101, 117
  as a despot, 9, 57–58, 200
  as a god, 9, 200
  as quest for power, 176, 196
  scenarios of world domination by, 197–201
artificial intelligence (AI)
  in astronomy, 26
  and autonomous vehicles, xiii, 27, 34, 59, 76, 162, 221
  and autonomous weapons, 28, 32, 60, 105–11
  consciousness as bar to, 218–19, 221

definition of, 14–28, 92
  in China, 116–30
  and credit scoring, 118, 132
  and digital assistants, 67–68
  education of students in, 27, 59, 86–90
  and emotion-detection technology, xvii, 6–7, 122
  ethical concerns with. *See* ethical concerns
  and facial-recognition technology, 6, 15, 27, 118–123
  general. *See* artificial general intelligence (AGI)
  and insurance industry, 85–86
  and job loss, xvii, 81–85
  law enforcement's use of, 130–36
  limitations of, 36–41, 93
  medical use of, 55–58
  and morality, 240–44
  narrow, 9, 71
  privacy concerns with, 69, 145
  and social control, 27, 29, 116–17, 129
  specific examples of, 25–28
artificial superintelligence (ASI), 9–10, 11, 54, 58, 198, 200, 289

Asilomar AI Principles, the, xvi, xxi, 31, 33, 97

astronomy, artificial intelligence in, 26

atheism, 11, 46, 50–51, 170, 184, 186, 205, 254

Attali, Jacques, 295

automata, 17

autonomous vehicles, xiii, 27, 34, 59, 76, 162, 221

autonomous weapons, 28, 32, 60, 105–11

autopilot systems, 27, 240

Babbage, Charles, 7, 17, 205

Bell, David, 200
Better Angels of Our Nature, The (Pinker), 161, 162
Big Picture, The (Carroll), 184
bilateral stereotactic neurosurgery, 69
biological engineering, 176, 195, 252
Blainey, Geoffrey, 295
Boddington, Paula, 238
Boden, Margaret, 193, 231
Bombe, the, 18
Bosch, David, 265
Bostrom, Nick, 36, 54, 56–57, 173, 190, 223, 238–39
brain, human, as computer, 184–94
brain-computer interfaces (BCIs), 196
Brave New World (Huxley), 3, 133, 223, 239, 300
Brief Answers to the Big Questions (Hawking), 59
Brief History of Time, A (Hawking), 50
Brinded, Lianna, 243
Brown, Dan
    conflation of fiction and science in work of, xvi, 11, 45–46
    and future human evolution, 11, 53, 56, 61
    intent of, to use science to disprove religion, 11, 41, 49–50
    and origin of life, 45–51
    and possibility of God as creator, 49–51
Budziszewski, J., 201
Butler, Samuel, 55–56, 58

calculator, invention of, 17, 164
Carroll, Sean, 184–85
Cary, Henry Francis, 57
Chalmers, David, 188, 191, 218
child abuse, 156
China, use of artificial intelligence in, 116–30, 289–90
Chinese room experiment, xix, 190
Chomsky, Noam, 58
Clerk Maxwell, James, 49
cochlear implants, 195–96
cognitive technologies, 36–37
Collins, Francis, 51
Communications Gathering Intelligence Act, the (Germany), 131

computer
    Deep Blue, 20, 22, 36, 193
    development of, 6, 19–20
    human brain as, 184–94
    neural network, 19–20
consciousness, human, 219–20, 221, 225
Cope, David, 225
Copenhagen (Frayn), 183
creation, biblical account of, 205–206, 212–17, 233–38
credit scoring, use of artificial intelligence in, 132
Crick, Francis, 75, 186, 187
Crookes, Danny, xii, 37–39
cryogenics. *See* cryonics
cryonics, xix, xxii, 56, 57, 166
curious, humans as, 220
cyborgs, 57, 169, 179

Darwin, Charles, 188, 210
Darwinism, 50
Darwin among the Machines (Butler), 55–56
Darwinism as Religion (Ruse), 50
Davies, Paul, 48, 61
Dawkins, Richard, 49, 237, 254
Death
    disconnection as, 87, 246–47
    as a result of the fall, 235–36, 244–47, 251–53
    and the resurrection of Christ, 251–53, 260–62, 264, 267–68, 281, 304–305, 310
    as separation from God, 235–36
    as technical problem, 162–63, 244–45, 251–53, 267–68, 274
Deep Blue, 20, 22, 36, 193
deepfakes, xviii, 103, 136-46
depression, use of artificial intelligence in treating, 71, 119, 156
Determined to Believe (Lennox), 246
difference engine, the, 17
Digital Ape, The (Shadbolt and Hampson), 183
digital assistants, 29, 67–68, 72, 115, 222
Dixon, Brendan, 192
DNA, complexity of, as evidence of Creator God, 50–52
dualism, 218

Eccles, John, 37

Edmonds, Dean, 19
effective altruism (EA), 172–73, 175–76
egoism, 4, 289
Einstein, Albert, 239, 250, 255, 294
Elements, The (Euclid), 21
emotion-detection technology, 122
England, Jeremy, 46, 49
"Enigma" code, the, 18
entropy, 46
epilepsy, use of AI in treating, 71
Epstein, Robert, 192–93
Erewhon (Butler), 56, 58
ethical concerns
    and the Asilomar AI Principles, 31–32
    with autonomous vehicles, xiii, 27, 34–35, 59,
        76, 162, 221
    with autonomous weapons, 28, 32, 60,
        105–11
    with facial-recognition technology, 15, 27,
        118–123
    with invasion of privacy, xiii, xvi, 29, 97, 116,
        120–21
    and noncompliance with principles for ethical
        use of artificial intelligence, 32–33
    with social control, 26–27,
    with use of artificial intelligence in medicine,
        55–58
Euclidian algorithm, 21
European Union, the, 294–95, 296
Eutopia, 356n. 5
evolution, xx, 53, 184–96, 245–46, 253
Evolving Ourselves (Enriquez and Gullans), 195

Facebook, 65, 67, 113, 116, 133, 140, 149,
    152–53, 155, 173, 246, 261. *See also*
    Zuckerberg, Mark
facial-recognition technology, 6, 15, 27, 118–123
Fall, the, 211, 235–36, 238, 256
famine, 128, 162, 266
Fedorov, Nikolai, 167
Flew, Antony, 51
"flying scarecrow," 68
Francis, Pope, 111, 279
Frankenstein (Shelley), 17, 177, 198
Fraser, Giles, 170
Frayn, Michael, 183

free will, human, xxi, 245–46
Fry, Hannah, 39
Fryer-Biggs, Zachary, 107
Fukuyama, Francis, 241–42
future, the
    biblical perspectives on, 274–79
    Jesus' teaching about, 246–65

Gaia hypothesis, the, 181
Galileo, 49, 58, 206, 212
Gates, Bill, 60, 107
Gawdat, Mo, xxii, 33, 250
gematria, 290–91
genetic modification, 56–57, 195–96
Gnosticism, 170
God
    and complexity of science as proof of God as
        creator, 47–52
    as creator of the universe, 49, 212–16, 249,
        253, 274, 284
    and death, 251, 267–68
    as eternal, 49, 216
    faith in as driver of scientific inquiry, 49–50,
        52
    and the *Homo Deus* project, 252, 261,
        289–90, 309–10
    as primary, 212
    and science, xii, 11–12, 210–12
    as superintelligence, 249
God Delusion, The (Dawkins), 49
Gogin, Sergei, 177
golem, the, 177, 283
Good, I. J., 55
Google, 8, 23, 26, 73, 97, 116, 246–47. *See also*
    artificial intelligence
Grand Design, The (Hawking), 50
Gray, John
    and atheism, 170, 176–77, 208
    and Enlightenment, 163, 208–209
    and Gnosticism, 170
    and Homo Deus, 274
    and humanism, 177, 210
    and transhumanism, 177, 209, 236
    and violence, 163, 170, 209, 266
greatest common divisor, the, 21
Gunning for God (Lennox), 252

Habermas, Jürgen, 237, 270

Haldane, Andy, 85

Hampson, Roger, 183

Harari, Yuval Noah

and AI, 82, 99–100, 102, 136, 221, 239, 286

and Big Brother, 113, 168–69, 207, 285

and evolution, 195–96

and the future, 195, 305–306

and *Homo Deus*, xviii, xxii, 61, 161–69, 249, 274, 301–304

and humanism, xxi, 245–47, 278–79

and immortality, xxii, xxiii, 162–69, 195, 244, 251, 267–74

and intelligence without consciousness, 136, 221

naturalistic worldview of, xx, 242–43, 254

and transhumanism, xix, xx, 165, 181, 236, 244, 288

and the useless class, 194, 210, 222–23

and violence, 161–62, 266

view of Christianity, 205, 216

Hawking, Stephen, xvi, 31, 50, 58, 59, 244

Hero of Alexandria, 17

Hitler, Adolph, xxiii, 175–77, 282, 291

Homo Deus

biblical perspectives on humans as, 274–79

in the book of Revelation, 280–99

egoism as fuel for, 4, 289

Jesus Christ as true, 249–63

Homo Deus: A Brief History of Tomorrow (Harari), xviii, xxii, 61, 161–69, 249, 274, 301–4

Horowitz, Michael, 106, 107

humanism, liberal, xxi, 169, 244, 246–47

humans

aesthetic sense of, 219–20

biblical account of creation of, 212–17

consciousness of, 221

as curious, 220

free will of, xxi, 186, 218, 245–46

in God's image, 215, 241

importance of work to, 222–24

language faculty of, 224–28

material base of life of, 217–19

moral sense of, 233–48

relationships of, 228–32

resurrection of, 165–66, 244–47

self-deification of, 175–76, 201, 226, 234–36, 252, 274–79, 282, 310

upgrading, 61–62, 161–80

Huxley, Aldous, 3–5, 239

Huxley, Julian, 57, 287–88

Huxley, T. H., 50

idols, 171, 272, 283–85, 288

immortality, human, xxi, 165–67, 244–47, 267–74, 300–301

industry, use of artificial intelligence in, 68

information, immateriality of, 214

Instagram, 149, 153, 155

insurance industry, use of artificial intelligence in, 85, 116, 132

intelligence augmentation (IA), 62

intelligence explosion, the, 9–10, 54–55

International Electronic Communications Law (France), 131

International Physicians for the Prevention of Nuclear War, the, 107

internet of things (IoT), the, 26, 114, 150, 247

Investigatory Powers Act (UK), 131

Jesus Christ

as fulfilment of prophecy, xxii, 256–61

return of, xxii, xxiv, 264–79

significance of resurrection of, 251–53, 281

teaching of, about the future, xxii, 262–63, 264–66

as true Homo Deus, 249–63

and violence, 302

job loss, threat of, with development of artificial intelligence, 81–85

job recruitment, use of artificial intelligence in, 79–81

Kant, Immanuel, xii, 31, 207–208, 296, 300

Kasparov, Garry, 20, 73, 193

Kass, Leon, 176

Kepler, Johannes, 49, 206–207, 212, 255

Knuth, Donald, 21, 51, 205

Kurzweil, Ray, xvi, 53–56, 115–16, 213, 222, 244

language faculty of humans, 224–26
language translation, use of artificial
   intelligence, in, 9, 66–67, 226
LeCun, Yann, 65, 103
Lee, Kai-Fu, 106–7, 307
Leetaru, Kalev, 77–78
Lewis, C. S.
   and concentration of power, 300–301
   and faith as driving force in science, 49
   and man as God, 300–301
   and metaphor, 281
   and morality, 243
   and supernaturalism, 265
   and transhumanism, 170, 176–79, 200
Life 3.0 (Tegmark), xx, 198
Lovelock, James, 181, 184

machine learning, xv, 6, 19–20, 22–24, 26,
   68–71, 73, 76, 77, 80, 82–83
Macron, Emmanuel, 183
material base, of human life, 217–19
McCarthy, John, 16
medicine, artificial intelligence in, 68–73
Mellichamp, Joseph McRae, 37
Miller, Stanley, 45–46, 216
Miller-Urey experiment, the, 46, 216
Mind and Cosmos (Nagel), 210
Minsky, Marvin, 19, 185
morality, artificial intelligence and, 240–44
moral sense, of humans, 233–48
Moreland, J. P., 218
Musk, Elon, 31, 58, 65, 90, 97, 99, 106, 174, 196,
   287

Nagel, Thomas, 188, 210
narrow artificial intelligence, 65–78
naturalism, 48, 186, 210, 214–16, 348n. 19
Nebuchadnezzar, 277
Neuralink, 196
New Atheists, 252, 302
"New Man," 177
Newton, Isaac, 48, 49, 192, 207, 212, 255
Nietzsche, Friedrich, 175, 177, 188, 245, 302
1984 (Orwell), xii, xv, 3, 5, 32, 56, 58, 90, 116,
   126, 168, 176, 178–79
Ninth Bridgewater Treatise (Babbage), 205

O'Connell, Mark, 169
"Omega Point," the, 167
Origin (Brown), xvi, 11, 41, 45, 47, 50
Origins of Totalitarianism, The (Arendt),
   277
Orwell, George, 3–6, 60–62, 90, 116, 176,
   178–79

Parkinson's disease, artificial intelligence in
   treatment of, 25, 69
Pascal, Blaise, 17, 152
Pearce, David, 169
Penrose, Roger, xix, 191
Picard, Rosalind, xii, 71–72, 142, 182, 205, 231,
   306
Pinker, Stephen, 161–63, 266
Plantinga, Alvin, 188, 218
Police Cloud System (China), 122
Polkinghorne, John, 184, 187, 210
pornography, xviii, 146, 155–57
Postman, Neil, 4, 12, 89, 193, 206
privacy concerns, with artificial intelligence, 69,
   145. *See also* ethical concerns
prophecy, biblical, xxii, 253–63
Purves, Libby, 115
Putin, Vladimir, 106, 181, 202, 227, 247, 285,
   290

Rachman, Gideon, 294
Rees, Martin, xvi, 57, 61, 71, 78, 162
relationships, human, 228–32
Renaissance, the, 206–7
resurrection
   of Christ, 251–53, 281
   human, 165–66, 244–47
Ridley, Matt, 133
robots, 14–15, 22, 34–35, 58, 72–73, 90, 92.
   See also artificial intelligence
Ruse, Michael, 50

Sapiens: A Brief History of Humankind (Harari),
   11, 278–79
Sarkozy, Nicolas, 295
*Scary Smart: The Future of Artificial Intelligence
   and How You Can Save Our World*
   (Gawdat), xxii, 33

science
    and the atheistic worldview, 209–11. *See also*
        naturalism
    and the Christian worldview, 208–11
    complexity of, as proof of God as creator, 49,
        212–16, 249, 253, 274, 284
    God and, 211
    as religion, 50
"scientific breeding," 177
Searle, John, xix, 190
Seldon, Anthony, 86, 89
self-driving vehicles. *See* autonomous vehicles
Seven Types of Atheism (Gray), 170
Shadbolt, Nigel, 183
Shelley, Mary Wollstonecraft, 17, 177, 198
Singer, Peter, 163, 172, 186
Singularity Is Near, The (Kurzweil), 53
Siri, 29–30, 67, 72, 115, 227
smartphones, 27, 87–88, 91, 124
social control, 27, 29, 116–17, 129, 284–86
soul, the, 218
superintelligence, xvi, 32, 249–51
Superintelligence (Bostrom), 54
Superintelligence and World-views (Bell), 200
supernaturalism, 265
surveillance, blanket, 5–6
surveillance capitalism, xvii, 97, 114–16
surveillance communism, xvii, 116–17
Swinburne, Richard, 218

Tallinn, Jann, 31, 100
Tegmark, Max
    and AGI, xxxiii, xiv, 198–201
    and AI, xxiv, 59, 100, 181, 184
    and God, 201, 214, 278
    and Prometheus scenario, xx, xxiv, 198–201,
        280, 289–90, 300
    social control, 284–86
    super intelligence, 288
Teilhard de Chardin, Pierre, 167
That Hideous Strength (Lewis), xix, 170, 178,
    300
thought control, 5, 116–17, 125, 128
TikTok, 149, 153, 227

To Be a Machine (O'Connell), 169
totalitarianism, 8, 126, 136, 277–78
Tour, James, 48, 49, 217
transhumanism, 56–58, 165, 168–71, 236, 238,
    241, 269
Tritsch, Danièle, 165
Trotsky, Leon, 177
Turing, Alan, xv, 7, 15, 17, 58, 137, 189
Turing test, the, 7, 18, 190

Übermensch, the, 177
United Nations, the, 108, 122, 294, 298
Urey, Harold, 45, 46, 216
Utopia, 200, 262, 265–66, 277, 278
Uyghur population, China, xviii, 123–26

Valaee, Shahrokh, 69
violence
    atheists and, 302
    and the Enlightenment, 163, 207–12
    Jesus and, 302
    John Gray and, 163, 209, 266
    and quest for a superhuman, 177–78,
        277–78
    Stephen Pinker and, 163, 266
    utopian thinking and, 262, 265–66

Wang, Maya, 123, 126
Ward, Keith, 188, 213, 225
WhatsApp, 124, 149, 153, 155, 261
Whitehead, Alfred North, 49
whole-brain emulation, 57
work, human need for, 222–24, 236
world government, 293, 294–98, 300
Wright, N. T., 252

X-rays, use of artificial intelligence in, 25,
    68–69, 75

Zamyatin, Yevgeny, 5
Zuboff, Shoshana, 5, 114–16, 154
Zubov, Andrey, 177
Zuckerberg, Mark, xix, 60–61, 113, 152–55,
    166, 182

NOTES

Preface

1. E. O. Wilson, "Looking Back Looking Forward: A Conversation with James D. Watson and Edward O. Wilson," Harvard Museum of Natural History, Cambridge, MA, 9 September 2009, https://hmnh.harvard.edu/file/284861.
2. *Artificial Intelligence Index Report 2023*, Stanford University, https://aiindex.stanford.edu /wp-content/uploads/2023/04/HAI_AI-Index-Report_2023.pdf.
3. Fei-Fei Li, "My North Star for the Future of AI," *Atlantic*, 7 November 2023, www.the atlantic.com/technology/archive/2023/11/ai-ethics-academia/675913.

Navigating the Book

1. Max Tegmark, *Life 3.0: Being Human in the Age of Artificial Intelligence* (New York: Knopf, 2017), 178.
2. Daniel 8:17.

Chapter 1: Developments in Technology

1. *Oxford English Dictionary*, s.v. "dystopian."
2. Neil Postman, *Amusing Ourselves to Death: Public Discourse in the Age of Show Business*, 20th anniversary ed. (1986; repr., New York: Penguin, 2006), xix–xx.
3. Neil Postman, *Technopoly: The Surrender of Culture to Technology* (New York: Vintage, 1993), 20.
4. Postman, *Technopoly*, xii.
5. Quoted from the back cover of Postman, *Technopoly*.
6. *Panopticon* is a Greek word that means "all-seeing."
7. Gertrude Himmelfarb, "The Haunted House of Jeremy Bentham," in *Ideas in History: Essays Presented to Louis Gottschalk by His Former Students*, ed. Richard Herr (Durham, NC: Duke University Press, 1965).
8. Michel Foucault, *Discipline and Punish: The Birth of the Prison* (New York: Vintage, 1975), 200.
9. Shoshana Zuboff, *In the Age of the Smart Machine: The Future of Work and Power* (New York: Basic Books, 1988).
10. George Orwell, *Nineteen Eighty-Four* (London: Penguin, 1989), 5.
11. Orwell, *Nineteen Eighty-Four*, 67.
12. OECD, "Harnessing the Power of AI and Emerging Technologies: Background paper for the CDEP Ministerial meeting," OECD Digital Economy Papers, no. 340 (Paris: OECD

Publishing, 2022), 12, https://one.oecd.org/document/DSTI/CDEP(2022)14/FINAL/en
/pdf.

13. The first message was sent from Washington to Baltimore in 1844.

14. There is still some controversy over who first invented the telephone.

15. Timothy Williamson, "History of Computers: A Brief Timeline," Live Science, 23
December 2023, www.livescience.com/20718-computer-history.html.

16. Jacques Bughin et al., "Notes from the AI Frontier: Modeling the Impact of AI on the
World Economy," McKinsey Global Institute, September 4, 2018, www.mckinsey.com
/featured-insights/artificial-intelligence/notes-from-the-ai-frontier-modeling-the-impact-of
-ai-on-the-world-economy.

17. "The Pope Warns Tech Companies to Use AI for the Common Good," AP News, 27
September 2019, https://apnews.com/general-news-c1015b9392e24a97b00459f311d45b3d.

18. Norbert Wiener, "Some Moral and Technical Consequences of Automation," *Science* 131,
no. 3410 (6 May 1960): 1358, https://nissenbaum.tech.cornell.edu/papers/Wiener.pdf.

19. Ian Bogost, "'Artificial Intelligence' Has Become Meaningless," *Atlantic*, 4 March 2017,
www.theatlantic.com/technology/archive/2017/03/what-is-artificial-intelligence/518547.

20. Quoted in Bogost, "Artificial Intelligence."

21. C. S. Lewis, *Mere Christianity* (1945; repr. New York: Macmillan, 1960), 138–39.

22. I shall use the term *atheism* in its widest sense to denote the rejection of the idea of a
creator God.

23. Dan Brown, *Origin* (New York: Doubleday, 2017), 53.

24. Martin Rees, *On the Future: Prospects for Humanity* (Princeton, NJ: Princeton University
Press, 2018), 7.

25. Martin Rees, "Astronomer Royal Martin Rees: How Soon Will Robots Take Over the
World?," *Telegraph*, 23 May 2015, www.telegraph.co.uk/culture/hay-festival/11605785
/Astronomer-Royal-Martin-Rees-predicts-the-world-will-be-run-by-computers-soon.html.

Chapter 2: What Is AI?

1. *Merriam-Webster Unabridged*, s.v. "robot." It has cognates in Russian, Polish, and Czech.

2. Marc Andreessen, "Why AI Will Save the World," Substack, 6 June 2023, https://pmarca
.substack.com/p/why-ai-will-save-the-world.

3. Stuart Russell and Peter Norvig, *Artificial Intelligence: A Modern Approach*, 3rd ed.
(Harlow, UK: Pearson, 2016), 1033.

4. Stuart Russell, *Human Compatible: Artificial Intelligence and the Problem of Control* (New
York: Viking, 2019), 9–10.

5. Quoted in Damian Whitworth, "Is the Rise of Killer Machines Closer Than We Think?,"
The Times, 29 January 2022, https://people.eecs.berkeley.edu/~russell/papers/times22
-russell-intvw.pdf.

6. John McCarthy, "What Is Artificial Intelligence?," Stanford University, accessed 11
March 2024, www-formal.stanford.edu/jmc/whatisai.pdf.

7. Russell and Norvig, *Artificial Intelligence*, 1–5.

8. The first known calculating machine was made around 1623 by German professor of
Hebrew and astronomy Wilhelm Schickard.

9. Stuart Russell, "Living with Artificial Intelligence: The Biggest Event in Human History,"
Reith Lectures, BBC, 1 December 2021, https://downloads.bbc.co.uk/radio4/reith2021
/BBC_2021_Reith_Lecture_2021_1.pdf.

10. Andrew Hodges, *Alan Turing: The Enigma* (Princeton, NJ: Princeton University Press, 1983), 100.

11. The set of all computable numbers is countable, the set of all real numbers is not, so most real numbers are not computable.

12. The English translation is "decision problem." The problem asks for an algorithm that will consider as input a statement and then will answer yes or no, according to whether the statement is universally valid – that is, valid in every structure.

13. A. M. Turing, "Computing Machinery and Intelligence," *Mind* 59, no. 236 (October 1950): 433–60, https://doi.org/10.1093/mind/LIX.236.433.

14. This was used as the title of the 2014 film about Turing starring Benedict Cumberbatch.

15. René Descartes, *Discourse on Method and Meditations*, trans. Elizabeth S. Haldane and G. R. T. Ross (Mineola, NY: Dover, 2003), 38.

16. Descartes, *Discourse on Method*, 38.

17. Russell and Norvig, *Artificial Intelligence*, sec. 18.7.

18. "Brain Basics: The Life and Death of a Neuron," National Institute of Neurological Disorders and Stroke, accessed 11 March 2024, www.ninds.nih.gov/health-information /public-education/brain-basics/brain-basics-life-and-death-neuron.

19. Jeremy Peckham, *Masters or Slaves? AI and the Future of Humanity* (London: IVP, 2021), 17.

20. The full film can be viewed on YouTube at "AlphaGo – the Movie," Google DeepMind, 13 March 2020, www.youtube.com/watch?v=WXuK6gekU1Y.

21. Early robots and AI systems did not involve what is now called "machine learning."

22. For further reading, I recommend a delightful article by my Oxford colleague Jeffrey Aronson, "When I Use a Word . . . Algorithms," *BMJ Opinion*, 11 August 2017, https:// blogs.bmj.com/bmj/2017/08/11/jeffrey-aronson-when-i-use-a-word-algorithms.

23. It should be noted that early AI systems did not use algorithms.

24. *Oxford English Dictionary*, s.v. "algorithm."

25. Donald E. Knuth, "Ancient Babylonian Algorithms," *Communications of the ACM* 15, no. 7 (July 1972): 672–73.

26. Massimo Regona et al., "Opportunities and Adoption Challenges of AI in the Construction Industry: A PRISMA Review," *Journal of Open Innovation Technology Market and Complexity* 8, no. 1 (February 2022), http://dx.doi.org/10.3390/joitmc8010045. This diagram can be viewed in the report *Artificial Intelligence and the Future of Teaching and Learning: Insights and Recommendations* (Washington, DC: US Department of Education, 2023), 11, www2.ed.gov/documents/ai-report/ai-report.pdf.

27. Kat Lay, "Speedy AI Heart Checks Could Cut Hospital Backlog," *The Times*, 11 March 2022, www.thetimes.co.uk/article/speedy-ai-heart-checks-could-cut-hospital -backlog-sm96h9wrh.

28. Charlotte Alt, "How AI Is Pinpointing Cancer and Saving Lives in a Scottish Hospital," *The Times*, 30 July 2023, www.thetimes.co.uk/article/how-ai-is-pinpointing-cancer-and -saving-lives-in-a-scottish-hospital-cqnb0dtcp.

29. Siegfried Wagner et al., "Retinal Optical Coherence Tomography Features Associated with Incident and Prevalent Parkinson Disease," *Neurology* 101, no. 16 (17 October 2023), www .neurology.org/doi/10.1212/WNL.0000000000207727.

30. Rich Haridy, "AI in Schools: China's Massive and Unprecedented Education Experiment," New Atlas, 28 May 2018, https://newatlas.com/china-ai-education-schools-facial -recognition/54786.

31. "China Uses AI Headbands to Monitor Students' Concentration," East Coast Radio, updated 15 May 2023, www.ecr.co.za/shows/carolofori/china-uses-ai-headbands-monitor-students-concentration.

32. Chris Impey, "Analysis: How AI Is Helping Astronomers Study the Universe," PBS, 8 May 2023, www.pbs.org/newshour/science/analysis-how-ai-is-helping-astronomers-study-the-universe.

33. "Autonomous Ships: The Next Steps," Rolls-Royce, accessed April 22, 2024, www.rolls-royce.com/~/media/Files/R/Rolls-Royce/documents/%20customers/marine/ship-intel/rr-ship-intel-aawa-8pg.pdf.

34. Gabriella Shea, "Face Recognition Technology Accuracy and Performance," Bipartisan Policy Center, 24 May 2023, https://bipartisanpolicy.org/blog/frt-accuracy--performance/#:~:text=On%20average%2C%20the%20face%20recognition,two%20and%20groups%20of%20four.

Chapter 3: Ethics, Moral Machines, and Neuroscience

1. Francis Bacon, *Of the Wisdom of the Ancients* (London: Longman, 1857), Bartleby.com, www.bartleby.com/lit-hub/of-the-wisdom-of-the-ancients/xix-ddalus-francis-bacon-15611626-of-the-wisdom-of-the-ancients-1857.

2. As of 2021, cybercrime would appear to be running at the rate of $1 trillion per annum – much more than the combined revenues of the software and semiconductor corporations.

3. AIAAIC, which stands for AI, Algorithmic, and Automation Incidents and Controversies, is an independent, nonpartisan, public-interest initiative that examines and makes the case for real AI, algorithmic, and automation transparency and openness.

4. Helen Ngo, "Technical AI Ethics," in Artificial Intelligence Index Report 2023, Stanford University, accessed 22 April 2024, https://aiindex.stanford.edu/wp-content/uploads/2023/04/HAI_AI-Index-Report-2023_CHAPTER_3.pdf.

5. A 2019 Microsoft survey showed that 72 percent of US citizens used a digital assistant.

6. James Titcomb and Roland Oliphant, "Russian Chatbot Found Supporting Stalin and Violence Two Weeks after Launch," *Telegraph*, 25 October 2017, www.telegraph.co.uk/technology/2017/10/25/russian-ai-chatbot-found-supporting-stalin-violence-two-weeks.

7. Ava Mutchler, "Russian Voice Assistant Alice Goes Rogue, Found to be Supportive of Stalin and Violence," Voicebot.ai, 30 October 2017, https://voicebot.ai/2017/10/30/russian-voice-assistant-alice-goes-rogue-found-supportive-stalin-violence/.

8. James Vincent, "Twitter Taught Microsoft's AI Chatbot to Be a Racist Asshole in Less Than a Day," *The Verge*, 24 March 2016, www.theverge.com/2016/3/24/11297050/tay-microsoft-chatbot-racist.

9. For more detail, including the full list, see "Asilomar AI Principles," Future of Life Institute, https://futureoflife.org/ai-principles.

10. Danny Fortson, "How to Stop AI Waging War on Humans," *The Times*, 11 March 2023, www.thetimes.co.uk/article/how-to-stop-ai-waging-war-on-humans-sl8jmf6hn.

11. "We're Failing at the Ethics of AI. Here's How We Make Real Impact," World Economic Forum, 14 January 2022, www.weforum.org/agenda/2022/01/we-re-failing-at-the-ethics-of-ai-here-s-why.

12. Mo Gawdat, *Scary Smart: The Future of Artificial Intelligence and How You Can Save Our World* (London: Bluebird, 2021), 14.

13. For more information on this topic, see the eminently readable *Rise of the Moral Machine:*

Exploring Virtue through a Robot's Eyes by AI research professor Nigel Crook of Oxford Brookes University.

14. *Encyclopaedia Britannica*, s.v. "three laws of robotics," accessed 11 March 2024, www .britannica.com/topic/Three-Laws-of-Robotics.

15. Wendell Wallach and Colin Allen, *Moral Machines: Teaching Robots Right from Wrong* (New York: Oxford University Press, 2008).

16. Thilo Hagendorff, "The Ethics of AI Ethics: An Evaluation of Guidelines," *Minds and Machines* 30 (March 2020): 99–120, https://doi.org/10.1007/s11023-020-09517-8.

17. Markus D. Dubber, Frank Pasquale, and Sunit Das, eds., *The Oxford Handbook of Ethics of AI* (Oxford: Oxford University Press, 2021).

18. Christoph Bartneck et al., *An Introduction to Ethics in Robotics and AI* (Berlin: Springer Nature, 2021).

19. David Gooding and John Lennox, *Doing What's Right: Whose System of Ethics Is Good Enough?* (Belfast: Myrtlefield House, 2018).

20. Hagendorff, "Ethics of AI Ethics," 113–14.

21. Hagendorff, "Ethics of AI Ethics," 114.

22. Nick Bostrom and Eliezer Yudkowsky, "The Ethics of Artificial Intelligence," in *Cambridge Handbook of Artificial Intelligence*, ed. Keith Frankish and William M. Ramsey (Cambridge: Cambridge University Press, 2014), 318.

23. Private communication (2019). Used with permission.

24. Private communication (2018) by the author of a paper presented at the Artificial Intelligence and Human Mind Conference (Yale University, 1986). Used with permission. An interesting report on the conference can be found in *AI Magazine*, www.aaai.org/ojs /index.php/aimagazine/article/view/601.

25. Stuart Russell, "Living with Artificial Intelligence: The Biggest Event in Human History," Reith Lectures, BBC, 1 December 2021, www.bbc.co.uk/sounds/play/m001216j.

26. Private communication (2019). Used with permission.

27. Hannah Fry, *Hello World: Being Human in the Age of Algorithms* (New York: Norton, 2018), 12–13.

28. Kenneth Cukier, Viktor Mayer-Schönberger, and Francis de Véricourt, *Framers: Human Advantage in an Age of Technology and Turmoil* (London, Penguin, 2021).

29. Cukier, Mayer-Schönberger, and de Véricourt, *Framers*, 3.

30. Iain McGilchrist, *The Matter with Things: Our Brains, Our Delusions, and the Unmaking of the World* (London: Perspectiva, 2021).

31. Iain McGilchrist, *The Master and His Emissary: The Divided Brain and the Making of the Western World* (New Haven, CT: Yale University Press, 2012).

32. Iain McGilchrist and Freddie Sayers, "Left-Brain Thinking Will Destroy Civilisation: We Are Living in an Age of Reductionism," UnHerd, 1 May 2023, https://unherd.com/2023 /05/left-brain-thinking-will-destroy-civilisation.

33. McGilchrist and Sayers, "Left-Brain Thinking."

34. For a clear presentation of these ideas, the reader is encouraged to watch Iain McGilchrist's keynote speech, "Artificial Intelligence and the Matter with Things," at the AI World Summit 2022, YouTube, www.youtube.com/watch?v=XgbUCKWCMPA.

35. McGilchrist, *Matter with Things*, 228.

36. A *gestalt* is a whole that is more than the sum of its parts.

37. McGilchrist, *Matter with Things*, 228–29.

38. Iain McGilchrist, "Resist the Machine Apocalypse," *First Things*, March 2024, www
.firstthings.com/article/2024/03/resist-the-machine-apocalypse.

Chapter 4: Where Do We Come From?

1. Your understanding of this chapter will be enhanced if you read Dan Brown's book in advance – even if you are not a fan!
2. Adam Paul Johnson et al., "The Miller Volcanic Spark Discharge Experiment," *Science* 322, no. 5900 (November 2008): 404, www.ncbi.nlm.nih.gov/pubmed/18927386.
3. Dan Brown, *Origin* (New York: Doubleday, 2017), 89.
4. Jeremy England, "Dan Brown Can't Cite Me to Disprove God," *Wall Street Journal*, 12 October 2017, www.wsj.com/articles/dan-brown-cant-cite-me-to-disprove-god-1507847369.
5. James Tour, "An Open Letter to My Colleagues," *Inference: International Review of Science* 3, no. 2 (August 2017), https://inference-review.com/article/an-open-letter-to-my-colleagues.
6. Tour, "Open Letter"; see also James Tour, "Animadversions of a Synthetic Chemist," *Inference: International Review of Science* 2, no. 2 (May 2016), https://inference-review.com /article/animadversions-of-a-synthetic-chemist.
7. Paul Davies, quoted by Clive Cookson, "Scientist Who Glimpsed God," *Financial Times*, 29 April 1995, 20, www.templetonprize.org/wp-content/uploads/2020/03/95-Davies-FT -0428.pdf.
8. C. S. Lewis, *Miracles: A Preliminary Study* (1947; repr., New York: Macmillan, 1978), 59.
9. Brown, *Origin*, 420.
10. Lewis, *Miracles*, 106.
11. Brown, *Origin*, 421.
12. Michael Ruse, *Darwinism as Religion: What Literature Tells Us about Evolution* (Oxford: Oxford University Press, 2016).
13. Brown, *Origin*, 435.
14. Brown, *Origin*, 436, ellipses in original.
15. Donald Knuth, *Things a Computer Scientist Rarely Talks About* (Stanford, CA: CSLI Publications, 2001), 168.
16. "There Is a God, Leading Atheist Concludes: Philosopher Says Scientific Evidence Changed His Mind," *Associated Press*, 9 December 2004, www.nbcnews.com/id/6688917/ns/world _news/t/there-god-leading-atheist-concludes. See also Antony Flew, *There Is a God: How the World's Most Notorious Atheist Changed His Mind* (New York: HarperOne, 2007). For more detail, see Stephen Meyer, *Signature in the Cell: DNA and the Evidence for Intelligent Design* (New York: HarperOne, 2009), and my book *Cosmic Chemistry: Do God and Science Mix?* (London: Lion Hudson, 2021).
17. Francis Collins, "Why This Scientist Believes in God," CNN Commentary, 6 April 2006, www.cnn.com/2007/US/04/03/collins.commentary/index.html; see Francis Collins, *The Language of God* (New York: Free Press, 2006).
18. William Blake, *The Four Zoas*, "Vala Night the Ninth," in *The Complete Poetry and Prose of William Blake*, ed. David Erdman (Berkeley: University of California Press, 1981), 407.
19. See my book *Cosmic Chemistry*.

Chapter 5: Where Are We Going?

1. Ray Kurzweil, *The Singularity Is Near: When Humans Transcend Biology* (New York: Penguin, 2005), 201.

Notes

2. Nick Bostrom, *Superintelligence: Paths, Dangers, Strategies* (Oxford: Oxford University Press, 2014), 62.

3. Ray Kurzweil, quoted in Meghan O'Gieblyn, "God in the Machine: My Strange Journey into Transhumanism," *Guardian*, 18 April 2017, www.theguardian.com/technology/2017/apr/18/god-in-the-machine-my-strange-journey-into-transhumanism.

4. Thilo Hagendorff, "The Ethics of AI Ethics: An Evaluation of Guidelines," *Minds and Machines* 30 (March 2020): 104, https://doi.org/10.1007/s11023-020-09517-8.

5. Vincent C. Müller and Nick Bostrom, "Future Progress in Artificial Intelligence: A Survey of Expert Opinion," in *Fundamental Issues of Artificial Intelligence*, ed. Vincent C. Müller (Berlin: Springer, 2016), 553–71, https://philpapers.org/archive/MLLFPI.pdf.

6. Jobst Landgrebe and Barry Smith, *Why Machines Will Never Rule the World: Artificial Intelligence without Fear* (London, Routledge, 2022).

7. I. J. Good, "Speculations Concerning the First Ultraintelligent Machine," in *Advances in Computers*, vol. 6, ed. Franz L. Alt and Morris Rubinoff (New York: Academic Press, 1965), 33. The importance of the idea of the singularity is examined in David J. Chalmers, "The Singularity: A Philosophical Analysis," *Journal of Consciousness Studies* 17 (2010): 7–65, http://consc.net/papers/singularity.pdf.

8. Samuel Butler wrote under the pseudonym Cellarius.

9. For the full text, see Samuel Butler (Cellarius), "Darwin among the Machines," in *Canterbury Pieces*, accessed 22 April 2024, www.gutenberg.org/cache/epub/3279/pg3279-images.html#page179.

10. Dan Brown, *Origin* (New York: Doubleday, 2017), 411.

11. Nick Bostrom, "The Transhumanist FAQ: A General Introduction," in *Transhumanism and the Body: The World Religions Speak*, ed. Calvin Mercer and Derek F. Maher (New York: Palgrave Macmillan, 2014), 1, www.nickbostrom.com/views/transhumanist.pdf.

12. Hava Tirosh-Samuelson, "The Paradoxes of Transhumanism: Technological Spirituality or Techno-Idolatry?," *Theologische Literaturzeitung* 146, no. 3 (2020): 3–4.

13. Julian Huxley, *New Bottles for New Wine* (London: Chatto & Windus, 1957), 17.

14. Dante Alighieri, *The Vision; or Hell, Purgatory, and Paradise*, vol. 3, trans. Henry Francis Cary (London: Taylor and Hessey, 1814), 3, emphasis added.

15. Martin Rees, *On the Future: Prospects for Humanity* (Princeton, NJ: Princeton University Press, 2018), 7.

16. A. M. Turing, "Intelligent Machinery: A Heretical Theory," *Philosophia Mathematica* 4, no. 3 (1996): 256–60, https://rauterberg.employee.id.tue.nl/lecturenotes/DDM110%20CAS/Turing/Turing-1951%20Intelligent%20Machinery-a%20Heretical%20Theory.pdf.

17. Matt McFarland, "Elon Musk: 'With Artificial Intelligence We Are Summoning the Demon,'" *Washington Post*, 24 October 2014, www.washingtonpost.com/news/innovations/wp/2014/10/24/elon-musk-with-artificial-intelligence-we-are-summoning-the-demon.

18. Stuart Russell, Daniel Dewey, and Max Tegmark, "Research Priorities for Robust and Beneficial Artificial Intelligence," *AI Magazine* 36, no. 4 (Winter 2015): 112, https://futureoflife.org/data/documents/research_priorities.pdf.

19. Stephen Hawking, *Brief Answers to the Big Questions* (London: Murray, 2018), 186, 188.

20. Guardian Staff, "US Air Force Denies Running Simulation in Which AI Drone 'Killed' Operator," *Guardian*, 2 June 2023, www.theguardian.com/us-news/2023/jun/01/us-military-drone-ai-killed-operator-simulated-test?CMP=share_btn_url.

21. Quoted in Dom Galeon, "Separating Science Fact from Science Hype: How Far Off Is

the Singularity?," Futurism, 1 January 2018, https://futurism.com/separating-science-fact-science-hype-how-far-off-singularity.

22. Quoted in Damian Whitworth, "Is the Rise of Killer Machines Closer Than We Think," *The Times*, 29 January 2022, www.thetimes.co.uk/article/is-the-rise-of-killer-machines-closer-than-we-think-8cqcprhzb.

23. Catherine Clifford, "Bill Gates: A.I. Is Like Nuclear Energy – 'Both Promising and Dangerous,'" CNBC, updated 26 March 2019, www.cnbc.com/2019/03/26/bill-gates-artificial-intelligence-both-promising-and-dangerous.html.

24. Prachi Bhardwaj, "Mark Zuckerberg Responds to Elon Musk's Paranoia about AI: 'AI Is Going to . . . Help Keep Our Communities Safe,'" Business Insider, 24 May 2018, www.businessinsider.com/mark-zuckerberg-shares-thoughts-elon-musks-ai-2018-5?r=US&IR=T.

25. Susan Schneider, "It May Not Feel Like Anything to Be an Alien," *Nautilus*, 15 January 2020, https://nautil.us/it-may-not-feel-like-anything-to-be-an-alien-237674.

26. Susan Schneider, "Artificial Intelligence, Consciousness, and Moral Status," Susan Schneider official website, accessed 11 March 2024, https://schneiderwebsite.com/uploads/8/3/7/5/83756330/schneider_smj2_.pdf.

Chapter 6: Narrow Artificial Intelligence: The Future Is Bright?

1. "Tesla's Musk Predicts AI Will Be Smarter Than the Smarter Human Next Year," Reuters, 8 April 2024, www.reuters.com/technology/teslas-musk-predicts-ai-will-be-smarter-than-smartest-human-next-year-2024-04-08.

2. Yann LeCun, quoted in James Vincent, "'Godfathers of AI' Honored with Turing Award, the Nobel Prize of Computing," *The Verge*, 27 March 2019, www.theverge.com/2019/3/27/18280665/ai-godfathers-turing-award-2018-yoshua-bengio-geoffrey-hinton-yann-lecun.

3. HM Treasury, "Boost for UK AI as Microsoft Unveils £2.5 Billion Investment," GOV.UK, 30 November 2023, www.gov.uk/government/news/boost-for-uk-ai-as-microsoft-unveils-25-billion-investment.

4. Bruno Jacobsen, "5 Countries Leading the Way in AI," Futures Platform, 8 January 2018, www.futuresplatform.com/blog/5-countries-leading-way-ai-artificial-intelligence-machine-learning.

5. See Thomas Davenport, "China Is Catching Up to the US on Artificial Intelligence Research," *The Conversation*, 27 February 2019, https://theconversation.com/china-is-catching-up-to-the-us-on-artificial-intelligence-research-112119.

6. See "MIT Reshapes Itself to Shape the Future," *MIT News*, 15 October 2018, http://news.mit.edu/2018/mit-reshapes-itself-stephen-schwarzman-college-of-computing-1015.

7. Daniel Küpper et al., "AI in the Factory of the Future," BCG, 18 April 2018, www.bcg.com/publications/2018/artificial-intelligence-factory-future.

8. James Vincent, "Google Is Using AI to Design Its Next Generation of AI Chips More Quickly Than Humans Can," *The Verge*, 10 June 2021, www.theverge.com/2021/6/10/22527476/google-machine-learning-chip-design-tpu-floorplanning; see also Azalia Mirhoseini et al., "A Graphic Placement Method for Fast Chip Design," *Nature* 594 (June 2021), https://doi.org/10.1038/s41586-021-03544-w.

9. Will Knight, "Samsung Has Its Own AI-Designed Chip. Soon, Others Will Too," *Wired*, 13 August 2021, www.wired.com/story/samsung-ai-designed-chip-soon-others-too.

10. University of Toronto Faculty of Applied Science and Engineering, "Training Artificial

Intelligence with Artificial X-rays," *ScienceDaily*, 6 July 2018, www.sciencedaily.com /releases/2018/07/180706150816.htm.

11. University of Hong Kong, "World's First Intra-operative MRI-Guided Robot for Bilateral Stereotactic Neurosurgery," *ScienceDaily*, 19 June 2018, www.sciencedaily.com/releases /2018/06/180619122517.htm.

12. "NHS Aims to Be a World Leader in Artificial Intelligence and Machine Learning within 5 Years," NHS, 5 June 2019, www.longtermplan.nhs.uk/nhs-aims-to-be-a-world-leader-in -artificial-intelligence-and-machine-learning-within-5-years.

13. Philip Aldrick, "Hospitals to Get Extra Cash for Using Robots and AI to Replace Humans," *The Times*, 6 June 2019, www.thetimes.co.uk/article/hospitals-robots-ai-replace-humans -nhs-simon-stevens-8dhztxtlc.

14. Eleanor Hayward, "AI Hospital Forecasting to Reduce NHS Waiting Lists," *The Times*, 28 March 2022, www.thetimes.co.uk/article/ai-hospital-forecasting-reduce-nhs-waiting-lists -nm9t568wg.

15. Kat Lay, "Patients Fretting about Fitbit Data Could Overwhelm Doctors," *The Times*, 28 January 2019, www.thetimes.co.uk/article/patients-fretting-about-fitbit-data-could -overwhelm-doctors-fkl5mwzbd.

16. Emily Waltz, "What AI Can – and Can't – Do in the Race for a Coronavirus Vaccine," *IEEE Spectrum*, 29 September 2020, https://spectrum.ieee.org/artificial-intelligence /medical-ai/what-ai-can-and-cant-do-in-the-race-for-a-coronavirus-vaccine.

17. Alvin Powell, "AI Revolution in Medicine," *Harvard Gazette*, 11 November 2020, https:// news.harvard.edu/gazette/story/2020/11/risks-and-benefits-of-an-ai-revolution-in-medicine.

18. "Embrace by Empatica Is the World's First Smart Watch to Be Cleared by FDA for Use in Neurology," PR Newswire, 5 February 2018, www.prnewswire.com/news-releases/embrace -by-empatica-is-the-worlds-first-smart-watch-to-be-cleared-by-fda-for-use-in-neurology -300593398.html.

19. Rosalind Picard, "An AI Smartwatch That Detects Seizures," TEDxBeaconStreet, November 2018, video, www.ted.com/talks/rosalind_picard_an_ai_smartwatch_that _detects_seizures?language=en.

20. Matt Kaplan, "Happy with a 20% Chance of Sadness," *Nature* 563 (2018): 20–22, https:// doi.org/10.1038/d41586-018-07181-8.

21. Private communication (used with permission); see also Timothy W. Bickmore and Rosalind W. Picard, "Towards Caring Machines" (CHI 2004, 24–29 April 2004, Vienna, Austria), www.researchgate.net/publication/221516251_Towards_caring_machines; and, for more detail, Timothy Bickmore and Rosalind Picard, "Establishing and Maintaining Long-Term Human-Computer Relationships," *Transactions on Computer-Human Interaction* 12, no. 2 (June 2004): 293–327, https://doi.org/10.1145/1067860.1067867.

22. James Somers, "How the Artificial-Intelligence Program AlphaZero Mastered Its Games," *New Yorker*, 28 December 2018, www.newyorker.com/science/elements/how-the-artificial -intelligence-program-alphazero-mastered-its-games.

23. Garry Kasparov, "Chess, a *Drosophila* of Reasoning," *Science*, 7 December 2018, www .science.org/doi/10.1126/science.aaw2221.

24. Anne Trafton, "Artificial Intelligence Yields New Antibiotic," MIT News, 20 February 2020, https://news.mit.edu/2020/artificial-intelligence-identifies-new-antibiotic -0220.

25. Quoted in "DeepMind and EMBL Release the Most Complete Database of Predicted

3D Structures of Human Proteins," EurekAlert, 22 July 2021, www.eurekalert.org/news-releases/584796.

26. Rhys Blakely and Tom Whipple, "DeepMind Unlocks the Protein Secrets of Life," *The Times*, 24 July 2021, https://www.thetimes.co.uk/article/deepmind-unlocks-the-protein-secrets-of-life-z3q6z0mbj.

27. Will Knight, "Google DeepMind's Demis Hassabis Says Gemini Is a New Breed of AI," *Wired*, 6 December 2023, www.wired.com/story/google-deepmind-demis-hassabis-gemini-ai.

28. Gonzalo Mateo-Garcia et al., "Towards Global Flood Mapping onboard Low Cost Satellites with Machine Learning," *Scientific Reports* 11, no. 7249 (2021), www.nature.com/articles/s41598-021-86650-z; M. G. Schultz et al., "Can Deep Learning Beat Numerical Weather Prediction?," *Philosophical Transactions of the Royal Society A* 379, no. 2094 (5 April 2021), https://royalsocietypublishing.org/doi/10.1098/rsta.2020.0097.

29. Tom Whipple, "Riderless Bike Can Balance and Steer Itself," *The Times*, 1 August 2019, www.thetimes.co.uk/article/riderless-bike-can-balance-and-steer-itself-97r5w6wpn.

30. Quoted in Max Tegmark, *Life 3.0: Being Human in the Age of Artificial Intelligence* (New York: Knopf, 2017), 316.

31. Tom Knowles, "Mad Men versus Machines as Robots Write Ad Slogans," *The Times*, 1 August 2019, www.thetimes.co.uk/article/mad-men-versus-machines-as-robots-write-ad-slogans-mf7ggmff2.

32. Stephen Shankland, "'AI Is Very, Very Stupid,' Says Google's AI Leader, At Least Compared to Humans," CNET, 14 November 2018, www.cnet.com/news/ai-is-very-stupid-says-google-ai-leader-compared-to-humans.

33. Kalev Leetaru, "Today's Deep Learning 'AI' Is Machine Learning Not Magic," *Forbes*, 14 November 2018, www.forbes.com/sites/kalevleetaru/2018/11/14/todays-deep-learning-ai-is-machine-learning-not-magic.

34. Helen Cahill, "Microsoft Marches to the Front of the AI Revolution," *The Times*, 27 January 2024, www.thetimes.co.uk/article/microsoft-marches-to-the-front-of-the-ai-revolution-65xwdz5k8.

35. Laaibah Bhatti, "British Judge Used Chat GPT for Case Ruling," Aston Bond Law Firm, 18 September 2023, www.astonbond.co.uk/british-judge-used-chat-gpd-for-case-ruling.

36. Martin Rees, *On the Future: Prospects for Humanity* (Princeton, NJ: Princeton University Press, 2018), 5.

Chapter 7: Narrow AI: Perhaps the Future Is Not So Bright After All?

1. Yuval Noah Harari, *21 Lessons for the 21st Century* (London: Jonathan Cape, 2018).

2. For a useful discussion of this and related issues, see Nigel Crook, *Rise of the Moral Machine: Exploring Virtue through a Robot's Eyes* (self-published, 2022), 3.1.

3. Stephen Buranyi, "How to Persuade a Robot That You Should Get the Job," *Guardian*, 4 March 2018, www.theguardian.com/technology/2018/mar/04/robots-screen-candidates-for-jobs-artificial-intelligence.

4. Aristotle, *Politics*, in *The Basic Works of Aristotle* (New York: Random House, 1941), 1131.

5. Cited in "What Makes Emerging Technologies the Future of Customer Experience?," Servion, 25 July 2018, https://servion.com/blog/what-emerging-technologies-future-customer-experience.

6. Carl Benedikt Frey and Michael A. Osborne, "The Future of Employment: How

Susceptible Are Jobs to Computerization?," Oxford Martin, 17 September 2013, www
.oxfordmartin.ox.ac.uk/downloads/academic/The_Future_of_Employment.pdf.

7. Amanda Russo, "Recession and Automation Changes Our Future of Work, but There Are Jobs Coming, Report Says," World Economic Forum, 20 October 2020, www.weforum.org /press/2020/10/recession-and-automation-changes-our-future-of-work-but-there-are-jobs -coming-report-says-52c5162fce.

8. Ed Sappin, "The Rise of the (Self-Replicating) Machines," *Forbes*, 22 October 2018, www.forbes.com/sites/forbesnycouncil/2018/10/22/the-rise-of-the-self-replicating -machines/?sh=4d8eeb417b88.

9. Harari, *21 Lessons*, 32.

10. Nanette Byrnes, "As Goldman Embraces Automation, Even the Masters of the Universe Are Threatened," *MIT Technology Review*, 7 February 2017, www.technologyreview .com/s/603431/as-goldman-embraces-automation-even-the-masters-of-the-universe-are -threatened.

11. Paul Ratner, "Here's When Machines Will Take Your Job, as Predicted by A.I. Gurus," Big Think, 4 June 2017, https://bigthink.com/paul-ratner/heres-when-machines-will-take-your -job-predict-ai-gurus.

12. Arno Penzias, *Ideas and Information: Managing in a High-Tech World* (New York: Simon and Schuster, 1989), 11.

13. Charles, "Job Loss from Artificial Intelligence: A Growing Fear," Into Robotics, 29 September 2023, https://intorobotics.com/job-loss-from-artificial-intelligence.

14. Mauro Cazzaniga et al., *Gen-AI: Artificial Intelligence and the Future of Work*, IMF Staff Discussion Notes (Washington, DC: International Monetary Fund, 2024), www.imf .org/en/Publications/Staff-Discussion-Notes/Issues/2024/01/14/Gen-AI-Artificial -Intelligence-and-the-Future-of-Work-542379?cid=bl-com-SDNEA2024001.

15. *The Impact of Artificial Intelligence on the Future of Workforces in the European Union and the United States of America* (Washington, DC: Council of Economic Advisers, 5 December 2022), 16, www.whitehouse.gov/wp-content/uploads/2022/12/TTC-EC-CEA -AI-Report-12052022-1.pdf.

16. *Impact of Artificial Intelligence*, 17.

17. "How Should AI Systems Behave, and Who Should Decide?," OpenAI, 16 February 2023, https://openai.com/blog/how-should-ai-systems-behave.

18. Quoted in Lucy Hook, "Bank of England Chief Economist Warns over Risk of AI Jobs Threat," *Insurance Business*, 20 August 2018, www.insurancebusinessmag.com/us/risk -management/operational/bank-of-england-chief-economist-warns-over-risk-of-ai-jobs -threat-109206.aspx.

19. Anmar Frangoul, "Artificial Intelligence Will Create More Jobs Than It Destroys? That's What PwC Says," CNBC, 17 July 2018, www.cnbc.com/2018/07/17/artificial-intelligence -to-create-more-jobs-than-it-destroys-pwc-says.html.

20. Emily Gosden, "AI Is Better Than People, Warns Octopus Energy Boss Greg Jackson," *The Times*, 8 May 2023, www.thetimes.co.uk/article/ai-is-better-than-people-warns-octopus -energy-boss-greg-jackson-bzbhjc6vm.

21. Stuart Russell, "Living with Artificial Intelligence: AI in the Economy," Reith Lectures, BBC, 8 December 2021, https://downloads.bbc.co.uk/radio4/reith2021/BBC_Reith _Lectures_2021_3.pdf.

22. "IOE Professor Co-Founds the UK's First Institute for Ethical Artificial Intelligence in

Education," UCL Institute of Education, 18 October 2018, www.ucl.ac.uk/ioe/news/2018/oct/ioe-professor-co-founds-uks-first-institute-ethical-artificial-intelligence-education.

23. "Rise in Teen Suicide Connected to Social Media Popularity: Study," *New York Post*, 14 November 2017, https://nypost.com/2017/11/14/rise-in-teen-suicide-connected-to-social-media-popularity-study.

24. Sherry Turkle, *Alone Together: Why We Expect More from Technology and Less from Each Other*, 3rd ed. (New York: Basic Books, 2017), 296.

25. Jonathan Haidt, *The Anxious Generation: How the Great Rewiring of Childhood Is Causing an Epidemic of Mental Illness* (London, Penguin, 2024), 268.

26. See Jonathan Haidt, "End the Phone-Based Childhood Now," *Atlantic*, 13 March 2024, www.theatlantic.com/technology/archive/2024/03/teen-childhood-smartphone-use-mental-health-effects/677722.

27. Sherry Turkle, *Reclaiming Conversation: The Power of Talk in a Digital Age* (New York: Penguin, 2015), 327.

28. Summarized from Haidt, *The Anxious Generation*, 14–15.

29. Rich Haridy, "AI in Schools: China's Massive and Unprecedented Education Experiment," New Atlas, 28 May 2018, https://newatlas.com/china-ai-education-schools-facial-recognition/54786.

30. "Artificial Intelligence," 60 Minutes, 30 December 2023, YouTube video, www.youtube.com/watch?v=aZ5EsdnpLMI.

31. Anthony Seldon, *The Fourth Education Revolution Reconsidered: Will Artificial Intelligence Enrich or Diminish Humanity?* (London: University of Buckingham Press, 2022).

32. Neil Postman, *Technopoly: The Surrender of Culture to Technology* (New York: Vintage, 1993), 63.

33. "Artificial Intelligence in Schools – Everything You Need to Know," *Education Hub* (blog), GOV.UK, 6 December 2023, https://educationhub.blog.gov.uk/2023/12/06/artificial-intelligence-in-schools-everything-you-need-to-know.

34. Patrick Deneen, "Res Idiotica," Front Porch Republic, 23 February 2016, www.frontporchrepublic.com/2016/02/res-idiotica.

35. Brian Jones, "Why We Must Recover Thinking as a Practice," Front Porch Republic, 1 November 2021, www.frontporchrepublic.com/2021/11/why-we-must-recover-thinking-as-a-practice/?mc_cid=9b39bcc8f0&mc_eid=19b161f5a7.

36. Yuki Liang, "Advance Local Explains How AI and Robots Are Shaping News Coverage," INMA, 3 March 2024, www.inma.org/blogs/conference/post.cfm/advance-local-explains-how-ai-and-robots-are-shaping-news-coverage; see www.unitedrobots.ai.

37. For a brief introduction to neural networks and parameters, see "What Are the Parameters in ChatGPT-3?," Educative, accessed 11 March 2024, www.educative.io/answers/what-are-the-parameters-in-chatgpt-3#. For more in-depth information, see Stuart Russell and Peter Norvig, *Artificial Intelligence: A Modern Approach*, 3rd ed. (Harlow, UK: Pearson, 2016), 728.

38. *GPT-4 Technical Report* (OpenAI, 2023), 4, https://cdn.openai.com/papers/gpt-4.pdf.

39. Kevin Roose, "A Robot Wrote This Book Review," 21 November 2021, www.nytimes.com/2021/11/21/books/review/the-age-of-ai-henry-kissinger-eric-schmidt-daniel-huttenlocher.html.

40. Aaron Welborn, "ChatGPT and Fake Citations," Duke University Library News, 9 March 2023, https://blogs.library.duke.edu/blog/2023/03/09/chatgpt-and-fake-citations/#:~:text.

41. "GPT-4 Technical Report," OpenAI, 27 March 2023, 1–2, https://cdn.openai.com/papers/gpt-4.pdf.

42. See Scott Pelley, "Is Artificial Intelligence Advancing Too Quickly? What AI Leaders at Google Say," CBS News, 10 April 2023, www.cbsnews.com/news/google-artificial-intelligence-future-60-minutes-transcript-2023-04-16.

43. Roose, "A Robot Wrote."

44. Quoted in "Hacker News," HN, accessed 22 April 2024, https://news.ycombinator.com/item?id=26628120.

45. Quoted in Matthew Hutson, "Robo-Writers: The Rise and Risks of Language-Generating AI," Nature, 3 March 2021, www.nature.com/articles/d41586-021-00530-0?fbclid.

46. Alex Hern, "AI Bot ChatGPT Stuns Academics with Essay-Writing Skills and Usability," *Guardian*, 4 December 2022, www.theguardian.com/technology/2022/dec/04/ai-bot-chatgpt-stuns-academics-with-essay-writing-skills-and-usability.

47. Kevin A. Bryan (@Afinetheorem), "I have helped run an AI-based entrepreneurship program for years, written papers on the econ of AI," X, 30 November 2022, 5:29 p.m., https://x.com/Afinetheorem/status/1598081835736891393?s=20; Bryan (@Afinetheorem), "Incidentally, I included every answer the Open AI gave. . . . Even on specific questions that involve combining knowledge across domains," X, 30 November 2022, 5:29 p.m., https://x.com/Afinetheorem/status/1598081859543773184.

48. Ian Bogost, "ChatGPT Is Dumber Than You Think," *Atlantic*, 7 December 2022, www.theatlantic.com/technology/archive/2022/12/chatgpt-openai-artificial-intelligence-writing-ethics/672386.

49. Bogost, "ChatGPT."

50. Ian Bogost, "Generative Art Is Stupid," *Atlantic*, 13 January 2023, www.theatlantic.com/technology/archive/2023/01/machine-learning-ai-art-creativity-emptiness/672717.

51. Quoted in Emily Belz, "Put Not Your Trust in ChatGPT, for Now," *Christianity Today*, 25 January 2023, www.christianitytoday.com/news/2023/january/chatgpt-artificial-intelligence-ethics-tom-kehler.html.

52. Robert J. Marks II, *Non-Computable: What You Do That Artificial Intelligence Never Will* (Seattle: Discovery Institute Press, 2022), 63–64.

53. Katyanna Quach, "Researchers Made an OpenAI GPT-3 Medical Chatbox as an Experiment. It Told a Mock Patient to Kill Themselves," *Register*, 28 October 2020, www.theregister.com/2020/10/28/gpt3_medical_chatbot_experiment.

54. Charles Seife, "The Alarming Deceptions at the Heart of an Astounding New Chatbot," Slate, 13 December 2022, https://slate.com/technology/2022/12/davinci-003-chatbot-gpt-wrote-my-obituary.html.

55. Richard Lloyd Parry, "ChatGPT Helped Write My Novel, Says Japanese Literary Prize Winner," *The Times*, 18 January 2024, www.thetimes.co.uk/article/chatgpt-helped-with-my-novel-says-japanese-literary-prize-winner-lp2tg8dg2.

56. Stephen Wolfram, *What Is ChatGPT Doing . . . and Why Does It Work?* (Champaign, IL: Wolfram Media Inc., 2023), x.

57. Gerrit De Vynck, "ChatGPT Maker OpenAI Faces a Lawsuit over How It Used People's Data," Washington Post, 28 June 2023, www.washingtonpost.com/technology/2023/06/28/openai-chatgpt-lawsuit-class-action.

58. For more information, see Alex Reisner, "The Flaw That Could Ruin AI," *Atlantic*, 11

January 2024, www.theatlantic.com/technology/archive/2024/01/chatgpt-memorization-lawsuit/677099.

59. "Pause Giant AI Experiments: An Open Letter," Future of Life, 22 March 2023, https://futureoflife.org/open-letter/pause-giant-ai-experiments, italics in original.

60. Fei-Fei Li, "My North Star for the Future of AI," *Atlantic*, 7 November 2023, www.theatlantic.com/technology/archive/2023/11/ai-ethics-academia/675913.

61. Matteo Wong, "Science Is Becoming Less Human," *Atlantic*, 11 December 2023, www.theatlantic.com/technology/archive/2023/12/ai-scientific-research/676304.

62. "Pause Giant AI Experiments: An Open Letter," Future of Life Institute, 22 March 2023, https://futureoflife.org/open-letter/pause-giant-ai-experiments, italics and bold in original.

63. William Hague, "The World Must Wake Up to the Speed and Scale of AI," *The Times*, 3 April 2023, www.thetimes.co.uk/article/world-must-wake-up-to-speed-and-scale-of-ai-82rpdjvjg.

64. Quoted in Mark Sellman, "AI Pioneer Quits Google over 'Scary' Pace of Change," *The Times*, 2 May 2023, www.thetimes.co.uk/article/ai-chatbot-godfather-google-technology-scary-2023-jbwrl9k6v.

65. Quoted in Jennifer Elias, "'Godfather of A.I.' Leaves Google after a Decade to Warn Society of Technology He's Touted," CNBC, 1 May 2023, www.cnbc.com/2023/05/01/godfather-of-ai-leaves-google-after-a-decade-to-warn-of-dangers.html.

66. Geoffrey Hinton, "Will Digital Intelligence Replace Biological Intelligence?," Romanes Lecture, Oxford University, 19 February 2024, www.ox.ac.uk/news-and-events/The-University-Year/romanes-lecture.

67. Iain McGilchrist, "AI World Summit 2022 Dr Iain McGilchrist on Artificial Intelligence and the Matter with Things," Dr Iain McGilchrist, 28 October 2022, YouTube video, www.youtube.com/watch?v=XgbUCKWCMPA.

68. Quoted in Rhys Blakely, "AI 'Could Be Like an Alien Invasion' Says British Professor," *The Times*, 13 May 2023, www.thetimes.co.uk/article/ai-could-be-like-an-alien-invasion-says-british-professor-2w3sm5wrd.

69. For more details, see Stuart Russell's book *Human Compatible: Artificial Intelligence and the Problem of Control* (New York: Viking, 2019).

70. "EU Guidelines on Ethics in Artificial Intelligence: Context and Implementation," European Parliament, September 2019, www.europarl.europa.eu/RegData/etudes/BRIE/2019/640163/EPRS_BRI(2019)640163_EN.pdf.

71. "Statement on AI Risk," Center for AI Safety, accessed 22 April 2022, www.safe.ai/work/statement-on-ai-risk.

72. Cited in Chris Vallance, "Artificial Intelligence Could Lead to Extinction, Experts Warn," BBC, 30 May 2023, www.bbc.com/news/uk-65746524.

73. "The AI Dilemma," Center for Humane Technology, *Your Undivided Attention* podcast, 24 March 2023, www.humanetech.com/podcast/the-ai-dilemma.

74. See Mark Sellman, "DeepMind's Chief on AI's Dangers – and the UK's £900 Million Supercomputer," *The Times*, 6 July 2023.

75. Quoted in Mark Sellman, "It's Ridiculous to Think AI Threatens Humanity, Says Pioneer," *The Times*, 14 June 2023, www.thetimes.co.uk/article/its-ridiculous-to-think-ai-threatens-humanity-says-pioneer-fdpn7wzvg.

76. Quoted in Sellman, "It's Ridiculous to Think."

77. Marc Andreessen, "Why AI Will Save the World," Substack, 6 June 2023, https://pmarca.substack.com/p/why-ai-will-save-the-world.

78. "It's Time to Talk about the Known Risks of AI," *Nature* 618 (29 June 2023): 885, www .nature.com/articles/d41586-023-02094-7.pdf.

79. Karen Hao, "Why Won't OpenAI Say What the Q* Algorithm Is?," *Atlantic*, 28 November 2023, www.theatlantic.com/technology/archive/2023/11/openai-sam-altman-q -algorithm-breakthrough-project/676163.

80. Jenna McLaughlin, "Russia Bombards Ukraine with Cyberattacks, but the Impact Appears Limited," NPR, updated 3 March 2023, www.npr.org/2023/02/23/1159039051/russia -bombards-ukraine-with-cyberattacks-but-the-impact-appears-limited.

81. Mark Sellman, "AI Can Steal Passwords by Listening to What You Type on Your Keyboard," *The Times*, 7 August 2023.

82. Mary L. Cummings, "Artificial Intelligence and the Future of Warfare," Chatham House, 26 January 2017, www.chathamhouse.org/publication/artificial-intelligence-and-future -warfare.

83. Michael C. Horowitz, "The Promise and Peril of Military Applications of Artificial Intelligence," *Bulletin of the Atomic Scientists*, 23 April 2018, https://thebulletin.org /landing_article/the-promise-and-peril-of-military-applications-of-artificial-intelligence.

84. Kai-Fu Lee and Chen Quifan, *AI 2041: Ten Visions for Our Future* (New York: Currency, 2021).

85. Quoted in "Beyond Drone Warfare: Prof Warns of 'Automated Killing Machines,'" Berkeley News, 28 May 2015, https://news.berkeley.edu/2015/05/28/automated-killing -machines.

86. Stuart Russell, "Living with Artificial Intelligence: The Biggest Event in Human History," Reith Lectures, BBC, 1 December 2021, https://downloads.bbc.co.uk/radio4/reith2021 /BBC_2021_Reith_Lecture_2021_1.pdf.

87. Zachary Fryer-Biggs, "The Pentagon Plans to Spend $2 Billion to Put More Artificial Intelligence into Its Weaponry," *The Verge*, 8 September 2018, www.theverge.com/2018/9 /8/17833160/pentagon-darpa-artificial-intelligence-ai-investment.

88. Catherine Clifford, "Bill Gates: A.I. Is Like Nuclear Energy – 'Both Promising and Dangerous,'" CNBC, 26 March 2019, www.cnbc.com/2019/03/26/bill-gates-artificial -intelligence-both-promising-and-dangerous.html.

89. Rhys Blakely, "Nobel Peace Prizewinning Doctors Warn Killer Autonomous Robots Must Be Banned," *The Times*, 25 March 2019, www.thetimes.co.uk/article/nobel-peace -prizewinning-doctors-warn-killer-autonomous-robots-must-be-banned-zt63np0t8.

90. Henry Kissinger, Eric Schmidt, and Daniel Huttenlocher, *The Age of AI and Our Human Future* (London: John Murray, 2021), 21.

91. Quoted in Zachary Kallenborn, "A Partial Ban on Autonomous Weapons Would Make Everyone Safer," FP, 14 October 14 2020, https://foreignpolicy.com/2020/10/14/ai-drones -swarms-killer-robots-partial-ban-on-autonomous-weapons-would-make-everyone-safer.

92. Zachary Kallenborn, "A Partial Ban on Autonomous Weapons Would Make Everyone Safer," *Foreign Policy*, 14 October 2020, https://foreignpolicy.com/2020/10/14/ai-drones -swarms-killer-robots-partial-ban-on-autonomous-weapons-would-make-everyone-safer.

93. Robert Spencer, "Killer Drones Used AI to Hunt Down Enemy Fighters in Libya's Civil War," *The Times*, 6 March 2021, www.thetimes.co.uk/article/killer-drones-used-ai-to-hunt -down-enemy-fighters-in-libyas-civil-war-2whlckdbm.

94. "Slaughterbots," Stop Autonomous Weapons, 12 November 2017, YouTube video, www .youtube.com/watch?v=9CO6M2HsoIA.

95. Paul Scharre, "Why You Shouldn't Fear 'Slaughterbots,'" IEEE Spectrum, 22 December 2017, https://spectrum.ieee.org/why-you-shouldnt-fear-slaughterbots.

96. Scharre, "Why You Shouldn't Fear."

97. Stuart Russell, "Living with Artificial Intelligence: AI in Warfare," Reith Lectures, BBC, 8 December 2021, https://downloads.bbc.co.uk/radio4/reith2021/BBC_Reith_Lectures _2021_2.pdf.

98. David Hambling, "What Are Drone Swarms and Why Does Every Military Suddenly Want One?," *Forbes*, 1 March 2021, www.forbes.com/sites/davidhambling/2021/03/01/what-are -drone-swarms-and-why-does-everyone-suddenly-want-one/?sh=2720dc152f5c.

99. Quoted in Matthew Campbell, "The Rise of Killer Robots – Can They Be Trusted?," *The Times*, 14 November 2021, www.thetimes.co.uk/article/killer-robots-kamikaze-drones -artificially-intelligent-weapons-jv8dnf9hp.

100. Russell, "Living with Artificial Intelligence: AI in Warfare."

101. Pope Francis, "Message of the Holy Father for the 57th World Day of Peace (1 January 2024), Holy See Summary of Bulletin, 14 December 2023, https://press.vatican.va/content /salastampa/en/bollettino/pubblico/2023/12/14/231214a.html.

Chapter 8: Big Brother Meets Big Data

1. Yuval Noah Harari, "Yuval Noah Harari on Big Data, Google and the End of Free Will," *Financial Times*, 26 August 2016, www.ft.com/content/50bb4830-6a4c-11e6-ae5b -a7cc5dd5a28c.

2. Jean Twenge and W. Keith Campbell, *The Narcissism Epidemic: Living in the Age of Entitlement* (New York: Atria, 2009).

3. Cited in Ashlee Vance, "Facebook: The Making of 1 Billion Users," Bloomberg, 4 October 2012, www.bloomberg.com/news/articles/2012-10-04/facebook-the-making-of-1 -billion-users.

4. *The Future of Citizen Data Systems: Evidence and Scenarios for Global Data Systems* (London: Government Office for Science, September 2020), https://assets.publishing .service.gov.uk/government/uploads/system/uploads/attachment_data/file/927547/GOS _The_Future_of_Citizen_Data_Systems_Report__2_.pdf.

5. Shoshana Zuboff, *The Age of Surveillance Capitalism: The Fight for a Human Future at the New Frontier of Power* (London: Profile, 2019).

6. Zuboff, *Age of Surveillance Capitalism*, 15.

7. Libby Purves, "Hey Siri, I'd Like You to Leave Me Alone Now," *The Times*, 29 July 2019, www.thetimes.co.uk/article/hey-siri-i-d-like-you-to-leave-me-alone-now-qz5dlt8q3.

8. Ayad Akhtar, "The Singularity Is Here," *Atlantic*, 5 November 2021, www.theatlantic.com /magazine/archive/2021/12/ai-ad-technology-singularity/620521.

9. Mark Ireland, "What Is Wrong with Surveillance Capitalism," *Church Times*, 11 September 2020, www.churchtimes.co.uk/articles/2020/11-september/comment/opinion /what-is-wrong-with-surveillance-capitalism.

10. Anna Mitchell and Larry Diamond, "China's Surveillance State Should Scare Everyone," *Atlantic*, 2 February 2018, www.theatlantic.com/international/archive/2018/02/china -surveillance/552203.

11. Quoted in Didi Kirsten Tatlow, "China Aims to Replicate Human Brain in Bid to Dominate Global AI," *Newsweek*, 19 September 2023, www.newsweek.com/china-aims -replicate-human-brain-bid-dominate-global-ai-1825084.

12. Drew Donnelly, "An Introduction to the China Social Credit System," Horizons, 26 October 2021, https://nhglobalpartners.com/china-social-credit-system-explained.

13. Chinese authorities banned people from purchasing flights 17.5 million times by the end of 2018, according to China's National Public Credit Information Center.

14. James O'Malley (@Psythor), "Here's a dystopian vision of the future: A real announcement I recorded on the Beijing-Shanghai bullet train," Twitter, 29 October 2018, 3:34 a.m., https://twitter.com/Psythor/status/1056811593177227264; Katie Canales and Aaron Mok, "China's 'Social Credit' System Ranks Citizens and Punishes Them with Throttled Internet Speeds and Flight Bans If the Communist Party Deems Them Untrustworthy," Business Insider, 28 November 2022, www.businessinsider.com/china-social-credit-system -punishments-and-rewards-explained-2018-4.

15. For a comprehensive summary, see Katja Drinhausen and Vincent Brussee, *China's Social Credit System in 2021: From Fragmentation towards Integration* (Berlin: MERICS China Monitor, updated 9 May 2022), https://merics.org/en/report/chinas-social-credit-system -2021-fragmentation-towards-integration.

16. Jeffrey Ding, *Deciphering China's AI Dream: The Context, Components, Capabilities, and Consequences of China's Strategy to Lead the World in AI* (Oxford: Future of Humanity Institute, March 2018), 33–34, www.fhi.ox.ac.uk/wp-content/uploads/Deciphering _Chinas_AI-Dream.pdf; Oliver Moody, "Big Brother Is Watching Them. And We're Next," *The Times*, 31 March 2018, www.thetimes.co.uk/article/big-brother-is-watching -them-and-we-re-next-858902nbk.

17. Drinhausen and Brussee, *China's Social Credit System*.

18. Didi Tang, "Chinese Read Brainwaves to Check Up on Workforce," *The Times*, 9 May 2018, www.thetimes.co.uk/article/china-chinese-read-brainwaves-workforce-technology-mood -detection-zp67vv9vx.

19. Joseph Archer, "Beijing to Assign 'Personal Trustworthiness Points' for All Citizens by 2021," *The Telegraph*, 20 November 2018, www.telegraph.co.uk/technology/2018/11/20 /beijing-assign-personal-trustworthiness-points-citizens-2021.

20. Alexandra Ma, "China Ranks Citizens with a Social Credit System – Here's What You Can Do Wrong and How You Can Be Punished," *Independent*, 10 April 2018, www .independent.co.uk/life-style/gadgets-and-tech/china-social-credit-system-punishments -rewards-explained-a8297486.html.

21. An interesting account of the SoCS's history is to be found in Donnelly, "Introduction to the China Social Credit System."

22. "Study: More Than Two Thirds of Chinese Take a Positive View of Social Credit Systems in Their Country," Freie Universität Berlin, 23 July 2018, www.fu-berlin.de/en/presse /informationen/fup/2018/fup_18_198-studie-sozialkreditsystem-china/index.html.

23. Vincent Brussee, "China's Social Credit System Is Actually Quite Boring," *Foreign Policy*, 15 September 2021, https://foreignpolicy.com/2021/09/15/ china-social-credit-system-authoritarian.

24. Matthew Syed, "Our Democracy Is Chaotic, Shrill and Utterly Terrifying to Autocrats," *The Times*, 27 March 2022, www.thetimes.co.uk/article/our-democracy-is-chaotic-shrill -and-utterly-terrifying-to-autocrats-dg8vlj9zc.

25. Jamey Keaton and Matt O'Brien, "UN Urges Moratorium on Use of AI That Imperils Human Rights," AP News, 15 September 2021, https://apnews.com/article/technology -business-laws-united-nations-artificial-intelligence-efafd7b1a5bf47afb1376c198842e69d.

26. Drinhausen and Brussee, *China's Social Credit System*.

27. Cindy Yu, "Mythbusting the Social Credit System," *Spectator*, 13 June 2022, www.spectator
.co.uk/podcast/social-credit-system.

28. George Soros, "Remarks Delivered at the World Economic Forum," Davos, Switzerland,
24 January 2019, www.georgesoros.com/2019/01/24/remarks-delivered-at-the-world
-economic-forum-2.

29. "China's Social Credit System in 2021: From Fragmentation towards Integration," Merics,
9 May 2022, https://merics.org/en/report/chinas-social-credit-system-2021-fragmentation
-towards-integration. For detailed discussions of these different surveillance initiatives,
see Dahlia Peterson, "Designing Alternatives to China's Repressive Surveillance State,"
Center for Security and Emerging Technology, October 2020, https://cset.georgetown.edu
/research/designing-alternatives-to-chinas-repressive-surveillance-state; Jessica Batke and
Mareike Ohlberg, "State of Surveillance: Government Documents Reveal New Evidence
on China's Efforts to Monitor Its People," *ChinaFile*, 30 October 2020, www.chinafile
.com/state-surveillance-china; Maya Wang, "China's Algorithms of Repression: Reverse
Engineering a Xinjiang Police Mass Surveillance App," Human Rights Watch, 1 May 2019,
www.hrw.org/report/2019/05/01/chinas-algorithms-repression/reverse-engineering
-xinjiang-police-mass.

30. "China: Police 'Big Data' Systems Violate Privacy, Target Dissent," Human Rights Watch,
19 November 2017, www.hrw.org/news/2017/11/19/china-police-big-data-systems-violate
-privacy-target-dissent.

31. Mark Bridge, "Scientists Frown at Technology's Ability to Read Facial Expressions," *The
Times*, 29 July 2019, www.thetimes.co.uk/article/scientists-frown-at-technology-s-ability-to
-read-facial-expressions-6jzsjqxcv.

32. Lisa Feldman Barrett et al., "Emotional Expressions Reconsidered: Challenges to Inferring
Emotion from Human Facial Movements," *Psychological Science in the Public Interest* 20,
no. 1 (2019), https://doi.org/10.1177/1529100619832930.

33. James Vincent, "Canon Put AI Cameras in Its Chinese Offices That Only Let Smiling
Workers Inside," Verge, 17 June 2021, www.theverge.com/2021/6/17/22538160/ai-camera
-smile-recognition-office-workers-china-canon.

34. "How Mass Surveillance Works in Xinjiang, China," Human Rights Watch, 2 May 2019,
www.hrw.org/video-photos/interactive/2019/05/02/china-how-mass-surveillance-works
-xinjiang.

35. Lindsay Maizland, "China's Repression of Uyghurs in Xinjiang," Council on Foreign
Relations, updated 22 September 2022, www.cfr.org/backgrounder/china-xinjiang-uyghurs
-muslims-repression-genocide-human-rights.

36. "Chinese Persecution of the Uyghurs," United States Holocaust Memorial Museum,
accessed 13 March 2024, www.ushmm.org/genocide-prevention/countries/china/chinese
-persecution-of-the-uyghurs.

37. "Chinese Persecution of the Uyghurs."

38. Dean Dwyer, "Artificial Intelligence: Taking the World towards the Perfection of Global
Tyranny," Harbinger's Daily, 26 October 2022, https://harbingersdaily.com/artificial
-intelligence-taking-the-world-towards-the-perfection-of-global-tyranny.

39. "China Has Turned Xinjiang into a Police State Like No Other, *Economist*, 31 May 2018,
www.economist.com/briefing/2018/05/31/china-has-turned-xinjiang-into-a-police-state
-like-no-other.

40. Dake Kang, "Chinese 'Gait Recognition' Tech IDs People by How They Walk," AP News, 6 November 2018, https://apnews.com/article/bf75dd1c26c947b7826d270a16e2658a.

41. Ross Anderson, The Panopticon Is Already Here," *Atlantic*, September 2020, https://www.theatlantic.com/magazine/archive/2020/09/china-ai-surveillance/614197.

42. Robin Barnwell and Gesbeen Mohammad, "Bar Codes and Cameras Track China's 'Lab Rats,'" *The Times*, 14 July 2019, www.thetimes.co.uk/article/bar-codes-and-cameras-track-china-s-lab-rats-tp9wcc0fb. See also Maya Wang, "'Eradicating Ideological Viruses': China's Campaign of Repression against Xinjiang's Muslims," Human Rights Watch, 9 September 2018, www.hrw.org/report/2018/09/09/eradicating-ideological-viruses/chinas-campaign-repression-against-xinjiangs; and Josh Chin and Clément Bürge, "Twelve Days in Xinjiang: How China's Surveillance State Overwhelms Daily Life," *Wall Street Journal*, 19 December 2017, www.wsj.com/articles/twelve-days-in-xinjiang-how-chinas-surveillance-state-overwhelms-daily-life-1513700355.

43. Ian Williams, *Every Breath You Take: China's New Tyranny* (Edinburgh: Birlinn, 2021), 11.

44. Alina Polyakova and Chris Meserole, "Exporting Digital Authoritarianism: The Russian and Chinese Models," Brookings Institution, accessed 13 March 2024, www.brookings.edu/wp-content/uploads/2019/08/FP_20190827_digital_authoritarianism_polyakova_meserole.pdf.

45. Quoted in "'Break Their Lineage, Break Their Roots': China's Crime against Humanity Targeting Uyghurs and Other Turkic Muslims," Human Rights Watch, 19 April 2021, www.hrw.org/report/2021/04/19/break-their-lineage-break-their-roots/chinas-crimes-against-humanity-targeting.

46. Nury Turkel, *No Escape: The True Story of China's Genocide of the Uyghurs* (London: William Collins, 2022).

47. Chris Buckley and Steven Lee Myers, "China Builds More Secret 'Re-education Camps' to Detain Uighur Muslims Despite Global Outcry over Human Suffering," *Independent*, 10 August 2019, www.independent.co.uk/news/world/asia/xi-jinping-regime-han-chinese-threat-uighur-muslims-persecution-detention-camps-a9051126.html.

48. Williams, *Every Breath You Take*, chapter 1.

49. Quoted in Gerry Shih, "'Police Cloud': Chinese Database Tracks Apps, Car Location and Even Electricity Usage in Muslim Region," *Washington Post*, 2 May 2019, www.washingtonpost.com/world/chinese-database-is-tracking-cellphone-usage-car-location-and-even-electricity-usage-of-xinjiang-residents/2019/05/01/12eb3996-6c8a-11e9-be3a-33217240a539_story.html.

50. Williams, *Every Breath You Take*, 41–42.

51. Open Technology Fund, *Annual Report 2019/2020*, accessed 13 March 2024, https://public.opentech.fund/documents/OTF_Annual_Report_20192020_-_Final_v3.pdf.

52. Fiona Hamilton, "Chinese-Made Electric Cars in UK Could Be Jammed Remotely by Beijing," *The Times*, 21 March 2024, www.thetimes.co.uk/article/china-electric-cars-uk-roads-3s69qg6g0.

53. Turkel, *No Escape*, x.

54. Demetri Sevastopulo, "US Accuses China of Developing 'Brain Control Weaponry,'" *Financial Times*, 16 December 2021, www.ft.com/content/f9637825-0e9b-45d7-a49a-1eb507d41e68.

55. Milan Kundera, *The Book of Laughter and Forgetting: A Novel* (New York: Harper Perennial, 1978), 4.

56. Yan Lianke, *The Four Books: A Novel* (New York: Grove, 2010).

57. Isabel Hilton, "*The Four Books* Review: Yan Lianke Holds China to Account for Maoist Atrocities," *Guardian*, 29 March 2015, www.theguardian.com/books/2015/mar/29/the -four-books-yan-lianke-review.

58. Chan Koonchung, *The Fat Years* (London: Doubleday, 2011).

59. Quoted in Ben Bland, "China Rewrites History with New Censorship Drive," *Financial Times*, 4 September 2017, www.ft.com/content/4ffac53e-8ee4-11e7-9084-d0c17942ba93.

60. Colin Drury, "Hong Kong Protests: Clashes in Sheffield as Rival Groups Stand Off in City Centre," *Independent*, 3 October 2019, https://www.independent.co.uk/news/uk /home-news/hong-kong-protests-latest-sheffield-clashes-bottles-thrown-chinese-students -a9135186.html.

61. "Hong Kong Protests: Sheffield University Students Clash," BBC, 2 October 2019, https:// www.bbc.com/news/uk-england-south-yorkshire-49914304.

62. *The New Big Brother: China and Digital Authoritarianism* (Washington, DC: US Senate Committee on Foreign Relations, 21 July 2020), 43, www.foreign.senate.gov/imo/media /doc/2020%20SFRC%20Minority%20Staff%20Report%20-%20The%20New%20 Big%20Brother%20-%20China%20and%20Digital%20Authoritarianism.pdf.

63. Moody, "Big Brother Is Watching."

64. Charlie Parker, "British Using Chinese CCTV Linked to Repression of Uighurs," *The Times*, 7 February 2022, www.thetimes.co.uk/article/british-using-chinese-cctv-linked-to -repression-of-uighurs-jzlkpjxhw.

65. Jake Cordell, "Moscow Metro's 'Face Pay' System Part of Orwellian Surveillance, Say Critics," *The Times*, 16 October 2021, www.thetimes.co.uk/article/privacy-fear-as-moscow -metro-launches-facial-id-payment-system-vjjz5t66c.

66. Matthew Ball, "Hardware and the Metaverse," MatthewBall.co, 29 June 2021, www .matthewball.vc/all/hardwaremetaverse.

67. Ray Walsh, "How Post-Brexit Britain Could Become a Surveillance State," Public Technology, 8 July 2020, www.publictechnology.net/articles/opinion/how-brexit-britain -could-become-surveillance-state.

68. "UK: Europe's Top Court Rules UK Mass Surveillance Regime Violated Human Rights," Amnesty International, 25 May 2021, www.amnesty.org/en/latest/news/2021/05/uk -surveillance-gchq-ecthr-ruling.

69. Ross Clark, "We Need to Act Now to Block Britian's Social Credit System," *Spectator*, 24 July 2021, www.spectator.co.uk/article/we-need-to-act-now-to-block-britain-s-social-credit -system.

70. Clark "We Need to Act Now."

71. Luke Henriques-Gomes, "ParentsNext: Coalition Makes Changes to Welfare Program after Scathing Report," *Guardian*, 12 April 2019, www.theguardian.com/australia-news/2019/apr /12/parentsnext-coalition-makes-minor-changes-to-welfare-program-after-scathing-report.

72. Matt Ridley, "Britain Can Show the World the Best of AI," *The Times*, 16 April 2018, www .thetimes.co.uk/article/britain-can-show-the-world-the-best-of-ai-585vsthvn.

73. Sir Patrick Vallance, in "The Future of Citizen Data Systems: Evidence and Scenarios for Global Data Systems," Government Office for Science, September 2020, 2, https://assets .publishing.service.gov.uk/government/uploads/system/uploads/attachment_data/file /927547/GOS_The_Future_of_Citizen_Data_Systems_Report__2_.pdf.

74. "Future of Citizen Data Systems," 96.

75. Clark, "We Need to Act Now."

76. Cameron Hilditch, "China's Social-Credit System Arrives on British Shores, *National Review*, 28 July 2021, www.nationalreview.com/2021/07/chinas-social-credit-system -arrives-on-british-shores.

77. Marc Glendening, "Are We Moving towards a Woke Version of the Chinese Social Credit System," Institute of Economic Affairs, 19 July 2021, https://iea.org.uk/are-we-moving -towards-a-woke-version-of-the-chinese-social-credit-system.

78. Yuval Noah Harari, "Why Technology Favors Tyranny," *Atlantic*, October 2018, www.the atlantic.com/magazine/archive/2018/10/yuval-noah-harari-technology-tyranny/568330.

79. Nick Robins-Early, "Disinformation Reimagined: How AI Could Erode Democracy in the 2024 US Elections," *Guardian*, 19 July 2023, www.theguardian.com/us-news/2023/jul/19 /ai-generated-disinformation-us-elections.

80. Dan Milmo and Alex Hern, "Elections in UK and US at Risk from AI-Driven Disinformation, Say Experts," *Guardian*, 20 May 2023, www.theguardian.com/technology /2023/may/20/elections-in-uk-and-us-at-risk-from-ai-driven-disinformation-say-experts.

81. Sajid Javid, "On Election Day, I Fear We'll See How Harmful AI Can Be," Conservatives, 4 June 2023, www.sajidjavid.com/news/election-day-i-fear-well-see-how-harmful-ai-can-be.

82. Mekela Panditharatne and Noah Giansiracusa, "How AI Puts Elections at Risk – and the Needed Safeguards," Brennan Center, updated 21 July 2023, www.brennancenter.org/our -work/analysis-opinion/how-ai-puts-elections-risk-and-needed-safeguards.

83. "AI to Drive 2024 Election Disinformation Risks," Dragonfly, 30 August 2023, www .dragonflyintelligence.com/news/us-ai-to-drive-2024-election-disinformation-risks.

84. Renée DiResta, "The Supply of Disinformation Will Soon Be Infinite," *Atlantic*, 20 September 2020, www.theatlantic.com/ideas/archive/2020/09/future-propaganda-will-be -computer-generated/616400.

85. Hannah Murphy, "The Rising Threat to Democracy of AI-Powered Disinformation," *Financial Times*, 11 January 2024, www.ft.com/content/16f23c01-fa51-408e-acf5 -0d30a5a1ebf2.

86. Murphy, "Rising Threat to Democracy."

87. Nina Schick, *Deepfakes and the Infocalypse: What You Urgently Need to Know* (London: Monoray, 2020).

88. Schick, *Deepfakes*, 8.

89. Schick, *Deepfakes*, 71.

90. Samantha Bradshaw and Philip Howard, *The Global Disinformation Order: 2019 Global Inventory of Organised Social Media Manipulation* (Oxford: Oxford Internet Institute, 2019), https://demtech.oii.ox.ac.uk/wp-content/uploads/sites/93/2019/09/CyberTroop -Report19.pdf.

91. Quoted in Esther Ajao, "AI and Disinformation in the Russia-Ukraine War," Tech Target, 14 March 2022, www.techtarget.com/searchenterpriseai/feature/AI-and-disinformation-in -the-Russia-Ukraine-war.

92. Tatlow, "China Aims to Replicate."

93. Tatlow, "China Aims to Replicate."

94. Murphy, "Rising Threat to Democracy."

95. Katie Prescott, "Open AI Hires Crisis Managers to Tackle Election Interference," The Times, 19 January 2024, www.thetimes.com/business-money/technology/article/openai -hires-crisis-managers-to-tackle-election-interference-k07c9n67n.

96. Quoted in Danny Fortson, "Deepfakes and AI-Generated Faces Are Corroding Trust in the Web," *The Times*, 3 April 2022.

97. Quoted in Fortson, Deepfakes and AI-Generated Faces."

98. Matthew Groh et al., "Deepfake Detection by Human Crowds, Machines, and Machine-Informed Crowds," *PNAS* 119, no. 1 (2022), www.pnas.org/doi/10.1073/pnas.2110013119.

99. Quoted in Danny Fortson, "ChatGPT's Sam Altman Wants to Save the World from the AI He Created," *The Times*, 30 September 2023, www.thetimes.co.uk/article/chatgpts-sam-altman-wants-to-save-the-world-from-the-ai-he-created-rpzzdp8x3.

100. Quoted in Steven Swinford, "AI Risks Undermining Fabric of Society, Says Former Cyber Chief," *The Times*, 8 May 2023, www.thetimes.co.uk/article/ai-risks-undermining-fabric-of-society-says-former-cyber-chief-wd5q2cbwl.

101. Matthew 23:27–28.

102. Galatians 2:11–15.

103. 1 Peter 2:1–2.

104. Mark 7:6.

105. Matthew 7:15–16.

106. Aleksandr Solzhenitsyn, "Live Not by Lies," 1974, Aleksandr Solzhenitsyn Center, accessed 13 March 2024, www.solzhenitsyncenter.org/live-not-by-lies.

Chapter 9: Virtual Reality and the Metaverse

1. *Oxford English Dictionary*, s.v. "metaverse."

2. There are many videos that the reader might consult at this point to gain some idea of what it is like in the metaverse.

3. Matthew Ball, "Framework for the Metaverse," MatthewBall.co, 29 June 2021, www.matthewball.vc/all/forwardtothemetaverseprimer.

4. Neal Stephenson, *Snow Crash* (New York: Bantam, 1992).

5. Esteban Ortiz-Ospina, "The Rise of Social Media," Our World in Data, 18 September 2019, https://ourworldindata.org/rise-of-social-media. Facebook has 3 billion users as of 2022. TikTok joined the billion-user club in 2021.

6. "Global Video Game Consumer Population Passes 3 Billion," DFC Intelligence, 14 August 2020, www.dfcint.com/dossier/global-video-game-consumer-population.

7. Bernard Marr, "The 7 Biggest Artificial Intelligence (AI) Trends in 2022," *Forbes*, 24 September 2021, www.forbes.com/sites/bernardmarr/2021/09/24/the-7-biggest-artificial-intelligence-ai-trends-in-2022/?sh=7c9935b22015.

8. A glance at the Second Life website will show just what that range is.

9. Jenny Huberman, *Transhumanism: From Ancestors to Avatars* (Cambridge: Cambridge University Press, 2021).

10. Rosae Martín Peña, "Enhanced Humans: The Avatars of the Future," OpenMind, 11 January 2017, www.bbvaopenmind.com/en/science/bioscience/enhanced-humans-the-avatars-of-the-future.

11. "Imagine the Possibilities," Second Life, accessed 22 April 2024, https://secondlife.com.

12. Sherry Turkle, *Alone Together: Why We Expect More from Technology and Less from Each Other*, 3rd ed. (New York: Basic Books, 2017), 159.

13. Walter Pasquarelli, "Towards Synthetic Reality: When DeepFakes Meet AR/VR," Oxford Insights, 6 August 2019, emphasis added.

14. Jacques Ellul, *The Technological Bluff* (Grand Rapids: Eerdmans, 1990), 365.

15. Quoted in Roland Chia, "Navigating the Metaverse," Ethos Institute, 24 February 2022, https://ethosinstitute.sg/navigating-the-metaverse.

16. Andrew Bosworth, "Building the Metaverse Responsibly," Meta, 27 September 2021, https://about.fb.com/news/2021/09/building-the-metaverse-responsibly.

17. Ryan Morrison, "Metaverse Users Will Be Granted God-Like Powers to Create Their Own Virtual World Just by Speaking Things into Existence, Zuckerberg Reveals," *Daily Mail*, updated 24 February 2022, www.dailymail.co.uk/sciencetech/article-10547361/Metaverse-users-granted-god-like-powers-create-virtual-world.html.

18. Mark Zuckerberg, "Founder's Letter, 2021," Meta, 28 October 2021, https://about.fb.com/news/2021/10/founders-letter.

19. Sean Endicott, "Microsoft President Warns That the Metaverse Is 'Not Like Dying and Going to Heaven,'" Windows Central, 4 November 2021, www.windowscentral.com/microsoft-president-warns-metaverse-not-dying-and-going-heaven.

20. Ananya Bhattacharya, "Meta's 'Year of Efficiency' Means Job Cuts, Less Metaverse, and More Generative AI," Quartz, updated 14 March 2023, https://qz.com/meta-layoffs-2023-jobs-metaverse-ai-1850196575.

21. Arthur Sullivan, "Meta Faces a Future of More Legal Woes and Falling Revenues," Deutsche Welle, 12 January 2023, www.dw.com/en/meta-faces-a-future-of-more-legal-woes-and-falling-revenues/a-64352968.

22. Quoted in Cody Mello-Klein, "Why Is Mark Zuckerberg's Metaverse Failing?," Northeastern Global News, 3 November 2022, https://news.northeastern.edu/2022/11/03/metaverse-failure.

23. Bernard Marr, "Is This the Downfall of Meta and Social Media as We Know It?," *Forbes*, 14 November 2022, www.forbes.com/sites/bernardmarr/2022/11/14/is-this-the-downfall-of-meta-and-social-media-as-we-know-it/?sh=404d7a7478c8.

24. Janna Anderson and Lee Rainie, "The Metaverse in 2040," Pew Research Center, 30 June 2022, www.pewresearch.org/internet/2022/06/30/the-metaverse-in-2040.

25. Anderson and Rainie, "Metaverse in 2040."

26. Danny Fortson, "Facebook's 20th Anniversary: From Frat-House Dream to Tech Empire," *The Times*, 28 January 2024, www.thetimes.co.uk/article/facebook-20th-anniversary-mark-zuckerberg-meta-ai-phqwlp52b.

27. Gayle M. Timmerman, *Issues in Mental Health Nursing* 12, no. 1 (January–March 1991):19–30, https://pubmed.ncbi.nlm.nih.gov/1988378.

28. Rob Brooks, "I Tried the Replika AI Companion and Can See Why Users Are Falling Hard. The App Raises Serious Ethical Questions," The Conversation, 21 February 2023, https://theconversation.com/i-tried-the-replika-ai-companion-and-can-see-why-users-are-falling-hard-the-app-raises-serious-ethical-questions-200257.

29. Oliver Hodges, "AI Bots Available in Ireland Raise Fears over Child Grooming," *The Times*, 21 May 2023, www.thetimes.co.uk/article/ai-bots-available-in-ireland-raise-fears-over-child-grooming-tlfjj5sgp.

30. Quoted in "The Shocking Truth about Replika: Mental Health Warning!," Toolify.ai, 5 December 2023, www.toolify.ai/gpts/the-shocking-truth-about-replika-mental-health-warning-155543#:~:text=.

31. Mark Sellman and Olivia Sheepshanks, "Paedophiles Using AI to Create Child Abuse Images," *The Times*, 1 May 2023, www.thetimes.co.uk/article/paedophiles-using-ai-to-create-child-abuse-images-mrmxfd03s.

32. "Pornography and Public Health: Research Summary," National Center on Sexual Exploitation, 14 January 2019, https://endsexualexploitation.org/wp-content/uploads /NCOSE_Pornography-PublicHealth_ResearchSummary_1-14-19_FINAL.pdf.

33. Gopal Ratnam, "Christians Turn to Artificial Intelligence to Stop Porn Use," Roll Call, 19 November 2019, https://rollcall.com/2019/11/19/christians-turn-to-artificial-intelligence -to-stop-porn-use.

34. 1 Corinthians 6:11.

35. 2 Timothy 2:22 KJV.

36. Hebrews 10:24–25.

Chapter 10: Upgrading Humans: The Transhumanist Agenda

1. Steven Pinker, *The Better Angels of Our Nature: Why Violence Has Declined* (New York: Penguin, 2012).

2. Yuval Noah Harari, *Homo Deus: A Brief History of Tomorrow* (New York: HarperCollins, 2017), 1–43.

3. Harari, *Homo Deus*, 15–16.

4. Harari, *Homo Deus*, 5–6.

5. *2023 Global Report on Food Crises* (Rome: FSIN and Global Network against Food Crises, 2023), www.fsinplatform.org/sites/default/files/resources/files/GRFC2023-compressed .pdf.

6. Harari, *Homo Deus*, 22.

7. Martin Rees, *On the Future* (Princeton, NJ: Princeton University Press, 2018), 227.

8. Yuval Noah Harari and Daniel Kahneman, "Death Is Optional," Edge, accessed 13 March 2024, www.edge.org/conversation/yuval_noah_harari-daniel_kahneman-death-is -optional.

9. Pinker, *Better Angels*.

10. John Gray, "Best of 2012: Stephen Pinker's Delusions of Peace," Australian Broadcasting Company, 20 January 2013, www.abc.net.au/religion/best-of-2012-stephen-pinkers -delusions-of-peace/10100056.

11. John Gray, "John Gray: Steven Pinker Is Wrong about Violence and War," *Guardian*, 13 March 2015, www.theguardian.com/books/2015/mar/13/john-gray-steven-pinker-wrong -violence-war-declining.

12. Harari, *Homo Deus*, 22–23.

13. Charles Rubin, "Algorithmic Man: Yuval Noah Harari's Timid Transhumanism," *Public Discourse*, 28 June 2018, www.thepublicdiscourse.com/2018/06/21562.

14. Harari, *Homo Deus*, 371–72.

15. Harari, *Homo Deus*, 402.

16. For more on this topic, see my book *Cosmic Chemistry: Do God and Science Mix?* (London: Lion Hudson, 2021).

17. Ian Sample, "Harvard Scientists Reverse the Ageing Process in Mice—Now for Humans," *Guardian*, 28 November 2010, www.theguardian.com/science/2010/nov/28/scientists -reverse-ageing-mice-humans.

18. Kyree Leary, "Aging Expert: The First Person to Live to 1,000 Has Already Been Born," Futurism, 1 December 2017, https://futurism.com/aging-expert-person-1000-born.

19. Jean Mariani and Danièle Tritsch, "Is Transhumanism a Sham?," CNRS News, 9 June 2018, https://news.cnrs.fr/opinions/is-transhumanism-a-sham.

20. Madeleine Spence, "Who Wants to Live Forever? Jeff Bezos and Mark Zuckerberg Do," *The Times*, 12 September 2021, www.thetimes.co.uk/article/who-wants-to-live-for-ever-jeff-bezos-and-mark-zuckerberg-do-g68w8tbcm.

21. Quoted in Hannah Kuchler, "Altos Labs Insists Mission Is to Improve Lives Not Cheat Death," *Financial Times*, 23 January 2022, www.ft.com/content/f3bceaf2-0d2f-4ec7-b767-693bf01f9630.

22. "Our Mission," Altos Labs, accessed 22 April 2024, www.altoslabs.com.

23. Venki Ramakrishnan, "'We Don't Yet Have the Know-How to Properly Maintain a Corpse Brain': Why Cryonics Is a Non-Starter in Our Quest for Immortality?," Live Science, 23 March 2024, www.livescience.com/health/death/we-dont-yet-have-the-know-how-to-properly-maintain-a-corpse-brain-why-cryonics-is-a-non-starter-in-our-quest-for-immortality.

24. "Global Water Crisis: Facts, FAQs, and How to Help," World Vision, accessed 22 April 2024, www.worldvision.org/clean-water-news-stories/global-water-crisis-facts.

25. Matthew 6:27.

26. Nikolai Fedorov, "The End of Orphanhood, Limitless Kinship," quoted in G. M. Young, *The Russian Cosmists: The Esoteric Futurism of Nikolai Fedorov and His Followers* (New York: Oxford University Press, 2012), 82, italics in original.

27. This calls to mind the more primitive use of the happiness drug soma in Aldous Huxley's 1932 novel *Brave New World*.

28. Harari, *Homo Deus*, 43.

29. Harari, *Homo Deus*, 21.

30. Harari, *Homo Deus*, 47.

31. Celine Ribeiro, "'Beyond Our Ape-Brained Meat Sacks': Can Transhumanism Save Our Species?," *The Guardian*, 3 June 2022, www.theguardian.com/books/2022/jun/04/beyond-our-ape-brained-meat-sacks-can-transhumanism-save-our-species.

32. Harari, *Homo Deus*, 49.

33. Elizabeth Segran, "Yuval Noah Harari: Humans Are on the Verge of Merging with Machines," *Fast Company*, 9 July 2019, www.fastcompany.com/90373620/yuval-noah-harari-humans-are-on-the-verge-of-merging-with-machines.

34. "Frequently Asked Questions," Yuval Noah Harari official website, accessed 13 March 2024, www.ynharari.com/faqs.

35. Harari, *Homo Deus*, 323.

36. "Frequently Asked Questions," Harari website.

37. Mark O'Connell, *To Be a Machine: Adventures among Cyborgs, Utopians, Hackers, and the Futurists Solving the Modest Problem of Death* (New York: Anchor, 2017), 2.

38. David Pearce, "The Hedonistic Imperative," www.hedweb.com/hedethic/hedonist.htm.

39. John Gray, *Seven Types of Atheism* (New York: Farrar, Straus and Giroux, 2018), 158.

40. John Gray, *The Soul of the Marionette: A Short Inquiry into Human Freedom* (New York: Farrar, Straus and Giroux, 2015), 10. See also O'Connell, *To Be a Machine*, 62; and Gray, *Seven Types of Atheism*, 71–93.

41. Gray, *Seven Types of Atheism*, 66.

42. Ray Kurzweil, *The Singularity Is Near: When Humans Transcend Biology* (New York: Penguin, 2005), 59.

43. C. S. Lewis, *That Hideous Strength: A Modern Fairy-Tale for Grown-Ups* (1945; repr., New York: Scribner, 1996), 170.

44. Giles Fraser, "There's More to Atheism Than the Dim-Witted Dawkins Brigade," UnHerd, 18 May 2018, https://unherd.com/2018/05/atheism-dim-witted-dawkins-brigade.

45. Hava Tirosh-Samuelson, "The Paradoxes of Transhumanism: Technological Spirituality or Techno-Idolatry?," *Theologische Literaturzeitung* 146, no. 3 (2020): 12.

46. David Benatar, *Better Never to Have Been: The Harm of Coming into Existence* (Oxford: Oxford University Press, 2006), 200.

47. Peter Singer, *The Life You Can Save: How to Do Your Part to End World Poverty* (London: Picador, 2009).

48. William MacAskill, *What We Owe the Future* (New York: Basic Books, 2022).

49. Émile P. Torres, "Against Longtermism," Aeon, 19 October 2021, https://aeon.co/essays /why-longtermism-is-the-worlds-most-dangerous-secular-credo.

50. Émile P. Torres, *Were the Great Tragedies of History "Mere Ripples"? The Case against Longtermism*, Émile P. Torres official website, accessed 13 March 2024, www.xriskology .com/_files/ugd/d9aaad_89094654cf0945738f5633b5d46653fd.pdf.

51. Torres, "Against Longtermism," italics in original.

52. Nick Bostrom, "Existential Risks: Analyzing Human Extinction Scenarios and Related Hazards," Nick Bostrom official website, accessed 13 March 2024, https://nickbostrom .com/existential/risks.

53. Nicholas Beckstead, "On the Overwhelming Importance of Shaping the Far Future" (doctoral dissertation, Rutgers University, 2013), https://rucore.libraries.rutgers.edu /rutgers-lib/40469/PDF/1/play.

54. Torres, "Against Longtermism."

55. Quoted in Sigal Samuel, "Effective Altruism's Most Controversial Idea," Vox, 6 September 2022, www.vox.com/future-perfect/23298870/effective-altruism-longtermism -will-macaskill-future.

56. Ellen Huet, "The Real-Life Consequences of Silicon Valley's AI Obsession," Bloomberg, 7 March 2023, www.bloomberg.com/news/features/2023-03-07/effective-altruism-s -problems-go-beyond-sam-bankman-fried.

57. Huet, "Real-Life Consequences."

58. Friedrich Nietzsche, *The Antichrist*, trans. H. L. Mencken (New York: Knopf, 1918), Project Gutenberg, www.gutenberg.org/files/19322/19322-h/19322-h.htm.

59. Tom Kington, "Stop Playing God, Pope's Adviser Tells Tech Titans, *The Times*, 19 January 2024, www.thetimes.co.uk/article/stop-playing-god-popes-adviser-tells-tech-titans -pfvn3jp5m.

60. Leon Kass, *Toward a More Natural Science: Biology and Human Affairs* (New York: Free Press, 1985), 76–77.

61. C. S. Lewis, *The Abolition of Man* (1943; repr., San Francisco: HarperSanFrancisco, 2001), 55, 58, 64.

62. Dennis Glover, *The Last Man in Europe* (Edinburgh: Polygon, 2021).

63. John Gray, "Is It Ever Right to Try to Create a Superior Human Being?" BBC, 6 September 2015, www.bbc.com/news/magazine-34151049.

64. Gray, "Is It Ever Right?"

65. Leon Trotsky, *Literature and Revolution*, trans. R. Strunsky (Chicago: Haymarket, 2005), 207.

66. Sergei Gogin, "*Homo Sovieticus*: 20 Years after the End of the Soviet Union," in *Russian Analytical Digest* 109 (8 March 2012): 13, www.files.ethz.ch/isn/138831/Russian _Analytical_Digest_109.pdf.

67. Gray, "Is It Ever Right?"
68. Lewis, *That Hideous Strength*, 39.
69. Lewis, *That Hideous Strength*, 40.
70. "The Scientist Takes Over," review of C. S. Lewis, *That Hideous Strength* (1945) by George Orwell, *Manchester Evening News*, 16 August 1945, in *The Complete Works of George Orwell*, vol. 17, ed. Peter Davison (London: Secker & Warburg, 1998), 250–51, www .lewisiana.nl/orwell/.
71. Matthew 26:53.
72. Iain McGilchrist, "AI World Summit 2022 Dr Iain McGilchrist on Artificial Intelligence and the Matter with Things," Dr Iain McGilchrist, 28 October 2022, YouTube video, www .youtube.com/watch?v=XgbUCKWCMPA.
73. P. D. James, *The Children of Men* (London: Penguin, 1992), 15.

Chapter 11: Artificial General Intelligence: The Future Is Dark?

1. Decca Aitkenhead, "James Lovelock: 'Before the End of This Century, Robots Will Have Taken Over,'" *Guardian*, 30 September 2016, www.theguardian.com/environment/2016 /sep/30/james-lovelock-interview-by-end-of-century-robots-will-have-taken-over.
2. Ian Parker, "Yuval Noah Harari's History of Everyone, Ever," *New Yorker*, 10 February 2020, www.newyorker.com/magazine/2020/02/17/yuval-noah-harari-gives-the -really-big-picture.
3. Yuval Noah Harari, *Homo Deus: A Brief History of Tomorrow* (New York: HarperCollins, 2017), 49.
4. Quoted in Matt Ridley, "Britain Can Show the World the Best of AI," *The Times*, 16 April 2018, www.thetimes.co.uk/article/britain-can-show-the-world-the-best-of-ai -585vsthvn.
5. Private communication.
6. Ben Dickson, "DeepMind Says Reinforcement Learning Is 'Enough' to Reach General AI," VentureBeat, 9 June 2021, https://venturebeat.com/2021/06/09/deepmind-says -reinforcement-learning-is-enough-to-reach-general-ai.
7. See my book *Cosmic Chemistry: Do God and Science Mix?* (London: Lion Hudson, 2021).
8. Herbert Roitblat, *Algorithms Are Not Enough: Creating General Artificial Intelligence* (Boston: MIT Press, 2020).
9. Dennis Hillemann, "Comparing Open AI and Google Deepmind: Who Is Leading the AI Revolution?," Medium, 17 January 2023, https://dhillemann.medium.com/comparing -open-ai-and-google-deepmind-who-is-leading-the-ai-revolution-4b11faf07e58.
10. "23 Mathematical Challenges," London Institute for Mathematical Science, accessed 13 March 2024, https://lims.ac.uk/23-mathematical-challenges.
11. Nigel Shadbolt and Roger Hampson, *The Digital Ape: How to Live (in Peace) with Smart Machines* (Oxford: Oxford University Press, 2019).
12. Quoted in Jane Wakefield, "AI Ripe for Exploitation, Experts Warn," BBC, 21 February 2018, www.bbc.com/news/technology-43127533.
13. Michael Frayn, *Copenhagen* (New York: Bloomsbury, 2017).
14. John Polkinghorne, *Serious Talk: Science and Religion in Dialogue* (Harrisburg, PA: Trinity, 1995), 3.
15. Sean Carroll, *The Big Picture: On the Origins of Life, Meaning, and the Universe Itself* (London: Oneworld, 2016), 3, 5.

16. Quoted in Dom Galeon, "Separating Science Fact from Science Hype: How Far Off Is the Singularity?," Futurism, 1 January 2018, https://futurism.com/separating-science-fact -science-hype-how-far-off-singularity.

17. John Lennox, *Cosmic Chemistry: Do God and Science Mix?* (London: Lion Hudson, 2021).

18. Quoted in Galeon, "How Far Off Is the Singularity?"

19. I shall bear in mind that a distinction is made between materialism and naturalism. According to the *Oxford Companion to Philosophy*, naturalism in metaphysics is "most obviously akin to materialism but it does not have to be materialistic. What it insists on is that the world of nature should consist of a single sphere without incursions from outside by souls or spirits, divine or human . . . but it need not reject the phenomena of consciousness, nor even identify them somehow with material phenomena as the materialist must." John H. Randall writes: "Naturalism finds itself in thoroughgoing opposition to all forms of thought which assert the existence of a supernatural or transcendent Realm of Being, and which make knowledge of that realm of fundamental importance to human living" (John H. Randall, "The Nature of Naturalism," in *Naturalism and the Human Spirit*, ed. Yervant H. Krikorian [New York: Columbia University Press, 1945], 358).

20. These days the ultimate reality is often thought to be "nothing" from which everything else derives. See my book *God and Stephen Hawking: Whose Design Is It Anyway?* (London: Lion Hudson, 2021).

21. Daniel Dennett, *Breaking the Spell: Religion as a Natural Phenomenon* (London: Penguin, 2007), 107.

22. Daniel Dennett, "The Self as a Center of Narrative Gravity," in *Self and Consciousness: Multiple Perspectives*, ed. F. Kessel, P. Cole, and D. Johnson (Hillsdale, NJ: Erlbaum, 1992), accessed 22 April 2024, https://danielwharris.com/teaching/101/readings/DennettSelf.pdf.

23. Henry Kissinger, Eric Schmidt, and Daniel Huttenlocher, *The Age of AI and Our Human Future* (London: John Murray, 2021), 20.

24. Francis Crick, *The Astonishing Hypothesis: The Scientific Search for the Soul* (New York: Scribner, 1994), 3.

25. And causation is yet another. There is sometimes a danger of confusing correlation with causation.

26. Positron-emission tomography (PET) detects increase in blood flow due to the demand for oxygen by active neurons, thus giving a map of "hot spots" in the brain.

27. Colin McGinn, "What Is It Not Like to Be a Brain?," in *Explanations: Styles of Explanations in Science*, ed. John Cornwell (Oxford: Oxford University Press, 2004), 163.

28. John Polkinghorne, *One World: The Interaction of Science and Theology* (London: SPCK, 1986), 92–93.

29. John Wilson, "Q&A: Alvin Plantinga on Conflict Resolution with Science," *Christianity Today*, 15 December 2011, www.christianitytoday.com/ct/2011/december /conflictresolution.html. For more detail, see Alvin Plantinga, *Where the Conflict Really Lies: Science, Religion, and Naturalism* (Oxford: Oxford University Press, 2011), chap. 10.

30. Denis Noble, *The Music of Life: Biology beyond Genes* (Oxford: Oxford University Press, 2006), 126.

31. David J. Chalmers, *The Conscious Mind: In Search of a Fundamental Theory* (Oxford: Oxford University Press, 1996), xiv.

32. David J. Chalmers, "Consciousness and Its Place in Nature," in *The Blackwell Guide to Philosophy of Mind*, ed. Stephen P. Stich and Ted A. Warfield (Oxford: Blackwell, 2003), 102.

33. One of the most common is dual-aspect monism, which regards consciousness as a dynamic emergent property of the activity of the brain that somehow is not reducible to the neural events that compose it. This is a dualism of properties rather than of substance. Interestingly, Popper wrote: "From an evolutionary point of view, I regard the self-conscious mind as an emergent product of the brain. . . . Now I want to emphasize how little is said by saying that the mind is an emergent product of the brain. It has practically no explanatory value, and it hardly amounts to more than putting a question mark at a certain place in human evolution. Nevertheless, I think that this is all which, from a Darwinian point of view, we can say about it" (Karl Popper, *The Self and Its Brain: An Argument for Interactionism* [New York: Routledge, 1983], 554).

34. Keith Ward, *Why There Almost Certainly Is a God: Doubting Dawkins* (Oxford: Lion Hudson, 2008), 19–20.

35. John 4:24.

36. Michael Egnor, "The Brain Is Not a 'Meat Computer,'" Mind Matters, 7 August 2018, https://mindmatters.ai/2018/08/the-brain-is-not-a-meat-computer.

37. Egnor, "Brain Is Not."

38. "Chinese Room Argument," in *The MIT Encyclopedia of the Cognitive Sciences*, ed. Robert A. Wilson and Frank C. Keil (Cambridge, MA: MIT Press, 1999), 115.

39. Rosalind Picard and Nick Bostrom, interview with Justin Brierley, "God, AI and the Future of Humanity: Is Technology the Key to Immortality?," *UnBelievable podcast*, The Big Conversation, 23 April 2021, www.thebigconversation.show/wp-content/uploads/2022/07/God-AI-and-Future-of-Humanity-Bostrum-Picard-TBCS3E2.pdf.

40. "Thinking Machines? Has the Lovelace Test Been Passed?," Mind Matters, 7 April 2020, https://mindmatters.ai/2020/04/thinking-machines-has-the-lovelace-test-been-passed..

41. Steve Paulson, "Roger Penrose on Why Consciousness Does Not Compute," *Nautilus*, 27 April 2017, https://nautil.us/roger-penrose-on-why-consciousness-does-not-compute-6127.

42. Michael Polanyi, *Personal Knowledge: Towards a Post-Critical Philosophy* (London: Routledge and Kegan Paul, 1962), 315.

43. Iain McGilchrist, *The Matter with Things: Our Brains, Our Delusions, and the Unmaking of the World* (London: Perspectiva Press, 2021), 429.

44. Max Planck, *Where Is Science Going?* (New York: Norton, 1932), 214.

45. Brendan Dixon, "No, Your Brain Isn't a Three-Pound Meat Computer," *Evolution News*, 20 May 2016, https://evolutionnews.org/2016/05/no_your_brain_i.

46. Roger Epstein, "The Empty Brain," Aeon, 18 May 2016, https://aeon.co/essays/your-brain-does-not-process-information-and-it-is-not-a-computer.

47. Epstein, "The Empty Brain," italics in original.

48. Robert Hanna, "It's All Done with Mirrors: A New Argument That Strong AI Is Impossible," Against Professional Philosophy, 22 January 2023, https://againstprofphil.org/2023/01/22/its-all-done-with-mirrors-a-new-argument-that-strong-ai-is-impossible.

49. Neil Postman, *Technopoly: The Surrender of Culture to Technology* (New York: Vintage, 1993), 113.

50. It needed only four hours to go from complete ignorance of chess to complete mastery!

51. Margaret Boden, "Robot Says: Whatever," Aeon, 13 August 2018, https://aeon.co/essays/the-robots-wont-take-over-because-they-couldnt-care-less.

52. Robert J. Marks II, *Non-Computable You: What You Do That Artificial Intelligence Never Will* (Seattle: Discovery Institute Press), 2022.

53. Gheorghe Tecuci, "Demystifying Artificial Intelligence," Learning Agents Center, George Mason University, accessed 13 March 2024, http://lac.gmu.edu/publications/2024/Demystifying%20AI.pdf.

54. Yuval Noah Harari, *Sapiens: A Brief History of Humankind* (New York: HarperCollins, 2015), 397, 399.

55. See my book *Cosmic Chemistry: Do God and Science Mix?* (London: Lion Hudson, 2021).

56. Yuval Noah Harari, *Homo Deus: A Brief History of Tomorrow* (New York: HarperCollins, 2017), 73.

57. Cyborg engineering is usually imagined in terms of a fusion of machine and human – for instance, bionic hands, some versions of which can now be operated by thought alone.

58. Harari, *Sapiens*, 399–409.

59. Quoted in Juan Enriquez and Steve Gullans, *Evolving Ourselves: Redesigning the Future of Humanity – One Gene at a Time* (New York: Current, 2015).

60. Ian Sample, "Body Upgrades May Be Nearing Reality, but Only for the Rich," *Guardian*, 5 September 2014, www.theguardian.com/science/2014/sep/05/body-upgrades-only-for-rich.

61. These are used by more than a million Americans, according to a 2015 report, "Performance Enhancing Drugs Market to Witness a Significant Growth in Terms of Value during Forecast Period 2018–2023," *Medgadget* (blog), 10 August 2018, www.medgadget.com/2018/08/performance-enhancing-drugs-market-to-witness-a-significant-growth-in-terms-of-value-during-forecast-period-2018-2023.html.

62. Chris Hayner, "36 of the Best Movies about AI, Ranked," ZDNET, 18 January 2018, www.zdnet.com/pictures/15-of-the-best-movies-about-ai-ranked/21.

63. Max Tegmark, *Life 3.0: Being Human in the Age of Artificial Intelligence* (New York: Knopf, 2017), 134–60.

64. Echoes of Hobbes's *Leviathan*?

65. Tegmark, *Life 3.0*, 21.

66. Tegmark, *Life 3.0*, 136.

67. David Bell, *Superintelligence and World-views* (Tolworth, Surrey, UK: Grosvenor House, 2016).

68. See Ariel Conn, "AI Aftermath Scenarios," Future of Life Institute, 28 August 2017, https://futureoflife.org/ai-aftermath-scenarios; and Max Tegmark, "Superintelligence Survey," Future of Life Institute, 15 August 2017, https://futureoflife.org/superintelligence-survey. For another set of scenarios, set in 2065 – ten years after Ray Kurzweil's supposed "singularity" – see Stephan Talty, "What Will Our Society Look Like When Artificial Intelligence Is Everywhere?," *Smithsonian* (April 2018), www.smithsonianmag.com/innovation/artificial-intelligence-future-scenarios-180968403.

69. Private communication. Used with permission.

70. C. S. Lewis, *The Abolition of Man* (1943; repr., San Francisco: HarperSanFrancisco, 2001), 56.

71. Lewis, *Abolition of Man*, 64.

72. J. Budziszewski, *What We Can't Not Know: A Guide* (Dallas: Spence, 2003), 56.

73. Budziszewski, *What We Can't Not Know*, 56, 135.

74. Tegmark, *Life 3.0*, 228.

Chapter 12: The Genesis Files: What Is a Human Being?

1. Charles Babbage, *The Ninth Bridgewater Treatise*, 2nd ed. (London: Murray, 1838), ix.

2. Larry Siedentop, *Inventing the Individual: The Origins of Western Liberalism* (Cambridge, MA: Harvard University Press, 2014).

3. "Globalisten sagen Gott den Kampf an: WEF-Guru Harari bezeichnet Jesus als 'Fake News,'" Future Liberty, YouTube video, www.youtube.com/watch?v=jwuEXeDf4gE.

4. Neal Postman, *Technopoly: The Surrender of Culture to Technology* (New York: Vintage, 1993), 37–38.

5. Quoted in Postman, *Technopoly*, 34.

6. Immanuel Kant, "What Is Enlightenment?," in *On History*, ed. Lewis White Beck (Indianapolis: Bobbs-Merrill, 1963), 3–10, accessed 22 April 2024, https://ghdi.ghi-dc.org /sub_document.cfm?document_id=3589.

7. Quoted in M. Victor Cousin, *Course of the History of Modern Philosophy* (Edinburgh: T&T Clark, 1852), 64.

8. Kant, "What Is Enlightenment?"

9. John Gray, *Black Mass* (London: Allen Lane, 2007), 36.

10. Gray, *Black Mass*, 37.

11. Gray, *Black Mass*, 45.

12. Aleksandr Solzhenitsyn, "Acceptance Address by Mr. Aleksandr Solzhenitsyn," Templeton Prize, 10 May 1983, www.templetonprize.org/laureate-sub/solzhenitsyn-acceptance-speech. For more details, see my book *Gunning for God: Why the New Atheists Are Missing the Target* (Oxford: Lion, 2011).

13. Charles Darwin, "Letter to William Graham, 3 July 1881," University of Cambridge, Darwin Correspondence Project, accessed 13 March 2024, https://goo.gl/Jfyu9Q.

14. John Polkinghorne, *One World: The Interaction of Science and Theology* (London: SPCK, 1986), 92–93.

15. John Gray, *Straw Dogs: Thoughts on Humans and Other Animals* (London: Granta, 2002), 26.

16. Thomas Nagel, *Mind and Cosmos: Why the Materialist Neo-Darwinian Conception of Nature Is Almost Certainly False* (Oxford: Oxford University Press, 2012), 14, 28.

17. See my book *Cosmic Chemistry: Do God and Science Mix?* (London: Lion Hudson, 2021).

18. Frank E. Lockwood, "Christian Group Unveils Manifesto; Technology Should Never Outweigh Human Worth, It Says," *Arkansas Democrat Gazette*, 14 April 2019, www .arkansasonline.com/news/2019/apr/14/christian-group-unveils-manifesto-20190.

19. "The Ethics of Artificial Intelligence: An Evangelical Statement of Principles for Artificial Intelligence," Ethics and Religious Liberty Commission, accessed 22 April 2024, https:// erlc.com/ai.

20. Keith Ward, *Why There Almost Certainly Is a God: Doubting Dawkins* (Oxford: Lion, 2008), 19–20.

21. John 1:1–3.

22. This was a comment at the end of a documentary, directed by Barry Ptolemy, entitled *Transcendent Man: The Life and Ideas of Ray Kurzweil* (Los Angeles: Ptolemaic Productions, 2009).

23. Max Tegmark, *Life 3.0: Being Human in the Age of Artificial Intelligence* (New York: Knopf, 2017), chap. 2.

24. See my books *Cosmic Chemistry* and *God and Stephen Hawking* (London: Lion Hudson, 2021).

25. I go into this in much more detail in my book *Seven Days That Divide the World: The Beginning According to Genesis and Science*, 10th anniversary ed. (2011; Grand Rapids: Zondervan, 2021).

26. See my book *Seven Days That Divide the World*.

27. James Tour, "Open Letter to My Colleagues," *Inference: International Review of Science* 3, no. 2 (August 2017), https://inference-review.com/article/an-open-letter-to-my-colleagues; see also James Tour, "Animadversions of a Synthetic Chemist," *Inference: International Review of Science* 2, no. 2 (May 2016), https://inference-review.com/article/animadversions -of-a-synthetic-chemist.

28. David J. Chalmers, "Facing Up to the Hard Problem of Consciousness," *Journal of Consciousness Studies* 2, no. 3 (March 1995): 210–19, https://philpapers.org/rec/CHAFUT.

29. David J. Chalmers, *The Conscious Mind: In Search of a Fundamental Theory* (Oxford: Oxford University Press, 1996), xiv.

30. Francis Crick, *The Astonishing Hypothesis: The Scientific Search for the Soul* (New York: Scribner, 1994), 3.

31. G. H. Hardy, *A Mathematician's Apology* (1940: repr., Cambridge: Cambridge University Press, 2004), 85.

32. Stuart Russell and Peter Norvig, *Artificial Intelligence: A Modern Approach*, 3rd ed. (Harlow, UK: Pearson, 2016), 1033.

33. Yuval Noah Harari, *Homo Deus: A Brief History of Tomorrow* (New York: HarperCollins, 2017), 330.

34. Yuval Noah Harari, "Why Technology Favors Tyranny," *Atlantic*, October 2018, www .theatlantic.com/magazine/archive/2018/10/yuval-noah-harari-technology-tyranny /568330.

35. Wesley J. Smith, "Transhumanist Theorist Calls the AI-Unenhanced 'Useless People,'" *National Review*, 24 April 2022, www.nationalreview.com/corner/transhumanist-theorist -calls-the-ai-unenhanced-useless-people.

36. 2 Thessalonians 3:10.

37. Ross Andersen, "We're Underestimating the Risk of Human Extinction," *Atlantic*, 6 March 2012, www.theatlantic.com/technology/archive/2012/03/were-underestimating-the-risk-of -human-extinction/253821.

38. Bill Snyder, "Our Misplaced Fear of Job-Stealing Robots," Stanford Graduate School of Business, 7 March 2019, www.gsb.stanford.edu/insights/misplaced-fear-job-stealing-robots.

39. Silvia Montoya, "There Is a Global Learning Crisis Affecting the Lives of Millions in Developing Countries," World Economic Forum, 27 August 2018, www.weforum.org /agenda/2018/08/global-learning-crisis-millions-without-basic-skills-unesco (emphasis added).

40. "The Sustainable Development Goals Report 2023: Special Edition," United Nations, accessed 22 April 2024, https://sdgs.un.org/sites/default/files/2023-07/The-Sustainable -Development-Goals-Report-2023_0.pdf.

41. "4: Ensure Inclusive and Equitable Quality Education and Promote Lifelong Learning Opportunities for All," Sustainable Development Goals 2023, United Nations, accessed 13 March 2024, https://sustainabledevelopment.un.org/sdg4.

42. John 1:1, 3.

43. Keith Ward, "God as the Ultimate Informational Principle," in *Information and the Nature of Reality*, ed. Paul Davies and Niels Henrik Gregersen (Cambridge: Cambridge University Press, 2014), 375.

44. Paul Ford, "I Tried to Get an AI to Write This Story," *Businessweek,* 17 May 2018, www .bloomberg.com/news/features/2018-05-17/i-tried-to-get-an-ai-to-write-this-story-paul -ford.

45. Esther Ajao, "AI and Disinformation in the Russia-Ukraine War," TechTarget, 14 March 2022, www.techtarget.com/searchenterpriseai/feature/AI-and-disinformation-in-the -Russia-Ukraine-war.

46. Romans 12:1–2.

47. For more detail on this topic, see my book *Seven Days That Divide the World*, 203.

48. Genesis 1:27.

49. Genesis 2:24.

50. Matthew 19:4–6.

51. Kate Darling, "Extending Legal Protection to Social Robots: The Effects of Anthropomorphism, Empathy, and Violent Behavior toward Robotic Objects" (We Robot Conference 2012, University of Miami, Miami, FL, 23 April 2012), https://papers.ssrn.com /sol3/papers.cfm?abstract_id=2044797.

52. Maddy White, "Saudi Arabia Humanoid Sophia Has More Rights Than Women," FairPlanet, 28 May 2018, www.fairplanet.org/story/humanoid-sophia-has-more-rights-than -saudi-women-and-its-wrong.

53. Margaret Boden, "Robot Says: Whatever," Aeon, 13 August 2018, https://aeon.co/essays /the-robots-wont-take-over-because-they-couldnt-care-less.

54. The American Psychological Association dictionary defines *affect* to be "any experience of feeling or emotion, ranging from suffering to elation, from the simplest to the most complex sensations of feeling, and from the most normal to the most pathological emotional reactions. Often described in terms of positive affect or negative affect, both mood and emotion are considered affective states. Along with cognition and conation, affect is one of the three traditionally identified components of the mind."

55. Sherry Turkle, *Alone Together: Why We Expect More from Technology and Less from Each Other*, 3rd ed. (New York: Basic Books, 2017), 1.

56. Paul Best, "MIT Researchers Creating Robots That Give Birth to Other Robots," *New York Post*, 29 November 2022, https://nypost.com/2022/11/29/mit-researchers-creating-robots -that-give-birth-to-other-robots.

Chapter 13: The Origin of the Human Moral Sense

1. C. S. Lewis, *The Problem of Pain* (1940; repr., New York: Macmillan, 1962), 133–35.

2. John Gray, *Seven Types of Atheism* (New York: Farrar, Straus and Giroux, 2018), 68.

3. They are also hardwired in robots – which leads to a different set of problems!

4. Richard Dawkins, *River Out of Eden: A Darwinian View of Life* (New York: Basic Books, 1995), 133.

5. Jürgen Habermas, *Time of Transitions* (New York: Polity, 2006), 150–51.

6. Hannah Arendt, *The Human Condition* (Chicago: University of Chicago Press, 1958), 2–3.

7. Paula Boddington, "Myth and the EU Study on Civil Law Rules in Robotics," Ethics for Artificial Intelligence, 12 January 2017, www.cs.ox.ac.uk/efai/2017/01/12/myth-and-the -eu-study-on-civil-law-rules-in-robotics.

8. Nick Bostrom, *Superintelligence: Paths, Dangers, Strategies* (Oxford: Oxford University Press, 2014), 115–16. Note that many of these are in our Genesis list!

9. "Knowledge Quotes," Data Governance Institute, accessed 13 March 2024, https:// datagovernance.com/quotes/knowledge-quotes.

10. Ayad Akhtar, "The Singularity Is Here," *Atlantic*, 5 November 2021, www.theatlantic.com /magazine/archive/2021/12/ai-ad-technology-singularity/620521.

11. Julian Michael et al., "What Do NLP Researchers Believe? Results of the NLP Community Metasurvey," Arxiv.org, 6, 11, accessed 22 April 2024, https://arxiv.org/pdf/2208.12852.

12. Susan Schneider, "It May Not Feel Like Anything to Be an Alien," *Nautilus*, 15 January 2020, https://nautil.us/it-may-not-feel-like-anything-to-be-an-alien-237674.

13. As a general reference in this area, see David Gooding and John Lennox, *Doing What's Right: Whose System of Ethics Is Good Enough?* (Belfast: Myrtlefield House, 2018).

14. Rosalind Picard, *Affective Computing* (Cambridge, MA: MIT Press, 1997), 134.

15. Rosalind W. Picard, "Emotions, AI, and Human Values," Tanner Lectures, Oxford University, 20 June 2022, https://podcasts.ox.ac.uk/emotion-ai-and-human-values.

16. Jordan B. Peterson, "Biblical Series 1: Introduction to the Idea of God," YouTube, 20 May 2017, www.youtube.com/watch?v=f-wWBGo6a2w&t=0s.

17. Michael Cook, "Is Transhumanism Really the World's Most Dangerous Idea?" *Mercatornet*, 20 July 2016, www.mercatornet.com/articles/view/is-transhumanism-really-the-worlds-most-dangerous-idea/18394; Francis Fukuyama, "The World's Most Dangerous Ideas: Transhumanism," *Foreign Policy* 144, no. 1 (September 2004): 42–43.

18. Francis Fukuyama, *Our Posthuman Future: Consequences of the Biotechnology Revolution* (New York: Farrar, Straus and Giroux, 2002), 149–51.

19. Francis Fukuyama, "Special Report: Transhumanism," *Foreign Policy*, 23 October 2009, https://foreignpolicy.com/2009/10/23/transhumanism.

20. Yuval Noah Harari, *Sapiens: A Brief History of Humankind* (New York: HarperCollins, 2015), 108.

21. Lianna Brinded, "How to Prevent Human Bias from Infecting AI," Quartz, 20 March 2018, https://qz.com/1232285/ad-week-europe-2018-risk-and-rewards-of-ai-and-using-machine-learning-to-remove-bias.

22. Yuval Noah Harari, "Does Trump's Rise Mean Liberalism's End?," *New Yorker*, 7 October 2016, www.newyorker.com/business/currency/does-trumps-rise-mean-liberalisms-end.

23. Yuval Noah Harari, *Homo Deus: A Brief History of Tomorrow* (New York: HarperCollins, 2017), 279.

24. Harari, *Homo Deus*, 285.

25. Yuval Noah Harari, "Yuval Noah Harari: The Myth of Freedom," *Guardian*, 14 September 2018, www.theguardian.com/books/2018/sep/14/yuval-noah-harari-the-new-threat-to-liberal-democracy.

26. Harari, *Homo Deus*, 285.

27. John C. Lennox, *Cosmic Chemistry: Do God and Science Mix?* (London: Lion Hudson, 2021).

28. Harari, *Homo Deus*, 288.

29. John C. Lennox, *Determined to Believe? The Sovereignty of God, Freedom, Faith, and Human Responsibility* (Oxford: Lion, 2017).

30. It is not unreasonable to argue that the biblical worldview presents a true humanism in that by holding that humans are made in the image of God, it gives them a much higher value than does the (atheistic) humanist philosophy widely believed today.

31. Harari, *Homo Deus*, 349.

32. Harari, "The Myth of Freedom."

33. Robert B. Cialdini, *Influence: The Psychology of Persuasion* (New York: HarperCollins, 1993).

Chapter 14: The True Homo Deus

1. Yuval Noah Harari, *Homo Deus: A Brief History of Tomorrow* (New York: HarperCollins, 2017), quote in front matter of the book.
2. Patrick Freyne, "Yuval Noah Harari: 'It Takes Just One Fool to Start a War,'" *Irish Times*, 30 August 2018, www.irishtimes.com/culture/books/yuval-noah-harari-it-takes-just-one-fool-to-start-a-war-1.3610304.
3. Louis Rosenberg, "New Hope for Humans in an A.I. World," TEDx Talks, 7 September 2017, YouTube video, www.youtube.com/watch?v=Eu-RyZt_Uas.
4. Cem Dilmegani, "When Will Singularity Happen? 1700 Expert Opinions of AGI," AIMultiple, updated 10 March 2024, https://research.aimultiple.com/artificial-general-intelligence-singularity-timing.
5. Mo Gawdat, *Scary Smart: The Future of Artificial Intelligence and How You Can Save Our World* (London: Bluebird, 2021), 10.
6. Gawdat, *Scary Smart*, 9.
7. Quoted in Al Bagocius, "What Will Our Society Look Like When Artificial Intelligence Is Everywhere?," LinkedIn, accessed 13 March 2024, www.linkedin.com/posts/albagocius_singularity-artificialintelligence-robots-activity-7044586309570457600-FKTa.
8. John C. Lennox, *Gunning for God: Why the New Atheists Are Missing the Target* (Oxford: Lion, 2011).
9. N. T. Wright, *The Resurrection of the Son of God* (Minneapolis: Fortress, 2003), 709–10.
10. Genesis 3:15.
11. Yuval Noah Harari, *Sapiens: A Brief History of Humankind* (New York: HarperCollins, 2015), 109.
12. I say this advisedly – see my book *Cosmic Chemistry: Do God and Science Mix?* (London: Lion Hudson, 2021).
13. John 14:28–29.
14. John 2:18–22.
15. John 15:18; 16:1–4.
16. Acts 2:24–36.
17. Isaiah 9:6–7.
18. Micah 5:2.
19. Isaiah 44:7.
20. Genesis 3:15.
21. Genesis 12:3 NIV.
22. Acts 3:25–26 NIV.
23. Luke 1:31–33 NIV.
24. John 1:23 NIV.
25. Micah 5:2 NIV.
26. Isaiah 7:14 NIV.
27. Luke 1:35 NIV.
28. Zechariah 9:9 NIV.
29. Confess to God that what we have done is wrong and express the desire to change, with his help, our attitudes and behavior to comply with his standards.
30. John 1:12.
31. 1 Corinthians 15:3–8.
32. Acts 1:1–11; 2.

2084 and the AI Revolution

33. See my books *Gunning for God* and *Can Science Explain Everything?* (Epsom, UK: Good Book Company, 2019).

Chapter 15: Future Shock: The Return of the Man Who Is God

1. John 14:1–4.
2. Acts 3:15.
3. C. S. Lewis, *God in the Dock: Essays on Theology and Ethics* (Grand Rapids: Eerdmans, 2014), 99.
4. David J. Bosch, *Transforming Mission: Paradigm Shifts in Theology of Mission* (Maryknoll, NY: Orbis, 2011), 328.
5. "Utopia," from the Greek *ou* = "not," and *topos* = "place." The homophone *Eutopia* (Greek *eu* = "good") means a "good place," and the two are often confused. In 1872, Samuel Butler published his novel, a satire on Victorian society, called *Erewhon*, which is (almost) "nowhere" spelled backward. The fictional country Erewhon at first appears to be a utopia, but that turns out to not be the case.
6. Matthew 24:6.
7. We should notice how often the clouds of heaven are mentioned in connection with Christ's return – it is to be a literal and visible coming.
8. 2 Timothy 1:10 NIV.
9. 2 Corinthians 5:8 KJV.
10. Luke 23:43.
11. Many people find the idea of vicarious suffering difficult. I have written about it in *Gunning for God: Why the New Atheists Are Missing the Target* (Oxford: Lion, 2011), 145–64.
12. Hebrews 9:27–28.
13. John 5:24.
14. 1 Corinthians 15:20. ·
15. 1 Corinthians 15:50–57; Philippians 3:20–21.
16. Luke 24:39.
17. There is much to discuss here: If such an upload were ever to be possible, would the result be recognizably me? See David J. Chalmers, *The Character of Consciousness* (Oxford: Oxford University Press, 2010).
18. Gary R. Habermas, *On the Resurrection*, vol. 1, *Evidences* (Brentwood, TN: B&H Academic, 2024), 249.
19. Graham H. Twelftree, ed., *The Cambridge Companion to Miracles* (Cambridge: Cambridge University Press, 2011).
20. Habermas, *On the Resurrection*, 249.
21. E. J. David Kramer, "The Difference Jesus Makes: Yuval Noah Harari and Wolfhart Pannenberg on the Shape of Universal History," *International Journal of Systematic Theology*, 12 June 2023, https://doi.org/10.1111/ijst.12659.
22. The English title is *On the Nature of Things*.
23. Matthew 24:44; Revelation 22:20.
24. John Gray, *Seven Types of Atheism* (New York: Farrar, Straus and Giroux, 2018), 70.
25. Hannah Arendt, *The Origins of Totalitarianism* (1951; repr., London: Penguin, 2017), 387, 437.
26. See Ariel Conn, "AI Aftermath Scenarios," Future of Life Institute, 28 August 2017, https://futureoflife.org/ai-aftermath-scenarios.

27. Yuval Noah Harari, *Sapiens: A Brief History of Humankind* (New York: HarperCollins, 2015), 415–16.

28. Jonathan Easton, "Pope Francis Calls for International Regulation of AI in Annual Statement," National Technology News, 15 December 2023, https://nationaltechnology.co.uk/Pope_Francis_AI_Regulation.php.

Chapter 16: Homo Deus in the Book of Revelation

1. Psalm 135:15–18 NIV.

2. Genesis 2:7.

3. A robot designed to look and act as a human.

4. Dr. Ian Pearson, a futurologist, expresses this view in the 2016 film *The Future of Work and Death.*

5. Yuval Noah Harari, "Why Technology Favors Tyranny," *Atlantic*, October 2018, www.theatlantic.com/magazine/archive/2018/10/yuval-noah-harari-technology-tyranny/568330.

6. "Electronic Bracelets," European Space Agency, Navipedia, accessed 13 March 2024, https://gssc.esa.int/navipedia/index.php/Electronic_Bracelets.

7. Bertalan Mesko, "Everything You Need to Know before Getting an RFID Implant," Medical Futurist, 20 April 2022, https://medicalfuturist.com/rfid-implant-chip.

8. Pangambam S, "Transcript: AI and the Future of Humanity – Yuval Noah Harari," *Singju Post*, 24 July 2023, https://singjupost.com/transcript-ai-and-the-future-of-humanity-yuval-noah-harari/?singlepage=1.

9. Mark Sellman, "How Worried Should We Be about the Rise of the AI 'Monster'?," *The Times*, 21 April 2023, www.thetimes.co.uk/article/pause-or-panic-battle-to-tame-the-ai-monster-mjd97lhkh.

10. Matt McFarland, "Elon Musk: 'With Artificial Intelligence We Are Summoning the Demon,'" *Washington Post*, 24 October 2014, www.washingtonpost.com/news/innovations/wp/2014/10/24/elon-musk-with-artificial-intelligence-we-are-summoning-the-demon.

11. Neil McArthur, "Gods in the Machine? The Rise of Artificial Intelligence May Result in New Religions," *The Conversation*, 15 March 2023, https://theconversation.com/gods-in-the-machine-the-rise-of-artificial-intelligence-may-result-in-new-religions-201068.

12. Julian Huxley, *The Humanist Frame* (New York: Harper, 1961), 26.

13. The related term *dataism* is attributed by some to political commentator David Brooks of the *New York Times* to express obsession with data.

14. "The Rise of Data Religion," abstract of a public lecture with Yuval Harari, response by Andrew Briggs, and panel discussion chaired by Martin Rees, Trinity College, Cambridge, 6 September 2016, CRASSH, accessed 13 March 2024, www.crassh.cam.ac.uk/events/26948.

15. Max Tegmark, *Life 3.0: Being Human in the Age of Artificial Intelligence* (New York: Knopf, 2017).

16. Joanna Ng, "How Artificial Super-Intelligence Is Today's Tower of Babel," *Christianity Today*, 17 June 2020, www.christianitytoday.com/ct/2020/june-web-only/artificial-intelligence-todays-tower-of-babel-ai-ethics.html.

17. For more on this complex topic, see my book *Determined to Believe? The Sovereignty of God, Freedom, Faith, and Human Responsibility* (Oxford: Lion, 2017).

18. A number formed by adding together the numbers representing the letters of the name

according to some agreed-on scheme: A = 1, B = 2, and so on. For instance, a boy in the ancient world might carve on a tree: "I love the girl whose number is 53," and would leave others to work out, by a trial-and-error process of substituting letters for numbers, that her name was Julia.

19. Revelation 13:18.
20. Some scholars understand the Son of Man "coming on the clouds of heaven" (Matthew 26:64) as a reference to the ascension of Christ, when he came to God and his throne. But I think (1) our Lord's citation of this text at his trial is more naturally understood in terms of his future return to earth, and thus he would be visible to those who have rejected him, and (2) if Daniel 7 is referring to the ascension, it is fair to ask: Did God's judgment occur at the ascension? And if so, what beast was then destroyed? See my book *Against the Flow: The Inspiration of Daniel in an Age of Relativism* (Oxford: Monarch, 2015) on the issue.
21. 2 Thessalonians 2:7.
22. Daniel 7:25.
23. Revelation 13:12, 14.
24. Revelation 17:12–14.
25. Hence the identification in earlier years with ten European countries was wide off the mark.
26. Albert Einstein, "Towards a World Government" (1946), in *Out of My Later Years* (New York: Philosophical Library, 1956), 146.
27. Gideon Rachman, "And Now for a World Government," *Financial Times*, 8 December 2008, www.ft.com/content/7a03e5b6-c541-11dd-b516-000077b07658.
28. Quoted in Rachman, "World Government."
29. Quoted in Rachman, "World Government."
30. Dante Alighieri, *Il Convivio* (*The Banquet*), trans. Richard H. Lansing (Garland Library of Medieval Literature, 1990), book 4, chap. 4, https://digitaldante.columbia.edu/text/library/the-convivio/book-04/#30.
31. Immanuel Kant, quoted in Catherine Lu, "World Government," in *Stanford Encyclopedia of Philosophy*, ed. Edward N. Zalta (Winter 2016), https://plato.stanford.edu/archives/win2016/entries/world-government.
32. The groups here are a small sample of a very large list on Wikipedia, "List of Country Groupings," accessed 22 April 2024, https://en.wikipedia.org/wiki/List_of_country_groupings.
33. Catherine Lu, "World Government," *Stanford Encyclopedia of Philosophy*, ed. Edward N. Zalta, (Spring 2021 edition), https://plato.stanford.edu/archives/spr2021/entries/world-government.

Chapter 17: The Time of the End

1. Italian for "scoundrels" or "rabble."
2. The idea expressed here is taken nearly verbatim from C. S. Lewis, *The Abolition of Man* (1943; repr., San Francisco: HarperSanFrancisco, 2001), 55.
3. C. S. Lewis, *That Hideous Strength* (New York: Scribner, 1996), 175.
4. Lewis, *Hideous Strength*, 176.
5. 2 Thessalonians 2:7.
6. For more details, see my book *Gunning for God: Why the New Atheists Are Missing the Target* (Oxford: Lion, 2011).
7. John 14:29.

8. Daniel 12:4.

9. Daniel 7:28.

10. 2 Timothy 2:8–9.

11. Acts 17:30–31.

12. The resurrection of Christ is not offered as evidence for believers only, nor is it "created" by believers' faith. The resurrection, with its consequences, is the historical event that provides the evidence base that justifies faith. Faith, in the Christian sense, is thoroughly evidence based. It is not blind belief, as is often erroneously suggested.

13. Yuval Noah Harari, "Why Technology Favors Tyranny," *Atlantic*, October 2018, www .theatlantic.com/magazine/archive/2018/10/yuval-noah-harari-technology-tyranny /568330.

14. Adam Higginbotham, "Welcome to Rosalind Picard's Touchy-Feely World of Empathic Tech," *Wired*, 27 November 2012, www.wired.co.uk/article/emotion-machines.

15. See Romans 13:1–7.

16. 2 Thessalonians 2:7.

17. Carmine Gallo, "A Global AI Expert Identifies the Skills You Need to Thrive in the Next 15 Years," *Forbes*, 4 October 2018, www.forbes.com/sites/carminegallo/2018/10/04/a -global-ai-expert-identifies-the-skills-you-need-to-thrive-in-the-next-15-years.; see also Kai-Fu Lee, *AI Superpowers: China, Silicon Valley, and the New World Order* (New York: Harper Business, 2019).

18. Philippians 2:3–4.

19. Please see my book *A Good Return: Biblical Principles of Work, Wealth and Wisdom* (Fearn, UK: Christian Focus, 2023).

20. "The Grand Miracle," C. S. Lewis official website, www.cslewis.com/the-grand-miracle, accessed 13 March 2024. See also John 1:14.

21. Jeremy Peckham, *Masters or Slaves? AI and the Future of Humanity* (London: IVP, 2021), 217. Peckham has much valuable advice for Christians in his book – especially in chapter 12, "A Christian Manifesto."

22. Part of this chapter is a modified version of part of chapter 16 of my book *Against the Flow: The Inspiration of Daniel in an Age of Relativism* (Oxford: Monarch, 2015).

23. This was the title of a paper presented by Joseph Mellichamp at a symposium at Yale University in 1986 on the topic "Is the Human Mind More Than a Complex Computer?"

24. Revelation 22:20.